www.wadsworth.com

wadsworth.com is the World Wide Web site for Wadsworth and is your direct source to dozens of online resources.

At *wadsworth.com* you can find out about supplements, demonstration software, and student resources. You can also send e-mail to many of our authors and preview new publications and exciting new technologies.

wadsworth.com
Changing the way the world learns®

Essentials of Texas Politics

8th Edition

RICHARD H. KRAEMER

Emeritus Professor of Government
University of Texas at Austin

CHARLDEAN NEWELL

Regents Professor of Public Administration
University of North Texas

DAVID F. PRINDLE

Professor of Government
University of Texas at Austin

WADSWORTH

THOMSON LEARNING

Australia • Canada • Mexico • Singapore • Spain • United Kingdom • United States

WADSWORTH

THOMSON LEARNING

Political Science Editor: Clark G. Baxter
Development Editor: Sharon Adams Poore
Assistant Editor: Jennifer Ellis
Executive Marketing Manager: Diane McOscar
Marketing Assistant: Kirstin Anderson
Project Editor: Dianne Jensis Toop
Print Buyer: Barbara Britton
Permissions Editor: Joohee Lee

Production Service: Matrix Productions
Text Designer: Cynthia Bassett
Copy Editor: Vicki Nelson
Cover Designer: Margarite Reynolds
Cover Image: Michael A. Murphy
Cover Printer: Malloy Lithographing
Compositor: Parkwood Composition
Printer: Malloy Lithographing

Printed in the United States of America
  4 5 6 7 04 03 02

For permission to use material from this text, contact us by
Web: http://www.thomsonrights.com
Fax: 1-800-730-2215
Phone: 1-800-730-2214

Wadsworth/Thomson Learning
10 Davis Drive
Belmont, CA 94002-3098
USA

For more information about our products,
contact us:
Thomson Learning Academic Resource Center
1-800-423-0563
http://www.wadsworth.com

International Headquarters
Thomson Learning
International Division
290 Harbor Drive, 2nd Floor
Stamford, CT 06902-7477
USA

UK/Europe/Middle East/South Africa
Thomson Learning
Berkshire House
168-173 High Holborn
London WC1V 7AA
United Kingdom

Asia
Thomson Learning
60 Albert Street, #15-01
Albert Complex
Singapore 189969

Canada
Nelson Thomson Learning
1120 Birchmount Road
Toronto, Ontario M1K 5G4
Canada

Library of Congress Cataloging-in-Publication Data
Kraemer, Richard H.
     Essentials of Texas Politics/Richard H. Kraemer, Charldean Newell,
     David F. Prindle.—8th ed.
     p. cm.
     Includes bibliographical references.
     ISBN 0-534-55377-X
       1. Texas—Politics and government—[date]   I. Newell, Charldean.
       II. Prindle, David F. (David Forrest), [date]   III. Title.
JK4816 .K68 2001
320.9764—dc21   00-060025

CONTENTS

5 Voters, Campaigns, and Elections   69

PREFACE

In Texas, as in the rest of the United States, government and politics are important aspects of modern life. Government includes public institutions and policies, while politics encompasses political behavior and action. Both touch our daily lives in many ways. Getting a driver's license, adding extra pennies when we buy a hamburger, arranging for water service at home, paying tuition—all of these actions are ways that we deal with government on a routine basis. Government is the little things as well as a Big Eight Summit Conference on defense, keeping the economy vibrant while controlling inflation, or electing a president.

Texas continues to be a dynamic and fascinating state. Many readers of this book were not yet born when the first edition was published in 1980. Then, the book described the one-party Democrat-dominated state and a budget rooted in the oil and gas industry. The Texas population was a little over 11 million. Now, the state has more than 9 million new residents and the population is over 20 million. Republicans have moved from being a decidedly minority party to a dominant force. Oil and gas revenues now fuel less than 2 percent of the state budget.

Other differences abound. For example, a full-page political ad in a major daily newspaper costs five times as much as it did in 1980, although a 30-second spot ad on television costs only about 20 percent more. The governor's salary has risen from $69,100 to $115,345 a year. The state's biennial budget has risen from $16.8 billion to $98.1 billion.

Other aspects of government and politics have not changed much at all. The Texas Constitution is still a patchwork of detailed provisions and numerous amendments—in fact, more each year—rather than a streamlined document. Business and economic interests continue to be the dominant influences on the legislature. And the executive branch and the courts are both still a hodgepodge of different agencies and different types of courts that confuse most citizens. Change and the lack of it are what makes studying Texas politics interesting.

There are three themes that the reader will encounter in *Essentials of Texas Politics,* eighth edition. The overriding theme is a comparison of the reality of Texas government and politics to the democratic ideals of participation, majority rule, and protection of minority rights. Throughout, the authors ask whether a particular political action or institution serves the general public interest or only narrow private interests. The authors are political scientists, trained to be analysts, not merely observers, of politics. Our mission is not to offer a defense or apology for the present system, but to identify the differences between governmental practices and the sense of fair play and equity expected in a democratic system. Thus, we point out where the system works well, but we also examine the faults of the system and suggest needed changes.

A second theme is increasing conservatism even in a state that has always been conservative. The Democrats have long been divided into liberal and conservative wings, with the term *conservative* mainly meaning protection of business interests and a paternal attitude toward ethnic minorities and the poor. The Republicans seem headed toward a division between economic conservatives and social conservatives.

Because political ideologies are so different among the various political factions and because the ethnic and racial composition of the state is changing rapidly, a third theme is that of conflict. We particularly call attention to conflicts among the rich, the poor, and the middle class; among and between Anglos, Mexican Americans, and African Americans; between ideologies; and between religious traditions.

Essentials is a short book, and we cannot provide a comprehensive, in-depth analysis of all things political in Texas. We hope, however, that we can pique the interest of students to learn more about government and politics in the Lone Star State and can help them understand how much state and local governments affect them everyday.

We want to thank our colleagues across the state who reviewed the eighth edition and made valuable comments to aid us in revising the book. They are: Kenneth R. Durham, Jr., LeTourneau University; Gregory Edwards, Amarillo College; Johanna Hume, Alvin Community College; Valarie Martinez-Ebers, Texas Christian University; Richard Murray, University of Houston; and Albert C. Waite, Central Texas College. While space limitations and occasional conflicting recommendations made it impossible to incorporate all of their suggestions, we did include most of the ideas proposed. We are also grateful to David L. Dillman, Abilene Christian University, for preparing the instructor's material.

We also appreciate colleagues and students at our own institutions who have given us their observations, constructive criticisms, and expertise. At the University of Texas at Austin, Janice May, Bartholemew Sparrow, and Jasmine Farrier have been particularly helpful, as has Alexandra Huffaker, an undergraduate whose independent study of the Texas legislature has informed our discussion in Chapter 6. At the University of North Texas, Steve Poe and John Todd have been helpful, respectively, in offering suggestions and sharing information. Also, we thank the many elected officials, legislative staff members, and state agency staff members who provided us with the information, clarification, and graphics material. We particularly thank Ben Sargent, winner of the 1982 Pulitzer Prize for editorial cartooning, for again graciously permitting the use of his outstanding cartoons. And we thank Angie Prindle for practical and moral support. Of course, any errors of fact or interpretation are ours alone.

1

THE CONTEXT OF TEXAS POLITICS

f I owned Hell and Texas, I'd rent out Texas and live in Hell.

General Philip H. Sheridan
Fort Clark, 1855

If somebody's smart enough to move here, he must be all right.

Lynn Ashby, *newspaper columnist*
Houston, 1977

All government is bad, including good government.

Edward Abbey
The Journey Home, 1977

INTRODUCTION

Much has changed between the 1850s, when General Sheridan made his well-known evaluation of Texas, and the modern period, when journalist Lynn Ashby made his. In 1855, Texas was poor and offered few comforts to a soldier assigned to garrison an outpost against Indian raids. Today, Lynn Ashby's Houston is the center of an air-conditioned metropolitan area of almost 4 million people. Houston is one of only five American cities (the others being New York, San Francisco, Seattle, and Chicago) that supports four fully professional theatrical arts companies—opera, ballet, theater, and symphony.[1] It is also the only city in the country whose air pollution is ranked "severe" by the federal Environmental Protection Agency.[2] Yet in some ways the state has changed little since Sheridan's era. Texas is a mix of old and new.

Old habits of thought and behavior evolved to meet problems of the nineteenth century, when Texas was settled by Americans of Western European background. They persist today, despite serious new problems created in the latter decades of the twentieth century. As Texans prepare themselves to meet the problems of the twenty-first century, they have to ask themselves if the habits and institutions they have inherited are up to the job.

The first topic of this chapter will be a listing of the most important principles of democratic theory and an explanation of why it is vital to understand them. Next will be a discussion of Texas as one among fifty states in a federal system. Following that is an exploration of some of the social and political attitudes that have been of historical importance in the state. Next will be a discussion of the economy of Texas and the way it interacts with the state's political system. As an introduction to some topics later in the book, the origin and distribution of the people of Texas will be summarized. Finally we will present a brief outline of the agenda for the rest of the book.

TEXAS AS A DEMOCRACY

Part of the task of this book is to discuss the concept of **democracy** and evaluate the extent to which Texas measures up as a democratic state. A democracy is a system of government the legitimacy of which is based on the people's participation. **Legitimacy** is the belief people hold that their government is moral, fair, and just and that therefore they should obey its laws. According to the moral theory underlying a democratic system of government, because the people themselves (indirectly, through representatives) make the laws, they are morally obligated to obey them.

Complications to this theory abound, and a number of them will be explored later. Because some means to allow the people to participate in the government must exist, free elections, in which candidates or parties compete for the citizens' votes, are necessary. There must be some connection between what a majority of the people want and what the government actually does. Nevertheless, majorities must not be allowed to take away certain rights from minorities, such as the right

---

1. Everett Evans, "Is Houston's Elite Arts Claim Legitimate?" *Houston Chronicle,* July 26, 1998, 'Zest' section, 12.

2. Ronnie Dugger, "Questions for George W.," *Texas Observer,* May 14, 1999, 23.

to vote, the right to be treated equally under the law, and the right to freedom of expression.

Although many of them could not state it clearly, the great majority of Americans, and Texans, believe in some version of the theory of democracy. That being so, it is possible to judge our state government (as it is also possible to judge our national government) according to the extent to which it approximates the ideal of a democratic society. Chapters in this book will frequently be comparing the reality of Texas government to the ideal of the democratic polity and asking readers to judge whether they think Texas is a successful democracy.

One of the major causes of shortcomings in democratic government, in Texas as elsewhere, is *private influence over public policy*. While ideally government decisions are made to try to maximize the public interest, too often they are made at the behest of individuals who are pursuing their own private interests at the expense of the public's. This book will often explore the ways that powerful individuals try to distort the people's institutions into vehicles of their own advantage. It will also examine ways that representatives of the public resist these selfish efforts to influence public policy. Part of the political process, in Texas as in other democracies, is the struggle to ensure that the making of public policy is truly a people's activity rather than a giveaway to the few who are rich, powerful, and well connected.

TEXAS IN THE FEDERAL SYSTEM

This book is about the politics of one state. Just as it would be impossible to describe the functions of one of the human body's organs without reference to the body as a whole, however, it would be misleading to try to analyze a state without reference to the nation. The United States has a **federal system.** Its governmental powers are shared among the national and state governments. A great many state responsibilities are strongly influenced by the actions of all three branches of the national government.

Education, for instance, is primarily a responsibility of state, not federal, government. Yet the national Congress influences Texas education policy with many laws that direct the state to govern the schools in a certain way or promise money in return for taking some action. The U.S. Supreme Court has often forced Texas schools to stop something they were doing—prayers in the classroom, for example. It has also made it necessary for them to do things they did not want to do—integrate racially, for example (see Chapter Three). Finally, the U.S. president makes many decisions that help or hinder the state in its pursuit of its own educational objectives. Recent chief executives have advocated the establishment of national education standards to which all the schools in all the states would have to conform.

The areas in which the federal government makes an impact on Texas government are several:

1. Nearly a third of state revenue each year comes from federal grants (see Chapter Nine).
2. The U.S. Supreme Court oversees the actions of the state government and, historically, has forced the state to make many changes in its behavior, especially in regard to civil rights and liberties (see Chapter Eight).

3. Congress allocates many of the "goodies" of government—military bases, veterans' hospitals, highways, and the like—that have a crucial impact on the state's economy.

4. Congress also mandates the state government to take actions, such as making public buildings accessible to physically disabled people or instituting background checks on gun purchasers, that force the Texas legislature to raise and spend money.

5. When Congress declares war, or the president sends troops to a foreign conflict without a declaration of war, Texans fight and die.

6. The president has many discretionary powers, such as cutting tariffs on imported goods or releasing federal disaster relief funds, that leave their mark, for good or ill, on the state's economy.

7. When the Federal Reserve Board raises or lowers interest rates, it constricts or stimulates Texas's economy along with the economies of the other forty-nine states. The changes thus created powerfully affect both the amount of money the state legislature has to spend and the demands on its allocation of resources.

Texas politics is thus both a whole subject unto itself and a part of a larger whole. While the focus will be on Texas in this book, there will be frequent references to actions by national institutions and politicians.

THE TEXAS POLITICAL CULTURE

Like the other forty-nine states, Texas is part of a well-integrated American civil society. It is also a separate and distinctive society with its own history and present-day political system.

Culture is the product of the historical experience of a people in a particular area. Our political system is the product of our political culture. **Political culture** is a shared system of values, beliefs, and habits of behavior in regard to government and politics. Not everyone in a given political culture participates in all of its assumptions, but everyone is affected by the beliefs and values of the dominant groups in society. Often, the culture of the majority group is imposed on members of a minority who would prefer not to live with it.

Not all Texans have shared the beliefs and attitudes that will be described here. Especially, as will be discussed in more detail in Chapter Three, African Americans and Mexican Americans have tended to be somewhat separate from the political culture of the dominant Anglo majority. Nevertheless, both history and present political institutions have imposed clear patterns on the assumptions that most Texans bring to politics.

Part of the larger American political tradition is a basic attitude toward government and politicians that was most famously expressed in a single sentence attributed to the revolutionary leader and president, Thomas Jefferson: "That government is best which governs least." Jefferson's aphorism is a summary of a political philosophy called conservatism that has dominated Texas politics in the twentieth century.

The term *conservative* is complex, and its implications change with time and situation. In general, however, it refers to a general hostility to government activity, especially in the economic sphere. Most of the early white settlers came to Texas to seek their fortunes. They cared little about government and wanted no interference in their economic affairs. Their attitudes were consistent with the popular values of the Jeffersonian Democrats of the nineteenth century: the less government the better, local control of what little government there was, and freedom from economic regulation, or *laissez-faire.*

Texas conservatism minimizes the role of government in society in general and in the economy in particular. It stresses an individualism that maximizes the role of businesspeople in controlling the economy. Like Edward Abbey, quoted at the beginning of this chapter, Texans suspect that even good government is bad. To a Texas conservative, a desirable government is one that mainly keeps taxes low.

Consistent with the emphasis on pseudo laissez-faire is a type of *Social Darwinism,* the belief that individuals who prosper and rise to the top of the socioeconomic ladder are worthy and deserve their riches, while those who sink to the bottom (or, having been born there, stay there) are unworthy and deserve their poverty. Social Darwinists argue that people become rich because they are intelligent, energetic, and self-disciplined, while those who become or remain poor do so because they are stupid, lazy, and/or given to indulgence in personal vices. Socioeconomic status, they argue, is the result of natural selection.[3]

3. For a description and evaluation of Social Darwinism in American culture, see Carl N. Degler, *In Search of Human Nature: The Decline and Revival of Darwinism in American Social Thought* (New York: Oxford University Press, 1991).

In practice, laissez-faire in Texas has often been **pseudo** (false) **laissez-faire.** Entrepreneurs don't want government to regulate or tax them, and they denounce policies to help society's less fortunate as "socialism." But when they encounter a problem that is too big for them to handle, they do not hesitate to accept government help. A good example is the city of Houston. Its leaders praise their city as the home of unrestrained, unaided free enterprise. In fact, however, Houston has historically relied upon government activity for its economic existence. The ship channel, which connects the city's port to the sea and thereby created it in an economic sense, was dredged and is maintained by government. Much of the oil industry, which was responsible for Houston's twentieth-century boom, was sustained either by state regulation by the Railroad Commission or by the federal government's selling facilities to the industry cheaply, such as occurred with the Big Inch and Little Inch Pipelines. Billions of dollars of federal tax money have flowed into the area to create jobs in the space industry (the Johnson Space Center and NASA).

Houston's business leaders have not resisted such government action on their behalf; quite the contrary. It is only when government tries to help ordinary people that the business community upholds the banner of laissez-faire.

SOURCE: Joe R. Feagin, *Free Enterprise City: Houston in Political-Economic Perspective* (New Brunswick, New York: Rutgers, 1988), passim.

Cartoonist Ben Sargent pokes fun at the conservative political culture, whose advocates often argue that government should be "run like a business." Junior Mosbacher, a wealthy Republican businessman, was appointed Commissioner of the Department of Human Services by Governor Bill Clements. In 1990, he failed to stay within his department's budget and was forced to substantially curtail services to the sick and poor.

SOURCE: Courtesy of Ben Sargent.

Of course, a person's success in life frequently *is* the result of his or her behavior and qualities of character. But it also depends on many other factors, such as education, race and ethnicity, proper diet and medical care, the wealth and education of one's parents, and luck. Nonetheless, Social Darwinism continues to dominate the thinking of many Texans. They strongly resist the idea that government has an obligation to come to the aid of society's less fortunate. This hostility to government aid to the needy has resulted in many state policies that mark Texas as a state with an unusually stingy attitude toward the underprivileged. For example, among the fifty states, in the late 1990s Texas ranked forty-seventh in its maximum weekly welfare payments to poor families and fiftieth in its per capita spending on health and welfare.[4]

Pseudo laissez-faire economic doctrine and Social Darwinism lead to a *trickle-down* theory of economic and social development. If business flourishes, so the theory goes, prosperity will follow and benefits will trickle down to the majority of Texans. In

4. Ronnie Dugger, "Questions for George W.," *Texas Observer*, May 14, 1999, 22; Mary Alice Davis, "Texas by the Numbers," *Austin American-Statesman*, May 25, 1999, A19.

other words, if government caters to the needs of business rather than attempting to improve the lives of the poor, everyone's economic situation can be improved. To a degree, the trickle-down theory does work—but only to a degree, since about 17 percent of the state's citizens existed at or below the poverty level in the late 1990s.[5]

There is another general attitude toward government, called *liberalism,* that accepts government activity—especially on behalf of the less fortunate—as often a good thing. Although conservatives have dominated Texas politics through most of its history, liberals have occasionally been elected to public office and liberal ideas have sometimes been adopted as state policy. The conflict between liberalism and conservatism underlies much political argument in the United States. Chapter Four explores the way these two ideologies have formed the basis for much of Texas politics.

ECONOMY, TAXES, AND SERVICES

When General Sheridan made his harsh evaluation of Texas in 1855, the state was poor, rural, and agricultural. In the twentieth century, however, its economy was transformed, first by the boom in the oil industry that began with the discovery of the great Spindletop oil field in 1901, then by its diversification into petrochemicals, aerospace, computers, and many other industries. Metropolitan areas grew along with the economy, and the state became the second most populous in the nation.

Political culture, however, has not changed as rapidly as the state's population and economy. The influence of the traditional conservative culture is evident in the treatment Texas affords to business and industry. In 1996, a private firm conducted a nationwide survey to determine how favorable a "business climate" each of the states had created. North Carolina was found to have the most favorable business climate, with Texas second.[6]

But while a "favorable business climate" in the short run consists of law taxes, weak labor unions, cheap labor, and an inactive government, in the long run these policies may create a fragile economy. In particular, the state's toleration of a mediocre public education system may be damaging its future.

The Corporation for Enterprise Development is a private organization that grades each state in terms not only of its economic health at any one time, but of its capacity for positive growth. Despite Texas's evidently booming economy, in 1998 the CED could rate it no better then "C" in its category of Development Capacity. Chief cause of the CED's lack of optimism about Texas's future was the state's mixed record on educating its children.[7]

Indeed, by the late 1990s, after a great deal of argument and tinkering with public policy, the Texas system of education could still not be termed a success. On the encouraging side, more students were passing the (very basic) Texas Assessment of

5. Molly Ivins, "National Media: Here's the Real Dirt on Bush," *Austin American-Statesman,* April 6, 1999, A9.

6. Steve Brown, "Texas No. 2 on List of Best Business Sites," *Dallas Morning News,* October 2, 1996, D1.

7. Corporation for Enterprise Development, "1998 Development Report Card for the States" [for details on this report, log on to the CED's website, listed at the end of the chapter].

Austin, home of one of the state's two flagship universities and a city that has pursued such education-dependent industries as computers, was greatly embarrassed in 1999 when the Texas Education Agency rated thirteen of the city's schools as "low performing" and rated its entire school district "unacceptable" for reporting fraudulent data to the agency. It is not clear whether Austin is typical of the Texas educational system as a whole.

SOURCE: Courtesy of Ben Sargent.

Academic Skills (TAAS) test every year, and in 1999 the state's eighth graders ranked fourth among the fifty states in a national writing test.[8]

On the discouraging side, however, 50 percent of the state's African-American and Hispanic youth and 30 percent of its Anglo youth were not graduating from high school. As a result, Texas ranked 49th among the fifty states in the percentage of teenagers who graduated from high school. It also ranked 43rd in how its high schoolers scored on the national Scholastic Aptitude Test. Surveys of employers suggested that their biggest concern was a lack of adequate skills in the workforce.[9]

For most of the twentieth century, Texas could rely upon its vast petroleum reserves to bring it prosperity. With seemingly endless gushers of black gold supplying them with jobs and their government with revenue, Texans believed that they did not have to worry about policies to educate a quality workforce or the taxes necessary to pay for such policies.

8. A. Phillips Brooks, "More Students Passing TAAS," *Austin American-Statesman,* May 28, 1999, B1; Jena Heath, "Texas Students No. 4 on U.S. Test," *Austin American-Statesman,* September 29, 1999, A1.

9. Richard Halpin, "High Dropout Rate Burdens Taxpayers With Enormous Costs," *Austin American-Statesman,* March 19, 1996, A13; Kendra A. Hovey and Harold A. Hovey, *State Fact Finder* 1999 (Washington, D.C.: Congressional Quarterly, 1999), 197; Davis, "Texas By the Numbers," op. cit., Bill Hobby, "Economically Robust Now, Texas Faces Uncertain Future," *Austin American-Statesman,* January 25, 1996, A11.

In 1985, however, the worldwide price of oil collapsed, dropping from over $30 a barrel to under $10 in the span of a few months. Thousands of wells in Texas, unable to turn a profit at such prices, were abandoned. With them went both private jobs and public revenues. Every time the price of oil dropped one dollar, Texas lost 13,500 jobs, $100 million in severance taxes, and $2.3 billion in gross state product.[10]

Despite the recovery of the state's economy in the early 1990s and its boom in the latter half of the decade, the fiscal problems caused by the decline of the petroleum industry have not been temporary. Oil production has continued to fall. Petroleum severance taxes, which in the 1970s had contributed about a third of state government's income, were producing less than 2 percent by the late 1990s.

And so the legislature has been forced to make unpopular choices. In 1984, 1986, and 1987 it raised state taxes. Texas's system of raising revenue, relying ever more heavily on the sales tax, became more regressive than ever (see Table 1.1). A *regressive* tax takes a larger percentage of the income of people the poorer they are, because they spend a larger portion of their income on commodities that are subject to a flat-rate tax. This is in contrast to a *progressive* tax, which takes a larger proportion of the income of people the wealthier they are, because the tax rate rises with their income.

Trying desperately to find a painless source of money, Texans established a state lottery in 1991. The same year the legislature restructured the state's corporation franchise tax and created other revenue-raising methods. All together, these measures brought in an extra $2.6 billion to the state treasury in their first year of operation. By mid-1990s, Texas state government was taking in more money than it was spending. The surplus continued in the second half of the decade.

Despite multiplying sources of income, however, Texas government continued to fund education, and various other state services, at levels below those that other states found desirable. Table 1.1 illustrates the point that on several measures of state services Texas continued to rank near the bottom.

Perhaps as a result of this relatively feeble government effort, Texas also continued to lag behind most other states in many rankings of quality of life. As Table 1.2 emphasizes, Texas scores low not only in some important measures of educational achievement, but also in child health protection, air pollution, and many other criteria of civilized living.

Texas state government is therefore faced with serious problems of preparing its citizens for the future. So far, it has demonstrated little inclination to deal with them. The greatest accomplishment of Texas government through the twentieth century was to keep taxes low. As we enter the twenty-first century, Texas citizens have to wonder if that is enough.

THE PEOPLE OF TEXAS

In many ways Texas is the classic American melting pot of different peoples, although it occasionally seems more like a boiling cauldron. The state was originally

---

10. "Texas A Net Loser From Falling Oil Prices, Economist Reports," *Energy Studies,* Vol. 11, #5, May/June 1986 (Newsletter of the Center for Energy Studies of the University of Texas at Austin), 1.

TABLE 1.1

Texas's Rank among States in Expenditure and Taxation

Category	Year	Rank
(a) Per capita state government expenditure	1997	50
(b) Teacher salaries	1997	38
(c) Maximum welfare benefits for a family of three	1998	47
(d) Per capita education expenditures	1995	30
(e) Per capita state funding for public health	1998	47
(f) Spending for parks and recreation	1998	48
(g) Tax rate on the poor	1996	6
(h) Tax rate on the rich	1996	40
(i) Progressivity of taxes	1996	44

SOURCES: (a) From Kendra A. Hovey and Harold A. Hovey, *State Fact Finder 1999* (Washington, DC: Congressional Quarterly, 1999), 173; (b) from Dave McNeely, "Everyone Wants to Raise Teacher Pay, But the Devil Is in the Details," *Austin American-Statesman,* March 25, 1999, A19; (c) from Mary Alice Davis, "Texas by the Numbers," *Austin American-Statesman,* March 25, 1999, A19; (d) from Hovey and Hovey, *State Fact Finder 1999,* 202; (e) and (f) from Ronnie Dugger, "Questions for George W.," *Texas Observer,* May 14, 1999, 22; (g) and (h) from Michael P. Ettinger, Robert S. McIntyre, Elizabeth A. Fray, John F. O'Hare, Julie King, and Neil Miransky, *Who Pays? A Distributional Analysis of the Tax System in All 50 States* (Washington, DC: Citizens for Tax Justice, Institute on Taxation and Economic Policy, 1996), 2 ("poor" here defined as the bottom 20% of the population) and Appendix I ("rich" here defined as the top 1% of the population); (i) from Hovey and Hovey, *State Fact Finder 1999,* 157.

populated by various Native American tribes. In the sixteenth and seventeenth centuries the Spaniards conquered the land, and from the intermingling of the conquerors and the conquered came the *mestizos,* persons of mixed Spanish and indigenous blood. In the nineteenth century Western European immigrants wrested the land from the heirs of the Spaniards. They often brought with them black slaves. Soon waves of immigration arrived from Europe and Asia, and more mestizos came from Mexico. The inflow continued into the 1980s and 1990s, with Vietnamese creating the state's first large Asian-American community.

The Census

At the end of each decade, the national government takes a census of each state's population. This census itself is a hot political topic because it is the basis for distributing money from many federal programs, and also for allocating seats in both the U.S. House of Representatives and the state legislatures. Critics of the census charge that it misses millions of poor people, especially those for whom English is not the first language.

The 1990 census was the subject of political wrangling, and the final figures eventually had to be ratified by the courts. Still, the federal General Accounting Office estimated that undercounting of Texas citizens cost the state $934 million in lost revenue.[11] Table 1.3 shows the official 1980 and 1990 figures for Texas as well as the Census Bureau's population projections. The increase in population indicated in the

11. "Unadjusted U.S. Census Cost Texas," *Austin American-Statesman,* March 3, 1999, A19.

TABLE 1.2

Texas's Rank in Measures of Quality of Life

Measure of Quality of Life	Year	Rank
(a) Percentage of children without health insurance	1998	1
(b) High school graduation rate	1996	49
(c) Toxic emissions	1995	1
(d) Percentage of population in poverty	1998	5
(e) Teen birth rate	1997	3
(f) Percent of population in prison	1996	1
(g) Murder rate	1996	16
(h) "Liveability index"	1997	40

SOURCES: (a) From Ronnie Dugger, "Questions for George W.," *Texas Observer,* May 14, 1999, 22; (b) from Kendra A. Hovey and Harold A. Hovey, *State Fact Finder 1999* (Washington, DC: Congressional Quarterly, 1999), 197; (c) and (d) from Mary Alice Davis, "Texas by the Numbers," *Austin American-Statesman,* March 25, 1999, A19; (e) from Andrew Park, "Texas' Teen Birth Rates among Nation's Highest," *Austin American-Statesman,* April 30, 1999, B2; (f) from *The Book of the States* (Lexington, KY: Council of State Governments, 1998), 400; (g) from Hovey and Hovey, *State Fact Finder 1999,* 250; Davis, "Texas by the Numbers" ("the liveability index" is created by combining a number of indicators of well-being; the "most liveable" state was Minnesota).

table entitled Texas to three additional seats in the U.S. House after 1990, bringing the state's total to thirty.

The U.S. Census Bureau makes unofficial population estimates between its counts at the end of each decade. By its 1999 estimate, the Texas population had soared past 20 million, making it the second largest state after California at almost 32 million, and the fastest growing of all fifty. It is very likely that Texas will be awarded still more House seats after the 2000 census.

More than two-fifths of the state's present population consists of African Americans (11 percent) and Mexican Americans (31 percent) together, and the 2000 census will probably show that these percentages have increased. By 2010, "minorities"

TABLE 1.3

The Texas Population, 1980, 1990, and 2000

Ethnic Group	1980	1990	2000 (Projected)	2000 Percent of Total
Anglo	9,350,299	10,291,680	11,100,000	55
Hispanic* or Latino	2,985,824	4,339,905	6,300,000	31
African American	1,710,175	2,021,632	2,300,000	11
Other	200,528	378,565	637,310	3
TOTAL	14,229,191	16,986,510	20,330,000	

* The great majority of Hispanics in Texas are Mexican American.

SOURCES: For 1980 and 1990, *1992–93 Texas Almanac and State Industrial Guide* (Dallas: A. H. Belo Corp., 1991), 137; for 2000, "Texas Projected Population," *Dallas Morning News,* September 20, 1999, A6 (source of the news report was the Texas State Data Center at Texas A&M).

are expected to account for one-half of the state's population and therefore will no longer be minorities.

The Distribution of Population

The distribution of population in Texas shows evidence of three things: the initial patterns of migration, the influence of geography and climate, and the location of the cities. The Hispanic migration came first, north from Mexico, and to this day is still concentrated in South and West Texas (Figure 1.1). Likewise, African Americans still live predominantly in the eastern half of the state (Figure 1.2).

As one moves from east to west across Texas, annual rainfall drops by about 5 inches per hundred miles. East Texas has a moist climate and supports intensive farming, while West Texas is dry and requires pumping from underground aquifers to maintain agriculture. The overall distribution of settlement reflects the food production capability of the local areas, with East Texas remaining far more populous. Cities developed at strategic locations, usually on rivers or the seacoast, and the state's population is heavily concentrated in the urban areas.

The Political Relevance of Population

The division of the Texas population into Anglos, Mexican Americans, and African Americans reflects political realities. All citizens are individuals, form their own opinions, and have the right to choose to behave as they see fit. No one is a prisoner of his or her group, and every generalization has exceptions. Nevertheless, it is a long-observed fact that people in similar circumstances often see things from similar points of view, and it therefore helps to clarify political conflict to be aware of the shared similarities. In this book, Anglos, Mexican Americans, and African Americans will often be discussed as groups, without an intent to be unfair to individual exceptions.

Historically, both minority groups have been treated badly by the Anglo majority. Today, the members of both groups are in general less wealthy than are Anglos. For example, according to the 1990 census, the mean household income for Anglos was about twice that for Mexican Americans. Foreign-born Mexicans, especially, were four times as likely to live below the poverty line as were Anglos.[12]

With economic differences come political conflict. As will be explained in Chapters Three, Four, and Five, Mexican Americans and African Americans tend to hold more liberal political opinions, and vote more liberally, than do Anglos. As the minority population increases in size relative to the Anglo population, its greater liberalism is sure to make itself felt, sooner or later, in the voting booth. Texas's changing mix of population is therefore constantly modifying its politics.

THE AGENDA OF THIS BOOK

The following chapters will examine how Texas organizes and operates politically to attempt to deal with its present social and economic problems and to plan for the

---

12. *Latinos in Texas: A Socio-Demographic Profile* (Austin: The Thomas Rivera Center, 1995), 66, 84, 111.

FIGURE 1.1

Texas's Hispanic Population as a Percentage of Total Population by Districts, 1990 SOURCE: Texas Legislative Council, based on 1990 census data.

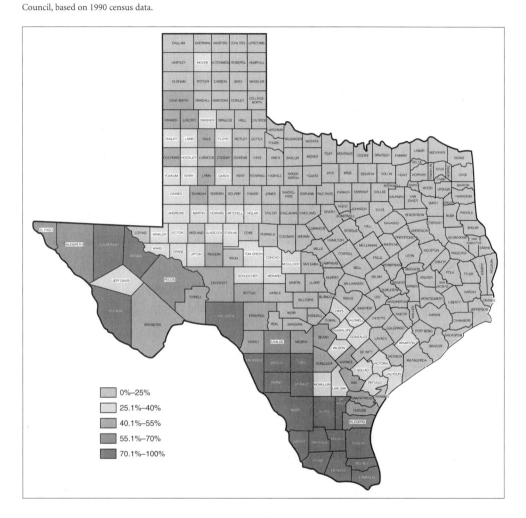

future. Every chapter will compare the reality of Texas politics to the democratic ideal and ask readers to decide how defensible the reality is. The book will consider, in order, the Texas Constitution, and then the inputs of politics: the state's important interest groups, the activities of political parties, and the individual voter within the context of campaigns and elections. The next subject will be the institutions of state government—the legislature, the executive branch, and the judiciary. Following that is an analysis of the outputs of politics, public policy, with a chapter devoted to state finance. Finally we will present a discussion of local government within Texas.

FIGURE 1.2

Texas's African-American Population as a Percentage of Total Population by Districts, 1990 SOURCE: Texas Legislative Council, based on 1990 census data.

SUMMARY

This chapter began with a summary of democratic theory, which holds that the legitimacy of a government rests upon the citizens' participation. The intention was announced to contrast the ideal of democracy with its actual practice in Texas. The topic then shifted to the way the Lone Star State is situated within the American federal system. The discussion turned to political culture and some of the implications of the general conservatism that has dominated Texas through much of its history.

Texas has a large and diverse population that continues to grow and change. Since minority citizens tend to have different political values than Anglo citizens, the state's changing population has implications for the present and future of its politics.

STUDY QUESTIONS

1. Could a king with absolute power be the head of a legitimate government? Why or why not?
2. Briefly summarize political conservatism and liberalism.
3. Would you say that the Texas political culture, as described in the text, is dominant in your family? Why or why not? In your community? Why or why not?
4. In general, what has been Texas's historical policy toward business (the economy)? Toward taxes? Toward education? Toward welfare? Toward environmental protection?
5. Would you say that the evidence supports the opinion that Texas is a better place to live than other states?
6. Why is the decennial census so important to Texas politics? In another ten to fifteen years, minority groups will constitute a majority of the Texas population. What effects might this have on the state's politics and government?

SURFING THE WEB

Students may access facts about Texas history at the "Lone Star Junction" website by logging on to the site and then clicking on any of several icons. The site is:

http://www.lsjunction.com/

To find facts about the Texas Assessment of Academic Skills (TAAS) test, log on to the following site:

http://www.tea.state.tx.us/student.assessment/release.htm

To access more facts than anyone could use from the United States census, log on to the following site:

http://www.census.gov/

To find out more about the Corporation for Enterprise Development and examine its ratings of all the states, log on to:

http://www.cfed.org

2

*ll political
power is inherent
in the people, and all
free governments are
founded on their
authority, and instituted
for their benefit.*

Article 1,
Texas Constitution

*It is very doubtful
whether man is enough of
a political animal to
produce a good, sensible,
serious and efficient
constitution. All evidence
is against it.*

George Bernard Shaw,
Irish dramatist

THE CONSTITUTIONAL SETTING

INTRODUCTION

Since its ratification in 1788, the Constitution of the United States has been used frequently as a model by emerging nations. State constitutions, however, seldom enjoy such admiration. Indeed, the Constitution of the State of Texas is more often ridiculed than praised because of its length and its outdated, unworkable provisions.

Texas is far from the only state whose constitution draws such criticism. The political circumstances that surrounded the writing of the national **Constitution** differed considerably from those existing at the times when the constitutions of the fifty states, especially the states of the old Confederacy, were written. State constitutions tend to be very rigid and to include too many specific details. As a result, we find that Texas and many other states must resort to frequent **constitutional amendments,** which are formal changes in the basic governing document.

In **federal systems,** which are systems of government that provide for a division and sharing of powers between a national government and state or regional governments, the constitutions of the states complement the national constitution. In the United States specifically, the state constitution cannot conflict legally with the U.S. Constitution. Article VI of the U.S. Constitution provides that the Constitution, laws, and treaties of the national government take precedence over the constitutions and laws of the states. Nevertheless, state constitutions are important because state governments are responsible for many of the basic programs and services, such as education, that daily affect citizens. A major difference between the U.S. and Texas constitutions is the generality of the national document and the statutelike specificity of the state charter.

The basic purposes of all constitutions are the same. This chapter will examine those purposes, then outline the development of the several Texas constitutions, elaborate the principal features of the state's current document, and illustrate the problems that have led to numerous amendments and revision efforts.

PURPOSES OF CONSTITUTIONS

The first purpose served by a constitution is to *give legitimacy* to the government. A government has legitimacy when the governed accept its acts as moral, fair, and just, and thus believe that they should obey its laws. This acceptance cuts two ways, however. On one hand, citizens will allow government to act in certain ways that are not permitted to private individuals. For example, citizens cannot legally drive down a city street at 60 miles an hour, but police officers may do so when in the act of pursuing wrongdoers. On the other hand, citizens also expect governments not to act arbitrarily; the concept of legitimacy is closely associated with limited government. If a police officer sped down a city street at 90 miles an hour just for the thrill of doing so, this behavior would fall outside the bounds of legitimacy.

What citizens are willing to accept is conditioned by their history and political tradition and by their civic culture. In Texas and the rest of the United States, democratic practices including citizen participation in decision making and fair processes are a part of that history and culture.

The second purpose of constitutions is to *organize government.* Governments must be organized in some way that makes it clear who the major officials are, how they are selected, and what the relationship is among those charged with basic governmental functions. And again, to some extent, the American states have been guided by the national model. Both national and state constitutions incorporate **separation of powers** with a system of **checks and balances** to ensure that each branch of government can be restrained by the others. In reality, we have separate institutions and defined lines of authority that lead to a sharing of power more than to a literal separation of powers. For example, passing bills is thought of as a legislative function, but the governor can veto a bill.

The Constitution of the United States expressly grants certain powers to the national government and implies a broad range of additional powers through Article I, Section 8, the "necessary and proper clause." This clause, also known as the "elastic clause," enables Congress to execute all its other powers by providing broad authority to pass needed legislation. Thus, *granting specific powers* is the third purpose of constitutions. The powers not explicitly or implicitly granted to the national government were reserved for the people or for the states by the Tenth Amendment. As the national Constitution has been developed and interpreted, many powers actually exist concurrently at both the federal and state levels of government—for example, the power to assess a tax on gasoline. Within this general framework, which continues to evolve, the Texas Constitution sets forth specific functions for which the state maintains primary or concurrent responsibility. Local government, criminal law, and regulation of intrastate commerce are among the diverse activities over which the state retains principal control.

American insistence on the fourth purpose of constitutions, *limiting governmental power,* reflects the influence of British political culture, our ancestors' dissatisfaction with colonial rule, and the extraordinary individualism that characterized our national development during the eighteenth and nineteenth centuries. The most famous and important limitations on governmental power are the guarantees of individual rights found in the national Bill of Rights. In Texas, the conservative political tradition resulted in a heavy emphasis on limiting government's ability to act. For example, the governor has very little power to remove members of state boards and commissions except by informal techniques such as an aggressive public relations campaign against a board member.

As we assess the degree to which democratic theory is actually applied in practice, one measure is how well a constitution accomplishes all these purposes. A constitution that only organizes government and assigns power could be very undemocratic, since it could allow for arbitrary governmental action. A constitution that provided only for limiting government power, even though that single purpose might be enough to achieve legitimacy, would still fall short since government would be unable to act effectively on behalf of the citizens.

TEXAS CONSTITUTIONS

The United States has had two fundamental laws: the short-lived Articles of Confederation and the present Constitution, which was written in 1787. Texas is

TABLE 2.1

Constitutions of Texas

Constitution	Dates
Republic of Texas	1836–1845
Statehood	1845–1861
Civil War	1861–1866
Reconstruction	1866–1869
Radical Reconstruction	1869–1876
State of Texas	1876–present

currently governed by its sixth constitution, ratified in 1876. The fact that the 1876 constitution had five predecessors in only forty years illustrates the political turbulence of the mid-1800s in Texas. Table 2.1 lists the six Texas state charters.

Texas was under the formal governance of Spain for 131 years, although only San Antonio and El Paso received any attention since the rest of the colony was sparsely populated. It became a Mexican state for fifteen years after Mexico declared its independence from Spain in 1821. Among several events leading Texians—as they were called—to seek their own independence, the assumption of power in Mexico by Antonio López de Santa Anna in 1834, the temporary incarceration of Texas colonizer Stephen F. Austin, and the exercise of greater control over Texans were paramount. Texans issued a Declaration of Independence on March 2, 1836, stating that "the people of Texas, do now constitute a Free, Sovereign, and Independent Republic, and are fully invested with all the rights and attributes which properly belong to independent nations. . . ." After a brief but bitter war with Mexico, Texas gained independence on April 21 after the Battle of San Jacinto. Independence was formalized when the two treaties of Velasco were signed by President Antonio López de Santa Anna of Mexico and President David Burnet of Texas on May 14, 1836. By September, the Constitution of the Republic of Texas, drafted shortly after independence was declared, had been implemented. Major features of this charter paralleled those of the U.S. Constitution, including a president and a congress; however, unlike the U.S. Constitution, the document also guaranteed the continuation of slavery.

The United States had been sympathetic to the Texas struggle for independence. Nevertheless, Texas's admission to the Union was postponed for a decade because of northern opposition to the admission of new slave states. After nine years of nationhood, Texas was finally admitted to the Union. The Constitution of 1845, the "statehood constitution," was modeled after the constitutions of other southern states. It was regarded as one of the nation's best at the time. The 1845 constitution not only embraced democratic principles of participation but also included many elements later associated with the twentieth-century administrative reform movement and was a very brief, clear document.[1]

The Constitution of 1845 was influenced by Jacksonian democracy, named for President Andrew Jackson. Jacksonians believed in an expansion of individual

1. See, for example, Fred Gantt, Jr., *The Chief Executive in Texas: A Study in Gubernatorial Leadership* (Austin: University of Texas Press, 1964), 24.

participation in government, at least for white males.[2] Jackson's basic beliefs ultimately led to the spoils system of appointing to office those who had supported the victors in the election ("to the victors belong the spoils"). Jacksonian democracy also produced long ballots with almost every office up for popular vote, short terms of office, and the expansion of voting rights. Thus, while participatory, Jacksonianism was not flawless.

When Texas joined the Confederate States of America in 1861, its constitution was again modified. This document, the Civil War Constitution of 1861, merely altered the Constitution of 1845 to ensure greater protection for the institution of slavery and to declare allegiance to the Confederacy.

Texas was on the losing side of the Civil War and was occupied by federal troops. President Andrew Johnson ordered Texas to construct yet another constitution. The 1866 document declared secession illegal, repudiated the war debt, and abolished slavery. However, it did not provide for improving conditions for African Americans. In other words, the only changes made were those necessary to gain presidential support for readmission to the Union.

Radical postwar congressional leaders were not satisfied with these minimal changes in the constitutions of southern states. They insisted on more punitive measures. In 1868–1869, a constitution that centralized power in the state government, provided generous salaries for officials, stipulated appointed judges, and called for annual legislative sessions was drafted. It contained many of the elements that present-day reformers would like to see in a revised state charter. However, because the constitution was forced on the state by outsiders in Washington and by carpetbaggers—northerners who came to Texas with their worldly goods in a suitcase made out of carpeting—white southerners never regarded the document as acceptable. They especially resented the strong, centralized state government and the powerful office of governor that were imposed on them. Moreover, because all former rebels were barred from voting, the 1869 constitution was adopted by Unionists and African

---

2. The Jacksonians supported slavery and devised an Indian policy that led to the brutal treatment of Native Americans.

Because Texas was an independent republic when the United States annexed it, the annexation agreement reflected compromises by both the state and national governments. For example, Texas gave up its military property but kept its public lands. The national government refused to assume the state's $10 million debt but provided that four additional states could be carved out of the Texas territory should the state desire such a division.

In the 1990s, a radical group calling itself the Republic of Texas contended that Texas remains a nation and that the United States illegally annexed Texas in 1845. Pursuing this belief, members of the movement harassed state officials in a variety of ways, including filing liens against the assets of public agencies and regularly accusing state officials of illegally using their powers.

Americans. Ironically, this constitution least accomplished the purpose of legitimacy—acceptance by the people—but was the most forward-looking in terms of granting power and organizing government.

The popular three-term Governor Elisha Pease resigned in the fall of 1869 after the radical constitution was adopted. After a vacancy in the state's chief executive office lasting more than three months, Edmund J. (E. J.) Davis was elected governor and took office at the beginning of 1870. The election not only barred the state's Democrats and traditional Republicans, both conservative groups, from voting but exhibited a number of irregularities. Davis was an honest man, but the radical state charter, Davis's Radical Republican ties, and his subsequent designation as provisional governor by President Ulysses Grant combined to give him dictatorial powers.[3]

THE PRESENT TEXAS CONSTITUTION

Traditionally Democratic and conservative, Texans began to chafe for constitutional revision as soon as the Democrats regained legislative control in 1872. An 1874 reform effort passed in the Texas Senate but failed in the House. This constitution would have provided flexibility in such areas as how tax dollars could be spent and terms of office. It also would have facilitated elite control and a sellout to the powerful railroads, which were hated by ordinary citizens because of their pricing policies and corruption of state legislatures.[4]

In 1875 the legislature called a constitutional convention, and ninety delegates were elected from all over the state. In the 1870s, farming and ranching dominated the state's economy, and one particular farmers' organization, the Grange, was a dominant force during the convention. The elected delegates overwhelmingly reflected a rural conservatism that embodied a belief in white supremacy and a strong emphasis on the constitutional purpose of limiting government. Other factors at work during the convention included Jacksonian democracy, the like-mindedness of the delegates; and a general lack of faith in government. The administration of Governor E. J. Davis contributed greatly to this cynicism.

Accordingly, the new constitution, completed in 1875, emphasized curbing the powers of government. The governor's term was limited to two years, a state debt ceiling of $200,000 was established, salaries of elected state officials were fixed, the legislature was limited to **biennial** sessions, and the governor was allowed to make very few executive appointments.

When this document went to the people of Texas for a vote in February 1876, it was approved by a margin of 136,606 to 56,652; 130 of the 150 Texas counties registered approval. The twenty counties that did not favor the new charter were urban areas. Understandably, modern critics of the Texas Constitution are also primarily urban, since the constitution does little to help solve the problems of the state's cities.

3. Jim B. Pearson, Ben Procter, and William B. Conroy, *Texas, The Land and Its People,* 3d ed. (Dallas: Hendrick-Long, 1987), 400–405; *The Texas Almanac, 1996–1997* (Dallas: *Dallas Morning News,* 1996), 499.

4. Historical perspectives are based on remarks of John W. Mauer, "State Constitutions in a Time of Crisis: The Case of the Texas Constitution of 1876," Symposium on the Texas Constitution, sponsored by the University of Texas Law School and the *Texas Law Review,* October 7, 1989.

General Features

The Texas Constitution of today is very much like the original 1876 document, in spite of numerous amendments and some major changes in the executive article. It includes a preamble and seventeen articles, with each article divided into subsections.

The Lone Star State almost can claim the record for the longest constitution in the nation. Only the constitution of Alabama contains more words than the roughly 81,000 in the Texas charter.[5]

Overall, the Texas Constitution reflects the factors, outlined earlier, that influenced the constitutional convention. It reflects the state's conservative political tradition. Changes in the national Constitution, both by amendment and by judicial interpretation, have necessitated alterations of the state constitution, although "deadwood" provisions—those that cannot be made operational and that conflict with federal law—still remain. The public has voted on 565 proposals to amend the constitution, with the result that 390 amendments had been added by the end of 1999 (see Table 2.2). These amendments, necessary because of the basic document's restrictiveness, have produced a state charter that is poorly organized and difficult to read, let alone interpret—even by the courts.[6] In effect, the constitution is both fundamental law and a legislative code—that is, it incorporates provisions that in other states are usually found in statutes. Such matters as state university capital funding

5. The Alabama Constitution had approximately 220,000 words as of 1998. This and other comparative information can be found in *The Book of the States, 1998–99*, vol. 32 (Lexington, KY: Council of State Governments, 1998), 3.

6. A full discussion of poorly organized sections and provisions in conflict with federal law can be found in *Reorganized Texas Constitution without Substantive Change* (Austin: Texas Advisory Commission on Intergovernmental Relations, 1977).

TABLE 2.2
Texas Constitutional Amendments, 1879* to Present

Decade(s)	Proposed	Adopted	Cumulative Total
1870s–1880s	16	5	5
1890s	15	11	16
1900s	20	10	26
1910s	35	9	35
1920s	26	12	47
1930s	45	34	81
1940s	35	25	106
1950s	43	33	139
1960s	84	55	194
1970s	67	44	238
1980s	99	88	326
1990s	80	64	390
Total through 2000	**565**	**390**	**390**

*The first amendment to the 1876 Texas Constitution was adopted in 1879.

SOURCE: Compiled by C. Neal Tate and Charldean Newell.

(buildings and equipment, for example), the creation of hospital districts, and the land program for veterans are all found in the constitution.

Specific Features

The Texas Constitution is similar to the U.S. Constitution in many ways, particularly the way in which the purposes of organizing and limiting government and legitimacy are addressed. That is, each government has executive, legislative, and judicial branches. Each has a system of shared powers. Each includes provisions against unequal or arbitrary government action, such as restricting freedom of religion. The two documents are less alike in terms of providing power to government—the national Constitution is much more flexible in allowing government to act than is the state document. Texas legislators, for example, cannot set their own salaries or determine when their business is finished and adjournment is appropriate.[7] Details of these features can be found in the later chapters of this book.

Bill of Rights.   Similar to the **Bill of Rights** in the U.S. Constitution, Article I of the Texas Constitution provides for equality under the law; religious freedom, including separation of church and state;[8] due process for the criminally accused; and freedom of speech and of the press. The state constitution further provides protection for the mentally incompetent and several specific guarantees, such as a prohibition against deporting an individual from the state, among the thirty protections cited in the document. It includes an Equal Rights Amendment for all Texans.

Citizens generally support the U.S. and Texas bills of rights. However, just as the public sometimes gets upset with the U.S. Bill of Rights when constitutional protections are afforded to someone the public wants to "throw the book at"—an accused child molester, for example—Texans sometimes react against the protections provided in the state constitution. A 1992 Texas Poll revealed that if given a chance to vote on the Bill of Rights today, "a significant number of Texans would balk at several sweeping protections—including the rights to assemble and protest, to hold unpopular beliefs and to bear arms."[9] Nevertheless, modern efforts toward constitutional revision have left these protections intact.[10]

Separation of Powers.   Like the national Constitution, the state charter divides governmental functions among three branches: the executive, the legislative, and the judicial. The national government divides power between the nation and the states as well as among the three branches. Providing for a sharing of power should ensure

7. The definitive study of the Texas Constitution is Janice C. May, *The Texas State Constitution, A Reference Guide* (Westport, CT: Greenwood, 1996).

8. Article I, Section 4, stipulates acknowledgment of the existence of a Supreme Being as a test for public office; however, this provision is not enforced because it violates the U.S. Constitution.

9. Todd J. Gillman, "Bill of Rights Might Face Tough Ride Now," *Dallas Morning News,* August 22, 1992, 12F.

10. The extensive application of the U.S. Bill of Rights to the states through the vehicle of the Fourteenth Amendment is a modern occurrence. So long as citizens were legally perceived to be citizens of the state first and of the nation second, state guarantees were vital. In recent years, state courts have begun to reassert themselves as protectors of rights, as the federal courts have begun to be less protective in their own decisions.

that no one branch becomes too powerful. Article II outlines the separation of institutions, and the articles dealing with the individual "departments"—as these branches are labeled in the state constitution—develop a system of checks and balances similar to those found in the national Constitution. Examples of these checks include the governor's power to veto acts of the legislature and the legislature's power to impeach a governor.

Legislative Branch.   The Texas Legislature, like the U.S. Congress, consists of a senate and a house of representatives. The legislative article (Article III) establishes a legislative body, sets the qualifications for membership, provides its basic organization, and fixes its meeting times. This article also sets the salary of state legislators. A 1991 constitutional amendment created an Ethics Commission whose powers include recommending legislative salaries, but the recommendation still must be approved by the voters. The Ethics Commission has made no such recommendation. Until it does, a $7,200 annual salary prevails.

Rather than emphasizing the positive powers of the legislature, the article spells out those specific actions that the legislature cannot take, reflecting the fear of strong government brought about by Reconstruction. For example, the U.S. Constitution gives Congress broad powers to make any laws that are "necessary and proper." In contrast, rather than allowing lawmaking to be handled through the regular legislative process, the Texas Constitution forces state government to resort to the constitutional amendment process. Another illustration is that adding to the fund maintained by the state to help veterans adjust to civilian life by giving them good deals on the purchase of land requires an amendment. So does changing the percentage of the state budget that can be spent on public welfare.

Article III also sets limits on legislative procedure. It stipulates that the legislature may meet in regular session only every two years. It also specifies the number of days for introduction of bills, committee work, and floor action, although the governor, to permit early floor action, can declare an emergency.

Executive Branch.   Little similarity exists between provisions for the executive branch in Texas's charter and those in the national Constitution. The U.S. Constitution provides for a very strong chief executive, the president, and creates only one other elective office, the vice president, who runs on a ticket with the presidential candidate. Article IV of the state constitution provides that the governor is the "chief executive" of the state. However, the state constitution requires that the following individuals also be elected statewide, just as the governor is:

1. The lieutenant governor, who presides over the Texas Senate
2. The comptroller (pronounced con-TROL-ler) of public accounts, who collects the state's taxes and determines whether enough revenue exists to fund the state budget and who keeps the state's money
3. The commissioner of the General Land Office, who protects the state's environment and administers its vast public lands
4. The attorney general, who is the state's lawyer
5. Members of the Texas Railroad Commission, who regulate intrastate transportation and the oil and gas industry

Furthermore, statutory laws require that the agriculture commissioner and members of the State Board of Education be elected. Thus, quite unlike the president, who appoints most key federal executives, the governor is saddled with five other elected executives and two key elected policy-making boards. He or she has no formal control over these individuals.

The result is that Texas has a "disintegrated" or "fragmented" executive branch—that is, the governor has little or no control over other elected officials or most state agencies. Most of the more than 225 state agencies receive policy direction from a board or commission that is largely independent of the chief executive. Thus, we see that the executive article, like the legislative one, is overly specific and creates roadblocks to expeditious governmental action. When government is burdened with too many restrictions, it cannot act quickly, even when citizens need a fast response. The governor, however, does have significant legislative powers through control of special sessions and the veto.

Judicial Branch.   The national judicial system is clear-cut—district courts, appeals courts, the U.S. Supreme Court—but the Texas judicial system is not at all clear. There are three distinctive features of the judicial article of the state constitution. First, a rather confusing pattern of six different types of courts is established. Further complicating the picture is the fact that there are two supreme courts, one each for civil (Supreme Court) and criminal (Court of Criminal Appeals) matters.

Second, each level of trial courts has concurrent, or overlapping, jurisdiction with another level; that is, either level of court may hear the case. Additionally, there are trial courts established by statute that have different jurisdictions from those established by the constitution. For example, constitutional county courts have concurrent jurisdiction with justice of the peace courts in civil matters involving $200 to $5,000. County courts-at-law overlap district courts in civil matters up to $100,000. Although the legislature can adjust the jurisdiction of statutory courts, constitutional court authority can be altered only by constitutional amendment. Furthermore, the minimum dollar amounts stated in the constitution reflect economic values of the previous century. In an era of multimillion-dollar lawsuits, having a district court—the chief trial court of the state—hear a case when the disputed amount is $1,000 or less detracts from the more significant trial work of that court.

The 76th Legislature in 1999 proposed seventeen amendments to the Texas Constitution. One of the most interesting ones was Proposition 1, which established a procedure for succession to the lieutenant governor's office. Amid wide speculation that Governor George W. Bush might be the next U.S. president, the state wanted to ensure an orderly procedure if Lieutenant Governor Rick Perry moved up to the governor's office. The amendment established a procedure whereby the members of the Senate would elect one of their own members to act as lieutenant governor. The individual would remain a member of the Senate. Even before the vote on the amendment, political speculation began about which senator might be catapulted into the very powerful position of lieutenant governor and, thus, presiding officer of the Senate.

Third, qualifications of judges are stated so as to allow those with no legal training to be eligible for a justice of the peace or county court bench.[11] The problem of judicial qualifications is aggravated by the fact that judges are elected in Texas, so that, on occasion, vote-getting ability may be more important than the ability to render judgments.[12] In the national government, the president appoints all judges, who must be confirmed by the Senate.

Local Government. The Texas Constitution assigns considerable power to units of local government, especially municipalities. Local governments fall into three categories: counties, municipalities, and special districts. The constitution gives these governmental units varying degrees of flexibility. Counties, often regarded as administrative and judicial arms of the state, are most restricted. They are saddled with a commission form of government that combines executive and legislative authority and is headed by a judge. The powers vested in them and the services they offer are fragmented.

Cities whose population is 5,000 or over may become home-rule units of government. **Home rule** allows a city to write its own charter and make changes in it without legislative approval; general-law cities must operate under statewide statutes. The major constitutional handicaps for cities are the ceilings imposed on tax rates and debt and the limitations on the frequency of charter amendments.

Special districts are limited-purpose local governments that have taxing authority. The legislature generally authorizes the creation of special districts, although some water and hospital districts have been created by constitutional amendment. School districts are the best-known type of special district.

Suffrage. The provisions on voting and the apportionment of legislative bodies are interesting because many of them clearly conflict with federal law, which itself continues to evolve as the legal/political philosophy of federal judges changes. For example, Article VII of the Texas Constitution still contains references to 21 as the minimum voting age. As mentioned earlier, such provisions are known as "deadwood" because they cannot be made operational. In some cases, stopgap measures have been passed by the legislature to achieve compliance with federal law, but the retention of these constitutional provisions is certainly confusing.

Amendments. The framers of a constitution cannot possibly anticipate every provision that should be included. Consequently, all constitutions specify a procedure for amendment. In Texas, proposals for amendment may be initiated during a regular or special session of the legislature, and an absolute two-thirds majority—that is, 100 House and 21 Senate members—must vote to submit the proposed changes to the voters. The governor cannot veto a proposed amendment. The legislature also specifies the date of the election at which an amendment is to be voted on by the public. Whenever possible, amendments are placed on the ballot in general elections to avoid the expense

11. Contrary to popular opinion, a justice of the peace without legal training cannot become a judge on a superior (appeals) court. Qualifications for the superior courts include ten years as a practicing lawyer or a combination of ten years' legal practice and judicial service.

12. According to *Forbes* magazine, Texas and Alabama have the most expensive judicial elections in the country. With serious money—as much as $2 million for a Texas Supreme Court seat—on the line, vote-getting skills become especially important. See Laura Castaneda, "D.C. Worst, Utah Best on Litigious List," *Dallas Morning News,* January 3, 1994, 1D, 4D.

of a separate, called election. Only a simple majority of those citizens who vote—that is, half plus one—is needed for ratification, making it rather easy to add amendments.

CONSTITUTIONAL REVISION
Need for Reform

On the whole, state constitutions are long, restrictive, inclusive, and confusing and need frequent amendment to permit the provision of necessary services as well as to keep pace with contemporary needs. State constitutions tend to reflect the concerns of people with vested interests, who prefer the "security blanket" of constitutional inclusion to the insecurity of being left at the mercy of legislatures with changing party alignments, political persuasions, and political concerns.

The Texas document especially illustrates the problem of having to legislate by constitutional amendment because of the rigidity of the constitution. For example, in recent years amendments have included everything from legalizing bingo for church and fraternal organizations to allowing an East Texas farmer to keep the land he had bought almost fifty years earlier in spite of a technical defect in the title to the property to eliminating the tax on leased cars not primarily used to produce income.

Nevertheless, citizens often have little or no interest in constitutional revision. Like the legislators who would have to propose the constitutional overhaul, they are more concerned about the issues that regularly beset the Texas political system—education, health care, highways, air quality, and so on. Too, most Texans are politically conservative and prefer the basic governing document that they know to one that could cause sociopolitical-economic changes that they would not like.

Constitutions, like all laws, are political. What one group advocates may be strongly opposed by other interests. For example, should an amendment absolutely prohibiting a state income tax be added to the constitution, individuals who don't like income taxes would be satisfied, but governmental agencies, including colleges and universities, could suffer dire financial consequences, since virtually all the other tax sources are already in use.

Nevertheless, the advocates of **constitutional revision,** although not always agreeing on what the change should be, tend to focus on the following provisions of the current constitution:

1. *The biennial legislative session.* As state politics and finance become more complex, the short legislative sessions, held only every other year, become more of a handicap to developing long-range public policy.
2. *The judicial system.* The Texas judicial system, as previously discussed, is characterized by multiple layers of courts with overlapping jurisdictions. Many reform advocates would like to see the establishment of a streamlined, unified judicial system that ordinary citizens could understand.
3. *The disintegrated/fragmented executive branch.* The executive branch is characterized by a multiplicity of elected officials and policy-making boards. Reformers suggest an executive branch modeled on the national executive—that is, a single elected official and a series of executive departments responsible

to that official. Democratic theory requires that citizens be able to understand how to directly influence the agents of government. In a system in which one can reasonably ask, "Who's in charge here?" citizens have a hard time ensuring that they will be represented in or even heard by government.

4. *County government.* County government's structure and its lack of power to pass ordinances mean that counties cannot readily respond to problems; especially troublesome in urban counties. Reform advocates suggest that county government be streamlined and given at least limited ordinance power.

5. *Detailed provisions in the constitution.* For example, each time more funding is needed for welfare payments or the veterans' land program, a constitutional amendment must be passed. Thus, another area for reform is removing from the constitution details that are better left for statutory law, which can be changed more readily as situations demand.

Recent Reform Efforts

Attempts to modernize the Texas Constitution have been made from time to time since its adoption in 1876. Serious interest in constitutional change was evident in 1957–1961, 1967–1969, and 1971–1974, and to some extent in 1991–1993 and 1999, but the only reform effort that actually resulted in an opportunity for the electorate to decide on a new document came in 1975.

1971–1974. A 1972 constitutional amendment authorized the 63rd Legislature to convene itself as a constitutional convention. The Texas Constitutional Revision Commission, created by the same amendment, provided a detailed study of the state constitution that served as the basis for new constitutions proposed in 1974 and 1975. The constitutional convention was quickly labeled the "Con-Con." The proposal drafted by the convention was defeated when two issues—pari-mutuel (that is, racetrack) betting and right-to-work, which is an antiunion provision—were introduced that became the red herrings for foes of reform. They brought opposition from Bible Belt conservatives opposed to gambling and from organized labor opposed to the continuation of right to work. These and other groups made enough legislators skittish to prevent a favorable decision in the legislature (1974 was an election year). The proposal died without ever reaching the voters.

1975. Interest in constitutional reform remained high. When the 64th Legislature convened in January 1975, constitutional revision was a principal issue. Senate Joint Resolution (SJR) 11 (with amendments) emerged as the vehicle for accomplishing constitutional change. Although the legislature did not adopt all of the changes suggested by the 1973 revision commission, legislators did draw heavily on that work.[13]

13. A detailed analysis of the 1975 document is available in George Braden's *Citizen's Guide to the Proposed New Constitution* (Houston: Institute of Urban Studies, University of Houston, 1975). The University of Houston served as a research and information center during the revision efforts and published numerous reports beginning in 1973. Scholars from across the state were involved in the Houston research. One, Janice C. May, published a book-length study, *Texas Constitutional Revision Experience in the '70s* (Austin: Sterling Swift, 1975). A summary of the general literature on the revision efforts and of voting behavior can be found in John E. Bebout, "The Meaning of the Vote on the Proposed Texas Constitution, 1975," *Public Affairs Comment* 24 (February 1978): 1–9, published by the Lyndon B. Johnson School of Public Affairs at the University of Texas at Austin.

Highlights of SJR 11 included annual legislative sessions, a streamlined judicial system, modernization of county government, elimination of such details as the welfare ceiling, more power for the governor coupled with a limit of two terms, property tax relief, and a tax on petroleum refining.

Powerful interests lined up on both sides of this proposed constitutional reform, with vested economic interests and emotionalism acting as important components of the struggle for ratification of the document. Those whose interests were already protected in the constitution did not want to risk change; those who wanted equal protection or who simply wanted a more workable document eagerly sought change. In spite of the efforts of most state officials to convince the voters of the worth of the proposed state charter, the entire proposal was defeated by a two-to-one margin on November 4, 1975. Governor Dolph Briscoe, fearful of higher taxes and government expansion, and county officials, fearful for their jobs, helped bring about the defeat. Texans clearly preferred the old, lengthy, familiar document to one they saw as possibly promoting more spending and allowing greater governmental power.

1991–1993. In 1991, Senator John Montford drafted a proposed new constitution for introduction during the 1993 legislative session. The Montford proposal included such features as:

- Six-year terms for senators and four-year terms for House members, coupled with a limit of two consecutive terms for a senator and three for a House member
- A sixty-day budget session of the legislature in even-numbered years
- Empowerment of the legislature to meet to reconsider bills vetoed by the governor
- The only elected executives to be the governor, lieutenant governor, and comptroller, each with a limit of two terms
- Simplification of the court system and a provision of nonpartisan elections
- Creation of five regional university systems, each of which would share in the Permanent University Fund (PUF)
- Ordinance power for counties, subject to local voter approval[14]

As is so often the case, immediate problems such as the budget shortfall, school finance, and the inability of the prison system to cope with the volume of state prisoners crowded out constitutional revision in 1993. Additionally, the author of this proposal subsequently became head of Texas Tech University. Thus, the proposal lost its leading advocate.

After the 1997 legislative session, Representative Rob Junell, chair of the powerful House Appropriations Committee, expressed interest in constitutional reform. Junell liked some of the Montford ideas, particularly reducing the number of elected officials, including making judges subject to gubernatorial appointment. He was joined by Senator Bill Ratliff, chair of the equally powerful Senate Finance Committee. Their proposal included the following:

- Six-year terms for senators and four-year terms for House members

---

14. Draft resolution and "Comparison of Current and Proposed Constitutions" provided by the office of Senator John Montford, January 1992.

One of the thorniest constitutional problems was the determination by state courts that the Texas public education system did not provide "efficient and effective" education for all students. From 1989 to 1993, the legislature struggled to produce a funding scheme to equalize public education that was acceptable to the courts. Tax schemes in 1997 put such funding in the spotlight again. School funding is a perennial issue.

SOURCE: Courtesy of Ben Sargent.

- Limiting the elected executives to the governor, lieutenant governor, comptroller of public accounts, and attorney general
- Providing for an Executive Department that would consist of specified department heads, excluding elective officials and reporting to the governor
- Simplification of the court system, with judges to be appointed by the governor
- Establishing the possibility of a veto session for the purpose of reconvening to consider whether to override the governor's veto

Known as HJR 1 and SJR 1 in the 76th Legislature in 1999, the Junell-Ratliff proposal was withdrawn from committee in late April when the sponsors realized that their resolution had no chance of being considered by the full House or Senate. Opposition was widespread among both the Democratic and Republican state party organizations, the Texas AFL-CIO, and various other interest groups. Long-time political reporter Sam Attlesey characterized the demise of the proposal as due to "a lack of interest, excitement or crisis in state government."[15]

Twenty-nine states have constitutions newer than Texas's, and twelve have state charters written since 1950. Yet in spite of the occasional difficulty of governing

15. Sam Attlesey, "Texas Constitution Outlasts Plan for Rewrite," *Dallas Morning News,* April 25, 1999, 54A.

under the present state charter, only the League of Women Voters has shown a long-term concern for constitutional revision. Recent sessions of the legislature have faced too many problems demanding immediate solutions to allow legislators to give any consideration to a new constitution. Furthermore, many citizens fear that change may be for the worse rather than for the better. This conservative stance, reflecting once again the state's traditionalism, is encouraged by the major economic forces in the state.

SUMMARY

Texans were so unhappy with Reconstruction government that, given the opportunity to draft and ratify a new constitution in 1876, they concentrated their attention on two of the four purposes of constitutions: legitimacy and limiting government. The intent of the framers was to curb governmental power. Thus they largely ignored the importance of assigning sufficient power to governmental officials, and they subverted the purpose of organizing government by creating a fragmented set of institutions and offices designed to diffuse authority. Although this approach limits government, it also makes citizen participation more difficult because state government is confusing to most people.

Lacking the farsightedness of the framers of the U.S. Constitution, the authors of the Texas charter produced a restrictive document that today sometimes impedes the development and implementation of needed policies and programs. By the end of 1999, lawmakers have had to resort to amending the Texas Constitution 390 times to make possible programs that otherwise would have been consigned to legislative dreamland. In one sense, the element of democratic theory that holds that public input into policy is important is well satisfied by such a practice, but policies are very hard to modify once they are written into the constitution. Dynamic public issues such as funding for water quality, prison expansion, and public education could be handled more smoothly without the cumbersome amendment process. Now, if a policy proves to be ineffective, only another amendment can solve the problem.

The most cumbersome and/or unnecessarily restrictive provisions in the 1876 constitution and their consequences are summarized in the following list:

1. The governor, although held responsible by the public for overall state leadership and the actions of state agencies, in reality has little direct control over most major policy-making offices, boards, and commissions.
2. The legislature is caught between the proverbial "rock and a hard place." Constantly criticized by the citizenry for poor performance, it is operating in the stranglehold of poverty-level salaries, short and infrequent sessions, and innumerable restrictions on legislative action.
3. Texas judges are well aware of the lack of cohesiveness in the judicial system, but they are virtually powerless to provide simpler, more uniform justice because of the overlapping and parallel jurisdictions of the state's courts and the lack of effective supervision of the whole judicial system.
4. County governments, even when county commissioners are relatively progressive in attitude, are restricted by their constitutional structure and scope.

5. In spite of frequent amendments, the Texas Constitution still does not conform to current federal law.
6. The 390 amendments exacerbate rather than improve the poor organization of the charter, making it even more difficult for the laypersons to read.

Four modern legislatures have shown an interest in constitutional revision; two devoted time and energy to reform efforts. But the electorate still lacks sufficient understanding of and interest in the shortcomings of the present constitution to be intent on constitutional change. Citizens are also far too concerned about state taxes, public education, social services, crime and punishment, and many other pressing issues to give constitutional revision much attention. Although the current constitution "creaks and groans," the state still takes care of its business. A successful revision effort will have to wait until the citizens of Texas are more aware of the pitfalls of the present state charter and more convinced of the need for change. For now, "if it ain't broke, don't try to fix it" prevails.

STUDY QUESTIONS

1. What are the four purposes of constitutions? Which ones are most reflected in the Texas Constitution? Which ones are least reflected?
2. How many constitutions has Texas had? Why have there been so many? Do you think there needs to be yet another one? Why or why not?
3. Why is the Texas Constitution so frequently amended? What types of interests are involved when constitutional change is advocated?
4. What similarities and differences between the U.S. and Texas Constitutions do you see?
5. Do you think that you, personally, could get interested in constitutional revision? Why or why not?

SURFING THE WEB

View the entire Texas Constitution.
   www.capitol.state.tx.us/txconst/toc.html

Click on "Legislation–Amendments" for amendments proposed in the most recent legislative session.
   www.capitol.state.tx.us/

Type in "Constitution" to see articles on the various constitutions of the state.
   www.tsha.utexas.edu/handbook/online

3

INTEREST GROUPS AND LOBBYING

As soon as several of the inhabitants of the United States have taken up an opinion or a feeling they wish to promote in the world, they look around for mutual assistance; and as soon as they have found each other out, they combine. From that moment they are no longer isolated men, but a power seen from afar, whose actions serve for an example, and whose language is listened to.

Alexis de Tocqueville
Democracy in America, 1835

*Money doesn't talk,
it swears.*

Bob Dylan
*"It's Alright Ma
(I'm Only Bleeding)," 1965*

INTRODUCTION

Politics is concerned with the making of *public* policy, but a great many of its actions have *private* consequences. When government imposes a tax, or begins to regulate an industry, or writes rules about the behavior of individuals, it makes an impact, not just on the public in general, but on people in particular. Human nature being what it is, those people tend to judge the action not so much on the basis of its value to everyone in general but on the basis of its utility to themselves.

Seeking to obtain more favorable policies, people organize to try to influence government. When they do, they create a problem for democracy. We want our government to take account of the impact of its laws on individuals, but we do not want the special wants of some people to be more important than the common needs of us all. To the extent that public policy is made or modified at the behest of private interests, democracy is crippled.

In Texas, as elsewhere in the United States, special organized interests are always busy trying to influence what government institutions do. As citizens, we have to decide if these groups are merely presenting their point of view to public authorities or if they are instead corrupting the process of self-government.

The definition of interest groups is the first topic of this chapter. It describes and analyzes their activities and moves on to look at one of those activities, lobbying, in more detail. Four important groups are discussed out of the hundreds of possible ones that struggle for influence in Texas politics. Finally an evaluation of the state's interest group system will be presented in the light of democratic theory.

INTEREST GROUPS

Definition

In the broad sense, an interest group is a private organization of individuals who have banded together because of a common cause or interest. The concern here, however, is with *political interest groups*—those that try to influence politicians to make public policy that is consistent with their membership's personal interests or opinion about the public good.

Interest groups can be usefully contrasted with political parties. While the focus of a party is broad, encompassing many different interests, the focus of a group is narrow, comprising just one or a few similar interests. While parties attempt to gain power by running candidates in elections, groups try to affect power by influencing officeholders. Therefore, while parties are forced to appeal to the citizenry in order to marshal support, groups may work entirely behind the scenes. By joining groups, people gain the ability to affect government decisions beyond what they achieve with just their vote.

Who Is Organized?

The two most important things to understand about interest groups are that *not all interests are organized* and that *organized interests are much more powerful than unor-*

TX has the # lobby gps in US.
600+
then Ca. 300

ganized interests. Although the famous quotation from de Tocqueville at the beginning of this chapter might lead us to believe that every potential interest spawns an interest group, in fact some interests are far more likely to be organized than others. Those that are organized are relevant to policymaking; those that are not organized are usually irrelevant.

The general rules of interest group formation are (1) that economic producing groups are more likely to be organized than consuming groups; (2) that regardless of the type of group, people with more education and income are more likely to join than people with less education and income; and (3) that citizens who join groups out of personal involvement—as opposed to economic stake—tend to feel very strongly about the particular issue that is the group's reason for existence. Consequently, because they are more likely to be organized, producers tend to have more political influence than consumers, the middle and upper classes more influence than the working classes, and passionate believers more influence than citizens who are less emotionally involved.

Functions *more legal & protected by the Bill of Rights*

Interest groups attempt to *persuade* both the public and individual government officials to take a particular point of view on specific public policies. In trying to be persuasive, they perform five important functions in the political process:

1. They furnish information to officeholders in all branches of government. This activity consists of both communicating their collective opinion on public policy and of supplying policymakers with their version of the facts.
2. They politicize and inform members of their groups, as well as others.
3. They mediate conflict within their groups.
4. They engage both in electioneering, especially the contribution of money to candidates, and possibly in other interventions in the governing process, such as filing lawsuits.
5. By disseminating information supporting their own policy stands to citizens, they help to form public opinion.

Interest groups therefore enhance democratic government by supplying information to citizens, contributing to debates about issues, getting people involved in politics, and "shaking up" the established order by influencing institutions. But because they attempt to skew the process of government toward their own version of appropriate policy, these groups may also be a corrupting influence. A closer look at their activities will show the extent to which they may deflect public policymaking into private channels.

INTEREST GROUP ACTIVITIES

Electioneering

One of the most common ways that interest groups try to ensure that their future efforts at persuasion will be more effective is for them to support candidates for public

TABLE 3.1

Top Ten Recipients of Texas Medical Association Political Action Committee's 1998 Campaign Contributions

Candidate	Party	Amount
Attorney General John Cornyn	Republican	$86,800
Lt. Governor Rick Perry	Republican	$28,000
Senator David Bernson	Democrat	$16,000
Senator Michael Galloway	Republican	$15,000
Supreme Court Justice Deborah Hankinson	Republican	$12,500
Supreme Court Justice Harriet O'Neill	Republican	$10,000
Senator Steve Ogden	Republican	$10,000
Comptroller Carole Keeton Rylander	Republican	$10,000
Senator Tom Haywood	Republican	$ 8,500
Senator Mike Jackson	Republican	$ 8,500

SOURCE: Mary Flood, "Doctors' Orders: Medical Lobby Becomes a Powerhouse in Austin," *Wall Street Journal*, May 19, 1999, T1.

office. Interest groups that have helped to elect a politician can be confident that they will not be forgotten when the politician enters government.

Usually, the most effective way to help a candidate is to give him or her money. Because campaigning demands the purchase of advertising in expensive media (see Chapter Five), all candidates but the few who are personally rich need to beg wealthy individuals and groups for large amounts of money. Both the politicians and the contributors understand, if only tacitly, that what the interest groups expect is an exchange: The groups will give the candidates money, and if they win, the candidates give the groups public policy.

A politically active interest group that represents a wealthy industry can transfer impressive amounts of money to its favored politicians. Table 3.1 illustrates the donations of one group representing doctors during 1998. It can be assumed that doctors' views on public policy commanded great respect among Texas officials that year, and afterward.

There is no point in criticizing the integrity of public officials for being willing to accept large amounts of cash from groups that have their own, rather than the public's, interest at heart. It is the reality of electoral financing, not personal dishonesty, that makes politicians overly sensitive to private, as opposed to, public interests.

Lobbying

To *lobby* means to attempt to influence policymakers face to face. Everyone has the right to try to make an impact on what government does, and it is obvious that a personal talk with a government official has more impact than one anonymous vote. Because of the rules of interest group formation, however, some groups are much more likely to be able to afford to lobby than others.

Who Are the Lobbyists?   In 1999, there were 1,579 legislative lobbyists registered with the Texas Ethics Commission—nearly nine for every member of the House and

Senate. These lobbyists spent between $77 and $180 million attempting to persuade lawmakers on behalf of their clients.[1]

Lobbyists vary as much in their experience and competence as the legislators they are trying to influence. Topflight freelance lobbyists can make over $1 million per session. State legislators make $7,200.

Not all lobbyists serve special economic interests, and not all earn fortunes in their work. Some "public interest" lobbyists work for their conception of the common good and take home a modest salary for their efforts. But the biases in the interest group system mean that most of the people doing most of the lobbying will be serving narrow, wealthy interests.

What Lobbyists Do and How They Do It.   One effective lobbying technique is direct personal contact. Lobbyists try to see as many legislators as possible every day, buying a lunch, chatting for a few minutes, or just shaking a hand. Most lobbyists are able to get on a first-name basis with each legislator they think might be sympathetic to their goals. The speaker of the House and the lieutenant governor are key figures in the legislature, and lobbyists try, above all else, to ingratiate themselves with these two powerful officials.

Contributions or Bribery?   As discussed, the best way to assure the sympathetic concern of politicians is to give them money. Few lobbyists are as brazen as East Texas chicken magnate Lonnie "Bo" Pilgrim, who, during a fight over a new workers' compensation law in 1989, simply handed out $10,000 checks on the floor to senators who spoke on behalf of his favored legislation.[2] But the capitol is thronged during each legislative session by representatives of interest groups who are eager to give money in a less public manner, in the hope that their generosity will be rewarded with favorable laws.

For example, when the Texas Legislature passed a clean air bill in 1971, it "grandfathered" industries that were then existing by applying the rules only to newly

1. Michael Holmes, "Lobbyists Paying Plenty for Attention, Study Finds," *Austin American-Statesman,* May 24, 1999, B2.

2. Paul Burka, "Is The Legislature for Sale?" *Texas Monthly* (February 1991): 118.

It is common for a government official, after leaving his or her job representing the people, to go to work as a lobbyist, making very good money trying to persuade old colleagues on behalf of an interest group. In 1999, for example, 110 former legislators and other state officials were earning their living lobbying the legislature on behalf of clients. These professional persuaders earned an average of $397,000 each from their varied clientele.

SOURCE: Terence Stutz, "Key Lobbyists Held Government Jobs, Research Shows," *Dallas Morning News,* February 2, 1999, A15.

constructed plants. In 1999, these grandfathered plants were still spewing dozens of millions of pounds of toxic chemicals into the state's air. Environmentalists attempted to persuade the 1999 legislature to force these old plants to stop the pollution by repealing the 1971 loophole in the law. The polluting companies resisted the repeal with all their lobbying might.

The legislature passed a compromise bill, which refrained from forcing companies to stop polluting, but encouraged them to do so by gradually increasing, over several years, the fees they would have to pay for every pound of toxic chemicals they released into the air.

On the surface this outcome would appear to be a tolerable agreement, with both the private interests (business revenue) and the public interest (cleaner air) getting half a loaf. However, some of the grandfathered companies were exempted from the new fees. For example, an Aluminum Company of America (ALCOA) aluminum smelter near Rockdale was allowed to avoid reductions of sulfur dioxide, which causes acid rain, among other problems. Perhaps not coincidentally, ALCOA's political action committee had contributed $12,375 to state incumbent politicians from 1995 to 1998.[3]

Not all interest groups represent rich special interests. The Center for Public Policy Priorities is an example of a lobbying group that does not lobby for wealthy private interests and does not attempt to achieve its objectives through veiled bribery, yet still manages to influence the process of making public policy. Founded in the 1980s by a group of Benedictine nuns, the center attempts to speak on behalf of poor Texans, especially to the legislature. It provides high-quality analysis of the possible effects of proposed government policies on persons of middle and low income.

"They do very good research and very good work," says Republican Representative Harvey Hilderbran of Kerrville, who worked with the group on Texas's 1995 welfare reform law. "I view them as an important and credible resource."

During the legislative discussion of how the state should implement the new federal welfare reform law in 1997, the center managed to convince lawmakers to spend more money for adult education and job search programs that could help welfare recipients find jobs.[4]

Furthermore, campaign contributions are only one influence over politicians, and personal ideology, party spirit, and the arguments of journalists, scholars, or the public can sometimes sway votes away from the tendency of money. For example, during the 1998 state elections, interests in favor of installing a system of school vouchers, which would allow parents to use public money to put their children in private schools, spent more than $5 million supporting their favored candidates. Yet the 1999 legislature refused to pass a school voucher bill.[5]

Nevertheless, the power of money, day in and day out, to capture the attention of lawmakers makes wealth one of the great resources of politics and ensures that rich interest groups will tend, over the long run, to prevail over poor ones.

---

3. Texans for Public Justice and U.S. Public Interest Research Group, "Toxic Exposure: How Texas Chemical Council Members Pollute State Politics and Environment," 1999, sections IV and IV; Ralph K. Haurwitz, "Both Sides Settle for Less with Pollution Bill Compromise," *Austin American-Statesman,* May 31, 1999, A10.

4. Suzanne Gamboa, "Voice for Low-Income Texans Gains Influence in Legislature," *Austin American-Statesman,* March 28, 1997, B1.

5. "Caveat Emptor," *Texas Observer,* May 14, 1999, 3.

In concert with many other observers, cartoonist Ben Sargent believes that democracy is in danger from the concentrated power of special interest money in American, and Texan, politics.

SOURCE: Courtesy of Ben Sargent.

The importance of money in the interest group system brings up uncomfortable questions about democracy in Texas. Simply to give money to a politician for personal use is bribery and is illegal. Bribery is a danger to democracy because it means that private wealth has been substituted for public discussion in the making of public policy. When policy is made at the behest of a few rich interests working behind the scenes, then government is plutocratic, not democratic. The disturbing fact is that the line between outright bribery (illegal) and renting the attention of public officials with campaign contributions and entertainment (legal) is a very thin one. Money talks, and those with more of it speak in louder voices, especially in a state characterized by low legislative salaries and no public campaign finance (see Chapter Five).

Regulation of Lobbying.   It would be a violation of the constitutionally protected rights of expression and association for government to *prevent* individual citizens from organizing to influence the political process. However, government has the authority to *regulate* the manner in which citizens attempt to exercise their rights. This is especially true for the use of money, where the proper freedom to state one's case can easily evolve into the improper attempt to corrupt the system.

Nevertheless, aside from laws of general application regarding such crimes as bribery and conspiracy, Texas makes little attempt to regulate the activities of interest groups except in the area of lobbying. Early attempts at regulation in 1947, 1973, and 1981 were weak and ineffective because no state agencies were empowered to enforce the laws.

In 1991, however, the legislature passed a much-publicized "Ethics Bill," which limited the amount of food, gifts, and entertainments lobbyists can furnish legislators and required lobbyists to report the name of each legislator on whom they spend more than $50. Most important, it created an Ethics Commission that could hold hearings on complaints of improper behavior, levy fines, and refer violations to the Travis County district attorney for possible prosecution. Texas at last had a lobbyist-regulatory law with teeth.

The 1991 law was not perfect, however. It failed to require legislators to disclose the sources of their income and also neglected to ban the use of campaign contributions for living expenses. A three-quarters majority is required on the Ethics Commission for some important actions, which handicaps its activities. Finally, while the members of the commission are appointed by the governor, lieutenant governor, speaker of the House, and chief justice of the Texas Supreme Court, those who are chosen must come from a list of candidates furnished by the legislature. Reformers attempted to pass revisions of this law in subsequent legislators, but they failed.

After passage of the 1991 bill, Speaker Gib Lewis was quoted as saying that he doubted the new provisions would change life at the capitol very much.[6] Events during the rest of the decade suggested that he was correct. As long as legislators' salaries remain below the poverty line and as long as private money dominates public elections, the prospects for effective control of lobbying are poor.

Information.   Thousands of bills are introduced in the Texas Legislature every session, and legislators can have no more than a passing knowledge of most of the policy areas involved. Even those legislators who may have specialized knowledge need up-to-date, accurate information. Therefore, in Texas as in other states, information is one of the most important lobbying resources.

6. Gib Lewis, quoted in Laylan Copelin, "New Ethics Bill Sneaks Up on Lawmakers," *Austin American-Statesman*, May 28, 1991, B1.

The Texas Ethical Standards Task Force, a coalition of public interest and religious organizations, has created a list of "Seven Principles of Ethical Conduct" and has asked lawmakers and public officials to sign, display, and follow them. They are:
1. I will treat my office as a public trust.
2. I will use campaign contributions only for expenses directly related to my campaign.
3. I will make myself, my office, and my staff equally accessible to all persons.
4. I will deem it an abuse of the power of my office to seek favors or special treatment for myself, my family, clients and business associates or my contributors.
5. I will not use my position to enrich myself upon leaving office.
6. I will conscientiously avoid conflicts of interest, both real and perceived.
7. I will conduct my affairs with honesty and truthfulness, respecting the spirit as well as the letter of the law.

SOURCE: Denise Gamino, "Group Pushes Ethics Reform," *Austin American-Statesman*, November 27, 1996, B3.

Moreover, state agencies have a constant need for information and sometimes no independent means of finding it. They may come to rely on lobbying groups to furnish them with the facts they need. For example, in 1996, Elton Bomer, state insurance commissioner, chose the Texas Insurance Checking Office to gather the data the commission uses to determine auto insurance rates. The Checking Office is a subsidiary of an insurance industry lobbying group. An industry group is therefore supplying the information used to regulate the industry it represents.[7] Consumers might suspect that such data will not show that insurance companies are charging too much.

Persuading the Public

Although most interest group energy is expended in lobbying government directly, some groups also attempt to influence government policy indirectly by "educating" the public. They buy television commercial time in order to argue their public policy case to citizens, who, they hope, will then put pressure on their representatives to support the groups' agendas.

The 1999 legislative session was a good one for observing the efforts of interest groups to persuade the public on behalf of their private causes. Especially noteworthy was a $10 million advertising battle between phone giants Southwestern Bell and AT&T. Bell attempted to induce the legislature to pass a law giving it more freedom to raise and lower prices for its services, such as "Caller ID." For its part, AT&T wanted the legislature to force Bell to cut the access charges that long-distance companies must pay to complete their in-state calls.

In full-page ads in newspapers and half-minute spots on television, both companies urged consumers to demand that their legislators do the right thing, as they defined it. AT&T suggested that citizens oppose the "Bell rate hike law." Bell attacked AT&T for opposing legislation that would "keep rates among the lowest in the nation."

In the end, the legislature did nothing about telephones in 1999. The lobbying and public relations efforts of both companies seem to have canceled each other out.[8]

From the standpoint of democratic theory, the efforts of wealthy special interests to create public support through such media campaigns have both reassuring and troubling aspects. By expending their resources on propaganda aimed at ordinary citizens, interest groups greatly expand the amount of information available to citizens. Millions of people were exposed to arguments and information about telephone policy through the spots and ads who would otherwise have been ignorant that such fights were brewing in the legislature. Because an informed citizenry is a democratically competent citizenry, such campaigns are worthy additions to public debate. On the other hand, the arguments presented in the campaign completely reflect a private, one-sided viewpoint. Whereas the two sides in the telephone debate could choose to speak their positions on television, no one can afford to buy television time to speak for the general public interest. On balance, such campaigns probably do more good than harm, but it is a close call.

7. James E. Garcia, "Lobbying Group Subsidiary Will Gather Insurance Data," *Austin American-Statesman,* August 27, 1996, B1.

8. Bruce Hight, "Bell, AT&T Toss $10 Million in Ad Battle," *Austin American-Statesman,* May 12, 1999, D1.

Influencing Administrators and Coopting Agencies

The executive branch of government is also an interest group target. In order to implement many of its laws, especially those of a regulatory nature, any legislature often creates *administrative agencies* or *bureaus* as part of the executive branch of government. In seeking to carry out their administrative function, members of these agencies must interpret laws. Interest groups attempt to influence the interpretation of laws that apply to themselves.

The subject here is the regulatory agencies created to ensure that a particular industry provides good services at fair prices. Unfortunately, the usual history of these agencies is that, over time, they lose their independent role and become dominated by the interest they were created to control. This transition from guardian of the public interest to defenders of private interests, which has been well documented at the federal level, is called **cooptation.**

Cooptation has several causes. First, regulators tend to come from the industry being regulated, and therefore share its values and point of view. Second, it is almost impossible for even the best-intentioned regulators to remain independent from the interest to be regulated because they come to have cordial personal relationships with the people in the industry. Third, while a serious problem may cause an initial public outcry demanding regulation of a private interest—railroads, meat packers, or insurance companies, for instance—once regulatory legislation is passed, the public tends to lose interest and the spotlight of publicity moves elsewhere. From that point on, only the regulated industry is intensely interested in the activities of the government agency. Regulators find that representatives of the industry are constantly in front of them in person, bringing information, self-serving arguments, and the force of personality, while there is no one to speak up for the public.

This cooptation of government regulators in Texas is well illustrated by the history of the state board of insurance. With more than 2,200 companies and 130,000 agents collecting over $34 billion of premiums each year, the insurance business is a significant part of the Texas economy. The state began to regulate the industry in the late 1800s in order to protect consumers from unscrupulous practices. By the 1980s, however, the board was notorious among consumer representatives for always taking the side of the insurance industry in any dispute with customers.

In 1991, the Travis County grand jury issued a report of its investigation into the insurance industry and the board. The grand jury reported that it was

> shocked by the size of the problem, frightened by what it portends for our future economic health, and outraged by the ineffective regulation of the state board of insurance. . . . The potential exists for a savings-and-loan type of disaster in the insurance industry. As was true in the savings-and-loan arena, we see embezzlement and self-dealing by insurance company insiders and regulators who are asleep at the switch.

The report went on to say that "fraud in the insurance industry is widespread and deep and it is covered by falsified documents filed with the state board of insurance."[9]

9. Elyse Gilmore Yates, "Insure Integrity in the Insurance Industry," *Texas Observer,* February 8, 1991, 11.

Partly because of this report, by 1993 the board's practices had become such a scandal that it had become a political issue. That year the legislature abolished it, giving its former powers to a single commissioner, transferred some of its power to other state agencies, and renamed the agency the Texas Department of Insurance. Politicians and citizens hoped that because the new commissioner would have clear responsibility for promulgating and enforcing rules, he or she would be more easily held accountable to the public.

The jury is still out on whether the new Department of Insurance, under its single commissioner, is more independent of the industry than the old insurance commission. The fact that the commissioner, as discussed earlier, has picked an industry group to supply information to his department is not a good sign, however.

Interest Groups and the Courts

Like the legislative and executive branches, the judicial branch of government also makes policy by interpreting and applying laws. For this reason, interest groups are active in the judicial arena of politics. Groups representing important economic interests make substantial campaign contributions during judicial campaigns, hire lawyers to influence judges with legal arguments, and file suits. Money talks in courtrooms as well as in legislatures and the executive branch.

Nevertheless, courts can also be an avenue of success for underdog interest groups that have been unsuccessful in pressing their cases either in electoral politics or by lobbying the other two branches of government. An outstanding example is the National Association for the Advancement of Colored People (NAACP). Not only has this organization successfully argued such historically important national cases as *Brown v. Board of Education* (347 U.S. 483, 1954), in which segregated schools were declared unconstitutional, but it has won vital victories at the state level as well. In *Nixon v. Herndon* (273 U.S. 536, 1927), the U.S. Supreme Court held that a Texas law excluding African Americans from the Democratic primary was unconstitutional. The Texas Legislature attempted to nullify this decision by writing a new law authorizing party leaders to make rulings to the same effect, but this was struck down in *Nixon v. Condon* (286 U.S. 73, 1932). Later, in *Smith v. Allwright* (321 U.S. 649, 1944), the Texas NAACP struck another blow for equal citizenship when the Court held that racial segregation in party primaries on any basis whatsoever is unconstitutional. Thus, although dominant interest groups may win most of the time, the history of the NAACP in Texas proves that even the most downtrodden interests can sometimes prevail if they organize and know how to use the court system.

MAJOR INTEREST GROUPS IN TEXAS

Interest groups want publicity for their programs and goals, but they tend to hide their operations. Political scientists have not done extensive research on interest groups in Texas, and even under the best of circumstances the activities of such groups and the precise nature of their influence are difficult to discover. Nevertheless, what follows is an attempt to discuss a very few of the major interest groups in the state.

can't directly give $ to campaigns. So they form PACs (Pol. Action Committees)

The Oil and Gas Industry

As befitting its historical status as the most important sector in the economy of Texas, the oil and gas industry has a close working relationship with state government and is well represented by several interest groups. Principal among these are the Texas Midcontinent Oil and Gas Association (MOGA), which represents the industry as a whole but is dominated by the large producers, and the Texas Independent Producers and Royalty Owners (TIPRO), which represents the smaller producers and royalty owners.

MOGA, TIPRO, and other groups keep track of the voting of members of the legislature, contribute generously to the campaigns of representatives who are friendly to their interests, and are tireless in providing information to the legislative staff on conditions within the industry. Since oil and gas production is widely distributed within the state, its interest groups thus have a great deal of influence over a large majority of legislators, whether they are liberal or conservative on other issues.

This influence was demonstrated in the 1999 legislative session. Reacting to a depression in the business caused by a slump in worldwide oil prices, lawmakers passed a law giving small producers a $45 million tax break. Critics pointed out that world copper prices were also depressed, but the legislature did not offer tax relief to the small copper industry in the El Paso area. Copper simply does not have the organizational or financial clout of petroleum in Texas.[10]

Texas no longer dominates the world of petroleum, and petroleum no longer dominates Texas as it once did. Whereas in 1981 the oil and gas industry created almost 26 percent of the state's total gross product, by 1997 the total was down to 11 percent and falling.[11] Nevertheless, this diminished percentage still represents bil-

10. Molly Ivins, "Compassion Eases the Pain for Oil Bidness," *Austin American-Statesman,* February 20, 1999, A11.

11. Bruce Hight, "Oil Industry Gushing with Optimism," *Austin American-Statesman,* March 2, 1997, K1.

The legislature is by no means the only focus of attention of the petroleum industry. As the agency charged with regulating oil and gas production in Texas, the Railroad Commission is the subject of intense interest by people in that industry. A scholarly study of the 1970s concluded that winning Railroad Commission candidates received between 78 and 100 percent of their campaign contributions from people in the oil and gas industries. A journalistic investigation in 1999 concluded that, despite the many changes in Texas society and economy over the previous two decades, the situation in regard to Railroad Commission elections had not changed much. One sitting commissioner had raised almost 40 percent of his campaign money from people in the petroleum industry; another had gathered over two-thirds of his contributions from oil and gas. As a consequence, railroad commissioners of both parties have always been extremely sympathetic to industry problems, and have always made policies in line with industry desires.

SOURCES: David F. Prindle, *Petroleum Politics and the Texas Railroad Commission* (Austin: University of Texas Press, 1981), 169; Russell Gold, "Oil Money Greasing Races," *San Antonio Express-News,* September 28, 1999, A1.

lions of dollars, some of which go to interest groups and then to politicians. Although oil and gas are no longer dominant industries in Texas, MOGA and TIPRO will continue to be powerful groups in state government for many years to come.

Organized Labor Not very strong in TX.

Many Texans think of organized labor as a powerful interest group that has great influence on state policy, but there is little evidence to support this assumption. The primary explanation for this lack of power is cultural.

As discussed in Chapter One, the conservative political culture that dominates most of the southern states is hostile to labor unions. Texas is no exception. In 1999, the AFL-CIO had a national membership of 13.1 million, but only 230,000 in the Lone Star State. Second in size of population of the United States, Texas is only eighth in union membership.

Politically, unions have traditionally allied themselves with the Democratic party nationally and the liberal wing of that party within the state (see Chapter Four). But the relative weakness of liberals in Texas has meant that labor unions are even less powerful than their membership figures would suggest. Their weakness is reflected in the relatively anti-labor nature of Texas's laws. Workers' compensation insurance, unemployment insurance payments, and other benefits are lower than those of most other industrial states, and the laws regarding unions are restrictive rather than supportive. Unions are forced to make public disclosure of virtually all their major activities. This is not, of course, true of corporations. There are prohibitions against secondary boycotts, checkoff systems for union dues, mass picketing, and other activities, and the "right-to-work" law prohibits the closed shop and the union shop. In addition to these crippling regulations on organized labor in the private sector, Texas joins Georgia as the state with the most restrictive legislation dealing with public sector unions. Organized labor would like nothing better than to get rid of this array of restrictions, but it lacks the political power to do so.[12]

Developments in the 1990s do not suggest that the future will be brighter for Texas organized labor than the past. For one thing, the state's labor leaders cannot even control the political behavior of their members. The Texas AFL-CIO's own polls show that 45 percent of its members voted for Republican George W. Bush in 1994, despite the fact that the organization endorsed incumbent Democrat Ann Richards.[13] When Governor Bush appointed David Perdue, a labor official whom most union leaders considered a pro-business turncoat, to head the new Texas Workforce Commission in 1996, labor's utter lack of influence was dramatized.

12. A *secondary boycott* occurs when one union boycotts the products of a company being struck by another union. The *checkoff system* is a method of collecting union dues in which an employer withholds the amount of the dues from workers' paychecks. *Mass picketing* occurs when so many people picket a firm that traffic is disrupted and the firm cannot conduct business. A *closed shop* is in effect when workers must already be members of a certain union even to apply for work in a given firm. A *union shop* is in effect when workers do not have to be members of the union to apply for work but must join the union if they get a job.

13. Stuart Eskenazi, "Labor Unions Finding Friends in Former Foes," *Austin American-Statesman,* January 16, 1996, A1.

The Christian Right

In the late 1970s, a number of national organizations arose calling for a return to "Christian values," as they defined them, in American government and in society. The groups' purposes were to inform religious, politically conservative voters of a candidate's issue positions and to persuade them to participate more actively in local politics. By the 1990s, they were a formidable presence in virtually every level of American politics. These groups have been especially important in the south and thus are well represented in Texas. Together, the conservative religious interest groups are known as the *Christian Right*.

Although all Christian Right groups do not place the same emphasis on each individual issue, they share a cluster of positions on the substance of government. Kirk Ingels, Austin coordinator of the Christian Coalition, summarizes the movement's concerns by saying that "the primary focus" of his group "is to affect public policy so it reflects biblical truth."[14] Members interpret the Bible to be antiabortion, antigay rights, antigun control, antitax policies they view as subversive of families, and in favor of constitutional amendments that would mandate a balanced federal budget and permit organized prayers in public schools.

In the 1990s, the groups composing the Christian Right had a profound impact on Texas politics and society. One of the forums in which they are most active is in the arena of local schools. Elections to fill positions on the governing boards to Texas's school districts generally draw fewer than ten percent of the eligible voters to the polls. An organized, disciplined group can easily elect its favored members. Using their own organization and discipline, Christian Right groups have elected majorities to many of the state's 1,042 districts. They have also maintained a significant presence, although not a majority, on the State Board of Education.

The most dramatic flexing of the Christian Right's muscles occurred at the state Republican party conventions in 1994, 1996, and 1998. Delegates effectively took over the machinery of the party, writing Christian Right platforms and electing Christian Right party chairs (see Chapter Four).

The Christian Right has become so important in Texas and national politics that it may sometimes give the impression that all believing Christians are politically conservative. Such an interpretation would be far from the truth, however. Jim Wallis, a Washington, D.C. evangelical pastor, has founded Call to Renewal, a national group of liberal evangelicals. Within Texas, Cecile Richards, elder daughter of former Governor Ann Richards, has created the Texas Freedom Network to try to mobilize moderate and liberal Christian Democrats to run for local school boards. Liberal pastors have formed the Texas Faith Network to counter the efforts of the Christian Coalition.

In other words, organization among the Christian Right has sparked counterorganization among the Christian Left. Although the liberal Christian groups are unlikely to become as important in Texas as the conservative groups, they will provide a media counterpoint to Christian Right arguments. Interest group politics in Texas thus promises to be more fervently oriented toward moral questions than it has been in the past.

---

14. Quoted in Chuck Lindell, "Pulpit to Polls Movement Gathers Steam," *Austin American-Statesman,* March 6, 1994, A1.

LULAC

The most venerable of the Hispanic organizations, the League of United Latin American Citizens was formed in Corpus Christi in 1929.[15] Its members were much concerned about discrimination against Mexican Americans, especially in public education. In its first three decades, LULAC pursued the goal of equal education as both a private charitable organization and a public crusader. Privately, LULAC formed local self-help organizations to advance Latino education. Its "Little School of the 400" program of the 1950s, for example, which taught Spanish-speaking preschoolers the 400 English words they needed to know in order to survive in first grade in public schools, was so successful it inspired the national program Head Start. Publicly, the organization persuaded the U.S. Supreme Court to forbid Texas to segregate Mexican Americans in public schools in 1948.

Branching out to other issues, in 1953 LULAC won another suit against Texas's practice of excluding Mexican Americans from juries. Then in 1959 it persuaded the state legislature to sponsor its program to teach Latino preschoolers English. Soon the Texas Education Agency was paying up to 80 percent of the program's funding. LULAC may have represented a struggling minority, but it had become part of the state's political establishment; it was a success.

Into the 1970s, LULAC continued to be the standard bearer for Mexican-American aspirations for full citizenship in the United States in general and Texas in particular. But in that decade it began to falter. As an organization dispensing millions of dollars in foundation grants, it began to attract members who were more interested in advancing themselves than in advancing their ethnic group. Beginning in the mid-1970s, LULAC was rocked by a series of financial scandals. The worst of these scandals occurred in 1994, when the president, José Velez, together with three Taiwanese gangsters, was indicted by a federal grand jury on charges of collecting millions of dollars in a scheme to smuggle Asians and Hispanics into the United States illegally.

Given that Velez was under an ethical cloud, it might have been expected that his power in LULAC would be extinguished. But the national convention held in July 1994 provided several surprises. Rosa Rosales, a labor organizer from San Antonio, was the reform candidate and a favorite to be elected president. But Velez made a deal with a contingent of Puerto Rican delegates who bloc-voted for his hand-picked candidate, Belen Robles. Their support enabled Robles to beat Rosales by five votes. What the Puerto Ricans received in return for their loyalty to Velez was not made public.

Not only were many in LULAC outraged by the defeat of a reformer presidential candidate, but they were also stunned by the loss of power of Mexican Americans. Although words such as *Hispanic* and *Latino* may give the impression that everyone with a Spanish-language background is culturally the same, the terminology hides considerable differences of economic class and national origin. After the defeat of Rosales, many Mexican-American members of LULAC expressed their anger that the organization seemed to have been taken over by Puerto Ricans.[16] LULAC was no longer a league of *united* Latin American citizens.

15. This account of the history of LULAC through the 1980s relies upon Benjamin Marquez, *LULAC: The Evolution of a Mexican American Political Organization* (Austin: University of Texas Press, 1993), passim.

16. Lori Rodriguez, "LULAC Turning Puerto Rican," *Houston Chronicle,* July 9, 1994, 25A.

The cumulative effects of LULAC's troubles had a devastating effect on its prestige and membership. Once capable of mobilizing a quarter of a million citizens, by the late 1990s the organization could count on no more than 50,000 active members. At its 1999 national convention in Corpus Christi, there were few people in the audience for its workshops and fewer corporate sponsors. Whereas in 1987 eight presidential candidates had addressed its delegates, not a single one showed up in 1999.[17]

And so Texas's historically most important Hispanic organization is in trouble. LULAC may be an ethnic interest group that has outlived its usefulness.

CONCLUSION

Political interest groups present a dilemma to partisans of democratic government. By providing people a channel of input to government other than just their one vote, such groups broaden and intensify citizen participation and are therefore good for democracy. But by creating a means by which some people are much more influential than others, they often allow private perspectives to dominate public policymaking. This situation is bad for democracy. In Texas, where interest groups are very powerful, the dilemma is acute.

SUMMARY

Interest groups are influential in American and Texas politics because they provide two indispensable resources, money and information. Groups are active in every phase of politics: They engage in electioneering, lobby government officials, coopt agencies, litigate in the courts, and attempt to persuade the public to support their point of view. Organized groups are frequently effective; unorganized groups generally are not. Private interests thus often dominate public policy.

Although many efforts have been made to regulate lobbying, the results so far have not been encouraging. The Texas political system provides a nearly ideal setting for maximizing interest group influence. The most powerful groups tend to be those that represent major economic interests. This effect is consistent with the dominant role of the conservative political culture in Texas.

Interest groups are good for democracy in that they enhance debate about public policy and encourage citizens to participate in politics. But they also damage democratic government by substituting private influence for public deliberation in the creation of government policy. In Texas, where interest groups are very powerful, the negative qualities of the interest group system dominate.

---

17. James E. Garcia, "Latino Politics: Up to LULAC to Reform or Be Left Behind," *Houston Chronicle,* July 25, 1999, OUTLOOK, 1.

STUDY QUESTIONS

1. What do we mean by the terms *interest group, lobby,* and *lobbyist*? Are interest groups and lobbies the same thing? If you write a letter to your legislator, are you lobbying?
2. What functions do interest groups perform in a democratic society? How do they perform them?
3. What interests tend to be organized? What is the difference in political influence between organized and unorganized groups?
4. How can an interest group attempt to influence public opinion? From the perspective of democratic theory, what is good and what is bad about such efforts?
5. Do you think the 1991 ethics law will eventually succeed in eliminating the advantage wealthy private interests have in influencing public policy? Why or why not?

SURFING THE WEB

The recent activities of the National Association for the Advancement of Colored People (NAACP) are discussed under several different headings at its website. The court cases mentioned in this chapter, as well as its more recent judicial efforts, can be accessed by clicking the "History" icon. Its site is:

http://www.naacp.org/

To access other organizations discussed in this chapter:

Texas Independent Producers and Royalty Owners Association—

http://www.tipro.org/

Texas Mid-Continent Oil and Gas Association does not have a website.

Texas AFL-CIO—

http://www.texasaflcio.org/

Texas Christian Coalition—

http://www.texascc.org/

LULAC—

http://www.lulac.org/

4

*G*reat leaders like
*Franklin Roosevelt and
John Kennedy lift people
above themselves. Great
parties thrive by holding
together disparate
interests.*

Paul Samuelson
Nobel Prize–winning economist

*A political party is an
organization that takes
money from the rich and
votes from the poor under
the pretext of protecting
the one from the other.*

Anonymous

POLITICAL PARTIES

INTRODUCTION

Both Samuelson's favorable assessment of **political parties** and the anonymous cynical disparagement of their value are partly true. Parties are, indeed, the only organizations capable of holding together many fractious interests so that governing is possible. At the same time, in Texas and elsewhere parties frequently serve democracy badly.

This chapter opens with discussions of ideology and interests, the two bases for much party conflict. It proceeds to a brief history of the state's political parties, a consideration of the major functions of parties, and an outline of party organization in Texas. It then analyzes the "three-faction" system that often makes the state's two-party system confusing, and finally gives some attention to the state's occasional third-party efforts. As the discussion proceeds, it will contrast the reality of Texas's party politics with the democratic ideal.

IDEOLOGY—ONE BASIS FOR POLITICAL PARTIES

In Texas as elsewhere, party rivalry is often based upon differences in **ideology.** An ideology is a system of beliefs and values about the nature of the good life in the good society, about the relationship of government and the economy, about moral values and the way they should be achieved, and about how government is to conduct itself. The two dominant, and contesting, systems of beliefs and values in American and Texan life today are usually referred to as *liberalism* and *conservatism.*

Conservatives

The basic principle underlying **conservatism,** at least in economic policy, is laissez-faire. Conservatives prefer to allow free markets, not government, to regulate the economy. As noted in Chapter One, in practice conservative governments often pursue *pseudo laissez-faire* in that they claim to cherish free markets but actually endorse policies that deeply involve government in helping businesses overcome problems in their markets. Nevertheless, at the level of ideology, and certainly at the level of their argument with liberals, conservatives believe that economies run best if governments leave them alone. When contemplating economic problems such as poverty, pollution, unemployment, or health care, conservatives argue that government has caused most of them with overregulation and that the best way to deal with them is for government to stop meddling and allow the market to work. For example, local land developers don't want a city to tell them how high a sign should be or what kind of landscaping is required to hide ugly buildings or junk cars.

Liberals

Liberalism is the contrary ideology. Liberals are suspicious of the workings of unregulated markets and place more faith in the ability of government to direct economic activity. When thinking about economic problems, they are apt to blame "market failure" and suggest government activity as the solution. To continue the development example used with conservatism, a liberal would want a city government to protect the environment and would work for sign ordinances and landscaping policies. Also, liberals often want to redistribute wealth and power to help the less fortunate; conservatives want to leave the distribution of wealth and power as it is.

All this is relatively clear. When dealing with issues of personal belief and behavior such as religion, sexual activity, or drug use, however, liberals and conservatives switch sides. Conservatives are generally in favor of more government regulation; liberals are in favor of less. Liberals oppose prayer in school while conservatives favor it; liberals oppose laws regulating sexual behavior while conservatives endorse them and so on.

Thus, American ideological fights are confusing because liberals usually favor government activity in the economic sphere but oppose it in the personal sphere, while conservatives usually oppose government activity in the economic sphere but favor it in the personal sphere. This ideological split is the basis for a great deal of rhetorical argument and intense struggles over public policy (see Table 4.1).

As discussed in Chapter One, Texas has historically been dominated by political conservatism. The distribution of opinions in the population in the present day suggests that this domination does not misrepresent the center of gravity of state public opinion. A survey conducted in 1998 reported that only 14 percent of Texas adults were willing to label themselves liberals, while 46 percent called themselves moderates and 40 percent claimed the label "conservative."[1] The meaning of the simple self-reports is not completely clear, since by calling themselves conservative, people might be referring to economic issues, social issues, or both. Moreover, many years of national public opinion research have shown that a significant percentage of people will label themselves conservative in general but will endorse many specific liberal government programs. Still, the self-report numbers are sufficiently dramatic to emphasize the weakness of the liberal ideological tradition in the Lone Star State.

INTERESTS—A SECOND BASIS FOR PARTY CONFLICT

An **interest** is something of value or some personal characteristic that people share and that is affected by government activity—their investments, their race, their jobs, and so on. When there is a question of public policy on which the two parties take differing positions, people with conflicting interests often line up with the party favoring their interests, whether or not their political ideology is in line with that party's. Moreover, parties will often take positions to attract the money and votes of citizens with clashing interests. Thus parties put together **coalitions** of interests in order to attract blocs of voters and campaign contributions. Party positions are therefore almost always much more ambiguous and confusing than they would be if they simply divided according to ideology.

For example, Texan Republican party candidates in recent years have tended to criticize the state's tort laws—the statutes that allow people who believe they have been injured by a business to sue for damages. Republicans have argued that the state makes it too easy to file "frivolous" lawsuits and allows juries to award damages to injured parties that are too large. They have supported "tort reform" by the state legis-

1. We are grateful to O'Neill Provost of the Office of Survey Research at the University of Texas at Austin for supplying us with this information.

TABLE 4.1

Policy Differences between Liberals and Conservatives

Issue	Conservative Position	Liberal Position
Economic Issues		
Taxation	as little as possible and, when necessary, regressive taxes such as sales taxes*	more to cover government spending; progressive preferred*
Government spending	as little as possible, except for military	acceptable to provide social services
Nature of government regulation	more in personal sphere; less in economic	less in personal sphere; more in economic
Organized labor	anti-union	pro-union
Environment	favor development over environment	favor environment over development
Social Issues		
Crime	support more prisons and longer sentences; oppose gun control	support social spending to attack root causes; favor gun control
Abortion	"pro-life"	"pro-choice"
Affirmative action	oppose	support
Prayer in public schools	favor	oppose
Foreign Policy Issues		
Human rights as large component of foreign policy	no	yes
Free trade	more likely to favor	less likely to favor
Military spending	more	less
U.S. military intervention abroad	more likely to favor†	less likely to favor†

*A progressive tax is one that increases proportionately with income or benefit derived, such as a progressive income tax. A regressive tax, such as the sales tax, places proportionately less burden on wealthy taxpayers and more burden on those with lower incomes.

†However, liberals tended to support the U.S./NATO bombing war against Serbia in 1999, while conservatives tended to oppose it.

NOTE: Two words of caution are in order. First, this table presents an extremely brief summary of complex issues, and thus some distortion is inevitable. Second, it would be inaccurate to assume that every liberal agrees with every liberal position or that every conservative agrees with every conservative position. Even the most devout ideologues have inconsistencies in their beliefs and hitches in their logic.

lature. On the other hand, Democrats have tended to side with plaintiffs in lawsuits, arguing that wronged people should have easy access to the courts and should be entitled to large compensation for injuries. They have usually opposed tort reform.

As a result, the sorts of interests who tend to be the target of tort lawsuits, doctors and business owners, for example, have been inclined to support Republican candidates. The sorts of interests who tend to benefit from such suits, plaintiff's attorneys, for example, have tended to side with Democrats. This has very little to do with ideology and a great deal to do with who gets what from government.

Not all interests are economic. Mexican Americans, for example, have traditionally tended to support the Democratic party because they have perceived the

TABLE 4.2

Interests Generally Supporting the Two Major Parties

Type of Interest	Democrats	Republicans
Economic class	poor	middle; wealthy
	labor union	management
Professions	plaintiff's attorneys, public employees	physicians, business entrepreneurs
Development vs. environment	environmentalist	developers, rural landowners
Industry	entertainment	oil and gas, computers
Ethnic	African American, Mexican American	Anglo
Religion	Catholic, Jewish	Protestant, especially evangelical

Republicans as being less tolerant of ethnic diversity. Whether an interest arranges people in a politically relevant manner depends on what sorts of questions become issues of public policy.

Interests and ideologies tend to combine in different ways in different people, sometimes opposing and sometimes reinforcing one another. For example, a Mexican-American doctor in Texas would be drawn to the Republicans by her professional interest and drawn to the Democrats by her ethnic interest. She might have had trouble making up her mind about how to vote in the 2000 election. On the other hand, an Anglo oil company executive or an African-American labor union president would probably have experienced no such conflict. In each case, the personal ideology of the citizens might either reinforce or contradict one or more of their interests. The way interests and ideologies blend, conflict, and interact with candidates and parties is one of the things that makes politics complicated and interesting to study.

The partisan interest coalitions that have characterized recent Texas politics are summarized in Table 4.2. It is important to understand that not every person who has

Party conflict does not always consist of worthy and important arguments over ideology and interests. Sometimes it is petty squabbling over trivia.

An example is the dispute over nomenclature. For years, many Republicans have refused to call the Democratic party by its chosen name. Attempting to prevent their enemies from portraying themselves as the more democratic of the two, Republicans habitually say "the Democrat party" and "my Democrat opponent," instead of "Democratic."

After decades of annoyance, Democrats have run out of patience with Republican bad manners. The chair of the Texas Democratic party, Molly Beth Malcolm, has decided that "Turnabout is fair play. So from here on out I will be referring to the Republican party as the Republic party of Texas."

SOURCE: "'Democrat' Party Returns the Favor," *Austin American-Statesman*, February 21, 1999, B2.

Leaders of both major political parties argue constantly about what policy positions to adopt in order to attract the most voters. One of the common arguments, illustrated here, is that the party should be clearly liberal or conservative [left or right] in order to give the voter "a choice, not an echo."
SOURCE: Courtesy of Ben Sargent.

an interest agrees with every other person with the same interest, and so citizens who share interests are not unanimous in their partisan attachments. For example, although most of the people in the computer business who contributed large amounts to the parties in the 1990s gave to the Republicans, not all did. Similarly, although the great majority of African Americans who voted in those elections supported the Democrats, thousands did not. The table describes how interests lean, in general, not how every person with that interest behaves.

Politics would be fascinating enough if ideologies and interests, once they had arranged themselves into a party coalition, stayed that way. In fact, however, the party battle evolves as history changes the way people live. A hundred years ago, the Democratic party was the conservative party and dominated Texas almost completely. Today, the Republican party is more conservative and has won most recent elections. It is not too much of an exaggeration to say that the history of Texas is written in the story of her two major parties.

TEXAS POLITICAL PARTIES—A BRIEF HISTORY

Texas entered the United States in 1845 as a slave state. Nationally, the Democrats were pro-slavery, while their main opponents, the Whigs, ignored the issue.

Moreover, the Democrats had endorsed the admission of Texas to the Union in the 1844 election, while the Whigs had waffled. Thus, most Texans were Democrats.

Party divisions became intense when the Civil War ended in 1865. The Republican administration of Abraham Lincoln had defeated the Confederacy, of which Texas was a member, and freed the slaves. Reconstruction, or Union occupation, settled on all the southern states. White southerners found themselves under the rule of northerners, the military, and African Americans. Rightly or wrongly, they believed themselves to be subject to tyranny by a foreign conqueror. They identified this despotic occupation with the Republican party. In this emotionally searing experience, the southern politics of the next century were forged. The Democratic party became the vehicle of southern resistance to northern domination and of white opposition to full citizenship for blacks. As a result, when Reconstruction ended in 1875, Texas, like the other former members of the Confederacy, was a solid one-party Democratic state. It remained a **one-party state** through most of the twentieth century.

Beginning in 1932, the national Democratic party became dominated by liberals. Southern states such as Texas objected, but it took decades for the national realignment of party ideology to work its way through the South. For many decades, southern politicians and southern voters remained a slowly dissolving conservative faction in the largely liberal Democratic party.

It was conservative Republican President Ronald Reagan's landslide reelection in 1984 that finally broke the hold of the Democrats in Texas. Dozens of Republican candidates rode Reagan's coattails to victory in local elections, as did Phil Gramm, the Republican candidate for U.S. Senate. Some of the local officeholders subsequently lost their reelection bid, but by then Texas could no longer be considered a Democratic monopoly.

By 2000, Texas was a competitive two-party state that seemed to be moving toward domination by Republicans. The governor, lieutenant governor, land commissioner, comptroller, agriculture commissioner, both U.S. Senators, a majority of state senators and members of the board of education, and all three railroad commissioners belonged to the GOP ("Grand Old Party," a nickname from the post–Civil War era). Moreover, Texans gave decisive majorities of their major party vote to Republican presidential candidates in 1992, 1996, and 2000. Democrats were clinging to a majority of the delegation to the U.S. House of Representatives and another majority in the state house. Table 4.3 illustrates the spectacular growth of Republican officeholders in Texas from 1974 to 1998.

The story of the climb of the Republicans to majority party status is somewhat more complicated among the citizens. According to a survey conducted in 1998 by the Office of Survey Research at the University of Texas at Austin, 35 percent of Texans considered themselves Republicans, compared to 30 percent who identified as Democrats. But 35 percent also proclaimed themselves independents or adherents of some other party.[2] Although this poll indicates that Republicans lead Democrats in terms of self-identification, it also shows that the balance of power in the state is held by people who feel allegiance to neither major party. If Republicans have been win-

---

2. We are grateful to O'Neill Provost of the Office of Survey Research at the University of Texas at Austin for supplying us with this information.

TABLE 4.3

Growth of Republican Officeholders in Texas

Year	U.S. Senate	Other Statewide	U.S. House	Texas Senate	Texas House	Other	Total
1974	1	0	2	3	16	53	75
1978	1	1	4	4	22	87	119
1982	1	0	5	7	35	166	214
1986	1	1	10	6	56	504	578
1990	1	6	8	8	57	722	802
1994	2	13	11	14	61	956	1,057
1996	2	18	13	17	69	1,154	1,273
1998	2	29	13	16	72	1,390	1,522

SOURCE: *Austin American-Statesman,* November 13, 1994, 16A for figures from years 1974 to 1990; Texas Republican Party Headquarters for years 1994, 1996, and 1998.

ning recent elections, it cannot be simply because they overbalance Democrats in party identification. As will be discussed in Chapter Six, some of the explanation for Republican success results from the fact that they tend to vote at higher rates than Democrats. But the party identification figures suggest that, in addition, at least some of the explanation for the Republican rise must be the result of their ability in recent years to attract independent voters.

The importance of independents in Texas was underscored in the 1990s by the rapid rise and fall of an organization created by Dallas billionaire H. Ross Perot. Perot entered the 1992 presidential race, winning a very respectable 22 percent of the state's popular vote. Afterward, Perot's quasiparty, "United We Stand America" (UWSA), expended considerable money and energy trying to organize citizen support around the country, including Texas. If UWSA had been able to keep the allegiance of the independent voters it attracted in 1992, it would have become an important force in the state's politics. But UWSA seemed to fizzle out in the mid-1990s, with Perot receiving only 7 percent of the state's vote in the 1996 presidential election.

In the 1996 and 1998 state elections, the independents evidently preferred Republicans over Democrats by a considerable margin in most races. Nevertheless, independents remain a large and volatile segment of the Texas population, and neither party can afford to take them for granted.

As party interests and ideologies evolve through history, so do their personnel. Texas passed some sort of a milestone in the late 1990s when both parties became chaired by women for the first time. Republican Susan Weddington is a former businesswoman from San Antonio. Democrat Molly Beth Malcolm is a former teacher and drug counselor from East Texas.

FUNCTIONS OF POLITICAL PARTIES

The basic purpose of parties is to win elections and thus gain the opportunity to exercise control over public policy. While pursuing this goal, they potentially perform several functions that make them valuable institutions in a democracy. These include:

- Involving ordinary people in the political process, especially persuading them to vote and teaching them the formal and informal "rules of the game"
- Recruiting political leaders and inducing them to restrain their individual ambitions so that the party can achieve its collective purposes
- Communicating to the leaders the interests of individuals and groups
- Providing factual information and persuasive argument during public discussion of policy alternatives
- Structuring the nature of political conflict and debate, including screening out the demands of certain people and groups—usually fringe individuals or groups that lack significant public support
- Moderating differences between groups, both within the party and in the larger society
- Partially overcoming the fragmented nature of the political system so that "gridlock" can be overcome and coherent policy made and implemented

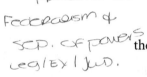

"FRAGMENTED"
Federalism &
SEP. OF POWERS
leg/Ex/Jud.

Political parties in any democracy can be judged according to the extent to which they fulfill these functions well or badly. How do Texas parties measure up?

PARTY ORGANIZATION

All parties are organizations, but they follow many different patterns of structure. In general, American parties, when compared to those in foreign democracies, are weak. They are not structured so that they can function easily as a cohesive team. Those in Texas are especially weak. As a result, Texas parties do not perform the function of overcoming gridlock and making coherent policy very well. Frequently they fail to structure conflict so as to make it sensible to most ordinary citizens. A review of state party organization will suggest why this is so.

In Texas, as in most states, parties are divided into a permanent organization and a temporary one (see Figure 4.1). The **permanent party organization** consists of little more than a skeleton force of people who conduct the routine but essential business of the party. The party's primary purpose of winning elections requires far more people and much greater activity. The party comes alive in election years in the form of a **temporary party organization** geared to capturing power.

The Temporary Party Organization

The temporary party organization is focused on the spring primary and the fall general elections. It attempts to choose attractive candidates and to mobilize voters to support them.

In Texas, party membership is determined by the act of voting; there are no permanent political party rolls. If a citizen votes in the Democratic party primary, for ex-

FIGURE 4.1

Major Party Organization in Texas

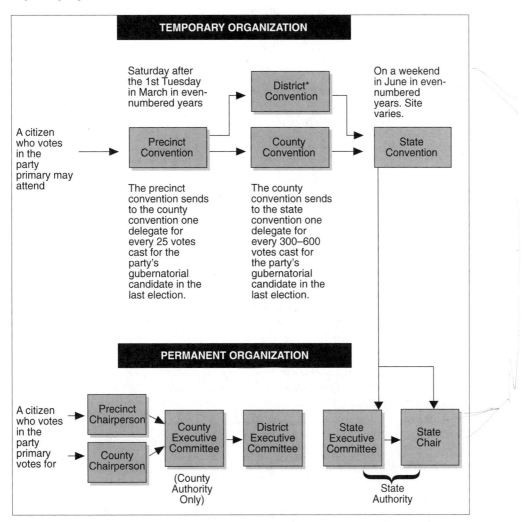

*District conventions are held in counties with more than one senatorial district.

ample, his or her registration certificate is stamped, an act that legally prohibits voting in any other party's primary or participating in any other party's conventions.

Precinct and County Conventions. In the 254 counties of Texas are more than 6,000 precincts, each having from 50 to as many as 3,500 voters. Each voter is entitled to have a voice in choosing the precinct chairperson and proposing and voting on resolutions that will establish party policy, but voter participation in party affairs is low. Normally only a small fraction of those who vote in the primaries, who are themselves only a fraction of the total number of registered voters, who are themselves only a fraction of the voting-age citizens, participates in conventions or other party affairs.

The main function of the precinct convention is to select delegates to the county convention, which is the next echelon of the temporary party organization.[3] And the main function of the county convention is to select delegates to the state convention. Both precinct and county conventions can be either short or long, peaceful or filled with conflict, productive of resolutions or not.

The State Convention.   Both major parties hold their state conventions over a weekend in June during even-numbered (election) years. The party state executive committee decides when and where the convention is held. Depending on the year of the election cycle in which it occurs, the June convention performs some or all of the following activities:

1. It certifies to the secretary of state the party nominees for the general election in November.
2. It writes the party platform.
3. It selects the members of the state executive committee.
4. It names the Texas committeeman and committeewoman to the national party committee.
5. It makes the final selection of delegates to the national party convention.
6. It selects a slate of presidential electors to serve in the electoral college in the event that the party's candidates for president and vice president win in Texas.

Party conventions have tended, over the past several decades, to travel in opposite directions, the Democrats from argument to harmony, the Republicans from agreement to acrimony. Until the 1980s, the liberal and conservative wings of the Democrats often fought viciously over party planks and leadership positions. In the 1990s, however, the party has come to be dominated more and more at its organizational level by the liberal faction. In conventions the delegates now tend to adopt liberal platforms and save their criticisms for the Republicans.

In contrast, when the Republicans were a small minority, they rarely argued over policy in their conventions. As they grew in state influence, however, Republicans generated greater and greater internal disagreement, especially between social and economic conservatives. The climax came in 1994, when delegates from the Christian Right (see Chapter Three) dominated the convention, electing their favored party chair and writing a platform to their own liking. Among other provisions, the Republicans supported federal and state initiatives to outlaw abortion under all circumstances and recommended that the public schools teach "creation science" in biology classes. The socially conservative platform and the convention's choice of a party chair sparked vigorous opposition from delegates who were economically conservative but more moderate on social issues.

Again in 1996 and 1998, the Christian Right dominated Republican state conventions, writing platforms that began with the words, "We believe in you! We believe that you are a sacred being created in the image of God."[4] Again, the religious social

---

3. Several of the larger counties—Bexar, Dallas, Harris, and Tarrant—are so populous that they are entitled to more than one state senator. In such counties each state senatorial district holds its own district convention rather than a countywide convention.

4. *1996 State Republican Party Platform*, 1; *1998 State Republican Party Platform*, 1.

conservatives elected their favored people to run the party, and again economic conservatives objected without effect.

Although events in the Democratic and Republican state conventions engender much publicity, their importance should not be exaggerated. Because candidates for public office in Texas are nominated in primaries rather than in caucuses or conventions (see Chapter Five), and because candidates typically raise their own campaign funds independently of the party, the state convention and platform are actually of little importance to what nominees say and do.

In 1994, the two most important Republican candidates, George W. Bush, running for governor, and Kay Bailey Hutchison, running for U.S. Senate, pointedly ignored the state Republican platform and disassociated themselves from its abortion plank. Bush distributed his own "platform" that disagreed with his party's at several points and strongly differed from it in emphasis. In 1996, Governor Bush publicly disagreed with party chair Tom Pauken on campaign strategy.

In summary, if students want to know what candidates plan to do if elected, they may want to ignore their party's platform and instead pay attention to the positions of the candidates themselves.

The Permanent Party Organization

Precinct Chairpeople. The citizen who votes in the primary has an opportunity to participate in the selection of precinct and county chairpeople of his or her party. The precinct chairperson is the lowest-ranking permanent party official. Elected for a two-year term, he or she is expected to be the party leader at the precinct level, recruiting candidates, arranging for the precinct convention, getting out the vote, and in general beating the drum for the party.

County Executive Committees. Together the precinct chairs comprise the County Executive Committee, which is charged with two major responsibilities: (1) conducting the party primary elections, and (2) conducting the county convention. It is presided over by the county chairperson, the most important official at the local level. Elected for two years to a demanding job, this official is unpaid, although some receive private donations. County chairs are compensated by the state for the expense of conducting their party's primary elections. After the primary election has been held, the County Executive Committee canvasses the vote and certifies the results to the State Executive Committee.

The District Executive Committee. The district executive committee is the least important permanent party organization. It meets only after the primary to fill vacancies in district offices. Membership varies according to the number of counties and sections of counties that comprise the senatorial district.

The State Executive Committee. The highest permanent body in the state party is the State Executive Committee, and the highest state party official is the party chair. Both are elected by the state convention. If the party controls the governorship, the chair usually works closely with the governor and is likely to be a friend and political ally. The

Republicans in 1996 were an exception, as there was notable friction and lack of cooperation between party chair Tom Pauken and Governor George Bush during the campaign.

In a similar fashion, the chair of the state committee of the party out of power usually has a close relationship with that party's top leaders. By law, the executive committees are responsible for staging the state conventions and for certifying the parties' candidates. They may also perform other functions such as raising funds, distributing information, and assisting with problems at the county level. In recent years the State Democratic Executive Committee has taken on new importance because of its rule-making authority, and Democratic politicians compete for membership.

The (Un) Importance of Party Organization

American political parties are not "responsible parties"—that is, they neither have centralized control over nominations and financing nor the power to impose the party platform on members. In Texas, parties are especially weak because it is, in fact, the primary election, not the party organization, that is important in determining who is nominated to office. Furthermore, candidates normally rely on their own fundraising and organizing ability more than they rely on their party to help them get elected.

As a result, when candidates succeed in capturing an office, they mostly have themselves and the individuals and groups who contributed to their campaign fund to thank for their achievements. They therefore have very little loyalty to the party; they are more likely to feel beholden to some wealthy interest group. Officeholders are often ideologically friendly with others of the same party, but they are not obligated to cooperate with each other. The parties have no discipline over them. The formal and informal party organizations have some ability to fashion a "party attitude" on public policy because they are centers of information flow and personal interaction, but they are incapable of forging a disciplined governing team.

As previously mentioned, in the 1990s Governor George W. Bush and Senator Kay Bailey Hutchison went their own way and pretty much ignored the official state party organizations. In return, that Republican organization showed no love for them. The 1996 state Republican convention at first refused to choose Hutchison as a delegate to the party's national presidential nominating convention. She was finally named a delegate only after some intense arm twisting by Governor Bush. In 1997, state party chair Tom Pauken actually took out ads in newspapers in East Texas urging Republicans to write their legislators, requesting them to "Say No to the Bush Tax Cut!"[5]

The consequence of this lack of organizational cohesion is that Texas parties fail to perform many of the functions that make parties elsewhere useful to democracy. By and large, they cannot recruit political leaders, structure the nature of public debate, or overcome the fragmented nature of the political system by forming officials into disciplined groups. Instead of thinking of parties in Texas as two stable, cohesive teams, therefore, it would be more realistic to imagine them as two (or, as we shall soon see, three) loose confederations of citizens, interest groups, and officeholders who sometimes cooperate because of occasional ideological agreement and temporarily parallel interests.

5. "Political Intelligence," *Texas Observer,* September 26, 1997, 16.

TWO PARTIES, THREE FACTIONS

Republicans

Ideologically, the Texas Republican party tends to be strongly conservative, usually opposing government involvement in the economy but sometimes endorsing such involvement in personal life. This ideological devotion to laissez-faire, of course, occasionally slides into pseudo laissez-faire under the pressure of actual politics. Nevertheless, under most conditions Republicans can be counted on to favor a cheaper, less active government than the Democrats. Both of Texas's U.S. Senators, Phil Gramm and Kay Bailey Hutchison, are good representatives of this ideological position, as is Governor George W. Bush.

Geographic Distribution.   While the Republicans are now greater than Democrats statewide in voter strength, their numbers are still unevenly distributed. Republicans tend to be found in cities and the wealthier suburbs, with Dallas and Harris County (Houston) containing about four out of every ten of the state's Republican voters. Other concentrations are found in the East and West Texas "oil patches," the German hill country north of San Antonio, and the Panhandle. Republicans are also steadily gaining ground in East Texas.

Socioeconomic and Ethnic Distribution.   GOP activists come from a relatively narrow socioeconomic and ethnic base. Most candidates and party activists are Anglo middle- or upper-class businesspeople or professionals. Although a sprinkling of African Americans and Latinos can be found among active Republicans, the party has not appealed to significant numbers of minorities since the end of Reconstruction in 1875. In his reelection of 1998, Governor George Bush may have received the votes of as many as 49 percent of Mexican Americans, but this number is under dispute. At any rate, the Hispanic support for Bush would seem to have been for his person, not his party.[6] Furthermore, the Republican party's traditional opposition to policies such as welfare and job-training programs aimed at helping the poor has generally ensured that its activists, if not always its voters, would be fairly wealthy.

Conservative Democrats

Despite the fact that Texas officially has a two-party system, it has generally offered three voting options to its citizens, for the Democrats are traditionally split into two factions. This three-faction system has the advantage of making more choices available to the voters, and the disadvantage of making Texas politics more confusing than it might otherwise be.

Conservative Democrats are the representatives of habits of thought and behavior that survive from Texas as it was when it was part of the Old South. This Old South culture is very conservative on social issues, but tends to be conflicted and indecisive on economic issues. Many southerners are normally conservative economically but

6. Various studies have concluded that 33%, 37%, or 49% of Hispanic voters supported Bush. See Ken Herman, "How Many Hispanics Voted for Bush? Depends Whom You Ask," *Austin American-Statesman*, November 13, 1998, A11.

can be aroused to a fervent belief in the ability of government to protect the little people of society from wealthy individuals and corporations—an attitude that has historically been known as *populism.* This populist streak makes the Old South part of Texas hard to predict on economic issues.

At the level of the party activists and officeholders, the conservative faction of the Democratic party is slightly less devoted to laissez-faire than Republicans, but much more so than is the liberal faction. It tends to be conservative on social issues, although conservative Democratic candidates have been known to bend to the left on social issues in order to attempt to persuade minority citizens to vote for them. Former U.S. Senator and Secretary of Commerce Lloyd Bentsen and the late former Lieutenant Governor Bob Bullock are good examples of conservative Democrats.

Geographic Distribution.   Support for the conservative Democrats is more widespread than for the Republicans, although there is considerable overlap. Its traditional base is the piney woods of East Texas, where the Old South culture is strongest. This wing of the party also can usually count on support from the Panhandle, from several counties in the Midland-Odessa area, from the German hill country north and west of San Antonio, and from Dallas, Lubbock, Midland, and Abilene. It is relatively weak in North Texas, in the sparsely settled counties of West Texas, and in larger urban areas, except those already noted. Small cities and rural areas often remain conservative Democratic in their affiliation.

Socioeconomic and Ethnic Distribution.   Representing the Old South political culture and the historically dominant wing of the party, conservative Democrats have traditionally drawn support from all classes in Texas, although that pattern is changing as Republicans continue to increase their support among the wealthy. Like the Republicans, they have historically been strong among the Anglo middle and upper classes, business and professional people, and white-collar workers. Unlike the Republicans, they have also drawn substantial support from farmers, ranchers, and workers, especially those in rural areas and small cities. Again, this pattern is changing as Republicans grow in popularity.

Although African Americans, Mexican Americans, and other minorities have strongly favored liberal over conservative Democrats, they often end up furnishing support for the conservatives. The reasons are twofold. First, machine politics prevail in several South Texas counties. Mexican-American leaders are able to deliver a substantial ethnic vote and frequently make deals to deliver it to conservative Democratic candidates. Second, many minority citizens vote a straight Democratic ticket without regard to the ideology of the candidate. Thus, conservative Democrats, without catering to the wishes of ethnic groups, frequently win their votes in the general election. Today, with serious competition from Republicans, conservative Democrats are paying more attention to ethnic groups and seeking their support.

Liberal Democrats

Liberals usually recommend policies that depend upon a government that is active in economic affairs, especially on behalf of those who have less wealth and power. They

Ben Sargent illustrates the magnitude of the Republican defeat of the Democrats in the elections of the 1990s. The name on the truck refers to Bob Slagle, chair of the state Democratic party in 1994. The Republican victories were equally decisive in 1996 and 1998.

SOURCE: Courtesy of Ben Sargent.

tend, however, to oppose government intervention in personal life. Former Governor Ann Richards, former Agriculture Commissioner (and now radio commentator) Jim Hightower, and former mayor of San Antonio (and also former U.S. Secretary of Housing and Urban Development) Henry Cisneros are good examples of Texas liberal Democrats.

Geographic Distribution.   Democratic voting strength in urban areas recently has been more or less equally divided between liberals and conservatives. Liberals are strong where labor unions are a factor: in far southeast Texas, in central Texas, and in much of the Gulf Coast. Considerable support also comes from South Texas, the south plains, and the trans-Pecos area of the state. Liberals can usually rely on doing well in Austin, the Beaumont–Port Arthur–Orange complex, Corpus Christi, Houston-Galveston, and Waco.

Socioeconomic and Ethnic Distribution.   Identifying the socioeconomic components of liberal Democratic strength in Texas is a more complex task than in the case of Republicans or conservative Democrats. Liberals form, at best, an uneasy coalition. White middle- and upper-class liberals can support African Americans and Mexican Americans in their quest for equal treatment, but labor unions have been noticeably cool in this area. African Americans and Mexican Americans usually give little support to reform legislation—of campaign spending and lobbying, for example—or efforts to protect the natural environment, which energize Anglo liberals. Many Mexican Americans are reluctant to vote for African-American candidates, and vice versa. While it can be said, therefore, that liberal strength comes mostly from labor unions, African Americans, Mexican Americans, and certain educated Anglos, the mix is a volatile one that does not make for stable cooperation.

Liberal leadership comes largely, but not exclusively, from the legal, teaching, and other professionals. In earlier years union officials provided leadership for the liberal faction and in some areas still do. But officials of the state unions have become more conservative in recent years. Leading the liberal Democrats is an uncertain business.

The Future of the Three-Faction System

The future does not look bright for conservative Democrats in Texas. They are being drained from the right and squeezed from the left. As Republicans steadily draw away their voting support, they continuously lose power within the Democratic party to liberals. It is possible to foresee a day in the not-too-distant future when Texas has only a conservative Republican party and a liberal Democratic party. Where will the conservative Democrats go? If they become Republicans, then that party will dominate Texas politics for a long time. If, however, they only become independents, casting their votes according to the candidates and issue stands offered by each party in each election, the future is much less predictable.

THIRD PARTIES IN TEXAS

Texas has had its share of **third parties.** The Know-Nothing party made a brief appearance before the Civil War, representing those who objected to Roman Catholics and immigrants. After the Civil War, the Greenback party, a cheap-money party, made an equally brief appearance. More important was the Populist or People's party, which represented widespread discontent among farmers and other "little people." The Populists advocated an extensive program of government regulation of big business and social welfare reform. The Populist candidate for president drew 100,000 votes in Texas in 1892—almost 20 percent of the votes cast. The major parties, especially the Democrats under Governor Jim Hogg, adopted some of the Populist positions, and the party ultimately disappeared. As mentioned, however, the populist spirit has not entirely disappeared from Texas politics.

The Populists were typical of third parties in America. Such parties tend not to achieve permanent status for themselves, but they can be important in influencing the major parties to adopt some of their positions and platforms. Since the Populist era, Texas has seen candidates from the Prohibitionists, Socialists, Socialist-Laborites, Communists, Progressives, Jacksonians, States' Righters, George Wallace's American Independence Party, the Citizens' Party, and Libertarians. In 1992, Ross Perot's candidacy for the presidency generated quite respectable support in Texas, but this support has since declined and he does not appear to be an important force for the future.

SUMMARY

I deology is one of the most important bases for political parties everywhere, but in Texas, where parties have historically been weak, ideology has been more important than party affiliation. The major ideological conflict has been between conservatives and liberals.

Liberals tend to favor government regulation of the economy but oppose it in personal life, while conservatives tend to favor regulation of personal life but oppose it in the economy. These basic differences lead to differences in many areas of public policy, from taxation to abortion. The Texas Republican party is consistently strongly conservative, but the Democratic party is split into a conservative and a liberal faction.

The other major basis for political parties is interests, which are based on economic, ethnic, religious, or almost any other characteristic of citizens. Interests combine and conflict with ideologies to make politics complicated and constantly changing.

From 1875 to the 1970s, Texas was a one-party Democratic state. Today, Republicans and independents each have the affiliation of slightly more than a third of the state's voters, and Democrats can claim the loyalty of a bit less than a third. The ongoing historical trend seems to be for the conservative faction of the Democrats to shrink and for Republicans to become the majority party in Texas.

Our political parties are characterized by both temporary and permanent party organizations. Since nominations are made in primaries, however, and since party leaders have no control over candidates or officeholders, party organization is much less important than ideology in explaining the politics of the state. This lack of organizational strength means that Texas's parties are not "responsible" and hence are incapable of fulfilling some of the functions that they perform in other democracies.

Texas has given birth to a number of third parties, none of which achieved permanency but several of which influenced public policy in the state.

STUDY QUESTIONS

1. What are the basic ideological differences between liberals and conservatives? What are the more important policy differences between them?
2. Of these interests, which would be most likely to draw the support of a political party—owners of French Impressionist paintings, people with Lou Gehrig's disease, Irish Americans, heroin addicts? Why?
3. What are the functions of political parties? How well do Texas parties perform them?
4. Discuss current trends in voter support and party organization in relation to the three factions. Who is growing stronger? Who is getting weaker?
5. Describe briefly the temporary and permanent party organizations in Texas. What political institution renders both of them relatively unimportant in determining the activities of the parties?
6. Are you a Democrat, a Republican, or an independent? Why?

SURFING THE WEB

Each national and state party organization has a website full of factual information and propaganda touting its candidates and policy stands:

Texas Republican Party—
    http://www.texasgop.org/

Texas Democratic Party—
    http://www.txdemocrats.org/

United We Stand, America, national headquarters—
    http://www.uwsa.org/

Texas Libertarian Party—
    http://www.tx.lp.org/

5

*S*uppose they gave an
election and nobody
came?

Bumper sticker from the 1960s

*Politics has got so
expensive that it takes
lots of money to even get
beat with.*

Will Rogers,
American humorist, 1931

VOTERS,
CAMPAIGNS,
AND ELECTIONS

INTRODUCTION

Nothing is more basic to the concept of democratic government than the principle of elected representatives freely chosen by the majority of the people, with each person's vote counting equally. And few things are more disturbing to observers of democracy than elections in which a large percentage of the people do not vote or in which control of wealth makes a few campaign contributors far more important than the great mass of their fellow citizens.

This chapter will first look at the reasons why voting is important to democracy. Then it will examine Texas's registration procedures and discuss its shockingly low voter turnout. The focus turns to election campaigns, with special attention to the impact of money on the outcome. A description of the various types of public elections in Texas follows. Having discussed some important principles about Texas elections, the chapter will then briefly examine the way some of them are illustrated by the 1994, 1996, 1998, and 2000 elections. Last come a comparison of our portrait painted of Texas elections with the democratic ideal and an argument that there is much room for improvement.

VOTERS

Why Vote?

As is the case with many important questions, the answer to this one is, "It depends." It depends on whether we view voting from the perspective of the *individual voter* or of the *candidates* or of the *political system.*

From the standpoint of the individual voter, there may seem to be no logic in voting, for public elections are almost never won by the margin of a single vote. The individual voter has very little hope of affecting the outcome of an election. Why, then, do so many people bother to register and vote?

The main reason is that people don't think of voting in completely logical terms. Like other political behavior, voting is governed not only by reason but also by emotion, custom, and habit. Most of us vote primarily because we have been taught that it is our duty as citizens (as, in fact, it is). And even though our single vote is unlikely to affect the outcome of an election, our participation in the governing of the community is important to the self-development of each of us.

Occasionally, in small towns and in elections held in conjunction with special districts, a single voter is decisive. In one municipal utility district (MUD) election in the northern part of the state, a vote was held in 1986 to elect directors of the MUD. Only one qualified voter lived in the district and, thus, one person decided the outcome of the election. A decade later in the same community, a single citizen moved his house trailer onto an industrial site and proceeded to cast the one vote to create an economic development district around the site. Suppose they gave those elections and nobody came?

From the standpoint of the candidate, voting is extremely important. There is a saying among politicians: "Votes are counted one by one by one." It expresses the insight that although citizens may seem to be part of a mass, it is a mass of individual personalities, each with his or her own motivations, ideology, and hopes for the future. Politicians who forget that each potential supporter is an individual soon find themselves forcibly retired.

From the standpoint of the political system, elections are crucial. In democratic theory, it is the *participation of the citizens* that makes government legitimate (that is, morally right and worthy of support). When citizens neglect or refuse to vote in large numbers, it raises questions about the most fundamental underpinnings of political authority.

Voting also performs other functions in a democratic society. The act of participating in an election decreases alienation and opposition by making people feel that they are part of the system. Further, the electorate *does* have some effect on public policy by choosing one set of candidates who endorse one set of policies over another. While one person's vote is very unlikely to swing an election, groups of like-minded citizens who vote the same way can be decisive. Finally, large-scale voting has the added virtue of helping to prevent dishonesty. It is relatively easy to rig an election when only a few people bother to go to the polls. One of the best guarantees of honest government is a large turnout on election day.

So, despite the fact that one vote almost never matters, **democracy depends upon each citizen's acting as if it does.** When people take their vote seriously and act as responsible citizens, the system works. When they refuse to participate and stay home on election day, they abdicate control over the government to the elites and special interests who are happy to run things. We can partly judge the extent to which a country or state has a decent government by the level of voter turnout among its citizens. How does Texas stack up?

This question will be answered shortly. First, however, must come a look at the legal context of the voting act. The most important part of that context is the system of registration.

Registration

Every political system has a **voter registration** procedure to distinguish qualified voters from those who are ineligible because of immaturity, lack of citizenship, mental incapacity, or other reasons. In most countries of the world, registration is easy; in many countries, the government goes to great lengths to make sure that all citizens are registered before every election.

Like the other former slaveholding states of the old Confederacy, however, for most of its history Texas deliberately limited voting. Through a series of devices—the grandfather clause, white primaries, property qualifications, the poll tax, and others—Texas prevented voting by African Americans, Mexican Americans, and poor whites.[1]

1. The *grandfather clause* was a law that prevented anyone from voting unless his or her grandfather had been eligible to vote. Since the grandparents of African Americans had been slaves, this rule disenfranchised them. White primary laws and rules prevented voting in primary elections by anyone who was not caucasian. Although the 15th Amendment to the U.S. Constitution guaranteed the right of all citizens of any color to vote in general elections, it did not apply to primaries. Property qualifications prevented voting by those who did not own property in the voting district. The poll tax required a voter to pay for a ballot months in advance of the election. Other similar devices were used in various localities.

Through the 1960s, however, the federal government, especially the courts, invalidated and squashed the whole tricky system of registration in Texas. By 1971, the state legislature was forced to write an honest law making the ballot box accessible to all citizens. Its major provisions, as amended, are:

1. *Initial registration:* The voter may register either in person or by mail. A parent, child, or spouse who is registered may register for the voter.
2. *Permanency:* The voter remains registered as long as he or she remains qualified. A new voter registration card is issued every two years.
3. *Period of registration:* Voters may register at any time and may vote in any election, provided that they are registered thirty days prior to the election.

To vote in Texas today, one must:

1. Be a United States citizen 18 years of age by election day.
2. Be a resident of the state and county for thirty days immediately prior to election day.
3. Be a resident of the election precinct on election day.
4. Have registered to vote at least thirty days prior to election day.

The Texas Voter—Government by the People?

Despite the fact that registration has been relatively easy in Texas for over two decades, voter turnout in the state, while it has been climbing erratically, is still below national levels. **Voter turnout** means the proportion of eligible citizens who actually cast ballots. Table 5.1 shows that the percentage of Texans voting in both presidential and off-year congressional elections is considerably lower than the percentage voting nationally. An average of 45.8 percent of eligible Texans turned out for presidential balloting in the quarter century since the new registration law went into effect, and an average of 26.8 percent turned out for off-year congressional elections. Other elections often attract even fewer voters; the June 1993 runoff between Kay Bailey Hutchison and Bob Krueger for U.S. Senate drew only 20.5 percent of the state's eligible electorate, for example.[2]

2. "Political Intelligence," *Texas Observer,* June 18, 1993, 24.

In 1994, the U.S. Congress passed and President Bill Clinton signed the "motor voter bill." This act mandates that states devise a registration system that allows an individual to register to vote whenever a driver's license is renewed. The hope of those creating the law was that easier registration would result in more citizens being registered, which in turn would mean more people in the ballot box on election day. The law's advocates were disappointed, however, when voter turnout *declined* from 1992 levels in 1996 and from 1994 levels in 1998.

TABLE 5.1

Percent of Voting-Age Population Voting in National Elections, 1972–1998

			Presidential Elections				
	1972	*1976*	*1980*	*1984*	*1988*	*1992*	*1996*
U.S.	55.5	54.3	51.8	53.1	50.2	55.2	50.8
Texas	45.4	47.3	44.7	47.2	44.2	49.0	43.0
			U.S. House of Representatives (Off-Year Elections)				
	1974	*1978*	*1982*	*1986*	*1990*	*1994*	*1998*
U.S.	36.1	35.1	38.0	36.4	35.0	38.9	36
Texas	18.4	24.0	26.2	29.1	26.8	35.0	28

SOURCES: *Statistical Abstract of the United States,* 101st ed. (Washington, DC: U.S. Department of Commerce, Bureau of the Census, 1980), 517, 106th ed. (1985), 254, 109th ed. (1989), 259; Federal Election Commission, Washington, DC; "Political Intelligence," *Texas Observer,* November 27, 1992, 8; Walter Dean Burnham, Department of Government, University of Texas at Austin.

In other words, government in Texas is never "by the people." At best, it is by half the people; often it is by a quarter of the people or even fewer.

Why Don't Texans Vote?

Americans in general are not known for high voter turnouts, but Texans seem to be even less participatory than the residents of many other states. Why?

Texas is a rather poor state with a very uneven distribution of its wealth. The poverty rate is important because the poor and less educated, in the absence of strong parties to persuade them to go to the polls on election day, have a tendency to stay home. When the poor don't vote, the overall turnout rate remains low.

The difference between rich and poor citizens is strongly related to differences between turnout rates for ethnic groups. Consider, for example, the turnout rates for the three dominant ethnic groups in the 1993 runoff for U.S. Senate:[3]

Anglo	*African American*	*Hispanic*
24%	13%	12%

Other studies confirm that Texas's low voter turnout rate is partly caused by the tendency of its minority citizens to stay home on election day. Thus, those who vote tend to be richer, better educated, and white; those who abstain tend to be poorer, uneducated, and minority.

The variations in voter turnout have major consequences for public policy. Minority citizens tend to have more liberal opinions on what government should be doing. These differences partly result from the fact that minorities are more likely to be poor than are Anglos. When they fail to go to the polls, however, their views become irrelevant. Because the more conservative white citizens vote at higher rates, their preferences are usually the ones that determine which candidates win and therefore which policies are pursued by government. Low minority turnout is one of the major explanations for conservative public policy in Texas.

3. "Political Intelligence," 24.

TABLE 5.2

Anglo and African-American Public Opinion, 1989–1997

Issue	Percent Agreeing among	
	Anglos	African Americans
1989: Think that government should do something to reduce differences between rich and poor (those most willing to redistribute)	29	47
1992: Feel that homosexuality should be considered an acceptable alternate lifestyle	37	50
1996: Favor government health insurance	35	53
1996: Agree that government should ensure that all citizens have a job	22	47
1997: Agree that affirmative action should be continued	35	80

SOURCES: Top item from National Opinion Research Center surveys, *An American Profile: Opinions and Behavior, 1972–1989,* (New York: Gale Research, 1990), 572; second item from Gallup poll of June 12, 1992; third and fourth items from 1996 National Election Study, reported in William Lasser, *American Politics: The Enduring Constitution,* 2nd ed. (Boston: Houghton Mifflin, 1999), 184; fifth item from Howe Verhouck, "In Poll, Americans Reject Means But Not Ends of Racial Diversity," *New York Times,* December 14, 1997, A32, reported in Paul C. Light, *A Delicate Balance: An Introduction to American Government,* 2d ed. (New York: Worth Publishers, 1999), 614.

Copyright © 1992 by Westview Press. Used by permission of Westview Press.

For example, minorities as a whole identify with the Democratic party in far greater percentages than do Anglos. According to a survey by the Survey Research Center at the University of Texas at Austin in August, 1998, 22 percent of the state's Anglos identified as Democrats, 41 percent of Hispanics, and 65 percent of blacks.[4] When minorities don't vote, it hurts Democrats.

But it is not just any Democrats who suffer. The liberal wing of the party needs minority support to win. As Tables 5.2 and 5.3 illustrate, African Americans and Mexican Americans tend to hold views on at least some public policy issues that are clearly more liberal than the opinions of whites. It seems obvious that if minorities had higher turnout rates, liberal Democrats would win elections much more often.

4. We are grateful to O'Neill Provost of the Office of Survey Research at the University of Texas at Austin for supplying us with these figures.

TABLE 5.3

Anglo and Mexican-American Public Opinion, Early 1990s

Question	Percent Agreeing among	
	Anglos	Mexican Americans
Government spending should increase on:		
Programs to help blacks (percent agreeing)	23.5	53.7
Programs for refugees and legal immigrants	16.4	41.3
English should be the official language (strongly agree)	45.6	13.7
The basis of job hires and college admissions should be:		
Government quotas	1.7	19.4
Strictly merit	52.0	29.3

SOURCE: Rodolfo O. de la Garza, Louis DeSipio, F. Chris Garcia, John Garcia, and Angelo Falcon, *Latino Voices: Mexican, Puerto Rican, and Cuban Perspectives on American Politics* (Boulder, CO: Westview Press, 1992), 91, 97, 110.

That would mean that government policy in Texas would be more liberal. As it is, the liberals rarely go to the polls, so state government remains conservative.

ELECTION CAMPAIGNS

Democracies do not hold elections unannounced. There is a period of time before the voting day in which the candidates attempt to persuade potential voters to support them. This period is the **campaign.** In Texas, would-be officeholders run initially during the primary campaign. Those who win nomination in the primary then campaign to win the general election.

Candidates for public office must have two essential resources: people and money. The people who are needed are both professionals and volunteers. The professionals plan, organize, and manage the campaign, write the speeches, and raise the money. Volunteer workers are the active amateurs who distribute literature, register and canvass voters, and get supporters to the polls on election day. No major election can be won without competent people who are brought together early enough to plan, organize, and conduct an effective campaign or without a sufficient number of volunteers to make the personal contacts and get out the vote.

People

The act of volunteering to work on a campaign is not only useful to the candidate; it is of great importance to the volunteers and to the democratic process. People who work on a campaign learn about the stupendous exertions, the difficult decisions, and the painful blunders that make up public life in a free society. They learn tolerance for other points of view, how to argue and evaluate the arguments of other people, and why the media are important. Finally, they learn that when they win, all the faults of the republic are not corrected, and that when they lose, civilization does not collapse. They learn, in other words, to be good citizens. In Texas as elsewhere, political campaigns are the most intense means of creating the truly participatory society.

Money

Voluntary participation, the first major resource of campaigns, is thus entirely uncontroversial. Everyone endorses it. But about the second resource, money, there is great controversy.

Except in municipal elections, where volunteers are most important, money is the most important campaign resource. Politicians need money to publicize their candidacies, especially over television. Table 5.4 illustrates the costs of buying advertising in major state media outlets in the late 1990s. The need to buy campaign advertising repeatedly over the course of months in many such media outlets makes the cost of running for office in Texas formidable. For example, George Bush and Ann Richards each spent about $13 million in their 1994 gubernatorial campaigns.[5] The

5. Laylan Copelin and David Elliott, "Small Group of Contributors Gives Large Share of Funds Raised," *Austin American-Statesman,* November 6, 1994, A15.

TABLE 5.4

Costs of Political Advertising in Selected Texas Cities, 1999

		Television	
City	Station	Cost of 30-Second Spot	Cost of 10-Second Spot
Houston	KHOU (CBS)	$6,000	$4,500
Dallas/Fort Worth	KDFW (CBS)	$12,000	$7,200
Austin	KVUE (ABC)	$2,400	$1,440
Lubbock	KCBD (NBC)	$1,100	$550
		Newspapers	
City	Paper	Cost of Full-Page Black & White Ad	Full-Page Color Ad
Fort Worth	Star-Telegram	$30,413.04	$32,640.04
San Antonio	Express-News	$7,489.44	$9,016.44
El Paso	Times	$3,780.00	$4,898.00
Amarillo	Daily News	$6,013.98	$6,753.98

SOURCE: Compiled by David F. Prindle, Professor of Government, University of Texas at Austin.

1994 election was much more typical than the 1998 contest, in which incumbent George W. Bush outspent his Democratic opponent, Garry Mauro, by about thirteen to one.[6] Altogether, candidates for statewide office and the legislature spent a total of about $115 million during their 1998 campaigns.[7]

This money must come from somewhere. A very few candidates, such as Clayton Williams, who ran for governor in 1990, and H. Ross Perot, who tried to win the presidency as an independent in 1992 and 1996, are so rich that they are able to finance their own campaigns. The great majority of candidates, however, must get their funding from somewhere else than their own pockets.

The United States is one of the few democracies in the world that does not have **publicly funded campaigns.** In other countries, the government gives tax money to the parties for their campaigning expenses. This practice ensures that the parties, if their candidates are successful, are relatively free of obligation to special interests. In the United States at every level except the presidency, however, we rely upon **private** money to **fund campaigns.** Candidates and parties must persuade private citizens to part with checks, or their campaigns will fail.

The candidate with the most money does not always win *every* election. In 1990, for example, Clayton Williams outspent Ann Richards two to one and still lost.[8] But the best-financed candidate does win *most* of the time. And just because a victorious candidate spent less than the loser does not mean that money was unimportant in his or her campaign. Ann Richards spent over $10 million in the 1990 campaign, which is a large chunk of cash by anyone's accounting. In other words, although money may

6. Ken Herman and Juan B. Elizondo, Jr., "Bush Outspends Mauro About 13-to-1," *Austin American-Statesman,* October 6, 1998, A1.

7. "State Office Hopefuls Raised $115 Million," *Austin American-Statesman,* May 14, 1999, B2.

8. Laylan Copelin and David Elliott, "Williams Outspending Richards 2–1," *Austin American-Statesman,* October 30, 1990, A1.

not be a *sufficient* resource to ensure political victory, it is still a *necessary* resource. People who are willing to contribute large amounts of money to campaigns, therefore, are extremely important to candidates.

Where Does the Money Come From?   Most of the money given to candidates comes from wealthy donors who represent some sort of special interest. Individual contributions of $5,000 to $20,000 or more are common in campaigns for major state offices, and people and organizations with wealth or access to wealth are able to rent the gratitude of candidates by helping to fund their campaigns. Ordinary people who have to worry about paying their bills are not able to contribute nearly as much and therefore cannot ensure candidates' attention to their concerns. In this way, private funding of campaigns skews public policy in favor of special interests.

Table 5.5 displays the major contributors to George W. Bush and Ann Richards during their contest for the governorship in 1994. Following the election, the people and interests who supported the winner, Bush, had more influence over public policy than the people and interests who supported Richards. (A similar chart is not

TABLE 5.5

Major Contributors to George Bush and Ann Richards, 1994

Name	Interest	Amount
Bush		
Donald Carter	Business	$115,000
Dennis Berman	Business	108,092
Richard Rainwater	Investments	100,000
Nathan Crain	Computer software	97,092
Lonnie Pilgrim	Poultry	80,236
Bradford Freeman	Banking	79,188
Louis Beecherl	Oil, Investments	65,000
Richard Heath	Cosmetics	64,949
Charles Wyly	Computer software	64,273
Walter Neuls	Insurance	58,736
Richards		
Arthur Schechter	Attorney	$138,000
John Moore	Computer software	135,000
Robert Bass	Oil	125,000
John O'Quinn	Attorney	110,000
Daniel Robinowitz	Real estate, gambling	108,000
Shelton Smith	Attorney	95,613
Walter Umphrey	Attorney	90,680
Steven Spielberg	Movie producer	90,000
Lee Godfrey	Attorney	80,129
Edward Gaylord	Business	76,000

SOURCE: Wayne Slater, "Big Donors Fuel Governor's Race," *Dallas Morning News,* November 3, 1994, 21A. Used by permission.

shown for the 1998 election because so few interests supported Democratic challenger Garry Mauro that there would be almost nothing on his side of the ledger.)

Control of Money in Campaigns.

The power of money in campaigns disturbs partisans of democracy because it seems to create an inequality of citizenship. Everyone has only one vote, but some people are millionaires. Those with more money to contribute seem to be "supercitizens" who can wield influence denied to the rest of us. For this reason, for decades many people have been trying to control the impact of money in both the states and the nation. Their success at both levels is spotty at best.

In Texas several laws have been passed to control the use and disclosure of the money collected by candidates. These laws have been made steadily tougher over the years, but they still allow wealthy individuals to purchase more political influence than is available to their fellow citizens.

The Texas Campaign Reporting and Disclosure Act of 1973.   As amended, this act outlines procedures for campaign reporting and disclosure. It appears to strengthen the election code in several areas where previously it was deficient. The act's major provisions are:

1. Every candidate for political office and every political committee within the state must appoint a campaign treasurer before accepting contributions or making expenditures.
2. Contributions exceeding $500 by out-of-state political committees can be made only if the names of contributors of $100 or more are disclosed.
3. Detailed financial reports are required of candidates and managers of campaign committees. They must include a list of all contributions and expenditures over $50.
4. Violators face both civil action and criminal penalties.

The 1973 law sounds like a genuine attempt to force the public disclosure of the financial sponsors of candidates. Its great flaw, however, is that it contained no provision for enforcement. Since laws do not enforce themselves, the public reporting of private contributions was at best a haphazard affair. Moreover, the law failed to impose any limits on the amount that individuals or organizations could contribute to campaigns; as long as they reported the amount, they could attempt to purchase as much influence as they could afford.

The 1991 Texas Ethics Law.   In 1991 the legislature passed another ethics bill designed to regulate and moderate the impact of private wealth on public policy in campaigns and at other levels of Texas politics. This law created an Ethics Commission that could hold hearings on public complaints, levy fines, and report severe violations to the Travis County (Austin) district attorney for possible prosecution.

Again, however, the law failed to place any limits on campaign contributions. Further, it required a "super majority" of six out of eight commissioners for important actions, a provision that was practically guaranteed to prevent the vigorous investigation of violators. As John Steiner, the Ethics Commission's executive director, stated publicly, "There's very little in the way of real enforcement . . . in most of the laws we administer. It's just an unenforced statute—except that if people don't [obey the law], it gets some bad press."[9] There were attempts made to toughen this law during the 1993, 1997, and 1999 legislatures, but the attempts failed.

In summary, then, there is virtually no control over, and very little effort to ensure the public disclosure of, the influence of money in Texas political campaigns. As a consequence, people with money have more influence over politicians than do ordinary citizens.

PUBLIC ELECTIONS

A public election is the only political activity in which large numbers of Texans—although, as we have seen, not a majority—are likely to participate. The state has three types of elections: primary, general, and special elections.

Primary Elections

A **primary** election is an election held within a party to nominate candidates for the general election or choose delegates to a presidential nominating convention. It is because primaries are so important in Texas that parties are weak. Because they do not

9. Quoted in Jeff South and Jerry White, "Computer Network Tracks Politicians' Funds," *Austin American-Statesman,* August 16, 1993, B1.

Cartoonist Ben Sargent points out that there is more than one way to corrupt democratic government.

SOURCE: Courtesy of Ben Sargent.

control nominations, party "leaders" have no discipline over officeholders and so, in reality, cannot lead.

The Texas Election Code provides that any political party whose candidate for governor received 20 percent or more of the vote in the most recent general election must hold a primary to choose candidates for upcoming elections. Parties whose candidates polled less than 20 percent may either hold a primary or choose their candidates by the less expensive method of a nominating convention. In effect, Republicans and Democrats must hold primary elections, while smaller third parties may select their candidates in conventions.

Under Texas law, a candidate must win the nomination with a majority vote in the primary. If there is no majority winner—as there frequently is not if there are more than two candidates—the two leading votegetters meet thirty days later in a primary runoff election.

There are two types of primary elections:

1. The **open primary** is one in which any registered voter may participate in a party's primary.
2. The **closed primary** is one in which only registered members of a party may participate in that party's primary.

Technically, Texas laws provide for a closed primary. In practice, however, voters may participate in any primary so long as they have not already voted in the primary of another party. The only realistic sense in which Texas has a closed primary is that once voters have recorded their party affiliation by voting in one party's primary, they cannot participate in the affairs—the runoff primary or the conventions—of another party during the same year.

General Elections

The purpose of a **general election** is to choose state and national executives and legislators. They are held in even-numbered years on the Tuesday after the first Monday in November. Beginning in 1974, Texas joined the group of states that elect their governors and other state officials in the *off year*, the even-numbered year between presidential election years. At the same time, the state adopted a constitutional amendment that extended the terms of office for the governor and other state officials from two to four years.

Unlike primary elections, which are conducted by officials of the political parties, general and special elections are the responsibility of the state. The secretary of state is the principal election officer, although the election organization is decentralized and most of the actual work is performed at the county level. The county commissioners' court appoints election judges, chooses the method of voting—paper ballots or some type of voting machine—and pays the bills. The county clerk conducts absentee balloting and actually performs many of the functions charged to the commissioners' court.

Nominees of established parties are placed on the ballot when they win a party primary or are chosen by a party convention. New parties and independent candidates get on the general election ballot by presenting a petition signed by a specified number of qualified voters who have not participated in the primary election of another party. The number of required signatures varies with the office. At the local level, it need not exceed 500; at the state level, it is 1 percent of the votes cast in the last gubernatorial election.

There is no standard election ballot in Texas. Primary ballots vary from party to party, and general election ballots vary from county to county. Sometimes citizens are asked to vote by making small holes in a punchcard, sometimes by marking a ballot with a special pencil.

The ballot lists the offices that are to be filled, beginning with the president (in an appropriate year) and continuing to the lowliest local position. Candidates' political party affiliations are listed beside their names, and candidates of the party that polled the most votes in the most recent gubernatorial election are listed first. Other parties' candidates appear in descending order of that party's polling strength in the prior gubernatorial election. A space is provided for write-in candidates. Constitutional amendments, if any, are listed separately, usually near the bottom of the ballot, followed by local referendum questions.

Special Elections

In Texas a number of special elections are held in addition to primary and general elections. They may be called at the state level to fill vacancies in Congress or in the state legislature, or to vote on proposed constitutional amendments. At the local level, most cities choose their councils in special elections, with one important variation— they are nonpartisan. Party labels do not appear beside the candidates' names, and no party certification is needed to get on the ballot.

Absentee or Early Voting

Texas citizens may vote absentee in any election. Voting may be done for a period of two weeks before the election, at the county clerk's office or at a variety of polling places throughout the county. In the past, one needed a reason to vote absentee, such as a planned trip from the county, or illness. Beginning in 1987, the legislature removed the restrictions, and anyone can now vote early. Twenty-five to 40 percent of the voters now typically cast early ballots.

ELECTIONS OF 1994, 1996, 1998, AND 2000

Elections of 1994

In both the nation as a whole and in Texas in particular, the 1994 election was a great victory for the Republican party. Nationally, this outcome seemed to be the result of Democratic President Clinton's unpopularity. Within Texas, however, it seemed to be the result of a long-term trend toward Republican domination of the state. Republicans successfully defended a U.S. Senate seat, picked up two seats in the U.S. House of Representatives, increased their representation in the Texas legislature, and garnered more than 900 local offices (see Table 5.3). They won both vulnerable

Railroad Commission seats and captured majorities on the state supreme court and the state board of education. Most important, George W. Bush defeated incumbent Democrat Ann Richards to become Texas's governor.

Democratic balloting continued to be based on lower-income Anglos, Mexican Americans, and African Americans. As Table 5.6 illustrates, voting for governor in Houston precincts followed the familiar economic and ethnic lines. Middle- and upper-income Anglos supported Bush by large majorities, while he lost African American and Mexican American districts and barely beat Richards in low-income Anglo neighborhoods.

It was perhaps at the level of the judiciary that the Republican party made the most significant gains in 1994. GOP candidates won every seat they contested on the state court of criminal appeals and supreme court, gaining their first majority on the supreme court since the days of Reconstruction. Republicans captured nineteen local judgeships from the Democrats in Harris County alone. The major long-run impact of the Republican court victories was to replace plaintiff-oriented, pro-lawsuit judges with business-oriented, anti-lawsuit judges.

Not every Democratic candidate failed. Relatively conservative politicians such as Lieutenant Governor Bob Bullock and Attorney General Dan Morales were reelected. Democrats also managed to hold on to nineteen of thirty U.S. House seats, despite the defeat of 42-year incumbent Jack Brooks in the ninth District (Galveston to Beaumont).

Republicans also failed to capture the Texas legislature. Although the Democrats lost ground, they still retained their majorities, keeping 17 of 31 seats in the senate and 89 of 150 in the house.

Elections of 1996

Nationally, President Clinton surprised almost everyone by outmaneuvering the Republican Congress in 1995 and 1996 and regaining his popularity. In the balloting, he defeated Republican challenger Robert Dole and independent Ross Perot handily. At the congressional level, Democrats cut into the Republican majority in the House of Representatives without winning a majority themselves, while the Republicans slightly increased their majority in the Senate, from fifty-three to fifty-five seats. At the national level, therefore, the voters sent a confused and confusing message in 1996.

TABLE 5.6

Economic and Ethnic Voting in 1994 Gubernatorial Election, Selected Houston Precincts

Group	% Richards	% Bush	% Other
Low-income Anglo	48.3	50.6	1.1
Middle-income Anglo	35.9	63.7	0.4
Upper-income Anglo	27.7	71.9	0.3
Low-income African American	97.4	2.4	0.2
Middle-income African American	93.6	6.3	0.1
Mexican American	75.6	23.8	0.7

SOURCE: *Houston Chronicle*, November 11, 1994, 20A.
Copyright 1994 Houston Chronicle Publishing Company. Printed with permission.

There was nothing confusing, however, about the voters' message in Texas. Texans gave victories to Republican candidates in all ten statewide races, bucking the national trend by supporting Dole for president, returning U.S. Senator Phil Gramm to Washington, awarding the GOP four seats on the Texas Supreme Court and three on the court of criminal appeals, and reelecting a Republican railroad commissioner. Further, after some victories in runoffs a month later, they won a majority in the state senate for the first time since Reconstruction. Democrats managed to keep control of Texas's congressional delegation and of the state house of representatives, but these were small consolations. Republicans seemed to be the party of the present and the future.

The actual voting, however, was not quite the whole story. As is usually the case with Texas elections, differences in voter turnout provide much of the explanation for the results. Statewide turnout fell six percentage points from 1992 to 1996, but the decline was not evenly distributed. Political scientists Richard Murray and Kent Tedin analyzed 149 precincts in Bexar (San Antonio), Harris (Houston), Tarrant (Fort Worth), Travis (Austin), and Dallas counties in both years. They concluded that turnout fell off 28 percent in working-class white areas between the two elections, 24 percent in Hispanic areas, and 14 percent in African-American areas. In other words, while the citizens who tend to favor Republicans were going to the polls, the citizens who tend to favor Democrats were staying home. The conservatives won because the liberals did not vote.[10]

Elections of 1998

Nationally, voters again sent Washington an ambiguous message in the congressional elections of 1998. Refusing to penalize Democratic candidates for President Clinton's personal troubles, citizens chose an extra five Democrats to take House seats in 1999, while defeating two Democrats and two Republican senators. These choices left the Republicans with a small majority of twelve seats in the House, while they maintained their 55 to 45 margin in the Senate. Because the party that controls the White House usually loses congressional seats in the sixth year of a president's term, these results were widely interpreted as a defeat for the Republicans, despite their continued majority in both houses.

In Texas, however, Republicans continued their march toward complete dominance of the state's politics, although they were halted just short of that goal. As in all previous state elections, the small voter turnout (28 percent), greatly skewed in favor of upper-income Anglos, gave a strongly conservative cast to the balloting.

Governor George W. Bush was never seriously threatened by his Democratic challenger, Garry Mauro, leading by roughly 2 to 1 margins in public opinion polls all during the campaign. Bush received endorsements from the great majority of organizations that voiced opinions, including some, such as the Texas Association of School Administrators, that had never before taken sides in a gubernatorial contest. Greatly outspending Mauro, he saturated the television and radio airwaves with courteous, positive ads, while his challenger was reduced to trying to create support by walking door to door.

10. Suzanne Gamboa, "Low Turnout of Democrats Led to GOP Sweep, Researchers Say," *Austin American-Statesman*, November 9, 1996, A10.

Mauro attempted to offer his own alternative to Bush's education policies and to criticize the governor for not attempting to squelch a proposed nuclear waste dump near Sierra Blanca (the dump was eventually vetoed by the Texas Natural Resource Conservation Commission), but neither of these issues caught fire with the voters. A booming state economy, a falling crime rate, a record of success with the legislature, and a genial personality made Bush unbeatable. On election day, amid speculation about his plans to run for the Presidency in 2000, Bush garnered 69 percent of the vote.

Often appearing to ride Bush's coattails, Republicans swept into every other statewide office. GOP candidates also won every seat on the state Supreme Court and Court of Criminal Appeals.

Democrats salvaged something from the wreckage by holding on to a 78-to-72 seat majority in the state house of representatives, and maintaining their margin of 17 to 13 in the U.S. House.

One of the lesser known but more interesting aspects of the 1998 campaign was the latest attempt by the Christian Right (see Chapter Three) to win a majority on the state Board of Education. In the pivotal battle in District 1 (Far West Texas), Democrat Rene Nunez defeated Republican Donna Ballard, thus ensuing that christian conservatives would only control seven seats on the fifteen-member board.

Elections of 2000

Nationally, the election of 2000 was one of the closest in history. Despite garnering about 200,000 fewer popular votes than Democratic Vice President Al Gore, Texas Republican governor George W. Bush seemed to have survived recounts and court challenges in Florida to capture 271 electoral votes and thus the presidency. As this book went to press, the Gore forces were still pursuing judicial intervention, and there was a small possibility that the election was not decided. Nevertheless, it appeared probable that Bush would eventually enter the White House. Bush's accession to the presidency would cause a shuffling at the top of the Texas power pyramid, with Lieutenant Governor Rick Perry becoming governor and the Senate set to choose a new lieutenant governor as its first order of business in January 2001.

The national congressional contest was also close. Although an ongoing recount in Washington state at press time created some uncertainty about the winner of that state's U.S. senatorial election, the Democrat was ahead, making it likely that the Senate would be divided 50–50 for the next two years. This balance represented a net gain of 5 seats for the Democrats. The Senate results were made more interesting by the victory of First Lady Hillary Rodham Clinton in New York—the first wife of a president to be elected to public office. Her win, combined with those of other women across the country, meant that 13 of the 100 senators in the 2001 Congress would be female, an all-time record. Meanwhile, the Democratic party netted two seats in the House of Representatives to shave the Republican majority to 221–211, with two independents and a cliffhanger in New Jersey still undecided at press time. The number of women in the House also set a record, rising from 56 to 60.

In contrast to the exciting national campaign, the Texas election was without much suspense. Because the Democratic leadership decided not to contest statewide offices, most Republicans ran against opponents from only the Reform or Green parties. Thus Republican candidates for the state's two highest courts, the Railroad Commission, and the Board of Education coasted to victory. In the campaign for U.S. senator, Democrat Gene Kelly ignored his party's advice and challenged incumbent Kay Bailey Hutchison. Utterly unfunded, Kelly was unable to mount any sort of media campaign, and Hutchison squashed him with 65% of the vote. Republicans also defended their 16–15 margin in the state senate. This slim majority ensured that Republicans would exercise the decisive voice in determining who became the next lieutenant governor. Although they had thrown in the towel early on statewide offices, Democrats defended their positions in more narrow constituencies, managing to keep both their 17–13 margin in the U.S. House of Representatives and their 78–72 majority in the state house.

CONCLUSION

All in all, a survey of voters, campaigns, and elections in Texas does not form a pretty picture. If the legitimacy of government in a democracy depends upon the participation of the citizens, then the appallingly low voter turnout in state elections raises serious questions about the legitimacy of state government. Moreover, the great disparity in turnout between ethnic groups most certainly skews public policy away from the patterns that would prevail if all citizens voted. Looking beyond voting, the great impact of money on political campaigns and elections suggests the possibility, if not the certainty, that wealthy elites control the policy process, rendering whatever citizen participation exists irrelevant. A cynical view of democracy finds much support in Texas electoral politics.

There is, however, some cause for optimism. The old barriers to participation that kept people from exercising their citizenship are gone, and in fact voter turnout has been rising slowly and unsteadily in recent years. It is possible that time and education will bring more people to fulfill their potential as citizens. Further, the gubernatorial campaign of 1990 proved that money is not the only thing that counts in Texas politics, although subsequent campaigns have done nothing to change the impression that money is the single most important political resource.

The system, then, is imperfect but not completely depraved. For anyone trying to make a better state, there are many flaws but some reason to hope that they can be corrected.

SUMMARY

Voting, campaigning, and elections are important to study because in a democracy the legitimacy of the government depends upon the people's participation. Thus, despite the fact that single votes almost never determine the outcome of elections, voting is important to the individual, the candidate, and the political system.

Consistent with its Old South political history, Texas until recently attempted to suppress voting by all but wealthy whites. Today, voter turnout is still below the national average, which is itself comparatively low. Turnout of black and brown citizens is generally lower than the turnout of whites. This disparity makes public policy more conservative than it would otherwise be.

In campaigns, candidates attempt to persuade voters to support them. In order to do so, they are forced to spend large amounts of money, which means they become dependent on wealthy special interests who contribute to their causes. This dominance of campaigns by money has consequences for public policy. Money is not absolutely decisive in campaigns, however, and candidates who are outspent by their opponents sometimes win.

There are three kinds of elections in Texas. Primary elections are held to choose candidates for general elections. General elections are held to determine who will serve in public office. Special elections are held when they are needed between general elections, often to either fill unexpected governmental vacancies or ratify constitutional amendments.

A comparison of the reality of Texas electoral politics with the ideal of the democratic polity suggests that Texas falls very far below the ideal, but offers some reasons for hope.

STUDY QUESTIONS

1. In the days when Texas deliberately suppressed voter turnout of everyone but wealthy whites, was its government legitimate?
2. What sorts of consequences are the result of differences in turnout between ethnic groups in Texas?
3. What effects does money have on campaigns? Are these good or bad for democratic government?
4. Why have Texas's laws so far largely failed to curb abuses of private campaign financing?
5. What are the consequences for public policy of the importance of primary elections in Texas?

SURFING THE WEB

The central source for information on voters, campaigns, and elections in Texas is the Secretary of State's Office:

http://www.sos.state.tx.us

You can access this site and then click on the "Elections Division" icon, or access the Elections Division directly at:

http://www.sos.state.tx.us/about/aboutelec.htm

6

f you can't walk into a room and tell right away who's for you and who's against you, you have no business in politics.

Sam Johnson,
Lyndon Johnson's father

They're often criticized, rarely understood, complain about being unappreciated and yet are never ignored. They serve under the banner of the public good and usually view their career choice as an opportunity to effect change. And when one of their own stumbles, the whole profession suffers.

Gene Rose
State Legislatures, 1999

THE TEXAS LEGISLATURE

INTRODUCTION

STRUCTURE OF THE LEGISLATURE

MEMBERSHIP CHARACTERISTICS

STRUCTURAL CRITICISMS AND SUGGESTED REFORMS

THE PRESIDING OFFICERS

POWERS OF THE PRESIDING OFFICERS

LIMITS ON PRESIDING OFFICERS

HOW A BILL BECOMES A LAW IN TEXAS

LEGISLATIVE HANDICAPS

SUGGESTED PROCEDURAL REFORMS

CONCLUSION

SUMMARY

STUDY QUESTIONS

SURFING THE WEB

INTRODUCTION

L egislative bodies are meant to represent the people and to reflect the differing views of a community, state, or nation. At the same time, they are meant to enact public policy, to provide funds for government operations, and to perform a host of other functions on behalf of the people who elected them. The Texas Legislature is still not completely representative of the state as a whole, but, especially from the mid-1980s on, it has increased its diversity along party, ethnic, and gender lines. Achieving greater diversity helps the state to meet more clearly the most fundamental tests of democratic government: representation and fairness. The legislature is particularly important in democratic theory because it institutionalizes the people's choices and translates the people's wants into public policy.

Texas's biennial legislative sessions are the focal point of the state government. In these sessions, legislators must wrestle with important economic and social issues, define public morality and provide methods to enforce it, and attend to strictly political chores, such as redistricting. They are handicapped in these endeavors, however, by a number of structural weaknesses in the legislative system and by a historic lack of public confidence and support.

The Texas Legislature, like other legislative bodies, is not very easy to understand because it operates under myriad procedural rules as well as informal norms of behavior for its members. Nevertheless, because the state constitution vests the legislature with considerable power, understanding at least the basics of legislative operation is important.

This chapter examines the organization of the legislature: the constitutional, statutory, and informal aspects of legislative structure; the less formalized internal organization of the two houses; and the support staff. It then looks at the legislature in action, with emphasis on important influences on legislation.

STRUCTURE OF THE LEGISLATURE

Size, Elections, and Terms

With the exception of Nebraska, which has a unicameral (single-house) legislature, the American states have patterned themselves on the **bicameral** model of the U.S. Congress. Article III of the Texas Constitution stipulates that the legislature is composed of a senate, with 31 members, and a house of representatives, with 150 members.

Key features of the system for electing legislators include:

1. Selection in the November general election in even-numbered years
2. Election from single-member districts
3. Two-year terms for House members and four-year staggered terms for senators
4. A special election called by the governor to fill a vacancy caused by death, resignation, or expulsion from office

Newly elected legislators take office in January. Whenever reapportionment to establish districts of approximately equal population size occurs—at least every ten years—all senators are elected in the same year. They then draw lots to determine who will serve for two years and who will serve the full four-year term.

Sessions

Regular Session.   The constitution provides for regular biennial sessions, beginning on the second Tuesday in January of odd-numbered years. These sessions may run no longer than 140 calendar days. Six other states (all considerably less populated than Texas) also have biennial sessions; the rest have either annual or effectively continuous sessions.

The truncated biennial legislative session accentuates all the formal and informal factors that influence legislation in Texas. For example, insufficient time for careful consideration of bills heightens the power of the presiding officers, the lobbyists, and the governor. Although there have been a number of changes in the specifics of the legislative sessions over the years,[1] voters have consistently rejected amendments providing for annual sessions. They fear increased governmental power and spending, a reflection of the antigovernment attitude implicit in a conservative political culture.

Called Sessions.   The governor can call the legislature into special session. Such a session is limited to a maximum of thirty days. The governor determines the agenda for this session. The legislature cannot call itself into special session to consider legislation, although it did convene itself to consider the impeachment of Governor James E. Ferguson in 1917. If either legislators or the governor wish to add items to the call for a special session agenda, they both must agree to do so. Thirty-one other state legislatures have mechanisms for calling themselves into special session.

The governor may call one special session after another if necessary. However, since the voting public has rejected annual sessions several times, Texas governors usually try to avoid calling numerous special sessions that might appear to function as annual sessions. The average $500,000 price tag is another discouragement.

Nevertheless, governors sometimes have little choice about calling a special session because too much legislative business—often including the state budget—is unfinished. For example, Governor Bill Clements called two special sessions in 1989 and four in 1990 to deal with school finance and workers' compensation. Six weeks before the regular 1991 session ended, Governor Ann Richards had already called a special summer budget session. An additional budget session was needed in 1991, and public

---

1. For example, at one time the legislature could spend an unlimited number of days in session, but the per diem—daily—expense coverage ended after 120 days.

The most common cause of a vacancy is resignation. A typical situation occurred in 1997 when Texas Senator Jim Turner was elected to Congress; he was then replaced in the Senate by Steve Ogden in a January special election.

After the 1980 census, redistricting efforts set in motion a gubernatorial veto and a spate of lawsuits in state and federal courts. After the 1990 census, redistricting brought about state and federal lawsuits and charges of judicial misconduct. Redistricting maneuvers promised to dominate the 2001 session after the 2000 census.

SOURCE: Courtesy of Ben Sargent.

school finance was the subject of a 1992 session. No special sessions were called from 1993 through 1999.

Legislative Districts

Mechanics.   Only one senator or representative may be elected from a particular district by the people living in that district. Although some districts are 300 times larger than others in geographical size, each senatorial district should have approximately 655,886 residents, and each House district, approximately 135,533 as of 2000.[2] Achieving equally populated districts does not come easily, however, since the task is a highly political one carried out by the legislature.

If the legislature fails to redistrict itself, the Legislative Redistricting Board (LRB) comes into play. The LRB is composed of five *ex officio* state officials; that is, they are

---

2. According to census estimates for 2000, Texas has a population of 20.33 million persons. Dividing that figure by 31 for senatorial seats gives the ideal district 655,886 citizens; dividing by 150 for representatives, the figure is 135,533. Obviously, citizens move in and out of districts, so the numbers are not exact, and they change as the population increases.

members by virtue of holding another office. These five are the lieutenant governor, the speaker of the House, the comptroller of public accounts, the general land commissioner, and the attorney general. Already powerful officeholders, once constituted as the LRB they are responsible for both legislative and congressional redistricting in Texas.

History. Prior to the mid-1960s, legislative districts were a hodgepodge, based partly on population, partly on geography, and largely on protecting rural interests. Members of the Senate have always been elected in single-member districts, but those districts reflected land area, not population. Indeed, the Texas Constitution once prohibited a single county, regardless of population, from having more than one senator. House districts were constitutionally based on population, but with limitations that worked against urban counties.[3] In addition, *gerrymandering*—drawing district lines in such a way as to give one faction or one party an advantage—was the norm.

The federal courts changed the ability of the state to artificially limit representation from urban areas and forced the drawing of legislative districts according to population. In 1962, *Baker v. Carr*[4]—the one-person, one-vote case—overturned a legislative districting system that gave one group substantial advantages over another. In 1964, in *Reynolds v. Sims,*[5] the Court laid down its first guidelines on conditions that would necessitate redrawing district lines, including a mandate that the membership of both houses be based on population. The Texas House of Representatives continued to use multimember legislative districts[6] until the courts forced some counties to abandon them in 1975 and others volunteered to do so. The **redistricting** battles that arose after the 1980 census are reflected in the Ben Sargent cartoon depicting a comedy of errors.[7]

Citizens in urban areas, Republicans, and ethnic minority groups have all been prominent in redistricting suits. As Table 6.1 shows, the predominant ethnic minorities in Texas—African Americans and Hispanics—have made some gains through population-based districting. Ethnic minority groups made up 28 percent of the legislation in 1999. However, at that time, the non-Anglo population of the state was 42 percent, with Hispanics accounting for about 30 percent and African Americans 12 percent. Table 6.2 shows the gains made by Republicans in the modern era, with most of these gains coming in urban areas.

In addition to ethnic, party, and urban pressures, legislators have to be concerned with the federal Voting Rights Act of 1965 and have to produce redistricting plans that the governor will not veto. With all these competing demands, it is no wonder that the legislature usually fails to produce a plan that pleases everyone. For example, after the 1990 census, while executive-legislative friction was minimal, the judiciary,

3. A county was entitled to a maximum of seven representatives unless its population exceeded 700,000; then one additional representative could be elected for each additional 100,000 in population.

4. 369 U.S. 186 (1962).

5. 377 U.S. 533 (1964).

6. A multimember district is one in which two or more representatives are elected by all of the people in that district. All the representatives represent all the people of the district. Multimember districts tend to reduce considerably the ability of ethnic minorities to win election, and the citizens tend not to be sure which representative is truly theirs.

7. See Steven Bickerstaff, "Legislative and Congressional Reapportionment in Texas: A Historical Perspective," *Public Affairs Comments* 37 (Winter 1991): 1–13, for a good review of redistricting developments.

TABLE 6.1

Ethnicity in the Texas Legislature, 1987–1997, by Percentage*

Year	Anglo	Hispanic/Mexican American	African American
1987	78.5	13.3	8.3
1989	77.9	14.4	7.7
1991	78.5	13.3	8.3
1993	73.5	17.7	8.8
1995	72.4	18.8	8.8
1997	73.0	18.5	8.4
1999	71.8	19.3	8.8

*Percentages do not always equal 100 because of rounding.

Republicans, and ethnic minority groups all attacked the redistricting handiwork. The disputes centered on the Texas House and Texas Senate districts. Redrawing the congressional districts proved to be easy, since the state had gained three new U.S. House seats. The legislature redistricted in 1991 and made adjustments in 1993. Thirteen House districts and three congressional districts were redrawn in 1996 based on the precedents of *Shaw v. Reno* (509 U.S. 630, 1993).

Redistricting after the 2000 census, which will be the job of the 2001 legislature, is likely to be controversial. By then, the non-Anglo population of the state is expected to be 45.3 percent, with Hispanics at 31 percent, African Americans at 11.3 percent, and other ethnic groups—principally of Asian and South Pacific origin—making up the other 3 percent. The U.S. Supreme Court, once quick to invalidate legislative districts that seemed to reflect ethnic or racial bias, raised the standard of proof in 1999 to include evidence of intentional, outright racial gerrymandering.[8] That higher standard may make for greater disputes on how the lines are drawn.

Party and Factional Organization

Historically, Texas was a one-party—Democratic—state (see Chapter Four). In the legislature, unlike the situation in the U.S. Congress and many other state legislatures, political party organization did not exist. As a one-party state, Texas saw factionalism within the Democratic party replace the party differences that characterized other legislative bodies.

Political party affiliation and party organization have grown in importance as Texas has become a two-party state. As Table 6.2 shows, Republican representation in the legislature has grown from minuscule in 1977 to a majority in the Texas Senate by 1997. Beginning in 1983, party members in the House designated floor leaders. In the 1989 session, House Republicans formed a formal caucus for the first time since Reconstruction, and today they regularly select *party whips*—the persons designated to line up votes on behalf of the official party position. However, in both houses, the presiding officers continue to deal with members on an individual basis, unlike the situation in the U.S. Congress, which is organized strictly along party lines.

8. *Hunt v. Cromarite*, Docket No. 98-85, U.S. Supreme Court, decided May 17, 1999.

TABLE 6.2

Political Party Membership in the Texas Legislature, 1977–1997, by Percentage

Year	Senate (N = 31)		House (N = 150)		Both Houses (N = 181)	
	Democrat	Republican	Democrat	Republican	Democrat	Republican
1977	90.3%	09.7%	87.3%	12.7%	87.9%	12.1%
1979	87.1	12.9	84.7	15.3	85.1	14.9
1981	77.4	22.6	74.7	25.3	75.0	25.0
1983	83.9	16.1	76.0	24.0	77.3	22.7
1985	83.9	16.1	65.3	34.7	68.5	31.5
1987	80.6	19.4	62.7	37.3	71.3	28.7
1989	74.2	25.8	62.0	38.0	63.9	36.1
1991	71.0	29.0	62.0	38.0	63.5	36.5
1993	58.1	41.9	61.3	38.7	60.8	39.2
1995	54.8	45.2	59.3	40.7	58.6	41.4
1997	45.2	54.8	54.7	45.3	53.0	47.0
1999	48.4	51.6	52.0	48.0	51.4	48.6

In the 76th and 77th Legislatures (1997–2000), the Republicans held the Senate while Democrats constituted a majority in the House. In 1999, Lieutenant Governor Rick Perry, the Republican presiding officer of the Senate, appointed nine Republicans and four Democrats as chairs of standing committees. To chair four permanent subcommittees and two special committees, he appointed three Republicans and three Democrats. The committee leadership appointed by Perry was slightly more partisan than Democrat Bob Bullock's 1997 appointees, but the Senate had more committees in 1997. The Democratic House of Representatives speaker, Pete Laney, who presided over the House in both of these sessions, appointed twenty-three Democrats and fourteen Republicans as chairs of standing committees in 1999. Neither presiding officer appointed a member of the opposition party as chair of a super-powerful committee such as Finance or Appropriations.

The almost equal party alignment in the Texas House and Senate was continued after the 2000 elections. In the Senate, the alignment remained at 16 Republicans and 15 Democrats. In the House, it was 78 Democrats and 72 Republicans. Thus, both parties held their status in each house.

The liberalism or conservatism of a legislator is often more important than the party label. Liberals versus conservatives and urban versus rural/suburban interests are typical divisions. These differences cut across party lines and are most evident on issues such as taxation, spending, and social welfare programs.

Compensation

Since 1975, members of the Texas Legislature have received a salary of $7,200 each year; this figure was established by constitutional amendment. (Texas is one of only six states that set legislative salaries by constitution.) They also receive a $118 per

FIGURE 6.1

Legislative Salaries, Per Diem in Ten Largest States, 1998 SOURCE: *The Book of the States, 1998–99 Edition,* vol. 32 (Lexington, KY: Council of State Governments, 1998), 80–81.

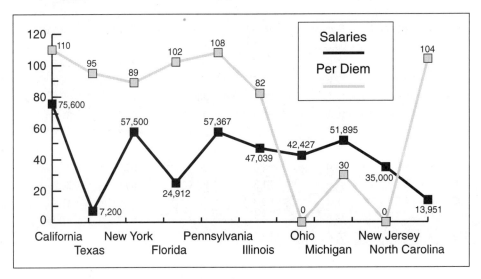

diem—daily—allowance when the legislature is in regular or special session to assist in paying for lodging, meals, and other expenses as of 2000. When they serve on a state board or council or conduct legislative business between sessions, legislators also are entitled to per diem expenses for up to twelve days a month. In addition, they receive a 28-cent mileage allowance so long as mileage charges do not exceed contracted airplane fares. The presiding officers receive the same compensation but also are entitled to apartments furnished by the state.

As Figure 6.1 shows, as of 1998—the last year for which comparative data were available—California paid legislators $75,600, ten times what Texas, the second largest state, pays. The Texas legislative stipend is not even half the federal minimum for a family of four to be above the poverty level! The low level of Texas salaries, which voters have repeatedly refused to change, makes legislators simultaneously more susceptible to lobbying tactics—at $7,200, a free lunch is important—and to diverting their attention to finding ways to earn a decent living. The latter task has become more difficult with the increase in committee work between legislative sessions and occasional special sessions. It also makes the per diem amount—$95 for the period shown in Figure 6.1—more important.

Under a 1991 state constitutional amendment, the Ethics Commission can convene a citizen advisory board to recommend changes in legislative salary; the proposal must then be submitted to the voters. By 2000, however, no such board had been formed. The Ethics Commission also was empowered to increase the per diem expense money and has done so twice.

The bottom line on legislative compensation is that the salary is very low, especially for a high-population state with a complex legislative agenda. The fringe benefits are rather generous, however. Some Texas legislators have manipulated salary, per diem, and travel reimbursements to bring in more than $70,000. The fundamentally undemocratic aspect of legislative compensation is that citizens have authorized only the $7,200 salary and might be surprised at the total compensation package.[9]

Legislators also receive an allowance for operating an office both during the session and in the interim between sessions. Members of the Senate receive $30,000 a month for office expenses; House members receive $9,750. These allowances compare quite favorably with those granted by other states. Additionally, legislators are entitled to retirement benefits if they serve at least twelve years and pay $48 a month. Those benefits are generous because they are pegged to the salary of a district judge, which is twelve times that of a legislator.

MEMBERSHIP CHARACTERISTICS

Formal Qualifications

The **formal qualifications** necessary to become a member of the Texas Legislature are stipulated in Article III of the constitution. They are those commonly required for elected officials: age, residency, U.S. citizenship, and voting status. Members of the Senate must be 26 years of age or older, qualified voters for five years, and residents of the senatorial district from which they are elected for one year. Members of the House must be at least 21 years old, qualified voters, legal residents of the state for two years, and residents of the district from which they are elected for one year.

Personal Characteristics

The formal qualifications are so broad that a substantial portion of the Texas citizenry is eligible to run for legislative office. However, individuals with certain personal characteristics tend to get elected more readily than individuals who lack these characteristics. These characteristics reflect political, social, and economic realities and traditions and confirm the state's conservative political tradition. That they exist does not mean that they are desirable. Indeed, they indicate that certain groups may be underrepresented in the Texas Legislature.

Not every legislator has all of these personal characteristics, but an individual elected without having any of them would be extraordinary indeed. In general, Texas legislators are middle-aged white male Protestant lawyers or businessmen who are married, have college educations, belong to a number of civic organizations, have considerable personal money as well as access to campaign funds, and have the support of the local media. Details of several of these characteristics are shown in Table 6.3.

White, Male.   Race, ethnicity, and gender are all factors in politics. Both ethnic minorities and women are considerably underrepresented in the Texas Legislature in terms of numbers though not necessarily ideologically. Although Texas's total minority population exceeded 45 percent by 2000 and minorities reach four-fifths of the population in some areas of the state, minority membership in the legislature is only

9. Ben Wear, "Salaries Are Just the Start at Capitol," *Austin American-Statesman*, April 2, 1995, A1, A20.

TABLE 6.3

Selected Characteristics of Members of the 76th Legislature, 1999–2000, by House, by Percentages*

Characteristics	Senate (N = 31)	House (N = 150)
Ethnicity		
Anglo/White	71.0%	72.0%
Hispanic/Mexican American	22.6	18.7
Black/African American	6.4	9.3
Gender		
Male	90.3%	80.7%
Female	9.7	19.3
Age		
Average age	52	NA
Oldest/youngest member	66/39	74/26
Education		
Graduate or professional degree	54.8%	54.7%
Some college up to bachelor's degree	45.2	40.0
No college or no answer	0	5.3
Marital Status		
Married	64.5%	78.0%
Nor married or not reporting	35.5†	22.0

*Percentages do not always equal 100 due to rounding.

†For the Senate, the greater percentage of those not stating they were married results from a lack of any statement about marital status in their Senate biographies.

28 percent. No Native Americans or Asian Americans are members. Although there are about 100 women for every 97 men in society, slightly less than 18 percent of Texas legislators are women.[10]

Lawyers and Businesspeople.   Law traditionally has been seen as preparation for politics. In fact, aspiring politicians often attend law school as a means of gaining entry into politics. The result is that attorneys, who make up less than 4 percent of the state's population, hold about one-third of Texas legislative seats. Their numbers have been waning in recent years, reflecting a national trend away from lawyers as legislators. The most frequent business fields are real estate, insurance, and investments. Table 6.4 shows the wide variety of occupations represented in the 76th Legislature in 1999–2000.

Fiftyish.   The average age of members of the Texas legislature has been creeping up to about the late forties in the House and to fifty-two in the Senate. The growing numbers of young adult and elderly citizens are not proportionately represented.

10. Lyn Kathlene, in "Power and Influence in State Legislative Policymaking: The Interaction of Gender and Position in Committee Hearing Debates," *American Political Science Review* 88 (September 1994): 560–76, reports that as the number of female legislators increases, the aggressiveness of their male colleagues also increases, presenting a serious challenge to the women's ability to participate on an equal basis.

TABLE 6.4

Occupations and Professions Represented in the Texas Legislature

Accounting	Insurance
Advertising	Investments
Aviation	Law
Business	Manufacturing
Chiropractic	Medicine/health professions
Civics/government/public service	Ministry
Communications	Oil and gas
Construction	Public finance
Consulting	Public relations
Customs brokering	Publishing
Dentistry	Ranching
Education	Real estate
Electronics	Sales and marketing
Engineering	Transportation
Farming	Veterinary medicine
Firefighting	

Other Factors. *Education, marital status, religion, organization, money,* and the *media* are additional factors in legislative elections. Since the late 1970s, virtually all members of the legislature are college educated, and slightly over half hold more than one degree—especially in law or business.

The preponderance of legislators are married, although the reporting system tends to make it appear that the legislature has a larger number of single members than is likely. In 1991, the legislature had its first (and still only) acknowledged gay man as a member.

The last year for which religion information on the House is available is 1991, when 54 percent of the members were Protestant, 26 percent were Roman Catholic, 4 percent were Jewish, and 16 percent did not respond. In 1997, the Senate included 68 percent Protestants, 29 percent Roman Catholics, and 3 percent Jews (one member). That the preponderance of legislators are Protestants merely reflects the religious composition of Texas society. The religious affiliations of the state's population are approximately as follows: Roman Catholic, 25 percent; Protestant, 67 percent; Jewish, 0.4 percent; other religions and those without religious beliefs make up the rest.[11]

Legislators also tend to be members of the "right" groups. Membership in civic associations, business and professional groups, and social clubs helps to convince voters that the candidate is a solid citizen.

Campaigning for office is expensive. In 1998, candidates for the state Senate spent $9 million and candidates for the House spent $23.6 million running for office—an

11. Helen Parmley, "Questions of Faith," *Dallas Morning News,* June 9, 1990, 1A, 14A. A later survey just of Dallas-area residents differs little: Roman Catholic, 29 percent; Protestant, 57 percent; Jewish, 4 percent; other, primarily Native American and Eastern religions, 10 percent; see "Religious Groups in Dallas Area," *Dallas Morning News,* November 4, 1995, 11C. Statewide, a smaller proportion of individuals outside the Judeo-Christian tradition can be expected outside the larger cities.

average of $562,500 for senators running that year and of $157,333 for House members.[12] Candidates with some personal money are better able to attract financial support than those of ordinary means, in part because they move in "money" circles.

Favorable media exposure—news coverage and editorial endorsements by newspapers, magazines, radio, and especially television—is of tremendous importance during a campaign. The media decide who the leading candidates are and then give them the lion's share of free news space. Texas media tend to be conservative and to endorse business-oriented candidates.

Experience and Turnover

Seniority has long been of great importance in the committee structure of the U.S. Congress, and Texas voters in many districts are accustomed to reelecting members of the Texas congressional delegation. However, rapid **turnover** of 20 to 25 percent has traditionally characterized the Texas Legislature, with the result that state legislators have been accused of being inexperienced and amateurish. In recent years, the turnover rate has been less—only 17 percent in 1999. Moreover, a typical freshman senator is likely to have had prior governmental experience in the House, and a typical freshman House member may have served on a county commissioners court, city council, or school board.

What causes legislative turnover? Running for higher office, retirement, moving into the more profitable private sector, and reapportionment/redistricting are among the causes. So are tough urban reelection races, changing party alignments, and voter perception—correct—that seniority is not so important in the state legislature as it is in the U.S. Congress. Nevertheless, seniority is important. Not only does it increase the probability that a legislator will be knowledgeable about policy issues, but also it means that the legislator will understand how the system works. In the Senate especially, the most senior members tend to chair committees.

STRUCTURAL CRITICISMS AND SUGGESTED REFORMS

Criticisms

The Texas Legislature seems caught in the proverbial vicious circle. Low salaries and short terms force legislators to maintain other sources of income, a necessity that leads to lack of attention to legislative business, especially between sessions. One legislator offered highly visible proof of the insufficiency of legislative salaries when he sought to live on his state salary and thus qualified for the food stamp program! The low salaries cause legislators to be vulnerable to lobbyists' pressures and "help" (see Chapter Three). Also, they contribute to turnover, since many legislators have difficulty earning a living between sessions, particularly if there are several sessions and interim committee work to be done.

12. See "State Office Hopefuls Raised $115 Million," *Austin American-Statesman*, May 14, 1999, B2, which reports the findings of Texans for Public Justice.

The electorate, on the other hand, views the legislature as a group whose members work only 140 days every two years and are paid $103 for each workday, or $14,400 for the two-year term, excluding per diem expense money. Voters consistently defeat proposals for both annual legislative sessions and salary increases. Also, legislators are reluctant to increase their own staff and expense budgets, knowing that the public prefers an image of frugality. Yet Texans seem to have little difficulty entrusting a *multibillion*-dollar budget to a poorly paid group of legislators whom they view as amateurs at best and scalawags at worst. Furthermore, they seem oblivious to the detrimental effect on legislation of inadequate salaries for both legislators and their staffs and the resulting dependency on special interests or on "gamesmanship" to maximize the per diem payments.

Suggested Reforms

Sessions.   The institution of annual legislative sessions has been a major element in all recent efforts at constitutional revision. Annual sessions would allow legislators time to familiarize themselves with complex legislation, permitting them, for example, to bring a little more knowledge to the chaotic guessing game that produces the state's biennial budget. Annual sessions would virtually eliminate the need for costly special sessions when a crisis arises between regular sessions. Annual sessions would provide time for the continual introduction of all those special resolutions such as declaring chili the official state dish that have negligible importance for the general public but take up so much valuable legislative time. They also would provide an opportunity for legislative oversight of the state bureaucracy. Coupled with adequate staff support, annual sessions would allow legislators to engage in more long-range planning of public policy.

The legislature also needs to be empowered to call itself into special session. At present, if legislative leaders see the need for a special session and the governor is reluctant to call one, the legislature is helpless. In thirty other states, legislators can initiate a special session either independently or in conjunction with the governor.[13] At a minimum, legislators need more freedom to add to the agenda of special sessions. Even though a session was called for a specific purpose, other significant items could be entered on the agenda and dispensed with, thus lessening the clutter of the next regular session's agenda.

The restrictions on both regular and special legislative sessions result in a high concentration of political power. The presiding officers dictate the flow of business during regular sessions, and the governor dominates special sessions.

Size and Salaries.   Some advocates have long recommended that the Texas House reduce its size to 100 members. Other advocates of reform have suggested that since both houses are now elected on the basis of population distribution, one house should be eliminated altogether and a unicameral legislature adopted. But tradition strongly militates against such a change. The physical size of the state poses another risk to reducing the size of the legislature: As population and thus district size continue to grow, citizens will increasingly lose contact with their representatives. A

13. *The Book of the States, 1998–99 Edition,* vol. 32 (Lexington, KY: Council of State Governments, 1998), 64–67.

reduction in the number of legislators would be a tradeoff between legislative efficiency and representativeness. Although efficiency is important to citizens, so is being represented by someone from a small enough geographic and population area to understand the needs of the people in the district.

More serious are recommendations for salary increases. The $7,200 salary is insufficient to allow legislators to devote their full energies to state business. A salary close to the median salary for the nine other largest states—$45,077—would not, of course, guarantee that legislators would be honest and conscientious and devote all of their working time to the business of the state. However, a decent salary level would ensure that those who wished to could spend most of their time on state business. It might also eliminate the retainer fees, consultant fees, and legal fees now paid to many legislators.

Terms of Office.   If Senate members had staggered six-year terms and House members staggered four-year terms, legislators could be assured of having time to develop expertise in both procedures and substantive policy. Moreover, the virtually continuous campaigning by legislators who represent highly competitive urban districts would be greatly reduced, leaving them more time to spend on legislative functions. Less campaigning also might serve to weaken the tie between legislators and the lobbyists who furnish both financial support for campaigning and bill-drafting services.

A new aspect of terms that is emerging in many states is term limitations.[14] Term limits have a chance of being adopted in Texas via constitutional amendment, but this outcome would be ironic. In an effort to place restrictions on legislators, enthusiasts are robbing future voters of the right to elect an incumbent. Thus, democracy today seeks to eliminate democracy tomorrow.

THE PRESIDING OFFICERS

The presiding officers of any legislative assembly have more power and prestige than ordinary members. In Texas, however, the lieutenant governor and the speaker of the House have such sweeping procedural, organizational, administrative, and planning authority that they truly dominate the legislative scene.

Although most state legislatures have partisan leadership positions analogous to the majority and minority leaders in the U.S. Congress, this is not yet the case in Texas because of the historical one-party tradition and the more recent tendency to have bipartisan leadership. The committee chairs hold the secondary positions of power, after the presiding officers. Chairs are appointed by the presiding officers and thus do not offer any threat to the power of either the speaker or the lieutenant governor.

The Lieutenant Governor

The lieutenant governor is elected independently by the citizenry, serves as president of the Senate but is not a member of it, and does not run on the ticket with the gu-

14. Virginia Gray, Russell L. Hanson, and Herbert Jacob, *Politics in the American States: A Comparative Analysis,* 7th ed. (Washington, DC: Congressional Quarterly Press, 1999), 168.

bernatorial candidate. The lieutenant governor rarely performs any executive functions and is chiefly a legislative official. The term of the office is four years.

Twenty-seven other states use the lieutenant governor as the presiding officer of the upper house. But these states (usually) also look to the governor for policy recommendations; their chamber rules are such that the lieutenant governor, far from exercising any real power, is generally in a position similar to that of the vice president of the United States—neither an important executive nor a legislative force. Such is not the case in Texas, where the lieutenant governor is a major force in state politics and the dominant figure during legislative sessions. The lieutenant governor orchestrates the flow of legislation in the upper house.

Rick Perry was elected as lieutenant governor in 1998, reflecting the Republican dominance of elections that year and the long coattails of Governor George W. Bush. Perry had served two terms as agriculture commissioner. He got fairly high marks in 1999 for the first session over which he presided, although his style was more that of referee than advocate and his issues were more classic partisan ones (abortion notification, school vouchers) than big, long-range ones.[15]

His style and issues stand in contrast to those of Democrat Bob Bullock, who ruled the Senate from 1991 until Perry took office in January 1999. Bullock was known as a master of the Texas political process, an elected official for twenty-two years and a political activist for forty-two, who wielded his influence as the most powerful politician in the state to influence big issues such as state finance. Bullock was also known for his "persuasiveness" and was characterized by two Austin political writers as having a "temper [that] could melt a brass doorknob."[16] Yet he was very good with people, and some of the highest praise for him when he died in June 1999 was from Republicans, including the governor.

Bullock's style, in turn, contrasted with that of his predecessor, William P. Hobby, who presided over the Senate for eighteen years until he got tired of the growing partisanship in the upper chamber. Hobby preferred to run things as if partisan lines were nonexistent—as they almost were when he first took the lieutenant governor's seat in 1973— and in a calm, dispassionate manner.

If the disputed 2000 presidential election finally resulted in a Bush victory, Perry moved up to governor based on a 1999 constitutional amendment. In turn, the Senate elected one of its members to serve as presiding officer.

Speaker of the House

The speaker of the Texas House of Representatives is an elected member of the House who is formally chosen as speaker by a majority vote of the House membership at the opening of the legislative session. The results of the election are rarely a surprise; by the time the session opens, everyone knows who the speaker will be. Candidates for speaker begin maneuvering for support long before the previous session has ended. And during the interim between sessions, they not only campaign for election to the

---

15. Dave McNeely, "Perry Receives Mostly Favorable Reviews This Session," *Austin American-Statesman,* June 7, 1999, A9, and Paul Burka and Patricia Kilday Hart, "The Best and the Worst Legislators, 1999," *Texas Monthly,* July 1999, 95.

16. Patrick Beach and Ken Herman, "A Texas Giant Is Gone," *Austin American-Statesman,* June 19, 1999, A1.

House in their home districts, but also try to secure from fellow House members written pledges of support in the race for speaker. If an incumbent speaker is seeking reelection, usually no other candidates run.

Until 1951, speakers traditionally served for one term; from 1951 to 1975, they served either one or two. The House seems to have abandoned the limited-term tradition, however. Billy Clayton served four terms as speaker (1975–1983), and his successor, Gib Lewis, served five (1983–1993). James E. (Pete) Laney, a West Texas cotton farmer, bested eight other House members to become speaker in 1993 and was elected to a fourth term in 1999. He campaigned for the leadership on the promises of reforming the rules and creating higher ethical standards.

Laney's style is very different from that of his predecessor or of his lieutenant governor colleague. A quiet individual with an equally quiet personal life, Laney has been a member of the House since 1973. He is known among House members as being dedicated to making the legislative process work. In the 1999 session, some conservative Republican lawmakers, who failed to achieve such items on their agenda as school vouchers, claimed that Laney had allowed liberal Democrats to dominate the session, but the reality seemed to be more the greater legislative expertise of the liberals in contrast to the skills of the conservatives.[17]

It is important for legislators to know whether the speaker is seeking reelection because they must decide whether to back the incumbent or take a chance on supporting a challenger. The decision is crucial: The speaker can reward supporters by giving them key committee assignments—perhaps even the opportunity to chair a committee—and by helping them campaign for reelection to the legislature. A House member who throws support in the wrong direction risks legislative oblivion.

Following the 1972 Sharpstown bank scandal, which involved prominent politicians receiving special favors in exchange for banking legislation, Speaker Price Daniel, Jr., dedicated the 1973 session to reform, emphasizing financial disclosure, restricting campaign contributions, and trying to eliminate some of the behind-closed-doors deals of former speakers. More recently, Speaker Pete Laney quickly moved to clean up the House after the Gib Lewis regime, which ended with the lodging of ethics charges against Lewis. Laney cut lobbyists' access to members inside the House chamber and placed restrictions on his staff's taking lobbying jobs after they left state government. He pushed for reform of the House rules on everything from early filing of bills to getting bills out of committee. This push included stopping the legislative freight train that traditionally occurred in the last three days of the session, when almost one-quarter of the bills would be voted on.[18] Laney insisted on earlier, more rational debate and voting. He made the ethical conduct of the speaker and the members a matter of high priority. He exercised his right to vote only five times and did not introduce bills. At the close of the 1993 session, lobbyists complained of how hard they had to work, and members praised him for refusing to dominate the legislative process.

17. Stuart Eskenazi, "Lane Walks Softly, Hides a Big Stick," *Austin American-Statesman,* January 5, 1997, A1, A8; "Interview: Pete Laney," *Dallas Morning News,* January 5, 1997, 1J, 10J; Scott S. Greenberger, "GOP Leaders Say Laney Let Liberals Loose in Legislature," *Austin American-Statesman,* June 2, 1999, B1.

18. See House Research Organization, *How a Bill Becomes a Law: Rules for the 73rd Legislature,* Special Legislative Report no. 180, February 26, 1993.

Pro Tempore Positions

Pro tempore ("for the time being") positions are largely honorific in Texas. At the beginning of the session, the Senate elects one member to serve as president pro tempore to preside when the lieutenant governor is absent or the lieutenant governor's office becomes vacant. At the end of the session, another individual is elected to serve as president pro tempore during the legislative interim; this person is usually one of the senior members. House rules also provide for the speaker to appoint someone to preside over the House temporarily or to appoint a speaker pro tempore to serve permanently. Whether to select anyone at all and who the individual will be are options left to the speaker.

POWERS OF THE PRESIDING OFFICERS

By constitutional mandate, the presiding officer in the Senate is the lieutenant governor, and the presiding officer in the House of Representatives is the speaker of the House. The powers the holders of these two positions enjoy are derived from the rules of the legislative body over which they preside and are of two basic sorts. The first has to do with the organization of the legislature and legislative procedure. In varying degrees, all presiding officers exercise this power of the chair. The second sort of power is institutional, and it has to do with the maintenance of the legislature as an organ of government.

A reform-oriented House or Senate can limit the powers of the presiding officers, and in fact did so in 1973 when some committee slots were reserved for seniority appointments. However, tradition and the realities of politics militate against any real

Presiding Officers' Powers of the Chair

Procedural Powers

1. Appointing half or more of the members of substantive committees and all members of procedural and conference committees (the House reserves half of the positions for seniority appointments; the Senate requires only that some members have prior experience)
2. Appointing the chairs and vice chairs of all committees
3. Determining the jurisdiction of committees through the referral of bills
4. Interpreting procedural rules when conflict arises
5. Scheduling legislation for floor action (especially important in the Senate, which lacks a complex calendar system)
6. Recognizing members who wish to speak, or not recognizing them and thus preventing them from speaking

Institutional Powers

1. Appointing the members of the Legislative Budget Board and serving as the chair and vice chair thereof
2. Appointing the members of the Texas Legislative Council and serving as chair and vice chair thereof
3. Appointing the members of the Legislative Audit Committee and serving as chair and vice chair thereof

overthrow of the powerful legislative leadership. So does the legislative amateurism that results from short sessions, low pay, and turnover in membership. Powerful leaders are a convenience, albeit sometimes a tiresome or costly one. The significance of some of the specific procedural and institutional powers of the lieutenant governor and speaker of the House is discussed in the following sections.

Procedural Powers

Legislative committees have life-or-death power over **bills.** Legislators' appointments to major committees, especially as chair or vice chair, largely determine their influence in the legislature as a whole. Presiding officers can thus use their power of appointment to reward friends and supporters with key positions on important committees and to punish opponents with insignificant positions on minor committees.

Committee Membership. In the House, half of the members of most substantive standing committees are appointed by the speaker and half gain their seats by seniority. The speaker also appoints all members of procedural committees dealing with the internal business of the House, as well as the members of the General Investigating Committee. When Pete Laney became speaker in 1993, he loosened the committee system by eliminating the budget and oversight chair that Gib Lewis had added to each committee to increase his appointment power and by eliminating five standing committees. In doing so, he reduced his own power. In the Senate, the lieutenant governor, as president of the Senate, plays an especially influential role in deciding committee membership because Senate rules stipulate only that a minority of the members must have prior service on a particular committee. The presiding officers appoint all committee chairs and vice chairs. The governor may make appointments to special interim study committees that function between legislative sessions, but the legislature has the power to approve or disapprove the appointments.

Representatives of special interests, as well as legislators, are frequently involved in the bargaining that eventually determines who will fill committee slots. Interest groups want friends on committees that have influence in their areas of interest, so they lobby the presiding officers in an effort to secure appointments favorable to them.

Conference Committees. A bill seldom passes both houses in identical form. Each time one fails to do so, a **conference committee** must be appointed to resolve the differences. Prior to 1973, conference committees could, and frequently did, produce virtually new bills. Since 1973 they have been limited to ironing out differences. This limitation is not followed closely, however, and it may be changed at any time because it must be readopted each session.

Five members from each house are appointed to conference committees by the respective presiding officer. Each house has one vote on the conference committee report—in other words, three members of each house's team of five must agree on the conference version of the bill—before the bill can be reported back to the House and Senate. The conference report must be accepted or rejected, without change, by each house. Thus conference committee members are key figures in the legislative process. Most conference reports, or versions of the bill, are accepted because of the press of time.

Appointees to conference committees usually share the viewpoints of the presiding officers on what should be done with the bill in question. Representatives of special interests often become involved in conference committee deliberations in an attempt to arrange tradeoffs or bargains with the presiding officers, making one concession in exchange for another. Sometimes, however, the main proponents of the two versions of the bill work out a compromise and the committee never meets.

Committee Chairs. The standing committees control legislation, and their chairs, who specify the committee agenda as well as subcommittee jurisdiction and assignments, control the committees. Lobbyists for special interest groups also work hard to influence the selection of chairs and vice chairs of committees. Their hope is that the chair will be someone who has been friendly in the past to interests represented by the lobbyists. The dynamics of lobby influence on the legislature were described in Chapter Three.

The reward and punishment aspect of committee appointments is especially evident in the appointment of chairs, for it is through them that the presiding officers control legislation. Seniority is relatively unimportant in determining chairmanships. Obviously, political enemies of the lieutenant governor or the speaker are not likely to chair standing committees. For example, Lieutenant Governor Bullock appointed only Democrats as committee chairs for the 1991 session in a futile effort to block growing Republican strength.

Referral. Which committee has jurisdiction over what type of legislative proposal is ill defined by the Texas Legislature because of the growth in the number of committees. In 1999, the House had thirty-seven committees—a number that continues to creep up. The Senate in 1999 had thirteen committees, plus four standing subcommittees. These numbers go up and down with different sessions. In both chambers, the presiding officers enjoy more discretion in referring bills to committees than do their counterparts in the U.S. Congress, where committee jurisdictions are relatively clear. The greater the degree of ambiguity, the more power the presiding officer has to refer a bill to a committee that will act favorably or negatively on it, depending on the wishes of the presiding officer. The presiding officer of the Senate may be overruled by the members, who can force a change in referral.

Some of the factors that the presiding officers consider when assigning bills to committees are (1) the position of their own financial supporters and political backers on the bill; (2) the effect of the bill on other legislation, especially with regard to funding; (3) their own ideological commitment to the bill; (4) the past record of support or nonsupport of the bill's backers, both legislators and special interests; and (5) the bargaining in which the bill's backers are willing to engage, including promises of desired support of or opposition to other bills on which the presiding officers have strong positions and a willingness to modify the bill itself.

Scheduling/The Calendar. In all legislative bodies, bills are assigned a time for debate. This scheduling—placing bills on a legislative calendar—determines the order in which bills are debated and voted on. In the U.S. Congress, the majority leader controls the two Senate calendars; the Rules Committee of the House assigns bills to one of five calendars. In Texas, the presiding officers heavily influence to which calendar, and where on that calendar, a bill will be assigned. The Texas House uses four calendars; additionally, the House uses seven categories to group bills and resolutions in these calendars. The Senate has one official calendar plus the intent calendar, explained later.

Scheduling is more important in Texas than in some other states or in Congress because of the short biennial legislative session. A bill that is placed far down on the schedule may not come to the floor before the session reaches its 140-day mandatory adjournment. In addition, the calendars are called in an order, and some calendars do not allow debate. For example, it is highly advantageous to have a bill placed on the Local, Consent, and Resolutions Calendar in the House, which is used for uncontested legislation. The timing of debate may well determine the outcome of the vote. Legislative strategies include trying to delay the call of a bill until negative votes can be lined up or, on the other hand, trying to rush a bill through before opposition can materialize. A bill can be slowed down by tacking on frivolous amendments. Another factor to be considered in Senate scheduling is the possibility of a **filibuster,** which is an effort by someone who does not have enough votes to defeat a bill to "talk it to death." A simple majority vote is necessary to stop debate. In the closing days of the session, when much important legislation still must be considered, a filibuster can be very ef-

Two Ways to Block a Bill

The Filibuster
Former Senator Bill Meier, who talked for 43 hours straight in 1977, holds the Texas and world records for filibustering. More recently in 1993, Senator Gonzalo Barrientos stopped just short of 18 hours in an unsuccessful effort to protect Barton Creek and its popular swimming hole.

The Technicality
One of the most bizarre events in the history of the Texas legislature occurred in 1997, when conservative Representative Arlene Wohlgemuth, angry at the blockage of a bill requiring parental notification before girls under 18 could get an abortion, raised a point of order about the calendar for May 26. The effect was to kill fifty-two bills that were scheduled for debate because the point of order concerned the calendar itself. Her fellow legislators referred to the incident as the "Memorial Day Massacre" and were irate that months of work, including the delicate negotiations between the House and Senate members to achieve compromise bills, apparently had been for naught. After tempers cooled, legislators began to find ways to resurrect some of the bills by tacking them onto other bills that had not been on the calendar for Memorial Day, and by using resolutions.

Pocketing
The presiding officers can also block bills by *pocketing* them; that is, they can decline to send a bill to the floor for debate even though a committee has given it a favorable report. Often, a presiding officer will pocket a bill because it virtually duplicates one already into the legislative pipeline or to keep an unimportant bill from cluttering up the agenda near the end of the session when major legislation is pending. In 1999, Speaker Laney pocketed twenty-five House bills and Lieutenant Governor Perry pocketed four Senate bills.

fective. In addition, senators can tag a bill. Tagging marks a bill and requires a delay of at least 48 hours before the proposed legislation can be heard in committee. Like the filibuster, such an action in the waning days of the session is usually sure death for a bill.

Although their power is great, the presiding officers do not have absolute control of the calendars. Bills can be—and usually are—taken off the single Senate calendar out of order by a two-thirds vote, although in many cases it is the lieutenant governor who wields the influence to arrange the change. For a member who wants to propose consideration of a bill out of order, the consent of the lieutenant governor, who can choose to recognize that member or not, is essential. Indeed, when Bill Hobby was lieutenant governor, he formalized this procedure of asking for a bill to be taken up out of order by establishing an *intent calendar*. In the House, the Calendars Committee and the Local and Consent Calendars Committee actually control the placement of bills on the calendars, making the speaker's power indirect. However, the speaker appoints both eleven-member committees, their chairs, and their vice chairs.

Recognition.   One of the prerogatives of the presiding officer of any assembly is to recognize individuals who wish to speak. In legislative bodies, with the occasional exception of presiding officers who are simply arbitrary, the recognition power is traditionally invoked in a fair and judicious manner.

In Texas the lieutenant governor actually has more formal recognition power than does the speaker. A quirk in Senate procedure stipulates that a bill must receive a two-thirds vote before floor consideration can actually begin. This procedure, rather than the calendar, has the effect of determining if and when a bill will be considered. The bill's sponsor must be recognized by the lieutenant governor before the bill can be moved for consideration. The sponsor also needs the presiding officer's support to garner the necessary two-thirds vote, for a lieutenant governor who opposes a piece of legislation can often influence eleven senators to block consideration of the bill. The consequence of this concentration of power is that the presiding officer almost single-handedly controls legislation in the Senate.

Procedures.   At the beginning of each regular session of the Texas Legislature, each house adopts the rules of procedure that will govern that session's legislative process. Although procedures can change considerably, many rules are carried over from one session to another or are only slightly modified. Numerous precedents determine how those rules that are carried over will be applied. Of course, all parliamentary rules are subject to interpretation by the chair.

The lieutenant governor/president of the Senate votes only in case of a tie; the speaker is a voting member of the House. One of the most extraordinary uses of speaker power occurred in 1967 when Speaker Ben Barnes voted to make a tie, then voted again to break the tie on a bill he favored. He thus cast two votes on the same bill.

Procedural interpretation, recognition of those wishing to speak, determination of the timetable for debate, referral of bills, and the appointment of committees and their chairs combine to make the presiding officers powerful indeed. Although none of these powers is unusual for a club president, they take on greater significance when we realize that they are used to determine the outcome of policy struggles within a major state. Moreover, the average legislator, who must contend not only with the tremendous influence of the presiding officers but also with other aspects of the Texas legislative system—short terms, short sessions, poor pay, marginal staff support—has no desire to try to wrest control from the presiding officers, even if such a move were politically feasible.

Institutional Powers

The presiding officers also appoint the members of three important arms of the legislature: the Legislative Budget Board, the Legislative Council, and the Legislative Audit Committee. Each of these bodies exists to serve the legislature as a whole, providing policy guidelines at the board level and technical assistance at the staff level. The fact that legislators' office budgets do not allow them to employ much in the way of professional (as opposed to clerical) staff makes these arms of the legislature even more important. Members of the legislature have only three basic sources of assistance and information: the three agencies described here, state bureaucrats, and lobbyists. Even major legislative committees have limited budgets for professional staff. Not only do the presiding officers control these three policy-setting and policy-recommending bodies but, for all three, the president of the Senate also serves as chair and the speaker of the House as vice chair.

The Legislative Budget Board.   At the national level, in most states, and even in most cities, the chief executive bears the responsibility for preparing the budget. In Texas, the governor and the legislature each prepare a budget, and state agencies must submit their financial requests to each. The legislative budget is prepared by the Legislative Budget Board (LBB), which is a ten-member joint Senate-House committee that operates continually, whether or not the legislature is in session. In addition to the presiding officers, there are four members from each house, including by tradition the chairs of committees responsible for appropriations and finance. Because of the importance of these "money" committees, their chairs sometimes develop power bases within the legislature that are independent of the presiding officers.

House members, especially, are always seeking staff assistance because their office budgets are less than those of senators. Students often volunteer and regularly become very responsible members of a representative's staff. Some become paid staffers.

A professional staff assists the board in making its budget recommendations, then often helps defend those recommendations during the session. The state appropriations act closely follows the LBB recommendations. Additionally, the staff assists the legislature in its watchdog function, overseeing state agency expenditures.

The Legislative Council.   The seventeen-member Legislative Council includes the presiding officers, five senators, and ten representatives who are appointed by their respective presiding officer. The council oversees the work of the director and professional staff. During the session, the Legislative Council provides bill-drafting services for legislators; between sessions, it investigates the operations of state agencies, conducts studies on problems subject to legislative consideration, and drafts recommendations for action in the next session. In short, it is the legislature's research office.

The Legislative Audit Committee.   In addition to the presiding officers, the other four members of the Legislative Audit Committee are the chairs of the taxing committees,[19] the House Appropriations Committee, and the Senate State Affairs Committee. The state auditor, appointed by the committee for a two-year term subject to two-thirds confirmation of the Senate, heads the professional staff. This committee oversees a very important function of all legislative bodies, the postaudit of expenditures of state agencies—to ensure their legality—by the auditor and his staff. The auditor's staff also checks into the level of quality of services and duplication in services and programs provided by state agencies, although the auditor's authority to issue management directives was severely curtailed in 1988. The work of the professional staff is highly detailed, involving a review of the records of financial transactions. In fact, the larger state agencies have an auditor or team of auditors assigned to them virtually year round.

LIMITS ON PRESIDING OFFICERS

It may seem that the presiding officers are nearly unrestrained in their exercise of power. However, there are several factors, both personal and political, that prevent absolutism on the part of the speaker of the House and the lieutenant governor.

Personality and Ambition

Although there is always the danger that presiding officers may become arbitrary or vindictive and thus abuse their office, generally speaking they are so powerful that they do not need to search for ways to gain influence other than persuasion, compromise, and accommodation. Arbitrariness is a function of personality, not of the office. Moreover, a presiding officer who is interested in higher governmental office or a lucrative executive position in the business world will not foolishly alienate special interests.

---

19. As is true in Congress, the taxing committees of the Texas Legislature are known as Finance in the Senate and Ways and Means in the House.

Legislators

State senators and representatives have their own power bases, without which they probably would not have been elected. Long-time members not only have supporters across the state, including influential special interests, but also have the advantage that seniority brings within the legislature itself. This is especially true if they have served as the chair of a major committee for more than one session. For example, Senator Bill Ratliff, already a seasoned committee chair as the head of the powerful Education Committee, became even more powerful when he was tapped to chair the Finance Committee in 1997 and 1999.

Although it may appear that the membership always seems to follow the lead of the presiding officers, in many cases there is an agreement in ideological positions to begin with. The leadership usually is conservative, and so are most legislators. In other instances, members will go along with the leadership in hopes of later being able to act independently on matters of importance to themselves or their districts. Finally, the powers of the presiding officers are largely granted by House and Senate rules. A totally arbitrary leader whose abuse of the system became intolerable could be stripped of power, as Speaker "Uncle Joe" Cannon was when the U.S. House revolted against him in 1910 because of his abuse of power.

Lobbies and State Administrators

Over the past fifty years, as the number of governmental agencies and bureaucrats at all levels has increased, alliances have developed between private and public interests. A presiding officer faced with such an alliance is seldom able to overcome it. Indeed, these coalitions and the presiding officers often share the same political viewpoint, making confrontation unlikely.

The public is seldom considered by these alliances, especially when some of the more powerful special interests of the state, such as oil and gas, insurance, banking, and real estate, are involved. An example of bureaucracy/private-interest alliances is that of the Texas Education Agency with the Texas State Teachers Association. When the legislative committees with jurisdiction over, say, roads or education join these alliances, the confederation is a very powerful one.

The Governor

Constitutionally, the governor is a weak chief administrator, and hence the alliance of state bureaucrats is with the lobbyists and not with the chief executive. But the governor is by no means a weak chief legislator. The governor's veto power is almost absolute because the legislature often adjourns before the governor has had to act on a bill. A governor who wants a particular piece of legislation enacted can threaten the legislature with a special session if the legislation seems to be in jeopardy. Because special sessions are costly to state legislators, in terms of both time and money, such a threat can be a powerful tool for the governor. The governor must be prepared to make good such a threat, as, for example, Bill Clements did when he called a special session on tort reform—that is, changes in the basis of civil lawsuits—in 1987 after failing to

The 1999 legislature passed 1,622 bills, although the governor later vetoed 31. This Ben Sargent cartoon reflects the hectic nature of the legislature's considering 5,766 bills in four and a half months.

SOURCE: Courtesy of Ben Sargent.

get action from the 1987 legislature. Another of the governor's strengths lies in the strong ties a conservative (usually the political orientation of a Texas governor) has to the same interest groups as the legislators. These ties often make it possible to call on these interests to support a gubernatorial position in conflict with the legislature.

The Electorate/The Constituents

Legislative bodies were created to be the people's voice in government. In reality, however, the citizens are usually unable to exert as much influence over the leadership and members of the Texas Legislature as state officials and private interests do. One reason for this situation is the strength of special interests; another is the lack of concern on the part of most citizens about what goes on in Austin. Public interest will perk up in the face of governmental scandal, but the ordinary day-to-day legislative events do not disturb the lethargy and complacency of most Texans. Public apathy and the lack of understanding of the legislature's work contribute mightily to the resistance to change that is so often manifested when efforts at constitutional reforms are made. Nevertheless, legislators are well aware that such issues as education reform and income tax will create public interest, and they live in dread of having to consider such provocative matters.

HOW A BILL BECOMES A LAW IN TEXAS

The Texas Constitution specifies that a bill be used to introduce a law or a change in a law. Bills that pass successfully through both houses become acts and are sent to the governor for signature or veto. In addition to bills, there are three types of resolutions in each house:

1. *Simple resolutions* are used in each house to take care of housekeeping matters, details of business, and trivia.
2. *Concurrent resolutions* are similar to simple resolutions but require the action of both houses. They are used for adjournment, for example.
3. *Joint resolutions* are of major interest to the public because they are the means of introducing proposed constitutional amendments.

Each bill or resolution is identified by an abbreviation that indicates the house of origin, the nature of the legislation, and a number. For example, S.B. 1 is Senate bill 1; S.J.R. indicates a joint resolution that originated in the Senate. Bills may originate in either house or in both simultaneously, with the exception of revenue bills, which must originate in the House. Legislators on average introduce over 5,000 bills and resolutions in each legislative session, but only 30 percent are passed. In 1999, a total of 5,766 bills and 140 proposed constitutional amendments were introduced. Of these, 1,622 bills were passed, and 17 proposed amendments were sent to the voters.

Because the smaller size of the Senate enables it to operate with less formality than the House, we will use the Senate to trace the path of a bill through the legislative process. In both houses, knowing "who's for you and who's against" as the opening chapter quotation says, is important.

The major differences in the procedures of the two houses are:

1. The House has more than twice as many committees as the Senate; therefore, the speaker has a greater choice in determining where to refer a bill.
2. The calendars are different (as explained earlier in this chapter).
3. Debate is unlimited in the Senate, whereas House debate is usually limited to ten minutes per member and twenty minutes for the bill's sponsor.

To be enacted into law, a bill must survive four legislative steps and a fifth step in the governor's office (see Figure 6.2). As a legislator attempts to get his bill passed, the opening quotation from Sam Johnson is particularly apt: Success depends on knowing who one's friends are.

Step One: Introduction and Referral

Every bill must be introduced by a member of the legislature, who is considered the sponsor. The bill may either be filed with the clerk if the legislature is not in session or be introduced by a member on the floor. If a bill has several sponsors, so much the better—its chances of survival will be greatly enhanced. Introducing the bill constitutes the first reading.

The lieutenant governor—in the House, the speaker—then refers the bill to a committee. If the bill is to survive, it must be assigned to a friendly committee.

FIGURE 6.2

How a Bill Becomes a Law in Texas

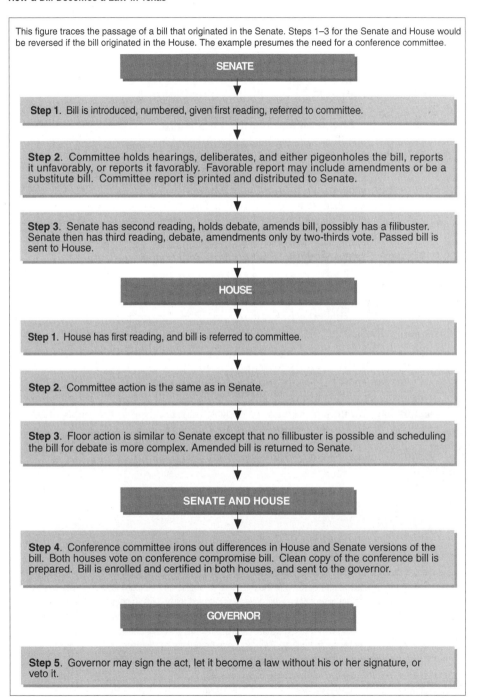

This figure traces the passage of a bill that originated in the Senate. Steps 1–3 for the Senate and House would be reversed if the bill originated in the House. The example presumes the need for a conference committee.

SENATE

Step 1. Bill is introduced, numbered, given first reading, referred to committee.

Step 2. Committee holds hearings, deliberates, and either pigeonholes the bill, reports it unfavorably, or reports it favorably. Favorable report may include amendments or be a substitute bill. Committee report is printed and distributed to Senate.

Step 3. Senate has second reading, holds debate, amends bill, possibly has a filibuster. Senate then has third reading, debate, amendments only by two-thirds vote. Passed bill is sent to House.

HOUSE

Step 1. House has first reading, and bill is referred to committee.

Step 2. Committee action is the same as in Senate.

Step 3. Floor action is similar to Senate except that no fillibuster is possible and scheduling the bill for debate is more complex. Amended bill is returned to Senate.

SENATE AND HOUSE

Step 4. Conference committee irons out differences in House and Senate versions of the bill. Both houses vote on conference compromise bill. Clean copy of the conference bill is prepared. Bill is enrolled and certified in both houses, and sent to the governor.

GOVERNOR

Step 5. Governor may sign the act, let it become a law without his or her signature, or veto it.

Step Two: Committee Action

Standing committees are really miniature legislatures, where the nitty-gritty of legislation takes place. Legislators are so busy—particularly in Texas, with its short, infrequent sessions—that they seldom have time to study bills in detail and so must rely heavily on the committee reports. A bill's sponsor, well aware of the committee's role, will do everything possible to ensure that the committee's report is favorable. It is particularly important to avoid having the bill pigeonholed—put at the bottom of the committee's agenda, with or without discussion, never to be seen again—or totally rewritten, either by the committee or, if the bill is referred to a subcommittee, by the subcommittee. If the bill can escape being pigeonholed, its sponsor will have a chance to bargain with the committee in an effort to avoid too many changes in the bill.

The committee may report the bill favorably, unfavorably, or not at all. An unfavorable report or none at all will kill the bill. Unless there is a strong minority report, however, there is little reason for the committee to report a bill unfavorably; it's easier to pigeonhole it and avoid floor action completely.

Step Three: Floor Action

Once a bill is reported out of committee, it must be scheduled for debate. The calendar is rarely followed in the Senate, so the sponsor moves to suspend the regular calendar order and consider the bill out of sequence. Before taking this action, the sponsor generally obtains an assurance from the presiding officer that she or he will be recognized and thus given an opportunity to make the motion. When the bill receives the necessary two-thirds vote on the motion, it can proceed to a second reading and floor debate. If the second reading has not occurred by the time the legislature is within seventy-two hours of adjournment, the bill dies.

Senators have unlimited privilege of debate; they may speak as long as they wish about a bill on the floor. Sometimes senators use this privilege to filibuster. If a bill is fortunate enough not to become entangled in a filibuster, debate proceeds. During the

One of the peculiarities of Texas legislative sessions is the constitutional provision for a "split session": The first thirty days are supposed to be devoted to the introduction of bills and resolutions, emergency matters, and confirmation of recess appointments by the governor; the next thirty days to committee hearings; and the final sixty days to floor action on bills and resolutions. The provision does not prescribe specific activities for the final twenty days of the session. The legislature may bypass this provision, however, by taking advantage of another constitutional provision that allows each house to determine its own schedule by a four-fifths vote, or the governor can declare an emergency. In practice, both houses require a four-fifths vote for the introduction of bills after the first sixty days or for voting on a bill during the first sixty days. A governor usually will use the emergency power sparingly—for example, when state government must take care of a crisis and cannot wait for a bill to take effect months later.

course of debate, there may be proposed amendments, amendments to amendments, motions to table, or even motions to send the bill back to committee. However, if a bill has succeeded in actually reaching the floor for discussion, it is usually passed in one form or another by simple majority vote. A third reading of the bill precedes the voting.

In the House: Steps One through Three Repeated

If it was not introduced in both houses simultaneously, a bill passed in the Senate must proceed to the House. There, under its original designation (for example, S.B. 341), it must repeat the same three steps as in the Senate, with the exceptions noted earlier. A bill has little chance of passing if a representative does not shepherd it through. This situation also is true in reverse, when a bill passes the House and then is sent to the Senate. In addition, the Laney reforms of 1993 included a series of deadlines concerning the final 17 days of a legislative session, and a bill must comply with those House rules. For example, after 135 days of regular session, the House cannot consider a Senate bill except to adopt a conference report, reconsider the bill to remove Senate amendments, or override a veto; the deadlines for consideration of various types of House bills are earlier.[20] The following assumes that the bill being followed has passed the House, but with one amendment added that was not part of the Senate's version.

Step Four: Conference Committee

Because the Senate and House versions of the bill differ, it must go to a conference committee, which consists of ten members, five appointed from each house by the presiding officers. If the House and Senate versions of the bill have substantial differences, the conference committee may attach several amendments or rewrite portions of the bill. The report of the conference committee must be voted on as it stands; neither house can amend it. It must be accepted, rejected, or sent back to the conference committee. If it fails at this time—or, indeed, at any other stage—it is automatically dead. No bill can be introduced twice during the same session. If the bill passes both houses, it is sent to the governor.

Step Five: The Governor

The governor has ten days, excluding Sundays, to dispose of acts. If the legislature adjourns, the ten-day period is extended to twenty days. There are three options available to the governor in dealing with an act. The first is to sign it, thus making it law.

The second is to allow the bill to become law without signing it (only three occurrences in 1999). If the governor does not sign it, a bill becomes law in ten days if the legislature is in session and in twenty days if it is not. By choosing this rather weak course of action, the governor signifies both opposition to the bill and an unwillingness to risk a veto that could be overridden by a two-thirds vote of both houses or that would incur the disfavor of special interests supporting the bill.

20. House Research Organization, *How a Bill Becomes a Law*, 24.

Third, the governor may veto the bill. A veto is a formal action requiring the governor to send a message to the legislature indicating disapproval of the bill. Although it is possible for the legislature to override a veto by a two-thirds vote, the governor often receives legislation so late in the session that the act of vetoing or signing it can be deferred until the session has ended. A veto then is absolute, since it must be overridden during the same legislative session in which the act was passed and the legislature cannot call itself into special session. Because recent legislative sessions have been faced with one crisis after another and too little time to deal with issues, the governor's powers have been strengthened through use of the veto and threats of a veto.

If the governor chooses to veto, the veto applies to the entire bill, except in the case of appropriations bills. On appropriations bills, the governor has the power of **item veto;** that is, specific items within the bill may be vetoed. This is a powerful gubernatorial tool for limiting state spending. Governor Richards used the item veto on relatively small matters. Governor Clements, in his first term, vetoed all the special appropriations for universities that underwrote such activities as student scholarships and research institutes. Governor Bush allowed several important bills to become law without his signature, disdaining the veto.

If a newly passed bill contains an emergency clause, it becomes effective as law immediately (or at whatever time is specified in the bill). If it does not, it becomes effective ninety days after the session ends. Again, there are special circumstances for appropriations bills, which always become effective September 1.

Public Policy, Legislative Style: A 1999 Sampler

The 1999 legislative session was dominated by a most unusual circumstance—how to make Governor George W. Bush look good in order to launch his bid for the presidential nomination in 2000. Bush wanted to emphasize education and tax cuts, as well as being tough on crime. The resulting legislation included measures designed to:

- Give public school teachers a $3,000 raise, lower school property taxes, and end social promotions
- Provide $506 million in tax breaks, including a three-day sales tax moratorium to help parents shop for back-to-school items, elimination of taxes on over-the-counter medications, and making baseline Internet services tax free
- Give low-level oil and gas producers a break on the severance tax
- Strengthen driving while intoxicated laws, anti-gang measures, and steps to avert youth violence
- Raise the speed limits on major highways, including ending the historical lower speed limits for trucks (related to gubernatorial support for NAFTA trade), but
- Lower the speed limits on beaches
- Require parental consent for a girl under 18 to have an abortion
- Protect consumers more from cramming and slamming by telecommunications firms (charging for services not requested and authorized switching of a long-distance carrier, respectively)
- Encourage industrial polluters to clean up the air
- Deregulate the electric generation business
- Restrict municipal annexation powers somewhat
- Give $100 a month raise to state employees

LEGISLATIVE HANDICAPS

The public often thinks that the legislature accomplishes very little. In fact, it is amazing that the legislature accomplishes as much as it does, given the limitations under which it must labor, as the *State Legislatures* quote at the beginning of this chapter notes. The forces influencing legislation are complex and varied—interest groups, the powers of the presiding officers, constitutional limitations, political parties, the role of committees, short and infrequent sessions, inadequate salaries, and the prerogatives of individual members.

Each legislator must face almost 9,000 bills and resolutions every time the legislature convenes in regular session, except that legislators traditionally file about 10 to 15 percent fewer bills when the agenda includes redistricting. Some of the almost 6,000 bills and most of the resolutions are substantively important; many are trivial matters that could more easily be left to administrative agencies. Nevertheless, in the short 140-day session, legislators must acquaint themselves with the proposals, try to push their own legislative programs, attend to a heavy burden of casework (tending to constituent problems and requests), spend countless hours in committee work, meet with hometown and interest-group representatives, and hear the professional views of state administrators who implement programs. All the while, they must try to avoid going into debt because their salaries are inadequate and their personal businesses or professions may slide when the legislature is in session.

Lenient lobbying laws—such as no grace period between leaving the legislature and becoming a lobbyist—lack of public support for adequate information services for legislators, and the need for continuous campaigning make the average legislator easy prey for special interests. Indeed, on many issues the interests of a legislator's district and of special interest groups often overlap and are difficult to distinguish.

Legislators' frustrations are especially evident when the biennial budget is considered. Appropriations are the real battleground of legislative sessions. There always are more programs seeking support than there is money to support them. Power struggles over money continue because each individual who promotes a program—be it for highways, public schools, higher education, law enforcement, utilities rates, environmental protection, lending rates, or welfare administration—believes in either its moral rightness or its economic justification. Who wins these struggles is determined not only by the power and effectiveness of the groups themselves but also by the political preferences of the legislators. Furthermore, the winners largely

Whose Bill Is It, Anyhow?

In response to a question posed by one of the authors, an Austin lawyer-lobbyist, a twenty-year veteran with the Texas Legislature, thought a moment. He then replied, "Here at the legislature, if you ask the question 'Whose bill is it?' what you mean is, which lobby wrote it. If you want to know which legislator is sponsoring the bill, you ask, 'Who's carrying the bill?' That'll give you some idea of how influential lobbyists are."

determine public policy for the state, since few government programs can operate without substantial amounts of money.

Lack of public understanding and support is another handicap for legislators. The public often criticizes politicians for being unprincipled and always willing to compromise. But the role of compromise in the political system, and especially in legislative bodies, is undervalued by the citizens. Caught in all the cross-pressures of the legislative system, members rarely have the opportunity to adhere rigidly to their principles. Those who watch closely what happens in the legislature are not the electorate back home but campaign supporters, lobbyists, and influential citizens. Members must satisfy these people as well as bargain with their colleagues if they are to have any chance of getting their own proposals through the legislature or, in fact, being reelected for another term.

Legislators may have to vote for new highways that they view as superfluous to get votes for issues that are important to them and their home districts. They may have to vote in favor of loan-sharking to gain support for tighter regulation of nursing homes. They may have to give up a home-district highway patrol office to obtain funds for needy children. Just as legislators who hope to be successful must quickly learn the procedural rules, they also must learn the art of legislative compromise and horse trading.

An additional difficulty legislators face is adjusting to the shifting trends within the legislature. Long dominated by rural Democratic conservatives, in recent years the legislature has become more urban and more Republican. When urban issues are at stake, temporary bipartisan alliances among big-city legislators are frequently formed.

Compounding the problem of party and geographic transition is the fact that the two houses have not changed in the same way. During the 1985 and 1987 sessions, the Senate was heavily Democratic and liberal politically; it became more Republican in 1989 and 1991, but it still was more progressive than the House. In 1993, the Senate had 18 Democrats and 13 Republicans; in 1995, 17 Democrats and 14 Republicans. In 1997, the Senate became Republican with 17 GOP members and 14 Democrats. In 1999, sixteen Republicans and fifteen Democrats made up the Senate, with a major struggle for party dominance slated for the 2000 elections. Since any 11 senators can block legislation through parliamentary procedures, the upper chamber ran the constant risk of being paralyzed into inaction.

The House has retained a Democratic majority, but the alliance of conservative Democrats and Republicans gave the House a distinctly conservative flavor beginning in the mid-1980s. However, since 1993 the House has been somewhat more liberal than the Senate. The Texas House of Representatives seemed to draw strength from the Laney reforms, which brought a higher sense of ethics as well as fairer procedures to the lower chamber. However, liberal-conservative skirmishes were plentiful in 1997 and 1999, and by 1999 the Democrats held only a six-vote margin.

SUGGESTED PROCEDURAL REFORMS

E arlier in this chapter, ways to improve the formal structure of the legislature were suggested. Improvements in legislative organization and procedures also are needed, especially in the areas of committees and ties to lobbyists.

Committees

The twenty-one House committees of 1973 were a more workable number than the thirty-seven of 1999, but fourteen or fifteen would be better. With fourteen or fifteen committees, less ambiguity about committee jurisdiction would occur. The Senate also must be alert to avoid further expansion of its committee system, given the increase from nine in 1985 to fifteen in 1997. The number dropped to thirteen in 1999, but with four standing subcommittees and two special committees for a total of nineteen committees for thirty-one members. It often seems that each new major state problem results in the creation of a new committee—and another committee chairmanship to use for political leverage. In addition, both houses could make more use of joint committees instead of submitting every issue to separate study and hearings; a joint budget committee if particularly needed. Fewer committee meetings would give legislators more time to familiarize themselves with the issues and the content of specific bills.

Fewer committees also might increase the chances for adoption of uniform committee rules throughout the two houses. Additional and more independent committee staff also are needed. Fewer committees would make paying for the staff more feasible. Currently, chairs can hire staff or elect to use their own, so that independence is also a political issue.

The Lobby

Until legislators are willing to declare their own independence from lobbyists and state administrators, the legislature cannot be truly independent of all interests but the public interest. Such a change depends on many factors: citizen attitudes, public willingness to allow adequate legislative sessions, pay and staff support for legislators, public financing of election campaigns, and a commitment on the part of legislators to give up the social and economic advantages of strong ties to the lobby. The likelihood of total independence from the lobby is not high: All legislative groups have some ties to special interests. At a minimum, however, Texas needs to abandon such blatant practices as allowing lawyer-legislators to accept retainer fees from corporations that subsequently send lobbyists to Austin to influence these same legislators. A starting point in reform was Speaker Laney's rule prohibiting members of his own staff from accepting a job as a lobbyist for a year after leaving the speaker's office.

CONCLUSION

The Texas Legislature is becoming more representative with each election. Moreover, unlike the U.S. Congress, where fragmentation of power makes coherent public policy virtually impossible, the powerful presiding officers in Texas make coherent public policy highly likely. Thus, for all its problems, the Texas Legislature can be highly effective. Since the Texas Legislature is centralized, it is capable of translating public preferences into policy. Because so few Texans vote, however, it often translates the preferences of the richer and better-educated minority into policy. Although liberals then criticize the content of public policy, they cannot deny that the policy is effective and that it is rational from the standpoint of most Texas voters.

SUMMARY

In many ways, the Texas Legislature is typical of state lawmaking bodies: its large size—181 members—its domination by Anglo males, its somewhat limited professional staff, its relatively short terms of office for its members (two years in the House and four in the Senate), and its reliance on legislative committees as the workhorses of the legislative process. Nevertheless, the following distinctive features of the Texas Legislature are atypical, especially when it is compared with the legislatures of other large urban states:

1. The legislature is restricted to one regular session of 140 days every two years.
2. Legislators are paid only $7,200 a year, although they receive a generous per diem payment for expenses.
3. The presiding officers—the speaker of the House and the lieutenant governor in the Senate—are preeminent in the legislative process. If either presiding officer is inclined to be arbitrary, democracy suffers.
4. A high turnover rate and the shifting memberships of the large number of committees—thirteen in the Senate and thirty-seven in the House in 1999—make it difficult for legislators to develop expertise in specific areas of legislation.
5. Special interests have an extraordinary influence on both the election and the performance of legislators. This dominance raises the issue of when and how constituents' voices are heard.
6. The short legislative session allows a conference committee to play a major role in shaping legislation and also gives the governor a chance to veto legislation with no opportunity for the legislature to override the veto. These procedures raise questions about citizen input and majority rule. In an institution that is designed to represent the public, such questions are inappropriate.

Texas legislators face the biennial task of developing sound public policy for a major state without jeopardizing the support of the presiding officers or of the special interests that are crucial to their reelection. Moreover, they operate in a highly constrained environment with both structural handicaps and lack of public confidence. They succeed better than one might expect given the many handicaps they face. Nevertheless, changes in legislative organization and procedure would improve legislative efficiency and independence. Recommendations for reform include the following:

1. Annual sessions
2. Higher salaries, in the $45,000 range
3. Four-year terms for House members and six-year terms for senators
4. Reduction in the number of legislative committees
5. Restrictions on the influence of the lobby coupled with more staff support

Were these reforms to be implemented, the Texas Legislature might be better prepared to govern the second-largest state in the nation.

STUDY QUESTIONS

1. What does "one person, one vote" mean? What have been its implications for Texas? Do you think this concept is responsible for the increases in ethnic minority representation in the legislature? Why or why not?

2. What are the characteristics of the average Texas state legislator? Is it significant that the legislature is in fact likely to underrepresent important groups in the state's population? Why? What role do you think legislative pay plays in underrepresentation of some groups?

3. What are the problems caused by a biennial legislative session?

4. In what ways are the presiding officers of the Texas Legislature extremely powerful? Why do you think this situation exists? What are the implications for democratic government?

5. You are a member of the Texas Senate and you are opposed to a bill that has been introduced. What strategies to defeat the bill are available to you at various stages in the legislative process?

SURFING THE WEB

An overview of Texas Legislative procedures.
   www.capitol.state.tx.us/capitol/legproc/sencal.htm

A membership profile of the Texas House of Representatives.
   www.house.state.tx.us/common/profile.htm

A list of House committees, complete with audio files of meetings.
   www.house.state.tx.us/house/commit/commit.htm

A membership profile of the Texas Senate.
   www.senate.state.tx.us/75r/Senate/Facts.htm

A list of Senate committees for the 75th and 76th Legislatures.
   www.senate.state.tx.us/75r/Senate/Commit.htm

7

THE GOVERNOR AND STATE ADMINISTRATION

hy does anyone want to be governor of Texas? The governorship is like the super-super gift in the Neiman-Marcus Christmas catalog— something for the man who has everything and absolutely unique!

Anonymous political scientist

He's [George W. Bush] a deal maker. He came out of the oil and gas business, from the front end—drilling—where you need acumen in deal making.

Texas Business

. . . governors as a group are riding higher and exerting more authority and influence than at any time since some of their predecessors led the Progressive movement of the early 1900s.

New York Times

INTRODUCTION

Democratic theory pays much more attention to the legislature than to the executive. Nevertheless, because chief executives and administrative agencies are important components of government, they too should be measured against the democratic ideal. In Texas, the legislature has been the dominant branch of state government through most of the state's history. Indeed, Texas is often cited for the weaknesses associated with the governor's office. However, a Texas governor with ideas and boldness can capture the support of the public and greatly enhance the limited constitutional and statutory powers of the office. Leadership, bargaining skills, and persuasive ability rather than the formal powers of the governorship are the keys to gubernatorial success.

This chapter first examines the basic structure of the governor's office, the formal qualifications for the office and the personal characteristics of those who are typically elected to it, the roles that the governor plays, and the limitations on those roles. It then examines the rise of big government in the state, the structure of state administration, and bureaucratic power.

BASIC STRUCTURE OF THE GOVERNOR'S OFFICE

Election, Term of Office, and Tenure

In Texas the governor is chosen in a statewide election held during the even-numbered years in which there is no presidential election. The candidates are selected in party primaries held earlier in the same year (see Chapter Five). The thinking behind holding the gubernatorial election in the "off year" is that national issues won't overshadow state ones. However, election contests for the Texas governor's office often focus on personalities, not issues, so that the importance of the off year is lost, and its main effect is that fewer people vote because they don't have the presidential election as a drawing card. In fact, voter turnout reached a modern low of 16 percent of registered voters during the 1994 primaries. The lieutenant governor is selected in the same manner but runs independently of the governor.

In 1974, when a 1972 constitutional amendment went into effect, the governor's term of office was extended from two to four years. There is no constitutional limit on the number of terms a governor may serve in Texas. Until World War II, Texas governors were routinely elected for two terms. During and after the war, three terms prevailed. Modern governors serving four-year terms have had difficulty being re-elected; the long-term likelihood is that governors will serve no more than two terms. The rise of the two-party system and the difficult and controversial problems governors face both suggest shorter service.

Impeachment and Succession

Impeachment.   In Texas a governor may be removed from office only through an **impeachment** proceeding. Impeachment is similar to a grand jury indictment; that is, it is a formal accusation. The state constitution is silent on what impeachable offenses are.[1] By implication and by the precedents set in the impeachment of Governor James E. Ferguson in 1917, however, the grounds are malfeasance, misfeasance, and nonfeasance in office—in other words, official misconduct, incompetence, or failure to perform.[2]

The impeachment procedure in Texas is similar to that at the national level. The House of Representatives, by a majority vote of those present, must first impeach the executive. Once the formal accusation is made, the Senate acts as a trial court; a two-thirds vote of the senators present is necessary to convict. Penalties for conviction are removal from office and disqualification from holding future governmental offices in the state. If there are criminal charges, they must be brought in a regular court of law.

Succession.   If a governor is removed from office by impeachment and conviction, dies in office or before taking office, or resigns, the constitution provides that the lieutenant governor shall become governor. A 1999 constitutional amendment further stipulated that, should the governor become disabled, the lieutenant governor would carry out the duties of the office; should the governor die or otherwise be unable to return, the lieutenant governor would become governor for the rest of the term of the governor who had vacated the office. If the lieutenant governor is unable to serve, the president *pro tempore* of the Senate would carry out the duties. Once the lieutenant governor becomes governor, the lieutenant governor's position is vacant. The vacancy would be filled within thirty days by the election of a member of the Senate to serve until the next general election. The amendment clarified some issues previously addressed by statute.

Compensation

A 1954 amendment allows the legislature to determine the salary of the governor and other elected executives. The legislature provided generous increments for many

---

1. The Texas Constitution does spell out the grounds for removing judges, however. Other officials subject to impeachment include the lieutenant governor, the attorney general, the commissioner of the General Land Office, the comptroller, and appellate court judges. The grounds stipulated for impeachment of judges include partiality, oppression, official misconduct, incompetence, negligence, and failure to conduct the business of the court. See Fred Gantt, Jr., *The Chief Executive in Texas* (Austin: University of Texas Press, 1964), 123.

2. Ferguson was impeached and convicted for mishandling public funds, conduct brought to light because funds for the University of Texas were involved.

The last governor to die in office was Beauford Jester in 1949, who was succeeded by Alan Shivers. The impetus for the 1999 amendment was to ensure a smooth transition in the event that Governor George W. Bush was elected president before his term expired in January 2002. The Bush run at the presidency also intensified Senate elections set to occur in 2000 since control of the Senate might mean not only control of redistricting (see Chapter Six) but also control of the all-powerful presiding officer's selection.

years, raising the governor's salary from $12,000 in 1954 to $99,122 in 1992–93. Then the state budget allowed no raises for state employees for five years. Beginning in 1997–98, other state employees received a $100-per-month raise while state executives received a 15 percent increase. Governor George Bush and Railroad Commissioner Carole Rylander turned down the raises. Bush commented through a spokesperson that he "does not believe he should accept the additional money [a salary of $113,990] because he feels he signed on for four years at" $99,122.[3] As of fiscal years 2000–2001, the governor's salary is $115,345. The salary of other elected executives is $92,217.

Once second only to New York, the Texas governor's salary has slipped to sixth. The Texas, California, and Washington governors all have taken voluntary reductions from the amount designated by statute.[4] The lieutenant governor is paid as a legislator—$7,200 a year—although he receives a salary supplementation for acting as governor whenever the governor leaves the state.

The governor also receives numerous fringe benefits. The constitution provides an official mansion, and other benefits include a travel and operating budget, a car, the use of state-owned aircraft, bodyguards furnished by the Texas Department of Public Safety, and offices and professional staff, including an executive assistant. These benefits compare favorably with those of other governors.

Staff

Like other chief executives, the governor alone is unable to perform all the functional and ceremonial tasks assigned to the governor's office. Assistance in fulfilling these obligations comes from a personal staff and from the professional staffs of the

3. Wayne Slater, "Bush, Railroad Commissioner Reject Pay Raises," *Dallas Morning News,* June 2, 1997, 17A–18A.

4. "The Governors: Compensation," *The Book of the States, 1998–99,* vol. 32 (Lexington, KY: Council of State Governments, 1998), 20–21.

Show Me the Money

Although well paid, particularly in comparison to legislators with their $7,200 salaries, the Texas governor is by no means the best-paid executive on the state payroll. Top-dollar honors belong to the larger universities in the state—University of Texas at Austin, Texas A&M University, the University of Houston/Main Campus, the University of North Texas, and Texas Tech University, all of which are the hub institutions of systems. The chancellors of the university systems and the presidents of the largest institutions receive base salaries of well over $200,000. Beyond that, they get all sorts of perquisites such as houses and cars. Some large institutions pay bonuses for successful fund raising, and some chancellors receive supplemental pay from individual institutions in the system—particularly medical schools. Dollars raised from local funds are used to supplement rather modest state-appropriated salaries. These large salaries often are matters of contention when university appropriations are discussed—and for that matter, among faculty when the president gets a raise but faculty members do not.

divisions that make up the Office of the Governor. Certain staff members are assigned to act as legislative liaisons—in effect, to lobby for the governor's programs—and often it is through them that the governor makes known an impending threat to veto a particular piece of legislation. Other staff members are involved in recommending candidates for the hundreds of appointments the governor must make to state boards, commissions, and executive agencies. The governor's aides also prepare the executive budget, coordinate the various departments and activities of the governor's office, and schedule appointments and activities.

Governor Ann Richards (1991–1995) got high marks for the highly diverse staff she assembled—45 percent female, 37 percent ethnic minority.[5] However, she found herself in some political difficulty when, after preaching to state agencies about the need to prune their budgets, she let her staff grow from the usual 225 or so to almost 400. She responded in 1994, an election year, by cutting back on personnel.

Governor George Bush pruned the size of the staff even more, to 190 by 1996. Even so, only New York (with 203) and Florida (with 264) had more gubernatorial staffers.[6] In 2000 Bush had only 137 full-time–equivalent staffers.

The comparison between Richards and Bush is somewhat deceiving, since the payroll changed very little between the two administrations. Richards followed a traditional populist approach of creating many jobs for "the people," although they didn't pay well. Bush followed a traditional businesslike approach of appointing fewer people but at much higher salaries.

QUALIFICATIONS FOR GOVERNOR

Formal Qualifications

Like the qualifications for members of the legislature, the formal qualifications for governor are so broad that several million Texans could legally run for the office. Article IV of the constitution stipulates that the governor must be at least 30 years old, be a citizen of the United States, and have been a resident of Texas for the five years immediately preceding the election.

Personal Characteristics

Formally qualifying for the governorship and actually having a chance at being considered seriously as a candidate are two very different matters. The social, political, and economic realities of the state dictate that personal characteristics, not stated in law, help to determine who will be the victors in gubernatorial elections. Some of these personal characteristics are based on accomplishments, or at least a positive involvement, on the part of the gubernatorial aspirant. Others are innate traits that are beyond the control of the individual.

These characteristics are similar to but even more stringent than those for members of the legislature. In short, *unless something unusual occurs in the campaign,* tradi-

5. "Governor Richards' Appointments/Demographic Analysis," governor's office information sheet, September 8, 1993.

6. *The Book of the States, 1996–97,* vol. 31 (Lexington, KY: Council of State Governments, 1996), 20.

Land Commissioner Garry Mauro ran against incumbent Governor George Bush in 1998. When his old mentor, Lieutenant Governor Bob Bullock, endorsed Bush, Mauro no doubt wondered who would desert him next.

SOURCE: Courtesy of Ben Sargent.

tion dictates that the successful candidate for governor will be a white Anglo-Saxon Protestant (WASP) male who is politically conservative, involved in civic affairs, and a millionaire. More than likely, but less inevitably, this individual will have held some type of office, usually attorney general or lieutenant governor, although being a professional politician is fast becoming a liability among voters with a penchant for electing "good ol' boys." The most atypical governor in more than a half century was Ann Richards, 1991–1995, who was the state's second female chief executive.[7] Even though Texas has had only two women governors, that is one more than any other state has had.

ROLES OF THE GOVERNOR AND LIMITS ON THOSE ROLES

The governor must play at least seven roles. Five are formal; that is, they are prescribed by the constitution and supplementing statutes. Two are informal and symbolic; that is, they derive from the Texas political setting (see Table 7.1). Governors of all states play similar roles, as does the president, who also has added responsibilities in the areas of diplomacy and economics.

7. The only other female governor was Miriam A. (Ma) Ferguson, who served two nonconsecutive terms, 1925–1927 and 1933–1935, the first as the successor to her husband, who had been impeached and convicted.

TABLE 7.1

Roles of the Governor

Constitutional and Statutory Roles	*Informal and Symbolic Roles*
Chief Executive	Chief of Party
Chief Legislator	Leader of the People
Commander in Chief/Top Cop	
Chief of State	
Chief Intergovernmental Diplomat	

The personality of the governor and the political and economic circumstances that prevail during a governor's administration largely determine which roles are emphasized. As the first opening quotation in this chapter indicates, the governorship is a unique office, and its distinctive qualities are further highlighted by the varied approaches taken by different governors.[8]

Let's look at the governors of the 1970s and 1980s as examples. Preston Smith (1969–1973) was an aggressive legislative leader who "called in his IOUs" from his days as lieutenant governor/presiding officer of the Texas Senate. Dolph Briscoe (1973–1979) was so low profile that *Texas Monthly* magazine pictured him on the cover as an empty chair in reference to his spending more time at his Uvalde ranch than at his Austin desk. He personified the quest for the office just to acquire something more for the man who has almost everything. Mark White (1983–1987) inherited a deteriorating economy and emphasized education and economic development as ways to shore up the state's financial picture. However, he was accused of being all style and no substance. Bill Clements (1979–1983, 1987–1991) emphasized tax reform, a war on drugs and crime, long-range planning, and better ties to neighboring states and Mexico during his first term. During his second, of necessity he emphasized economic diversification. Clements had a reputation as an obstructionist, making it difficult for public policy to be developed.

The governor acknowledged to be atypical, Ann Richards (1991–1995), was grounded in Travis County politics and got high marks for the quality and diversity of her appointments, for forcing changes in the controversial boards governing some state agencies—especially the State Insurance Board and the Board of Pardons and Paroles—and for exerting executive control over other agencies, such as the Texas Department of Commerce. Richards insisted on high standards of ethics, though some of her staff members stumbled later on. She also worked hard at economic diversification. However, Richards's approach to legislative relations was partisan and heavy handed, and she was not particularly popular among legislators. Her 1994 bid for reelection was inept, and she also faced the national Republican sweep. Richards lost handily to George W. Bush.

Bush, son of a former president,[9] operated very differently from Richards. The George Bush approach to legislators was nonpartisan, low key, and consensus build-

8. Thad L. Beyle, "Being Governor," *The State of the States* (Washington, DC: Congressional Quarterly Press, 1996), 77–107, discusses how governors might be evaluated, including the index developed by the National Governors Association.

9. Texas claims three former U.S. presidents: Dwight Eisenhower, who was born in the state; Lyndon Johnson, who was a life-long resident; and George Bush, who moved to Texas during an oil boom when he was a businessman, not a politician.

ing. As the second chapter opening quotation indicates, Bush saw himself as a deal maker. He campaigned on four issues—reform of the juvenile justice system, setting limits on civil lawsuits (tort reform), more flexible and better public education, and restrictions on welfare. These issues were common throughout the country in 1994. Once elected, Bush stuck with those issues and pushed each through the 1995 legislature. While he was successful in part by further expanding public school flexibility in the 1997 legislative session, his push for major changes in the Texas tax system was rebuffed. He had to settle for a proposed constitutional amendment to increase the tax exemptions for homesteads.

Speculation was keen already during the 75th Legislature in 1997 that George W. Bush was trying to create a platform from which to launch a presidential bid in the year 2000. By the time the 76th Legislature met in January 1999, no doubt existed about the governor's political plans. The *Wall Street Journal,* whose political philosophy is closely aligned to that of Bush's "compassionate conservatism," summarized the year by noting the total dominance of the capitol complex by a governor who was out of state campaigning much of the time. The *Journal* staff particularly noted the Bush "'Yellow Rose Garden' strategy of having potential presidential supporters and advisers, along with world leaders, come to Austin" as overshadowing "anything that was happening across the street at the state Capitol."[10]

FORMAL ROLES AND LIMITATIONS

The Texas Constitution was written at a time when concentrated power in the hands of a single state official was viewed with great apprehension. E. J. Davis, the last Republican governor before Clements, held office from 1870 to 1874 in an administration characterized by corruption and repression. Consequently, when the 1876 Constitution was drafted, the framers reacted against the Davis administration by creating a constitutionally weak governor's office (see Chapter Two).

10. "The Big Winners and Losers of 1999: The Governor Had a Banner Year, While Local Education Lost Out," *Wall Street Journal,* December 29, 1999, T1.

The 2000 elections showed that the speculation was correct. Bush was the Republican presidential nominee. The election was one of the closest and most disputed in American history so that, at the end of November, the winner remained uncertain. The Republicans retained narrow control of Congress, and each party retained control of one house in the Texas legislature.

Today the governor must still cope with a highly fragmented executive branch that includes five other elected executives, two elected boards, and a complex system of powerful policy-making boards and commissions. The Texas governorship has been judged to be one of the weakest in the country in terms of executive branch control and general institutional power.[11]

Chief Executive

News stories frequently describe the governor as the "chief executive," referring to gubernatorial control over the state bureaucracy and the governor's **appointment and removal,** budgeting, planning, supervisory, and clemency powers. Although this is one of the governor's most time-consuming roles, it also is one of the weakest, as the following discussion will illustrate.

Appointment.   Texas is said to have a long ballot because a large number of state officials are elected by the people rather than appointed by the governor. The list of officials elected on a statewide basis includes the lieutenant governor, whose major role is legislative; the attorney general; the comptroller of public accounts; the commissioner of the General Land Office; and the agriculture commissioner. In addition, members of the Texas Railroad Commission and the State Board of Education are elected. Since they are elected independently, they feel no obligation to the governor, and since they may want the governor's job, they may even wish to make the incumbent look bad.

The most visible executive appointments that the governor makes are those of secretary of state, commissioner of education, commissioner of insurance, commissioner of health and human services, and executive director of the Economic Development Department. The governor also appoints the director of the Office of State-Federal Relations and the adjutant general, who heads the state militia. He or she also fills any vacancy that occurs in one of the major elected executive positions, such as railroad commissioner. In such an event, the governor appoints someone to fill the vacancy until the next election. She or he also appoints all or some of the members of about two dozen advisory councils and committees that coordinate the work of two or more state agencies.

The governor has a major effect on state policy through appointments to approximately 121 policy-making, multimember boards and commissions. Examples include the University of Texas System board of regents, the Public Utility Commission, and the Insurance Board. The members of these boards are appointed by the governor, usually for a six-year term, but with the following limitations:

1. The terms of board and commission members are overlapping and staggered to prevent the governor from appointing a majority of the members until late in the first term of office.

11. See, for example, Thad Beyle, "The Governors," in Virginia Gray, Russell L. Hanson, and Herbert Jacob, *Politics in the American States,* 7th ed. (Washington, DC: Congressional Quarterly Press, 1999), particularly 209–19.

2. The statutes establishing the various boards and commissions are highly prescriptive and often specify both a certain geographic representation and occupational or other background characteristics of the members.[12]
3. Appointments to some boards and commissions must be made from lists supplied by members of professional organizations and associations.[13]

One other important use of the appointment power is filling vacancies in the judiciary. Although Texas has an elected judiciary, every legislature creates some new courts, and vacancies occur in other courts. The governor makes appointments to these benches until the next election. Indeed, more than half of the district court judges in the state are first appointed and subsequently stand for election.

The governor must obtain a two-thirds confirmation vote from the Senate for appointments; the president needs only a simple majority from the U.S. Senate. And, as in national politics, there is a practice of "senatorial courtesy" whereby the Senate will usually honor the objection of a senator from the same district as the nominee for appointment by refusing to approve confirmation.

Texas's short biennial legislative session, however, permits the governor to make many interim appointments when the legislature is not in session. This practice gives these appointees a free ride for periods as long as nineteen months. These recess appointments must be presented to the Senate within the first ten days of the next session, whether regular or called.

Another aid to the governor is incumbency. If a governor is reelected, he or she will be able to appoint all members of these boards and commissions by early in the second term. The governor will then have considerable influence over policy development.

Removal. The governor has only limited removal power in Texas. The governor can remove political appointees whom he or she has appointed, with the consent of the Senate, a power in effect only since a 1980 constitutional amendment. The governor also can remove personal staff members and a few executive directors, such as the one in the Department of Housing and Community Affairs. However, the governor cannot remove members of boards and commissions whom she or he did not appoint. This lack of removal power deprives the governor of significant control over the bureaucrats who make and administer policy on a day-to-day basis. As a result, the governor has difficulty implementing policies through the state bureaucracy.

The three general methods for removing state officeholders are:

1. *Impeachment,* which involves a formal accusation—the impeachment—by a House majority and requires a two-thirds vote for conviction by the Senate
2. *Address,* a procedure whereby the legislature requests the governor to remove a district or appellate judge from office (a two-thirds vote of both houses is required)
3. Quo warranto *proceedings,* a legal procedure whereby an official may be removed by a court

12. For example, three members (half of the total) of the Commission on Alcoholism and Drug Abuse must be recovering substance abusers.

13. This practice is most common with the licensing and examining boards in various health care fields.

Budgeting.   By law, the governor must submit a biennial budget message to the legislature within five days after that body convenes in regular session. This budget is prepared by the governor's Office of Budget and Planning. The Legislative Budget Board (LBB), however, also prepares a budget for the legislature to consider, and, traditionally, the legislature is guided more by the legislative budget than by the governor's. The executive budget indicates to the legislature the governor's priorities and signals items likely to be vetoed. With the exception of the item veto, the Texas governor lacks the strong budgetary powers not only of the president but also of many state executives (see Chapter Ten).

Planning.   Both modern management and the requirements of many federal grants-in-aid emphasize substate regional planning, and the governor directs planning efforts for the state through the Office of Budget and Planning. When combined with budgeting, the governor's planning power allows him or her a stronger hand in the development of new programs and policy alternatives. Though still without adequate controls over state programs, the governor has had a greater voice in suggesting future programs over the past two decades, mainly because many federal statutes designated the governor as having approval power for federal grants.

Especially in his first term, Bill Clements approached his job from the planning perspective, including the development of the Texas State Government Effectiveness Program to make state agency management more efficient and the creation of the Texas 2000 Commission to look at issues that will become increasingly more pressing in this century. During the Richards administration, Comptroller John Sharp—in part at the request of the governor to allow a more rational appropriations act for fiscal years 1992–93—developed an elaborate system for monitoring the performance of state agencies; in turn, state agencies had to engage in a massive strategic planning effort. The Texas Performance Review has continued as a vital part of state government.

Supervising.   The state constitution charges the governor with the responsibility of seeing that the laws of the state are "faithfully executed" but provides few tools for fulfilling this function. The governor's greatest supervisory and directive powers occur in the role of commander in chief (described later). Governors can request reports from state agencies, remove their own appointees, and use political influence to force hiring reductions or other economies. But lack of appointment power over the professional staffs of state agencies and lack of removal power over a predecessor's appointees do limit the governor's ability to ensure that the state bureaucracy does its job.

The governor thus must fall back on informal tactics to exercise any control over the administration. In this respect, the governor's staff is of supreme importance; if staff members can establish good rapport with state agencies, they may extend the governor's influence to areas where he or she does not have formal authority. They are aided in this task by two factors of which agency personnel are well aware: the governor's leadership of the party and his or her veto powers (both discussed later).

Clemency.   The governor's power with regard to acts of clemency (mercy) is restricted to one thirty-day reprieve for an individual sentenced to death. In cases of treason against the state (a rare crime), the governor may grant pardons, reprieves, and commutations of sentences with legislative consent. The governor also may remit fines or bond forfeitures and restore driver's licenses and hunting privileges. In addition, the governor has the discretionary right to revoke a parole or conditional pardon. Beyond these limited acts, the state's chief executive officer must make recommendations to the Board of Pardons and Paroles, which is part of the Department of Criminal Justice. Although empowered to refuse an act of clemency recommended by the board, the governor cannot act without its recommendation in such matters as full and conditional pardons, commutations, reprieves, and emergency reprieves.

Chief Legislator

Although the legislature tends to dominate Texas politics, the governor is a strong chief legislator who relies on three formal powers in carrying out this role: **message power, session power,** and **veto power.**

Message Power.   The governor may give messages to the legislature at any time, but the constitution requires a gubernatorial message when legislative sessions open and when a governor retires. By statute, the governor must also deliver a biennial budget message. Other messages the governor may choose to send or deliver in person are often "emergency" messages when the legislature is in session; these messages are a formal means of expressing policy preferences. They also attract the attention of the media and set the agenda for state government. Coupled with able staff work, message power can be an effective and persuasive tool. Examples of gubernatorial messages during the 1999 legislative session were a call for broad tax cuts, improvements in public schools, parental involvement in abortion decisions for girls under age 18, a crackdown on crime, electric deregulation, tort reforms, support for the North American Free Trade Agreement (NAFTA), and a continuing emphasis on the need to move people from welfare to work.

Session Power.   As discussed in Chapter Six, the legislature is constitutionally forbidden to call itself into special session; only the governor may do this. Called sessions are limited to a maximum duration of thirty days, but a governor who wants to force consideration of an issue can call one special session after another. The governor also sets the agenda for these sessions, although the legislature, once called, may consider other matters on a limited basis, such as impeachment or approval of executive appointments. As the complexity of state government has grown, legislators sometimes have been unable to complete their work in the short, biennial regular sessions. When they fail to complete enough of the agenda, they know they can expect a special session.

Special sessions offer a way around the restricted biennial legislative session of 140 days. The eight governors before Bush called a total of thirty-four special sessions. Bill Clements called six; Ann Richards called only two. Through 1999, Bush had called none, a reflection in part of his ability to get along with the legislative leadership and in part of the budget surplus.

Governor George Bush's number 1 issue for the 1997 legislature was reduction in school property taxes. Offsetting the lost revenue would have required new business taxes and additional sales taxes. Legislators "bailed out" rather than making key special interest groups angry.

SOURCE: Courtesy of Ben Sargent.

Veto Power.   The governor's strongest legislative power is the veto. Every bill that passes both houses of the legislature in regular and special sessions is sent to the governor, who has the option of signing it, letting it become law without signing it, or vetoing it.[14]

If the legislature is still in session, the governor has ten days—Sundays excluded—in which to act. If the bill is sent to the governor in the last ten days of a session or after the legislature has adjourned, the governor has twenty days—including Sundays—in which to act. If the governor vetoes a bill while the legislature is still in session, that body may override the veto by a two-thirds vote of both houses.

Because of the short legislative session, important bills are often sent to the governor so late that the legislature has adjourned before the governor has had to act on them. In such instances, the veto power is absolute. The legislature cannot override if it is not in session, and consideration of the same bill cannot be carried over into the next session. Short biennial sessions thus make the governor's threat of a veto an extremely powerful political tool.

---

14. Unlike the president, the governor does not have a "pocket veto." The governor must send a veto message to block a bill; laying it aside without a signature results in the bill's becoming law, even if the legislature adjourns.

The governor has one other check over appropriations bills, the **item veto.**[15] This device permits the governor to delete individual items from a bill without having to veto it in its entirety. The item veto may be used only to strike a particular line of funding, however; it cannot be used to reduce or increase an appropriation.

The item veto illustrates a reality of gubernatorial power in Texas. The governor's power over legislation is largely negative—he or she finds it easier to say no than to get his or her own legislative agenda adopted.

Commander in Chief/Top Cop

The state of Texas does not independently engage in warfare with other nations and thus would seem to have no need for a commander in chief. However, the governor does have the power to declare martial law, that is, to suspend civil government temporarily and replace it with government by the state militia and/or law enforcement agencies. Although seldom used, this power was invoked to quell an oil field riot in East Texas in the 1930s and to gain control of an explosive racial situation in North Texas in the 1940s. Additionally, the governor is commander in chief of the military forces of the state (Army and Air National Guard) except when they have been called into service by the national government. The head of these forces, the adjutant general, is one of the governor's important appointees. The governor also has the power to assume command of the Texas Rangers and the Department of Public Safety to maintain law and order. These powers become important during disasters such as a flood or tornado, when danger may exist from the aftermath of the storm or from unscrupulous individuals such as looters.

In routine matters, the governor is almost wholly dependent on local law enforcement and prosecuting agencies to see that the laws of the state are faithfully executed. When there is evidence of wrongdoing, the state's chief executive often brings the informal powers of the governor's office to bear on the problem, appealing to the media to focus public attention on errant agencies and officeholders.

Chief of State

Pomp and circumstance are a part of being the top elected official of the state. Just as presidents use their ceremonial role to augment their other roles, so also do

---

15. Congress granted the U.S. president the item veto in 1996; Bill Clinton used the power eighty-two times before the Supreme Court nullified it in 1998.

The governor's veto power was an important issue in the 1990 campaign between Clayton Williams and Ann Richards. Some supporters were drawn to Richards because she promised to veto anti-abortion legislation, while Williams picked up support from those who were comforted by his announced intent to veto any new taxes.

governors. Whether cutting a ribbon to open a new highway, leading a parade, or serving as host for a visiting dignitary, the governor's performance as chief of state yields visibility and the appearance of leadership, which facilitate the more important executive and legislative roles of the office. In the modern era, the governor is often the chief television personality of the state and sets the policy agenda through publicity. Ann Richards, for example, was a national TV celebrity, sometimes more popular outside the state than inside.

More and more, Texas governors are using the ceremonial role of chief of state, sometimes coupled with the role of chief intergovernmental diplomat, to become actively involved in economic negotiations such as attracting new plant locations. Efforts are directed toward both foreign and domestic investments and finding new markets for Texas goods. In such negotiations, the governor uses the power and prestige of the office to become the state's salesperson. Mark White and Bill Clements both made significant use of this role to attract new businesses to the state. Ann Richards strongly pushed for U.S. Senate approval of the North American Free Trade Agreement (NAFTA) because of the likelihood of expanded Texas-Mexico trade. Ironically, one historic function of the chief of state is tossing out the first ball at the opening baseball game; in George Bush's case, he was one of the team's owners until the beginning of 1998.

Chief Intergovernmental Diplomat

The Texas Constitution provides that the governor, or someone designated by the governor, is the state's representative in all dealings with other states and with the national government. This role of intergovernmental representative has increased in importance for three reasons. First, federal statutes now designate the governor as the official who has the planning and grant-approval authority for the state. This fact has given the governor's budgeting, planning, and supervising powers much more clout in recent years, and federal budget philosophy (see Chapter Ten) further enhances the governor's role.

Second, some state problems, such as water and energy development, often require the cooperation of several states. For example, in 1981–82, Governor Clements and five other governors tried to plan solutions for the water problems of the High Plains area. Additionally, although the U.S. Constitution precludes a governor from conducting diplomatic relations with other nations, Texas's location as a border state gives rise to

Governor George Bush used his commander-in-chief powers in an unusual way in late 1999 and 2000. In his bid for the Republican nomination for president, Bush traveled across the United States. During these campaign tours, he was protected by the Texas Department of Public Safety, which always protects the governor. Thus, a few state troopers and Texas Rangers got to see much of the country for a change. The protection was paid for by the Bush campaign.

social and economic exchanges with the governors of Mexican border states on matters such as immigration and energy, especially with growing NAFTA commerce.

Third, acquiring federal funds is always important, since they relieve the pressure on state and local government revenue sources. Often, the governor works in concert with other governors to try to secure favorable national legislation, including both funding and limits on unfunded federal mandates. Thus, Governor George Bush is an active member of the National Governors Association and a participant in the National Governors Conference. He also is active in regional and Republican party groups. He takes his place among the proactive governors described in the opening quotation from the *New York Times*.

A more traditional use of the governor's intergovernmental role is mandated by Article IV of the U.S. Constitution, which provides for the rendition (surrender) of fugitives from justice who flee across state lines. The Texas governor, like other governors, signs the rendition papers and transmits them to the appropriate law enforcement officials. Law officers are then in charge of picking up the fugitives and returning them to the appropriate state.

INFORMAL ROLES AND LIMITATIONS

In addition to the five "hats" described here, there are at least two others that the governor must wear. They have no basis in law, but they are nevertheless important to the job. The degree of success with which the governor handles these informal roles can greatly affect the execution of the formal ones.

Chief of Party

As the symbolic head of the Democratic or Republican party in the state, the governor is a key figure at state party conventions and usually is the leader of the party's delegation to national conventions. A governor may, however, have to compete with a U.S. senator from his party. Governors are able to use their influence with the party's State Executive Committee and at party conventions to gain a subsidiary influence over candidates seeking other state offices. An active, skilled governor can thus create a power relationship with state legislators and bureaucrats that the more formal roles of the office do not permit. The governor also wins some political influence by campaigning for other party candidates who are seeking state or national offices.

Governor Bill Clements, the first modern Republican governor of Texas, used the party role extensively to extend Republican influence through his appointment power. He appointed enough Democrats to maintain the good will of the majority leadership. Governor Ann Richards also made key executive and judicial appointments from among her Democratic party colleagues. While generally supporting the party position on redistricting, she also showed some willingness to deal with the Republicans in exchange for GOP support for legislation that she and the Democrats wanted, such as a state lottery.

Governor George Bush is the most interesting "study" of the three. In 1995, he operated on a nonpartisan basis and secured the support of both members and leaders of the Democrat-majority legislature for his legislative program. He also made his own Republican party angry by cooperating with the Democrats and by having a moderate position on a number of issues. For example, Governor Bush and Speaker of the House Pete Laney worked especially well together, and Bush told the state party bigwigs to back off from trying to defeat Laney in his 1996 reelection bid. Consequently, Bush was not included in the Republican delegation to the presidential nominating convention in 1996. In 1997, he fared somewhat less well with the legislature, even though the Senate had become Republican, in part because of resistance to his tax plan by conservative members of the GOP. In 1999, his obvious ambition to be president of the United States resulted not only in Republican party loyalty but also in considerable Democratic support for someone who could potentially influence national policy in the state's favor.

Leader of the People

Most Texans, unaware of the limitations on formal gubernatorial powers, look to the chief executive of the state for leadership in solving the state's problems and to serve as their principal spokesperson on major issues. A skilled governor can turn this role to substantial advantage when bargaining with other key figures in the policy-making process such as the presiding officers, legislators, and top bureaucrats in the state's administration. For example, through the media, the governor can rally public support for programs and policies. Choosing to accept invitations to speak is another way a governor can gain public exposure and thus support for programs and plans, including the budget. Public appearances usually serve as occasions for emphasizing gubernatorial accomplishments. They also allow a governor to show concern for ordinary citizens with extraordinary problems, as when the governor visits tornado or flood sites. In keeping with the traditionalistic tenor of the state, some governors use this role to show that they are "active conservatives."

Coupled with the strong legislative role, this informal role is critical to a governor's success. Leadership has been depicted as consisting of two parts: the ability to "transact"—that is, to make things happen—and the ability to "transform"—that is, to decide what things should happen.[16] The successful Texas governor is one who can both make things happen and decide what policies ought to happen.

A populist approach is consistent with the values of democracy. So is a more conservative approach that addresses issues that the public reiterates with each opinion poll. Thus, although having different positions—except that both wanted to improve public education—and using different styles, Ann Richards and George Bush both demonstrated leadership.

STATE ADMINISTRATIVE AGENCIES

Although we must concede that a state bureaucracy is needed to carry out government policy, we might be happier if the Texas administration were easier to understand. Even for the experienced observer, state administration in Texas is

16. James McGregor Burns, *Leadership* (New York: Harper and Row, 1978), 42–45.

TABLE 7.2

Types of Administrative Agencies in Texas

Agencies Headed by Elected Executives

  Office of the Attorney General

  Department of Agriculture

  Office of the Comptroller of Public Accounts

  General Land Office

Agencies Headed by Appointed Executives

  Examples: Office of the Secretary of State, Texas Department of Economic Development

Multimember Boards and Commissions

  Elected Board and Commission: State Board of Education, Texas Railroad Commission

  Example of Ex Officio Board: Bond Review Board

  Examples of Appointed Boards and Commissions: Department of Mental Health and Mental Retardation,
  · Texas Higher Education Coordinating Board

confusing; for the novice, it is perplexing indeed. There are three essential character-istics of the state administration that cause this confusion:

1. There is no single, uniform organizational pattern.
2. There are numerous exceptions to the traditional bureaucratic characteristic of hierarchy.
3. The number of state agencies depends upon one's method of counting.

There are at least five different types of top policymakers in state agencies: (1) elected executives, (2) appointed executives, (3) an elected commission and an elected board, (4) ex officio boards and commissions, and (5) appointed boards and commissions (see Table 7.2). Agencies headed by an elected or appointed executive fol-low traditional hierarchical principles in that a single individual clearly is "the boss" and thus is ultimately responsible for the operation of a particular department or of-fice. But the agencies that are headed by a multimember board or commission have three or six or even nineteen bosses, whatever number constitutes the membership of the board. Although there also is a hierarchical organization in these agencies, it be-gins with the professional staff of the agency, the level below the policy-setting board.

Another complication is that one office, board, or commission may be responsi-ble for the general policies of a number of separate agencies. For example, the Board of Regents of the University of Texas is the policy-making board for the entire University of Texas System, which includes fifteen agencies that are separately funded. Another example is the state Department of Mental Health and Mental Retardation, which has overall policy responsibility for more than thirty programs and agencies. As of fiscal years 2000–2001, at least 250 agencies, institutions, and independent pro-grams are funded by general appropriations. This list is not all inclusive, however, because not all agencies are budgeted, especially ex officio ones and regulatory commissions that derive their revenues from fines and fees. A rough count of just the policy-making boards, commissions, departments, and offices—excluding the courts and related agencies, the legislature and its staff agencies, and the offices of elected executives—yields about 121 agencies.[17] Community/junior colleges are excluded from the 121 because they have locally appointed boards. The reader, we hope, is beginning to see why the number of state agencies is usually expressed in approximate terms. In the space allotted here, there is no way to name, much less describe all state agencies, but a few of the most important are described briefly in the following pages.

Agencies with Elected Executives

Five state officials, in addition to the governor, are elected on partisan ballots for four-year terms. They are, in theory at least, directly accountable to the citizenry for their performance and their integrity in office. One of these, the lieutenant governor, presides over the Texas Senate and does not head any executive office. The lieutenant governor performs as an executive only when the governor is away from the state or upon succession to the governorship. The other four elected officials are department heads. The incumbents are as of early 2000.

Attorney General.   Along with the governor, the lieutenant governor, and the speaker of the House, the attorney general is one of the most powerful officers in Texas government. Although candidates for the position often run on an anticrime platform, the work of the office is primarily civil. As the attorney for the state, the attorney general and her or his staff represent the state and its agencies in court when the state is a party to a case. The Office of the Attorney General also is responsible for such varied legal matters as consumer protection, antitrust litigation, workers' compensation insurance, organized-crime control, and environmental protection. During 1996–97, the attorney general's efficiency in collecting child support payments was called into question, and the legislature placed this function under tighter scrutiny beginning in 1997.

The attorney general's greatest power, however, is that of issuing opinions on questions concerning the constitutionality or legality of existing or proposed legislation and administrative actions. These opinions are not legally binding, but they are rarely challenged in court, and thus they effectively have the same importance as a ruling by the state's Supreme Court (see Chapter Eight). Because the attorney general's opinions often make the headlines, and because the attorney general works with all state agencies, the office is second only to the governor's office in the public recognition it receives. Because the position is regarded as one of the stepping-stones to the governor's office, attorneys general often encourage publicity about themselves, their agency, and their support groups with an eye to possible future election campaigns. Republican John Cornyn was first elected in 1998. He stressed the child support function and open records.

Comptroller of Public Accounts.   The comptroller (pronounced "con-TROL-ler") is responsible for the administration of the state tax system and for performing

---

17. The numbers in this paragraph are based on an actual count of entries in the table of contents of the Appropriations Act for 2001–2002.

preaudits of expenditures by state agencies. In addition, as a part of the budget process, the comptroller certifies to the legislature the approximate biennial income for the state. Under the Texas Constitution, the legislature is precluded from appropriating more funds than are anticipated in state revenues for any biennial period. Texas, like most other states, must have a balanced budget. Since 1996, following the phaseout of the treasurer's office, the comptroller is also the state's banker. As such, the comptroller is the custodian of all public monies and of the securities that the state invests in or holds in trust. The office also issues the excise tax stamps used to indicate the collection of taxes on the sale of alcoholic beverages and cigarettes in the state. In short, the comptroller takes in the state's revenues, safeguards them, and invests them. This merger of the two offices made the comptroller's position even more powerful than it already was.

Republican Carol Keeton Rylander, a former mayor of Austin and Texas Railroad Commission member, was elected as the first woman comptroller in 1998. Calling herself "one tough grandma," she continued the rigorous examination of state agencies known as the Texas Performance Review established by her predecessor, John Sharp.

Commissioner of the General Land Office.

Only Texas and Alaska entered the Union with large amounts of public lands, and only they have land offices. About 22.5 million Texas acres, including the submerged lands extending from the coastline to the (marine) 3-league limit, are administered by the commissioner of the General Land Office, whose land management responsibilities include:

1. Supervising the leasing of all state-owned lands for such purposes as oil and gas production, mineral development, and grazing (over 11,500 leases)
2. Administering the veterans' land program, by which veterans may buy land with loans that are backed by state bonds
3. Maintaining the environmental quality of public lands and waters, especially coastal lands

Republican David Dewhurst was first elected as commissioner in 1998. He, like all land commissioners, must try to balance environmental interests with land and mineral interests. Dewhurst's background is in the energy industry.

Commissioner of Agriculture.

Farming and ranching are still important industries in the state, even though only about 1 percent of the population is engaged in agriculture. The Department of Agriculture, like its national counterpart, is responsible both for the regulation and promotion (through research and education) of the agribusiness industry and for consumer protection, although these functions may sometimes be in conflict. Departmental activities are diverse—for example, enforcing weights and measures standards, licensing egg handlers, determining the relative safety of pesticides, and locating export markets for Texas agricultural products. Pesticides illustrate the conflicting nature of the roles assigned to this office. Limiting pesticides to those that are safe for workers, consumers, and the environment may be detrimental to the profits of farmers. Election to this office is specified by statute rather than by the state constitution. Republican Susan Coombs, a fourth-generation rancher, was first elected in 1998.

Agencies with Appointed Executives

One example of an agency headed by an appointed executive is the Office of the Secretary of State. The state constitution stipulates that the governor shall appoint the secretary of state, whose functions include safeguarding the great seal of the state of Texas and affixing it to the governor's signature on proclamations, commissions, and certificates. In addition to this somewhat ceremonial duty, the secretary's duties include certifying elections (verifying the validity of the returns), maintaining records on campaign expenditures, keeping the list of lobbyists who register with the state, administering the Uniform Commercial Code, issuing corporate charters, and publishing the Texas Register—the official record of administrative decisions, rules, regulations, and announcements of hearings and pending actions. Governor George Bush appointed Elton Bomer, a former insurance commissioner, to the job in 1999.

The secretary of state's office, though appointive, can sometimes be a springboard to elective office. Lieutenant Governor Bob Bullock and former Governor Mark White both held the position, as did Mayor Ron Kirk of Dallas.

Boards and Commissions

Multimember boards or commissions head most state administrative agencies and make overall policy for them. These boards appoint chief administrators to handle the agencies' day-to-day responsibilities, including the budget, personnel, and the administration of state laws and those federal laws that are carried out through state governments. Two have elected members. The others have appointed or ex officio members.

Elected Boards and Commissions. As we have mentioned before, the Texas Railroad Commission (TRC) is one of the most influential agencies in the state, and the three persons who are its members are powerful indeed. The commission has tremendous political clout in the state because of its regulation of all mining and extractive industries, including oil, gas, coal, and uranium. Its control of intrastate surface transportation—railroads, buses, moving vans, and trucks—is of growing importance because of the importance of trucking rates to economic development. The commission even has national influence because of its authority over the national pipeline system through hookups to producing wells in Texas. Its members are chosen in statewide elections for staggered six-year terms. In 1994, the TRC became all-Republican for the first time.

The State Board of Education originally was created as an elected body. As part of the public school reforms of 1984, it was made an appointive board. In 1987 the voters overwhelmingly approved returning it to elective status. Fifteen members are chosen by the voters from districts across the state. A majority of the board's members are Republicans, a fact that has introduced a concern lest the long-standing controversy about the board's selection of textbooks for public schools resurface.

Ex Officio Boards and Commissions. There are many boards in the state administration whose members are all ex officio; that is, they are members because of another office they hold in the administration. When these boards were created, two purposes were served by ex officio memberships: The members usually were already in Austin (no small matter in pre-freeway days), and they were assumed to have some expertise in the subject at hand. An example is the Bond Review Board, which includes the governor, lieutenant governor, comptroller, and speaker of the House and ensures that debt financing is used prudently by the state.

Appointed Boards and Commissions.   Most of the state's laws are administered by boards and commissions whose members are appointed rather than elected and by the administrators the boards then appoint. The members of many boards are appointed by the governor, but some other boards have a combination of gubernatorial appointees and appointees of other state officials and/or ex officio members. They vary in size and, as a rule, have general policy authority for their agencies. Members serve six-year overlapping terms, without pay.

There are three broad categories of appointed boards and commissions: (1) health, welfare, and rehabilitation; (2) education; and (3) general executive and administrative departments. Examples from each category are (1) the Department of Mental Health and Mental Retardation, (2) the Texas Higher Education Coordinating Board, and (3) the Parks and Wildlife Department and the Public Utility Commission, respectively.

Appointed Boards and Citizens: The Case of the State Board of Insurance.   How do the 121 or so policy-making boards affect a citizen? One example is the State Board of Insurance, which regulates insurance companies and sets rates for auto, property, title, and workers' compensation insurance. The State Board of Insurance has long been perceived as a captive of the insurance industry. Governor Ann Richards had some success in turning the insurance board toward consumer interests early in her term. Her successor, Governor George Bush, helped the insurance industry by pushing for limitations on lawsuits, but in return demanded reasonable rate behavior. The board allowed increases in property insurance rates in the late 1990s, largely to cover a series of weather-related disasters. However, it forced vehicle insurance rates down after the insurers failed to prove the need for a rate hike. A little known fact is that not all insurers, for a variety of complex reasons, are regulated, and an increasing number of consumers are choosing these companies for insurance coverage. Anyone owning a car needs to be concerned when rates are set or when purchasing coverage from an unregulated carrier.

The Case of the College Governing Board.   Public community colleges, private universities, and public universities all have a board of trustees or boards of regents. These board members set policy for the college and appoint the president. At a typical board of regents meeting, the board members (1) renewed the president's contract, (2) approved a resolution increasing the amount of fees for most courses, (3) granted tenure to twenty faculty members, and (4) approved the hiring of a new dean of business. Each of these actions affected students—directly in the case of the fee increases, and indirectly in the case of the three types of personnel actions.

The Case of the Parks and Wildlife Board.   If one is an outdoors person who likes to camp, fish, or hunt, then the annual decisions of the Parks and Wildlife Board on what fees will be levied for each of these activities will be of interest. Texas traditionally has had very low parks and wildlife fees compared with other states. If that annual fishing license suddenly costs $100 instead of $19, one might have second thoughts about this form of recreation. Anglers also are affected by this board's decisions concerning what type of fish to release into the lakes of the state.

STATE ADMINISTRATION: WHAT IS IT?

This chapter has looked briefly at the types of state agencies that exist in Texas. Now, it will turn to the topic of **bureaucracy.** As often as not, *bureaucracy* becomes a dirty word when used to refer to the organization of government.

Few of us need an introduction to the concept of bureaucracy because public administration is a part of daily life. Traffic police, public school principals, highway workers, clerks in state and federal offices—they are all bureaucrats who apply and enforce public policies. Together, these bureaucrats make up the state administration. But what, really, is bureaucracy, and why does there seem to be so much of it?

Bureaucracy is a way of organizing people and activities in both government and business. The three characteristics we most associate with it are *hierarchy,* levels of power in an organization with maximum authority at the top; *specialization,* with everyone fitting into a niche and becoming an expert by performing the same tasks repeatedly; and *formal rules* and *regulations,* the notorious "red tape."[18]

When the United States was basically an agricultural nation, there was no need for either big government or big business. As people left farms and small towns and migrated to big cities to find work, the resulting urbanization of the nation created a host of problems: transportation, unemployment, sanitation, education, and so on. Federal, state, and local governments tried to solve these problems by providing services, and these services required numerous employees and organizations. For example, the federal Interstate Commerce Commission was created to tackle excessive railroad rates, while the Texas Employment Commission—now called the Texas Workforce Commission—was created to place workers into jobs. Later, agencies such as the Texas Department of Human Services and various county welfare agencies were created to deal with hard-core poverty. The result of these needs for more government has been the sprawling, powerful administrative state we know today.

As Figure 7.1 indicates, in recent years the number of state and local employees has fluctuated somewhat, actually dropping in 1987–1988, the worst years in the series of fiscal crises of the 1980s, and in 1992 and 1999, partially in response to citizen demands for greater productivity on the part of governments. However, the overall picture is one of growth in government employment. A poor economy will be reflected in private-sector employment figures, but it does not always lead to a downturn in public employment because governments must respond to the increased need for services during harsh times. This situation was particularly apparent at the national level during the Great Depression of the 1930s.

18. Max Weber is considered the classic expert on bureaucracy. See "Bureaucracy," in *From Max Weber: Essays in Sociology,* translated, edited, and with an introduction by H. H. Garth and C. Wright Mills (New York: Oxford University Press, 1946), 196–244.

FIGURE 7.1

State and Local Government Employment in Texas, 1980–1999* SOURCES: *Texas Almanac, 1982–83 through 2000–2001* eds. (Dallas: A. H. Belo Corporation, 1981–83–85–87–89–91–93–95–97–99), 410, 421, 597, 427, 502, 608, 467, 556, 548, and 582, respectively; *Fiscal Size Up: Texas State Services, 1998–99 Biennium* (Austin: Legislative Budget Board, 1996), 3–13.

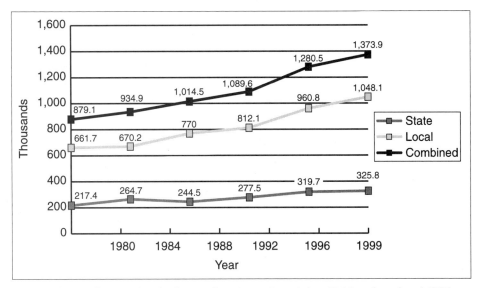

*Texas is 40th among the states in its ratio of state employees per 10,000 population, with 143 employees for each 10,000 citizens.

BUREAUCRACY: SURVIVAL TECHNIQUES

In the push and scramble of overlapping jurisdictions and overlapping authorities, agency personnel in Texas must fight for funds if they want their agency, and their jobs, to continue. Because the administrators operate in the political arena, they use political tactics to achieve their goals, just as state legislators and the governor do. Administrators must develop their own sources of political power if they want policies favorable to them enacted into law. In doing so, they rely occasionally on public good-will but more often on elected officials, interest groups, and their own expertise.[19]

Sources of Bureaucratic Power

Clientele Groups. The cornerstone of an agency's political clout is its relationship with its **clientele group** or groups—that is, the interest group(s) that benefit from the agency's programs. This relationship is mutually beneficial. Agency and clientele have similar goals, are interested in the same programs, and work together in a number of ways, including sharing personnel, information, and lobbying strategies. The greater the economic power of the interest groups, the stronger are the political ties between

---

19. An excellent study of bureaucratic power at the national level is Francis Rourke, *Bureaucracy, Politics, and Public Policy,* 4th ed. (Boston: Little, Brown, 1986). Rourke's framework is adopted here.

them and "their" agencies—so strong, in fact, that "regulation" often becomes promotion of the clientele group's interests. When this situation occurs, the agency is known as a "captive" agency; agency personnel and decision processes have been co-opted by the clientele group. When powerful legislators are added to the network in support of clientele-endorsed programs and budgets, an "iron triangle" of power occurs.

Among the better-known clientele/agency relationships are the relationships of the oil, gas, and transportation industries with the Texas Railroad Commission, the banking industry with the State Banking and State Depository boards, and the Texas State Teachers Association with the Texas Education Agency. By and large, the interest groups are seeking to use the agencies as protection against their competitors.

The Legislature.   Relationships with legislators are of two types: direct and indirect. First, agencies directly attempt to influence legislation and their budgets by furnishing information in writing and through testimony to legislative committees. In addition, agency executives work hard to get to know the speaker of the House, the lieutenant governor, and the members of the Legislative Budget Board and the Legislative Council, all of whom operate year-round, even when committee chairs and other legislators have gone home. Second, agencies use their clientele groups to try to influence legislation, budgets, and the selection of legislative leaders. During budget shortfalls, a number of state agencies—including higher education—became adept at finding powerful groups such as chambers of commerce and specially formed support groups to try to ward off agency budget cuts.

The Chief Executive.   As noted earlier in this chapter, the governor's power over state agencies is weak, but bureaucrats nonetheless want gubernatorial support. A governor who is a skillful chief legislator can help an agency get its budget increased or add a new program. The chief executive also can act as referee when an agency does not have the support of its clientele group and can give an agency visibility when it might otherwise languish in obscurity. The governor's legislative and party roles can be used to influence neutral legislators to look favorably on an agency, and the governor can greatly affect an agency's success or failure through appointments to the policy board or commission that oversees it. To state administrators, the chief executive is more powerful than the formal roles of the gubernatorial office would suggest. This power was demonstrated in 1991 when Governor Richards forced the reorganization of the Texas Department of Commerce, ending its practice of expensive foreign "economic development" trips.

Expertise and Information.   Expert information is a political commodity peculiar to bureaucrats, who enjoy a unique position in state government through their control of the technical information that the governor and legislators must have in order to develop statewide policies. Bureaucracies have a particularly strong advantage in Texas because the legislative committee system is inconsistent in producing legislative expertise. For the legislator who does not want to use the agency's information, the only alternative source is often the agency's clientele group. For example, if the legislature is trying to determine whether the state is producing enough physicians, the

Board of Medical Examiners, the Department of Health, and the Texas Medical Association are all ready to furnish the information.

Bureaucratic Involvement in the Policy-Making Process

Execution of the Laws.   The primary task of state bureaucrats is to execute the laws of Texas. In carrying out this task, however, they have considerable **administrative discretion;** that is, they are relatively free to use their own judgment as to just how the laws will be carried out. Regulatory boards illustrate most clearly the power of administrative agencies. When the Texas Railroad Commission determines the monthly oil allowable—the number of barrels of oil that can be pumped by each well during a particular month—it is making (administrative) rules that, like legislative statutes, have the force of law; it is, therefore, performing a quasilegislative function. And when the Alcoholic Beverage Commission decides who will be issued a license to sell beer, wine, and distilled spirits, it is performing a quasijudicial function by determining whether a person has the right to go into business.

Often, a statute passed by the legislature creates a general framework for implementing a program of regulation or service, but state agencies have considerable discretion in interpreting statutes. Consequently, the 121 or so policy-making boards, commissions, and authorities are very important in determining what government actually does. Especially in a state like Texas, which lacks a cabinet system and an integrated executive branch, the average citizen is affected on a daily basis by what these boards do, but that citizen may have little understanding of how these boards work or how to approach them. Compounding the problem is the fact that the chair is basically an equal member of the board, so that no single, readily identifiable person is in charge.

This board/commission structure makes it more difficult for citizens to participate. Moreover, these boards usually appoint an executive director, or college president, to carry out their policies, and that executive officer has considerable influence over board policies. For example, a college student may wish to protest the abolition of a popular major. Whose decision was it? The college's board of regents? The Texas Higher Education Coordinating Board's? Were the students consulted before the decision was made?

However, administrative discretion can be a positive factor in effective government. A common example is the decision of a Department of Public Safety law enforcement officer to allow one suspect to go free in the hope that he will lead criminal intelligence agents to a more important suspect.

Influencing Legislation.   Bureaucrats directly influence the content and meaning of statutes that are passed by the legislature, and they do so in three principal ways: by drafting bills, by furnishing information to legislators, and by lobbying.

During its short session, the Texas Legislature is under great pressure to draft, consider, and dispose of needed legislation. State bureaucrats are eager to aid the lawmakers, and two ways in which they do so are mutually beneficial: furnishing specialized information to legislative committees and drafting bills that individual legislators may then present as their own. Legislators thus gain needed assistance, and administrators are able to protect their agencies by helping to write their own budgets and developing their own programs.

Bureaucrats also influence legislation by lobbying legislators for or against proposed bills. Agencies usually work closely with their clientele group or groups in this endeavor. The governor also is lobbied not only for support of legislation favored by agencies and their clients but also for appointments to agencies that are acceptable to them and their clients. If successful, both these lobbying activities can greatly influence both the decisions of legislators and the policies set by boards and commissions. Moreover, the Texas Public Employees Association, especially strong among the state's classified employees, is an active lobby at budget time on matters of salary and fringe benefits.

HARNESSING THE ADMINISTRATIVE STATE

As part of the state's system of checks and balances, the governor has a veto over legislative acts and the legislature can impeach a governor or refuse to confirm gubernatorial appointments. As well as controlling various offices and agencies that report directly to them, all three traditional branches of government—executive, legislative, and judicial—have means of holding the bureaucracy, sometimes called the "fourth branch" of government, in check. Democratic theory posits that government should be elected by the people, but most administrators are not. The governor and other elected executives have legitimacy. State administrators must derive as much legitimacy (popular acceptance) as they can from these elected officials.

During the 1980s, the issue of bureaucratic accountability to the people through their elected representatives became increasingly important at both the state and national levels because of tight budgets and public desire to maximize each tax dollar, as well as a strong, conservative antigovernment trend. The importance of accountability was dramatically brought home in 1991 when the governor and the legislature agreed that no budget would be forthcoming for the 1992–93 biennium until all state functions were audited to determine whether money was being wasted. This effort, led by Comptroller John Sharp, received attention nationwide and was instrumental in a similar effort—the National Performance Review chaired by Vice President Al Gore—by the Clinton administration. Citizen demand for accountability and government response to it illustrate that both citizens and elective officials play a role in harnessing the administrative state.

How Much Accountability to the Chief Executive?

It would seem logical to make the bureaucracy accountable to the governor, the chief executive and nominal head of the state administration. But the governor's powers were intentionally limited to avoid centralizing governmental power in any one office. For example:

1. Appointment powers are restricted and removal powers are limited.
2. There is no true executive budget.
3. The executive is fragmented: Four departments, a major commission, and a major board are headed by elected officials, and many separate agencies deal

with related functional areas—over thirty policy-making boards are involved in the area of education alone.

Even if there were to be a complete reorganization of the executive branch, including the creation of consolidated departments headed by officials who constituted a governor's cabinet such as thirty-nine other states have, the sheer size and diversity of the bureaucracy, coupled with other demands on the governor's time and staff, would make executive control loose and indirect. Just as it is difficult to hold a president responsible for the actions of a Social Security clerk in Laramie, Wyoming, so also would it be difficult to hold a governor responsible for the actions of a college professor in Canyon or a welfare caseworker in El Paso.

Nevertheless, stronger supervisory control would allow the governor to exercise greater influence over major policy decisions. With a consolidated executive branch, unencumbered by elected administrators, and with managerial control over the state budget, the chief executive would have more hope of implementing policy. The advantage of a strong chief executive as the head of a more truly hierarchical structure of administration would be that overall responsibility would be vested in a highly visible elected official who could not so easily be dominated by special interests.

How Much Accountability to the Legislature?

Legislative Oversight. Legislatures traditionally have been guardians of the public interests with powers to oversee administrative agencies. These powers include budgetary control, the postaudit of agency expenditures to ensure their legality, programmatic control through the statutes, investigation of alleged wrongdoing, and impeachment of officials. Although traditional **legislative oversight** is somewhat effective in Texas, several factors militate against its total success. One is the tripartite relationship among legislators, bureaucrats, and special interest groups. Legislators may be reluctant to ruffle the feathers of groups that supply them with campaign contributions by pressing their oversight vigorously. These groups, in turn, often have strong connections to the bureaucracy. Another is the high turnover of legislative committee personnel. A third is the lack of ongoing supervision because legislators are on the job only part time as a result of Texas's short biennial legislative sessions. Much of the burden of oversight falls on the Legislative Budget Board, the Legislative Council, and the Legislative Audit Committee, although none of these has sufficient staff or time to do a thorough job, and none are well known to the general public.

A substitute for direct legislative oversight is legislation that micromanages an agency or set of agencies and requires some other agency to be the control force. A specific example is the highly specific legislation passed in the 1997 session that dictates the core curriculum, the admission standards, and the maximum number of credit hours at publicly assisted colleges and universities. The Texas Higher Education Coordinating Board was put in charge of enforcing these statutes.

Sunset Act. With the passage of the *Sunset Act* by the 65th Legislature in 1977, Texas established a procedure for reviewing the existence of all statutory boards, commissions, and departments—except colleges and universities—on a periodic basis. More than 200 agencies and advisory committees are included, and new ones are added as they are created. These reviews are conducted by a ten-member Sunset Advisory Commission made up of four senators and four representatives appointed by their respective presiding officers, who also appoint two citizen members. The chairmanship rotates between the House and the Senate every two years. The commission can determine the list of agencies to be reviewed before the beginning of each regular legislative session so long as all agencies are evaluated within a twelve-year period. The agencies must submit self-evaluation reports, and the commission coordinates its information gathering with other agencies that monitor state agencies on a regular basis, such as the Legislative Budget Board, legislative committees, and the offices of the state auditor, governor, and comptroller. After the sunset review, the legislature must explicitly vote to continue an agency, and it also may reorganize the agency or force it to modify its administrative rules and procedures.

At the end of the 1999 legislative session,[20] the sunset process had resulted in the following:

- Public membership on state boards and more public participation
- Stronger prohibitions against conflicts of interest
- Improved enforcement processes
- Elimination of overlap and duplication
- Abolition of twenty-nine agencies
- Abolition of eleven agencies, with functions transferred to other agencies
- Merger of nine agencies
- Approximately $621 million in savings and increased revenues to the state since inception of the sunset process

The Sunset Commission's 2001 agenda includes a mixed bag of twenty-five agencies and programs ranging from the Child Support Enforcement program in the attorney general's office to the General Services Commission to the natural resource and economic development agencies.

A continuing sunset issue is the several dozen quasi-state entities, such as the Texas High Speed Rail Authority, various river authorities such as the Lower Colorado River Authority, task forces, councils, and special districts. The concern is that they enjoy citizen support as public agencies but act with the independence of private organizations because they do not depend on general appropriations revenue. Support for including these entities in sunset review and/or in general state financial and performance audits has been slow to build.

How Much Accountability to the Public?

Elective Accountability.   Our government is based on the premise that it will be accountable to the people it governs. If accountability cannot be achieved directly by having all citizens of a political division meet to vote directly on laws and policies, theoretically it can be achieved through representatives who meet in government and report back to their citizen-constituents. But given the vast bureaucracy and the difficulty encountered by voters who try to make intelligent decisions regarding the

---

20. Sunset Advisory Commission, *Summary of Sunset Legislation, 76th Legislature, 1999,* available at www.sunset.state.tx.us/sunset/76.htm.

multitude of names on the long ballot in Texas, the elective process has become an unsatisfactory method of ensuring responsible administrative action. Long ballots tend to lead to confusion, not accountability, and once in office incumbents can usually count on being reelected simply because the voters recognize their names.

In view of these problems, Texas citizens need some way to check on the activities of particular administrators (and their agencies) on whom public attention, for whatever reason, is focused. Until the passage of the three acts described below, there was no ready way to gain the necessary information.

Open Records and Meetings.   Under the *Texas Open Records Act,* originally passed in 1973, the public, including the media, has access to a wide variety of official records and to most public meetings of state and local agencies. Sometimes called "sunshine" legislation because it forces agencies to shed light on their deliberations and procedures, this act is seen as a way to prevent or expose bureaucratic ineptitude, corruption, and unnecessary secrecy. An agency that denies access to information that is listed as an open record in the statute may have to defend its actions to the attorney general and even in court.

The 1987 *Open Meetings Act* strengthened public access to information by requiring governmental bodies to certify that discussions held in executive sessions were legal or to tape-record closed meetings. Closed meetings are permitted when sensitive issues such as real estate transactions or personnel actions are under consideration, but the agency must post an agenda in advance and submit it to the secretary of state, indicating what items will be discussed in closed session. Since 1981, the legislature also has required state agencies to write rules and regulations in understandable language. In recent years, the Texas Open Records Act has been frequently amended to permit exceptions. For example, many search committees looking for city managers, executive directors of agencies, and college presidents were being foiled by premature disclosure of the names of individuals they were considering and sought some protection from the act.

In 1999, the legislature strengthened open meetings provisions by placing firm restrictions on staff briefings that could be made before governing bodies at the state and local level. Two new types of exceptions emerged from the 76th Legislature—economic development and utilities deregulation—but these were seen as protections

Although most of the agencies abolished through the sunset process, such as the Pink Bollworm Commission, had outlived their usefulness, the State Board of Dental Examiners was eliminated in 1993 when the legislature failed to pass the statute authorizing its renewal. Its function of testing and licensing dentists and other dental personnel was taken over by the Texas Department of Health for two years until the dental board was recreated.

on behalf of the public when a government was in a competitive situation.[21] That is, while Texas government became even more open following the 1999 session, governments were allowed to have closed meetings when competitive issues were the topic of discussion.

Whistleblower Protection.   The 1983 legislature passed an act affording job security to state employees who spot illegal or unethical conduct in their agency and report it to appropriate officials. The national government established the precedent for "whistleblower" legislation in 1978. The term *whistleblower* comes from the fact that employees who report illegal acts are "blowing the whistle" on someone. The implementation of this act has not been promising, however. One spectacular case in which a whistleblower was fired from the Department of Human Services took five years to resolve.

SUMMARY

Although fairly well paid and endowed with a four-year term, the governor of Texas is still a constitutionally weak state officer, and the successful approval and implementation of the governor's budgetary and programmatic policies depend more on the incumbent's adroitness in developing leadership and political skills than on his or her formal powers. Although certain gubernatorial roles are strong, such as legislative, regional planning, and law enforcement powers, the governor is noticeably weak as a chief executive. The executive role is limited by:

1. Five other elected executives and two elected policy boards
2. Fragmentation resulting from the fact that the state bureaucracy is controlled by multimember boards and commissions
3. Restrictions on appointments and removals of state officials
4. The dual budget system

Since the governor's ability to control the bureaucracy is limited, we must look to other devices to control big government in Texas. Three recent measures—the Open Records Act, the Open Meetings Act, and the Whistleblower Act—have made strides in the direction of giving Texas citizens a responsible bureaucracy. These statutes are augmented by such traditional controls as the legislative audit and the legislature's power to investigate bureaucratic activities. Legislative control has also been bolstered by the Sunset Act.

Nevertheless, the fragmented nature of state administration allows bureaucrats considerable leeway to apply their own priorities in carrying out legislative mandates. The most obvious suggestions for reform would require consolidating agencies with similar functions in a single department headed by a single executive who reports to the governor. The result would be a cabinet system similar to those used by the national government and many other states. The new departments might include the following:

- Public and Higher Education
- Health and Human Services

21. See Alan J. Bojorquez, "New Open Government Legislation," *Texas Town & City* (October 1999): 11–14.

- Natural Resources
- Highways and Public Transportation
- Public Safety and Criminal Justice
- Commerce and Economic Development
- Administrative Services
- Professional and Occupational Licensing

Chapters Ten and Eleven cover the state budget and major policy issues in Texas. Together they provide a picture of state elected officials and state administration in action.

STUDY QUESTIONS

1. What are the formal qualifications to be governor of Texas? What personal characteristics do governors tend to have? Do you think any of the personal characteristics are likely to change soon? Why?
2. Why do you think many analysts regard chief legislator as the governor's most significant role?
3. What are the five types of policymakers in Texas administrative agencies? What do each of the elected executives and the two elected commissions do?
4. What are the sources of bureaucratic power? How are bureaucrats involved in the policy process?
5. What devices are available to both elected officials and the public to keep the bureaucracy in check?

SURFING THE WEB

The home page of the Texas governor.
   www.governor.state.tx.us

Information on the various divisions of the governor's office.
   www.governor.state.tx.us/office/index.html

The fast way to locate all state agencies and their home pages.
   www.state.tx.us/agency/agencies.html

A thorough look at the sunset process.
   www.sunset.state.tx.us

8

*I*f I asked you to design a criminal justice system and you came up with one like we have here in Texas, we'd have to commit you to Austin State Hospital because you'd be a danger to yourself and society.

Jim Mattox
Attorney General of Texas, 1988

The law, in its majestic impartiality, forbids the rich as well as the poor to sleep under bridges, to beg in the streets, and to steal bread.

Anatole France (Jacques Thibault)
French Nobel Prize–winning writer
Le Lys Rouge, 1894

THE JUDICIARY AND THE SYSTEM OF JUSTICE

INTRODUCTION

All over the United States, courts and the system of justice they administer are in distress. Texas's problems are among the more acute. In addition to many other ills, the state suffers from judicial inefficiency, high crime rates, a system of financing judge's campaigns that invites corruption, long delays in court proceedings, and unequal treatment of richer and poorer citizens.

Partly, these problems are caused by the high levels of lawlessness in American society (especially the traffic in illegal drugs) and are not the fault of Texas government. Partly, they are the result of a state judicial system that is chaotically organized and lacks the resources necessary to deliver as much justice to the poor as to the rich. Policymakers have attempted to address several of these problems over the course of the 1990s and have made some progress. Overall, however, both courts and the system of justice in Texas remain deeply troubled.

The first topic of this chapter will be an examination of the organization of the judiciary, followed by a look at its most serious problems. Next will come a description of some of the players in the judicial system. Last will be a consideration of the substance of the justice it produces. As the discussion proceeds, it will include evaluations of the Texas system of justice according to the ideal of democratic government.

THE JUDICIARY

Judiciary is a collective term that refers to both courts and judges. The judiciary derives its unique power not only from its reputation for wisdom and detachment but from its formal functions as final arbiter of the meaning and application of federal and state constitutions. It also interprets and applies all statutory law, settles many private disputes, punishes criminals, and awards damages in civil cases.

A Court System in Disarray

In 1973, the Texas Chief Justice's Task Force for Court Improvement wrote:

> The Texas Constitution prescribes the basic organizational structure of the Texas court system. That structure is essentially the same today as it was under the republic of Texas. The rigidity of the constitutional structure has led to the development, of necessity, of *one of the most complex and fragmented judicial systems of all the states.*[1]

Eighteen years later, the Texas Research League opened its study of the state's court system with the words:

> The Texas judiciary is in disarray with the courts in varying parts of the state going their own way at their own pace. . . . Texas does not have a *court system* in the real sense of the word.[2]

---

1. *Justice at the Crossroads: Court Improvement in Texas* (Austin: Chief Justice's Task Force for Court Improvement, 1972), 11.

2. *Texas Courts: A Study by the Texas Research League,* Report 2: "The Texas Judiciary: A Proposal for Structural-Functional Reform" (Austin: Texas Research League, 1991), xi.

These highly critical conclusions are typical. As the quote from Jim Mattox that begins this chapter attests, almost anyone who has looked closely at the state judicial system has been disheartened by its tangle of mixed jurisdictions, competing authorities, and inefficient allocation of resources. To present its organization in a textbook is almost inevitably to create more system on paper than exists in reality. Readers should keep this caveat in mind.

Texas State Courts

The following sections present a brief description of Texas's system of 2,570 courts and 3,024 judges from its lowest to its highest levels (see Figure 8.1).[3]

Municipal Courts.   City courts are authorized by the state constitution and by state laws to handle minor criminal matters involving a fine of $500 or less with no possibility of imprisonment (Class C misdemeanors), where jurisdiction is concurrent with justice of the peace courts. They also have **exclusive jurisdiction** over municipal ordinances and can impose fines of up to $2,000. Municipal courts have no **civil jurisdiction** and deal mainly with violations of traffic laws. Judges in these courts receive their salaries, which are highly variable, entirely from the city. In fiscal 1999, there were 1,126 municipal court judges who disposed of 6,933,398 cases.

Justice of the Peace (JP) Courts.   These are **original trial courts** with both civil and **criminal jurisdiction.** JP courts deal with misdemeanor criminal cases when the potential punishment is only a fine. They have exclusive jurisdiction over civil cases where the amount in controversy is $200 or less and **concurrent jurisdiction** with both county and district courts when the amount is at least $200 but less than $5,000. JPs also act as judges of small claims courts, as notaries public, and, like other Texas judges, are authorized to perform marriages. In all but the largest counties they may function as coroners, and in this role they may be required to certify cause of death, despite the fact that few if any JPs have any medical training.

Justices of the peace are elected by the voters of the precinct and, like other county officials, serve for four years. Salaries range from practically nothing to over $60,000 per year, depending on the size of the precinct, the volume of activity, and the generosity of the county commissioners. Texas's 838 JP courts disposed of 2,198,716 criminal cases and 198,461 civil cases in the fiscal year ending August 31, 1999.

County Courts.   The Texas Constitution requires each county to have a *court of record,* that is, a court where a complete transcript is made of each case. Judges of these 254 "constitutional" courts need not be lawyers but only "well-informed in the law of the state." Elected for four-year terms, they receive their salaries from the counties, and these salaries are highly variable. In the late 1990s, Harris was the most generous county, compensating its judges at a rate of more than $100,000 per year. At the other end of the scale, Motley County paid its judges only a little over $10,000. Vacancies are filled by appointments made by the county commissioners' court.

3. All information on Texas state courts in this section as of September 1, 1999 comes from *Annual Report of the Texas Judicial System For Fiscal Year 1999* (Austin: Office of Court Administration, 1999).

FIGURE 8.1

Court Structure of Texas

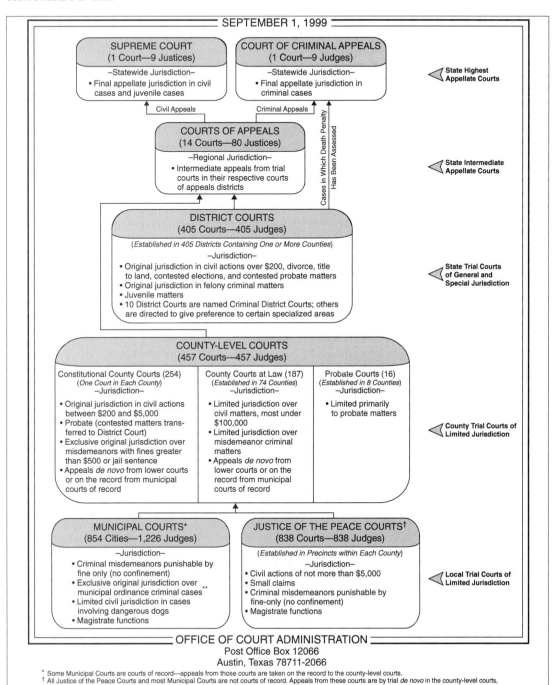

SEPTEMBER 1, 1999

SUPREME COURT
(1 Court—9 Justices)
–Statewide Jurisdiction–
• Final appellate jurisdiction in civil cases and juvenile cases

COURT OF CRIMINAL APPEALS
(1 Court—9 Judges)
–Statewide Jurisdiction–
• Final appellate jurisdiction in criminal cases

State Highest Appellate Courts

Civil Appeals   Criminal Appeals

COURTS OF APPEALS
(14 Courts—80 Justices)
–Regional Jurisdiction–
• Intermediate appeals from trial courts in their respective courts of appeals districts

State Intermediate Appellate Courts

Cases in Which Death Penalty Has Been Assessed

DISTRICT COURTS
(405 Courts—405 Judges)
(Established in 405 Districts Containing One or More Counties)
–Jurisdiction–
• Original jurisdiction in civil actions over $200, divorce, title to land, contested elections, and contested probate matters
• Original jurisdiction in felony criminal matters
• Juvenile matters
• 10 District Courts are named Criminal District Courts; others are directed to give preference to certain specialized areas

State Trial Courts of General and Special Jurisdiction

COUNTY-LEVEL COURTS
(457 Courts—457 Judges)

Constitutional County Courts (254)
(One Court in Each County)
–Jurisdiction–

• Original jurisdiction in civil actions between $200 and $5,000
• Probate (contested matters transferred to District Court)
• Exclusive original jurisdiction over misdemeanors with fines greater than $500 or jail sentence
• Appeals *de novo* from lower courts or on the record from municipal courts of record

County Courts at Law (187)
(Established in 74 Counties)
–Jurisdiction–

• Limited jurisdiction over civil matters, most under $100,000
• Limited jurisdiction over misdemeanor criminal matters
• Appeals *de novo* from lower courts or on the record from municipal courts of record

Probate Courts (16)
(Established in 8 Counties)
–Jurisdiction–

• Limited primarily to probate matters

County Trial Courts of Limited Jurisdiction

MUNICIPAL COURTS*
(854 Cities—1,226 Judges)
–Jurisdiction–
• Criminal misdemeanors punishable by fine only (no confinement)
• Exclusive original jurisdiction over municipal ordinance criminal cases**
• Limited civil jurisdiction in cases involving dangerous dogs
• Magistrate functions

JUSTICE OF THE PEACE COURTS†
(838 Courts—838 Judges)
(Established in Precincts within Each County)
–Jurisdiction–
• Civil actions of not more than $5,000
• Small claims
• Criminal misdemeanors punishable by fine-only (no confinement)
• Magistrate functions

Local Trial Courts of Limited Jurisdiction

OFFICE OF COURT ADMINISTRATION
Post Office Box 12066
Austin, Texas 78711-2066

* Some Municipal Courts are courts of record—appeals from those courts are taken on the record to the county-level courts.
† All Justice of the Peace Courts and most Municipal Courts are not courts of record. Appeals from these courts are by trial *de novo* in the county-level courts, and in some instances in the district courts.
**An offense that arises under a municipal ordinance is punishable by a fine not to exceed: (1) $2,000 for ordinances that govern the safety, zoning, and public health; or (2) $500 for all others.

County courts have both **original** and **appellate jurisdiction** in civil and criminal cases. Original jurisdiction extends to all criminal misdemeanors where the fine allowed exceeds $500 or a jail term may be imposed. County courts also hear appeals in criminal cases from either JP or municipal courts. In civil matters constitutional county courts share *concurrent jurisdiction* with JP courts when the amount in controversy is between $200 and $5,000.

The volume of cases in eighty-two of the state's larger counties has moved the legislature to establish a number of specialized county courts, with jurisdiction that varies according to the statute under which they were created. Some exercise jurisdiction in only civil, criminal, probate, or appellate fields, while others are in effect extra, generalist county courts. Judges for these "statutory county courts" must be attorneys.

Appellate jurisdiction from the decisions of county courts rests with the courts of appeals. County courts disposed of 111,909 civil, 774,252 criminal, and 8,094 juvenile cases in fiscal year 1999.

State Trial Courts: The District Courts.   In Texas, district trial courts are the principal trial courts in the state. There were 405 of these busy courts as of 1999. Each has a numerical designation—for example, the 353rd District Court—and each court has one judge. Most district courts exercise both criminal and civil jurisdiction, but in the metropolitan areas there is a tendency for each court to specialize in either criminal, civil, or family law cases.

District court judges must be attorneys who are licensed to practice in the state and have at least four years' experience as lawyers or judges prior to being elected to the district court bench. The basic salary of $101,700 paid by the state is supplemented by an additional sum in most counties. Terms are for four years, with all midterm vacancies being filled by gubernatorial appointment.

Cases handled by district court judges are varied. They usually have jurisdiction over felony criminal trials, divorce cases, suits over titles to land, election contests, and civil suits in which the amount in controversy is at least $200. They share some of their civil jurisdiction with county courts, depending on the relevant state statute and the amount of money at issue.

District court cases are appealed to a court of appeals, except for death penalty criminal cases, where appeal is made directly to the Court of Criminal Appeals. In fiscal year 1999, district courts disposed of 454,175 civil, 210,494 criminal, and 35,909 juvenile cases.

Intermediate State Appellate Courts: The Courts of Appeals.   The courts of appeals have intermediate civil and criminal **appellate jurisdiction.** Unlike the lower courts, appellate courts—the courts of appeals, the Court of Criminal Appeals, and the Supreme Court—are multijudge courts that operate without juries. Appellate courts consider only the written records of lower-court proceedings and the arguments of counsel representing the parties involved.

Texas's fourteen courts of appeals, each of which is responsible for a geographical district, have from three to thirteen justices per court for a total of eighty justices statewide. In each court the justices may hear cases *en banc* (together) or in panels of three. All decisions are by majority vote. Justices are elected for staggered six-year terms and must have the same qualifications as justices of the state's Supreme Court: Each must be at least 35 years of age and have ten years' legal experience either as practicing attorney or practicing attorney and judge of a court of record. Associate justices receive an annual salary of $107,350 and the chief justice, elected as such, receives $107,850. Within each district, counties are authorized to supplement the basic salary up to $1,000 less than the salary of judges of the highest state appellate courts.

Jurisdiction of the courts of appeals consists of civil cases appealed from district courts, county courts, and county courts at law, and of criminal cases, except for capital murder, appealed from lower courts. They both review the decisions of lower judges and evaluate the constitutionality of the statute or ordinance on which the conviction is based. Decisions of the courts of appeals are usually final, but some may be reviewed by the Court of Criminal Appeals or the Texas Supreme Court. The courts of appeals disposed of 5,255 civil and 7,895 criminal cases in fiscal year 1999.

Highest State Appellate Courts.   Among the states only Texas and Oklahoma have split their highest appellate jurisdiction between two courts: a *supreme court* that hears only civil cases and a *court of criminal appeals* for criminal cases. Each has responsibility not only for reviewing the decisions made by lower trial judges, but for interpreting and applying the state constitution. It is this last power of constitutional interpretation that makes each supreme court of vital political importance.

The Court of Criminal Appeals.   This is the state's final appeals court in criminal matters, although in rare instances its decisions may be appealed to the U.S. Supreme Court. It considers *writs of error,* filed by losing attorneys who contend that their trial judge made a mistake in applying Texas law and who wish to have the verdict

The task of interpreting laws may seem grand and noble, and often it is. But laws, as with all other works of humanity, are sometimes nonsensical. Imagine what you would do if you were asked to judge someone accused of breaking one of the following laws, which actually existed in Texas in the twentieth century:

1. At one time it was illegal to own a copy of the *Encyclopedia Brittanica* in the state—because it contained a formula for making liquor.
2. There was a law that prescribed that when two trains met at a railroad crossing, each had to come to a full stop, and neither could proceed until the other had gone.
3. The town of Princeton outlawed onion throwing.
4. In Clarendon, it was forbidden to dust any public building with a feather duster.
5. El Paso made it a crime to throw a faded bouquet into a trash can.
6. A law in Madisonville required persons to own at least two cows before they were permitted to tuck their trouser legs into their boot tops.

SOURCE: Dick Hyman, *The Trenton Pickle Ordinance and Other Bonehead Legislation* (Lexington, MA: Stephen Green Press, 1976), 2, 34, 44, 52, 80, 106).

overturned, and *writs of habeus corpus,* in which attorneys claim that a certain person has been unlawfully detained and should be released. It also creates rules of evidence and procedure in criminal trials. In fiscal year 1999, this court disposed of 377 cases in the process writing 798 opinions.

Qualifications for judges of the Court of Criminal Appeals and the justices of the Supreme Court are the same as for justices of the courts of appeals. The nine judges of the Court of Criminal Appeals are elected on a statewide basis for six-year staggered terms, and the presiding judge runs as such. Vacancies are filled by gubernatorial appointment. Cases are normally heard by a three-judge panel. The salary is $113,000 per year, with the presiding judge receiving $115,000.

The Supreme Court.   Like its counterpart at the national level, the Texas Supreme Court is the most prestigious court in the system. Unlike its national counterpart, it hears appeals only from civil and juvenile cases.

Qualifications for Supreme Court justices are the same as for the judges of the courts of appeals and Court of Criminal Appeals. There are nine justices on the bench, including a chief justice who campaigns for election as such. All are elected for six-year staggered terms, three justices elected every two years. Salaries are the same as for the Court of Criminal Appeals.

The Supreme Court has no authority in criminal cases. Its original jurisdiction is limited, and most cases that it hears are on appeal from the courts of appeals. Its caseload is somewhat lighter than other state courts, and it disposed of only 118 cases in fiscal 1999, in the process writing 165 opinions.

However, the Supreme Court also performs other important functions. It is empowered to issue *writs of mandamus*—orders to corporations or persons, including judges or other state officials, except the governor, to perform certain acts. Like the Court of Criminal Appeals, it spends much time considering applications for *writs of error,* which allege that the courts of appeals have wrongfully ruled on a point of law. It creates rules of evidence and procedure for civil courts, formulates codes of judicial behavior and conducts proceedings for removal of unfit judges, and makes administrative rules for all civil courts in the state.

The state Supreme Court also plays a unique role for the legal profession in Texas. It holds the power of approval for new schools of law; it appoints the Board of Law Examiners, which prepares the bar examination; it determines who has passed the exam; and it certifies the successful applicants as being entitled to practice law in Texas. It also supervises the State Bar of Texas and creates rules of operation for the Court Reporters Certification Board.

Salaries for Supreme Court justices are the same as for justices of the Court of Criminal Appeals.

THE COURTS UNDER PRESSURE

There is a common perception among observers of Texas government that its courts are inadequate, that they have lost the confidence of the population, and that they are on the brink of functional breakdown. Partly, this perception is caused by the fact that the complex, ambiguous, inefficient court structure does not make for swift and sure arbitration of society's conflicts. As important, however, are two other problems: the overwhelming caseload in the criminal justice system and the impact of campaign contributions on judicial decisions.

Too Much Crime, Too Many Criminals

Even if the Texas court system were perfectly organized, it would still be having major problems. There are simply too many accused criminals being arrested for any system to handle. From 1982 to 1992, the state's crime rate increased 12 percent; its citizens suffered through 44,583 robberies, 9,425 rapes, 86,106 aggravated assaults, and 2,239 murders in the latter year.[4] Throughout the rest of the 1990s, however, the crime rate declined. By 1998, even with an overall increase in population, the state's total numbers of murders and robberies had dropped by more than 36 percent in six years, its number of rapes 16 percent, and its number of assaults 14 percent. Nevertheless, even with fewer overall crimes, there were still enough offenses to cause the police to make 1,099,094 arrests in 1998.[5]

Something had to be done with all those accused criminals. Despite the drop in crime, Texas's 3,024 judges could not keep up with over a million yearly arrests. Although the legislature has created new courts, there are still not enough to make justice move efficiently.

In Harris County (Houston), for example, in October 1993 there were 219 capital murder cases pending for trial. Since there are twenty-two felony courts in Harris County, and each capital murder trial lasts about six weeks, it would have taken over a year to clear the county's docket, assuming that no new murders were committed in the meantime. Also, of course, while a murder trial is proceeding, the courtroom could not be used for anything else, so the backlog of nonmurder felony trials would grow huge while the county waited for the murder trials to end.[6]

Given this impossible situation, judges do what they can to keep the system functioning by accepting "plea bargains." A defendant pleads guilty to a lesser charge—say, manslaughter instead of murder—receives a lesser penalty (less time in prison, or a probated sentence), and a trial is avoided. More than nine out of ten criminal trials in Texas end in a plea bargain.[7] Since this agreement puts the criminal back on the streets quickly, it does almost nothing to make society safer. Ordinary citizens are often appalled at the swiftness with which violent criminals are recycled into their neighborhoods, but the courts cannot handle the problem of a crushing caseload any other way.

In the 1990s, Texas made a determined effort to deal with the problem of rampant crime. The state borrowed more than a billion and a half dollars and began a prison-building program. As of 1999, Texas was holding about 148,000 inmates in its prison system, making it the third largest jailer in the world after Russia and China.[8]

4. *Crime in Texas 1992* (Austin: Texas Department of Public Safety, Crime Records Division, 1993), 14, 63.

5. *Crime in Texas 1998* (Austin: Texas Department of Public Safety, Crime Records Division, 1996), 10.

6. "Capital Murder Cases Swamp Harris County Courts," *Dallas Morning News*, October 25, 1993, 12A.

7. *Texas Crime, Texas Justice* (Austin: Comptroller's Office, 1994), 51.

8. "Political Intelligence," *Texas Observer*, September 17, 1999, 17.

Whether because so many of the state's criminals are behind bars instead of out on the street, or for other reasons, the crime rate has declined. For many years Texas had the second highest rate among all the states, after Louisiana. By the late 1990s, however, the Texas crime rate had dropped to 13th among the states—not good, but still an improvement.[9]

Is Justice for Sale?

The second major public relations problem faced by the judicial system is the perception that many judges can be corrupted by campaign contributions. Unlike the situation in most states, where judges are appointed, in Texas they are elected. This practice is in line with democratic theory. Like legislators and executives, judges are government officials, and like them, they presumably serve the people. But when judges have to run for office like other politicians, it means that they also have to raise money like others. When lawyers who practice in the courtrooms of judges or others with a direct interest in the outcome of legal cases give them campaign contributions, it raises the uncomfortable suspicion that those judges' court rulings may be affected by the money. Wealthy private interests may taint the administration of justice just as they deform the public policy made by other institutions.

The possible corruption of justice is not just a theoretical problem. Texas and Alabama have the most expensive judicial races in the country.[10] Some individual law firms have contributed more than $100,000 to a single judicial candidate.[11] And some examples raise the strong suspicion that such donations have induced judges to commit improprieties.

Perhaps the most famous instance was a mammoth suit filed by Pennzoil in 1986 against Texaco. Claiming that Texaco had interfered with its takeover of Getty Oil, Pennzoil went to court, demanding $11 billion in compensation.

The trial lawyer hired by Pennzoil, Joe Jamail, gave District Judge Anthony Farris a $10,000 campaign contribution *after* Farris had been assigned to the case, and Farris then enlisted Jamail to raise $50,000 more. Farris subsequently ruled several times during the trial in favor of Jamail and Pennzoil, and they won the case, being awarded the largest judgment for damages in history. Texaco appealed, but the Texas Supreme Court refused to hear the case. Attorneys for both oil firms had contributed to members of the Court, but Jamail and Pennzoil's corporate lawyers had been much more generous, giving them more than $300,000 in 1986 alone. "The appearance," observed state senator Frank Tejada, chair of the Jurisprudence Committee, "is that perhaps justice is for sale." Indeed, the appearance was strong enough to bring critical attention from the national press, including a segment on the television program *60 Minutes*.

Responding to the public perception that justice might be for sale, in 1995 the legislature passed the Judicial Campaign Fairness Act (JCFA). This legislation limited individual contributions to statewide judicial candidates to $5,000 each election and

---

9. Kendra A. Hovey and Harold A. Hovey, *CQ's State Fact Finder, 1999: Rankings across America*, (Washington, DC: Congressional Quarterly Press, 1999), 248.

10. Laura Castaneda, "D.C. Worst, Utah Best on Litigious List," *Dallas Morning News*, January 3, 1994, 1D.

11. Lloyd Doggett, "Judicial Campaign Fairness Act Essential," *Austin American-Statesman*, May 26, 1993, 17A.

As this cartoon by Ben Sargent attests, the Texas public is skeptical that judges who take large campaign contributions from lawyers can render impartial verdicts.

SOURCE: Courtesy of Ben Sargent.

prohibited law firms from contributing more than $30,000 to individual Supreme Court candidates. Judicial candidates were also forbidden to accept more than $300,000 from all political action committees.

Although the intent of the JCFA was clearly to stop the contamination of the Texas judiciary by money, events almost immediately proved it to be ineffective. In 1996,

In 1988 the New York State Commission on Government Integrity made a thorough survey of methods of selecting state and local judges. In concluded that

1. There is "no persuasive evidence correlating systems of judicial selection with the quality and integrity of judges."
2. An appointive system does not "necessarily produce more qualified judges nor fewer corrupt ones."

In short, there is no proof that the way Texas chooses its judges is an unusually bad way, or that some other way would be better.

SOURCE: Frank D. O'Connor, "New York Should Continue to Elect Its Judges," *New York Times*, June 11, 1988, 14.

Justice James A. Baker of the Supreme Court allowed an attorney with a case pending before him to participate in his fundraising efforts.[12] When journalists reported this obvious conflict of interest, the bad publicity forced Baker to withdraw from the case. His withdrawal solved the immediate concern about one questionable case, but it did not address the basic problem. As long as attorneys are allowed to raise campaign funds for judges, there will be public doubts about the impartiality of the judiciary. The JCFA, while it was well intentioned, does not address this fundamental problem.

THE PLAYERS IN THE SYSTEM OF JUSTICE

The judiciary is part of an entire system that attempts to interpret and apply society's laws. A brief summary of the parts of this system, and some of its subject matter, follows.

The Attorney General (AG)

Over the years the attorney general has developed an unusual and highly significant power, the authority to issue **advisory opinions.** The constitution establishes the attorney general as Texas's chief legal officer and as legal adviser to the governor and other state officials. The legislature later expanded the scope of the AG's advisory activity. Out of this expansion has arisen the now firmly established practice that the legislature, as well as the agencies of the executive branch, will seek advice on the constitutionality of legislative proposals, rules, procedures, and statutes. In 1998, Attorney General Dan Morales handed down 164 "Letter Opinions," dealing with the constitutionality of proposed government laws or actions and his office issued 3,347 rulings that applied the Open Records Act to specific circumstances.[13]

Rather than filing a court action that is expensive and time consuming, Texas officials who go to the attorney general obtain a ruling on disputed constitutional issues in a relatively brief period of time and at almost no expense. The Texas judiciary and virtually everyone else in the state have come to accept these rulings, albeit sometimes with a good deal of grumbling.

The most publicized attorney general's ruling of recent years, and perhaps in history, dealt with the divisive subject of affirmative action. For some years prior to 1996, the University of Texas Law school had been favoring African-American and Latino applicants in its admissions process—that is, minority applicants were judged by a lower set of standards than were Anglo applicants. An Anglo woman, Cheryl Hopwood, had been turned down for admission to the law school despite the fact that her qualifications (grades and Law School Aptitude Test scores) were higher than those of some minority applicants who had been admitted. Hopwood sued in federal court. In 1996, the fifth circuit federal appeals court ruled in Hopwood's favor, deciding that such "reverse discrimination" against Anglos was unconstitutional.[14]

12. This is not the same James Baker who was Secretary of State under the administration of President George Bush and who is now a Houston attorney.

13. Texas Attorney General's Office, September 1999.

14. *Hopwood v. State of Texas,* 78 F. 3rd 932 (5th Circuit, 1996).

The fifth circuit court's decision was significant as it stood because it applied to the state's premier law school. Nevertheless, its scope did not extend to other schools. On February 5, 1997, however, Attorney General Dan Morales dismayed Texas's university community by issuing Letter Opinion 97-001, in which he decreed that the federal court's ruling had outlawed race as a consideration in any admissions process or financial aid decision at any public school. Affirmative action was therefore forbidden in all Texas public colleges.[15]

In September 1999, however, Morales's successor as attorney general, John Cornyn, issued another opinion that called Morales's ruling too broad and rescinded it. Cornyn stopped short of actually claiming that Morales's reasoning was wrong, merely stating that colleges should wait and see how an appeal of the Hopwood decision to the U.S. Supreme Court turned out.[16]

In other words, in one of the most important and intensely conflict-ridden issues in Texas, public policy is being set not by the state legislature, or the governor, but the attorney general. Such is the power of this institution in state government.

Lawyers

As it is in the rest of the country, the legal profession is a growth industry in Texas. In the fall of 1999, the state was home to 73,956 attorneys and was adding them at the rate of about 3,200 each year.[17]

The legal profession differs substantially in socioeconomic and other characteristics from the population in general. Most lawyers are white males who come from relatively wealthy families. In 1999, 23 percent of Texas lawyers were women, 3.5 percent were African American, and 5 percent were Hispanic. As is the case in many other areas of American life, however, the pool of attorneys is presently being broadened to be more diverse in its ethnic and gender background.

The State Bar of Texas

All lawyers who practice within the state are required to maintain membership in the State Bar and pay annual dues. The State Bar occupies a unique position: It is an agency of government, a professional organization, and an influential interest group active in state politics.

Judges

Even more than the legal profession as a whole, judges of the state courts have constituted an elite group. Until relatively recently, they were almost exclusively white males from middle- and upper-middle-class families who were members of the conservative faction of the Democratic Party. Today, however, Mexican Americans,

15. Attorney General's Letter Opinion 97-001, February 5, 1997.

16. Attorney General's Letter Opinion JC-107, September 3, 1999; Juan B. Elizondo, Jr., "Cornyn Rescinds Hopwood Opinion," *Austin American-Statesman*, September 4, 1999, A1.

17. Texas Bar Association, October 12, 1999.

African Americans, women, liberals, and Republicans are being increasingly represented on the benches of the Texas courts.

Despite having to stand for election to their seats on the bench, most Texas judges have until recently enjoyed substantial job security. Like other politicians, judges must run in partisan elections. When Texas was a one-party state (see Chapters Four and Five), all judges were Democrats, electoral defeat of an incumbent was rare, and vacancies were usually created only by the death, resignation, or retirement of the judge. Unexpired terms were then filled by appointments. State judges were and are appointed by the governor, county judges by county commissioners, and municipal judges in accordance with the provisions of individual city charters and statutes. Their comparative job security meant that judges were relatively insulated from democratic accountability compared to, say, members of the state legislature.

The rise of the Republican party to parity with the Democrats, however, has meant that judges are now no more secure in their jobs than other Texas politicians. What effect this fact might be having on their behavior on the bench is not yet clear.

In recent years a number of prominent judges and politicians have strongly criticized the state's system of partisan judicial elections and proposed that a new system be put in place. Although there are almost as many suggested reform plans as there are reformers, most involve either gubernatorial appointment of judges, nonpartisan elections, or some combination of the two. Prominent among the advocates of reform has been Tom Phillips, chief justice of the Texas Supreme Court. Many powerful Texans also endorse the system of partisan elections, however, including Governor George W. Bush. The opponents of reform argue that the present system is democratically responsive to the people's wants and therefore should be kept. It is worth noting that both Phillips and Bush are Republicans. There will be no major change in the Texas judicial system as long as the state's political establishment is thus divided.

Grand Juries

Grand juries meet in the county seat of each county and are convened as needed. Grand jurors are chosen from a list prepared by a panel of jury commissioners—three to five persons appointed by the district judge. From this list, the judge selects twelve persons who sit for a term, usually of three months' duration.

Grand jurors consider the material submitted by prosecutors to determine whether sufficient evidence exists to issue a formal indictment. Normally, the cases considered are alleged felonies—serious crimes. Occasionally persons are indicted for misdemeanors—minor crimes—as was Speaker of the House of Representatives Gib Lewis in December 1990. In Texas, grand juries are frequently used to investigate such problems as drug traffic within the community, increasing crime rates, alleged misconduct by public officials, and other subjects.

Trial Juries

Trial juries actually make decisions about right and wrong, truth and falsehood. Under Texas law, defendants in civil cases and anyone charged with a crime may demand a jury trial. While this right is frequently waived, thousands of such trials take

TABLE 8.1

Classification of Crimes in Texas, 1999

Crime	Maximum Fine or Other Penalty	Example of Offense
Class C misdemeanor	up to $500	gambling
Class B misdemeanor	up to $2,000—up to 180 days confinement	prostitution
Class A misdemeanor	up to $4,000—up to one year confinement	cruelty to animals
State jail felony	up to $10,000—180 days to two years confinement	credit card abuse
Third-degree felony	up to $10,000—two to ten years imprisonment	kidnapping
Second-degree felony	up to $10,000—two to twenty years imprisonment	arson
First-degree felony	up to $10,000—life imprisonment, or five to ninety-nine years	murder
Capital felony	life sentence or execution	murder of a peace officer

SOURCE: Marshall A. Shelsy, *Texas Law for Law Enforcement Officers: 1999* (Austin: Texas Municipal Courts Education Center; OMNI Publishers, 1999), 13–14, 22, 23, 33, 47–48, 77–78, 88.

place within the state every year. Lower-court juries consist of six people, while district court juries have twelve members. The call to duty on a trial jury is determined through the use of a jury wheel, a list generated from the county voter registration, driver's license, and state identification card lists.

Police

The state maintains an extensive organization primarily for the enforcement of criminal law. In addition to the judiciary and various planning and policy-making bodies, Texas has more than 42,000 law enforcement officers staffing state and local police agencies. Principal among these is the Texas Department of Public Safety (DPS). The DPS, with headquarters in Austin, employed 3,220 officers in 1999.[18] It is one of only eight state police agencies across the nation empowered to conduct criminal investigations.

The other law enforcement officers are employees of the 254 county sheriff's departments and more than 1,000 local police departments. Coordination and cooperation among these police agencies is sometimes haphazard and sometimes effective.

THE SUBSTANCE OF JUSTICE

The subject thus far has been an examination of the structure and personnel of the justice system. It is time to turn to some of the outputs of that system—civil liberties, civil rights, and criminal justice.

Civil Liberties and Civil Rights

By **civil liberties** are meant the basic freedoms that are essential to the survival of a democratic society—the rights to speak, write, worship, and assemble freely. The term **civil rights** refers to the rights of all citizens to fair and equal treatment under

18. Texas Department of Public Safety, October 12, 1999.

the law, including the rights of people accused of or convicted of crimes to be treated humanely. Civil rights also include electoral rights—the right to run for office and vote in honest elections.

Both the United States and Texas constitutions contain **bills of rights** that guarantee our basic freedoms, including those of speech, the press, and religion. But all constitutions have to be interpreted, and there are always disagreements about exactly what sort of activities are protected.

In regard to "freedom of speech," for example, does it include the right to plan to overthrow the government? Spout racist propaganda on a local cable TV access program? Wear a tee-shirt lettered with obscenities to high school? Publicly burn an American flag? Such questions generate disagreement among public-spirited citizens. When the disagreements lead to putting people in jail, courts are called upon to decide what bills of rights mean.

To take another example, virtually everyone believes in freedom of religion. But what, exactly, does that freedom mean? In Santa Fe (Texas, not New Mexico), a high school student prayed over a public address system prior to a football game in 1999. Was that prayer constitutional because it allowed her to exercise her right, or was it unconstitutional because it enabled her to impose her beliefs on others through official school technology? A recent Fifth U.S. Circuit Court of Appeals ruling had appeared to forbid such prayers, but a federal judge in Houston sided with the student. In 2000, the U.S. Supreme Court decided the specific case against the student and the school district, but the controversy will never die.[19]

Both the federal and state courts have intervened in Texas politics to protect civil rights and liberties. At the federal level, Judge William Wayne Justice ruled in 1980 that Texas's overcrowded prison system made it impossible to avoid subjecting prisoners to "cruel and unusual punishment," thus violating the Eighth Amendment to the U.S. Constitution. Justice, who is aptly named, virtually took over the prison system, ordering new facilities built and new rules enacted. Under Justice's guidance the prison system was greatly expanded and improved, but not enough to satisfy the judge. In 1999, he disappointed state officials by ruling that "systematic constitutional violations" remained in the manner that Texas treated its prisoners and that therefore the prisons must remain under court supervision.[20]

Historically, cultural traditions in the Old South were not particularly hospitable to civil rights and liberties. As reflections of this culture, until recently Texas courts

19. David Jackson, "High Court Rejects Pre-Game Prayer," *Dallas Morning News,* June 20, 2000, A1.

20. Mike Ward, "Courts Keep Control of Texas Prisons," *Austin American-Statesman,* March 2, 1999, A1.

Civil liberties refer to those actions that government cannot take. Civil rights refer to those actions that government must take to ensure equal citizenship for everyone.

did not much concern themselves with protecting any rights except property rights. Jim Crow laws, Black Codes, poll taxes, and other infringements of rights and liberties existed for decades undisturbed by the state judicial system. These blights on democracy were overturned by federal, not state, courts.

In the last two decades, however, the opening up of the Texas judiciary to new ideas and new people has caused a different spirit to pervade the courts, which have become more activist in this area. For example, the Texas Civil Liberties Union has successfully sued in state courts to secure a number of new rights, including workers' compensation benefits for migratory workers and protection of state employees against mandatory lie detector testing.[21] On this subject it would seem to be a new era in the Texas judicial system, and the rules of the past no longer apply.

Voting Rights

Along with its suppression of civil liberties, Texas, along with the other southern states, denied voting rights to large parts of its population for much of the twentieth century. Initially, the extension of voting rights came at the initiative of the national government, with state and local governments fighting rearguard actions. Attempts by states to keep African Americans from voting were slowly defeated by the tireless efforts of the National Association for the Advancement of Colored People (NAACP) in bringing suits in federal courts.

Two Texas cases were important in this fight to open the polls to all citizens. In 1944, in *Smith v. Allwright,* the federal courts struck down Texas's "white primary" laws that made African-American access to general elections meaningless. In 1971, highly discriminatory registration procedures were declared unconstitutional in *Beare v. Smith,* making much more open procedures possible.[22]

After such flagrant suppressions of minority voting rights were ended, the struggle over voting rights turned toward more ambiguous issues. One of the most contentious of these involved the system of electing local judges.

County judges in Texas are selected in **at-large elections,** in which all candidates receive their votes from the whole county. Such elections tend to make it difficult for minorities to be elected. If, for example, a quarter of the population of a county is Hispanic, and there is more or less bloc voting by the ethnic groups, then Hispanic candidates will be outvoted three to one every time. Although Hispanics represent 25 percent of the population, they will have zero percent of the judges.

The tendency of a political system to produce very few minority judges can be altered by instituting **district elections.** If the county is carved into a number of districts, with each district electing a single judge, then (assuming that people in different ethnic groups tend to live in different areas) the proportion of judges from each group should be roughly proportional to that group's representation in the population. If Hispanics have a quarter of the total population of the county, and a

---

21. The workers' compensation case is *Guadalupe Delgado v. State of Texas,* No. 356, 714 (District of Travis County, 147th Judicial District of Texas, modified May 22, 1985). The lie detector case is *Texas State Employees Union v. Texas Department of Mental Health and Mental Retardation,* 746 SW 2d 203, Texas, 1987.

22. 321 U.S. 649, 1944; 321 F. Supp. 1100, 1971.

quarter of the districts are largely Hispanic in population, then probably about a quarter of the elected judges will be Hispanic. Consequently, minority representatives almost always prefer district election systems over at-large systems.

In 1988, the League of United Latin American Citizens (LULAC; see Chapter Three) filed suit in federal court charging that Texas's system of electing county judges at large discriminated against minorities and thereby violated a section of the 1965 Voting Rights Act that attempted to ensure fair access to the electoral system by minorities. This case climbed step by step through the federal court system, with each level tending to reverse the ruling of the lower level. In August 1993, the Fifth U.S. Circuit Court of Appeals held that at-large elections were not discriminatory, and that therefore Texas's system could continue unchanged. In January 1994, the U.S. Supreme Court refused to hear an appeal of this ruling, thereby allowing it to stand.

Although the federal Supreme Court decision stopped the legal battle, it did not end the political struggle. Minority groups continued to press the state to change to single-member districts for judicial elections. As of the year 2000, they were not making progress with their quest but were persisting anyway.

Education—A Basic Right?

In 1987, Texas District Judge Harley Clark shocked the Texas political establishment by ruling in the case of *Edgewood v. Kirby* that the state's system of financing its public schools violated its own constitution and laws. Clark's ruling referred to Article VII, Section 1, which requires the "Legislature of the state to establish . . . an efficient system of public free schools," and part of Article 1, which asserts that "All free men . . . have equal rights." Additionally, the Texas Education Code in Section 16.001 states that "public education is a state responsibility," that "a thorough and efficient system be provided," and that "each student enrolled in the public school system shall have access to programs and services that are appropriate to his or her needs and that are substantially equal to those available to any similar student, notwithstanding varying local economic factors."

The state's educational system, however, did not begin to offer equal services to every child. During the 1985–86 school year, when the *Edgewood* case was being prepared, the wealthiest school district in Texas had $14 million in taxable property per student and the poorest district had $20,000. The Whiteface Independent School District in the Texas Panhandle taxed its property owners at $0.30 per $100 of value and spent $9,646 per student. The Morton I.S.D. just north of Whiteface taxed its

In addition to civil rights and liberties, civil law includes all types of cases that result in law suits or injunctions. For example, civil law is involved when you have a rent dispute with your landlord.

property owners at \$0.96 per \$100 evaluation, but because of the lesser value of its property was able to spend only \$3,959 per student.

Gross disparities such as these made a mockery of the constitutional and statutory requirements, as well as the demands of democratic theory, for equal educational funding. An estimated 1 million out of the state's 3 million school children were receiving inadequate instruction because their local districts could not afford to educate them.

Democracy requires only equality of opportunity, not equality of result. But inequality of education must inevitably translate into inequality of opportunity. The courts were following the dictates of democratic theory in attempting to force the rest of the political system to educate all Texas children equally.

The appropriate remedy was to transfer some revenue from wealthy to poorer districts. But given the distribution of power in the state, and especially the way it is represented in the legislature, this strategy was nearly impossible. As explained in Chapters Four and Five, because of the lack of voting participation by the state's poorer citizens, its wealthier citizens are over-represented in the legislature. Despite the fact that a badly educated citizenry was a drag on the state's economy, and therefore a problem for everyone, taxpayers in wealthier districts resisted giving up their money to educate the children of the poor in some other district. Their representatives refused to vote for some sort of revenue redistribution, regardless of what the court had said.

In October 1989, the Texas Supreme Court unanimously upheld Clark's ruling that the system was unconstitutional, and told the legislature to fix it. There followed four years of stalling, blustering, and complaining by the House and Senate. Several times the courts threw out laws that made cosmetic changes in the state's school system without addressing the central problems of unequal funding.

Finally out of evasions, in 1993 the legislature passed a law that would take about \$450 million property-tax dollars from ninety-eight high-wealth districts and give them to poor districts. In January 1995, the Texas Supreme Court upheld the new law by a bare five-to-four majority.

Although the number of dissenters on the court, plus the qualms evident in the majority opinion, suggested that the issue might not be over, one thing had become clear in eight years of litigation. The Texas judiciary, at least in this one area, had become the champion of the underdog. As will be shown in the next section, the legal system often discriminates against the poor, because there are not enough resources available to give them adequate justice. In the area of education, however, the Texas courts have somehow risen above the burdens of history and are attempting to force the people of Texas to live up to their democratic ideals.

Equal Justice?

The Texas criminal justice system does not affect all citizens equally. It imposes severe burdens on the poor and particularly on members of ethnic minorities—the same groups who are at a disadvantage in other areas of politics. Legal fees are expensive—well over \$100 per hour for most lawyers working on a case—and the system is so complex that accused people cannot defend themselves without extensive and expensive legal help.

In most Texas cities, a person charged with felony DWI or possession of drugs can expect to pay $5,000 or more for representation by a good attorney.

SOURCE: Courtesy of Ben Sargent.

The result is that the prisons, and death row, are full of poor people. Wealthier defendants can afford to hire attorneys to help them try to "beat the rap," and in any case they are often offered plea bargains that allow them to stay out of prison. But Texas lacks a system of *public defenders* to provide free legal assistance to alleged criminals who are too poor to pay a lawyer, except in the case of defendants who have been convicted of capital murder and sentenced to death. Judges, using county rather than state funds, appoint private attorneys to represent indigent defendants, but frequently these are inexperienced or already busy with paying clients.

Journalist Debbie Nathan spent time observing the way county-appointed attorneys interacted with their indigent clients. Her summary must be troubling to citizens who think that the poor, too, should be entitled to competent legal counsel when they are accused of a crime:

> What I witnessed was low-grade pandemonium. Attorneys rushed into court, grabbed a file or two, and sat down for a quick read; this was their first and often most lengthy exposure to their new client's case. Confused-looking defendants, most Hispanic or African American, met their counsel amid a hubbub of other defendants, defendants' spouses, and defendants' squalling babies.[23]

Reformers argue that if justice is to be done, Texas should have a system of public defenders equal in number and experience to the public prosecutors. Without such procedures, the system inevitably discriminates against poor defendants, who tend to be minority citizens. For example, in 1993 the Texas Bar Foundation sponsored a study by the Spangenberg Group of Massachusetts of the state's system of appointing attorneys for indigents accused of murder. The Spangenberg Group's conclusions about Texas justice were consistent and unambiguous:

> In almost every county, the rate of compensation provided to court-appointed attorneys in capital cases is absurdly low . . . the quality of representation in these cases is uneven and . . . in some cases, the performance of counsel is extremely poor.[24]

If such deficient legal representation is common for citizens accused of murder, which is a high-profile crime, then the representation afforded people accused of lesser crimes must be even worse. It stands to reason that defendants who receive inferior public legal representation would be convicted more often, and be given harsher sentences, than defendants who can afford to hire private attorneys. Indeed, a study in the early 1990s concluded that a white person convicted of assault had a 30 percent chance of drawing a prison sentence, while an Hispanic with a similar record had a 66 percent chance and an African American a 76 percent chance.[25]

In short, the ironic question posed by the judge in the previous cartoon, "How much justice can you afford?", is a challenge to the legitimacy of the Texas judicial system. The state is far from achieving the democratic ideal that everyone is equal before the law.

SUMMARY

Even if Texas's court system were organized with perfect efficiency, it would still be overwhelmed by the sheer volume of cases it must handle. In fact, however, it suffers from overlapping jurisdiction, vague responsibilities, and complexity. These defects make the problem of too many cases worse, so that the system as a whole does not function well.

---

23. Debbie Nathan, "Wheel of Misfortune," *Texas Observer*, October 1, 1999, 22.

24. The Spangenberg Group, *A Study of Representation in Capital Murder Cases in Texas* (Austin: State Bar of Texas, Committee on Legal Representation for Those on Death Row, 1993), 157, 163.

25. Jeff South, "Inequity Found in Sentencing," *Austin American-Statesman*, September 4, 1993, 1A.

Because Texas judges are elected, they must accept private contributions in order to be able to campaign. When those contributions come from lawyers and others with business before their courts, it raises the suspicion that money is able to impair judges' impartiality. Recently the legislature has attempted to regulate judicial campaign contributions in order to restore public confidence, but even the brief experience since the law went into effect suggests that the reform is not having its intended effect.

The Texas system of justice includes many players besides judges, including the attorney general, lawyers, police, and juries.

The output of the system has improved in some ways in recent years. Whereas Texas courts used to be inhospitable to claims that people's civil rights and liberties had been violated, they are now more open to such claims. They have also courageously taken on the rest of the political establishment, including especially the legislature, in ordering a more equitable distribution of school revenues. In the arena of criminal justice, however, the system in which they work discriminates against the poor, largely because it inevitably favors those defendants who can afford to pay private counsel. The situation could be improved with the introduction of a statewide system of public counsel to represent indigent defendants, but such a change is not on the immediate horizon.

STUDY QUESTIONS

1. What has been the most common criticism of the organization of the Texas judiciary?
2. What are the two main reasons that Texas's courts are perceived to be in crisis? Can you think of any changes that might improve the situation?
3. What is the attorney general's advisory opinion? How did it evolve? Why is it important?
4. What are civil rights and liberties? Why are they important? Why is it necessary to have courts protect them?
5. Do you favor a system of at-large or district elections for choosing Texas judges? Why?
6. In what ways has the Texas system of justice improved in the last few decades? In what ways has it deteriorated or remained unsatisfactory?

SURFING THE WEB

Much information on the organization of the Texas judiciary, as well as far more than anyone could hope to assimilate on the courts, is available from the state's Office of Court Administration:

http://www.courts.state.tx.us

Information on recent court cases is available from the TexLaw online service:

http://www.texlaw.com/

The Texas Law Pipeline contains a variety of information pertinent to the judiciary, including complete texts of the constitution and the Texas Penal Code:

http://www.sbot.org/pipe/tx_refer.html

9

LOCAL GOVERNMENT

he new city manager is (1) invisible, (2) anonymous, (3) nonpolitical, and (4) none of the above. Increasingly, modern city managers are brokers, and they do that brokering out in the open.

**Alan Ehrenhalt, 1990,
Deputy Editor, Governing:
*The States and Localities***

When Congress began swinging its ax in earnest . . . at the Federal deficit, somebody forgot to tell Amarillo to duck.

**Michael Wines,
1996, New York Times**

INTRODUCTION

In 1875, when the Texas Constitution was being written, only 8 percent of the state's population lived in urban areas. By the 1998 federal census estimate, Texas was 84 percent urban. The U.S. Bureau of the Census and the Texas State Data Center forecast that Texas will grow faster than any other state through 2000 and will have 83 percent more people in 2025 than it had in 1990. Much of this population growth will be in sectors that have specific problems—Hispanics and the elderly in particular[1]—and most of it will be in urban areas. Much of the state's history and many of its problems are linked to urbanization and population growth.

Once one of the most rural states, Texas is now one of the most urban. Most of the change has taken place since 1950, when the development of such industries as petrochemicals and defense began luring rural residents into cities. Like most American cities, Texas cities are virtually unplanned. Growth patterns are determined largely by developers, who give little thought to the long-range effects of their projects on the total community. Only in the past quarter century has community planning come to be taken seriously. In Texas and elsewhere, the nation's domestic problems—racial strife, unemployment, inflation, delinquency, crime, substance abuse, inadequate health care, pollution, inadequate transportation, taxation, and the shortage of energy—seem to be focused in the cities. But before we examine city government and its problems, we will step back in time and look at the first unit of local government: the county.

Local government is an especially rich field for exploring whether the tests of democratic government outlined in Chapter One have been passed. Americans have long viewed local government as the government closest and most responsive to them. In looking at the organization, politics, and finance of Texas's local governments, we also will look closely at whether citizens really are most involved at the local level.

COUNTIES: HORSE-DRAWN BUGGIES?

Historical and Legal Background

The county is the oldest form of local government in America, and in rural Texas it is still the most important. Today there are 3,043 counties in the 47 states that have this form of government. Texas has the largest number of counties—254—in the nation.[2]

In Texas, as in other states, the county is a creation of state government. Since citizens could not be expected to travel to the capital to conduct whatever business they had with the state, counties were designed to serve as units of state government that would be geographically accessible to citizens. Until city police departments assumed much of this role, the sheriff and the sheriff's deputies were the primary agents for the enforcement of state law. County courts still handle much of the judicial business

---

1. "Texas Projected Population," a graph published in the *Dallas Morning News*, September 20, 1999, 6A.

2. Our discussion of county government in Texas relies in part on Robert E. Norwood, *Texas County Government: Let the People Choose* (Austin: Texas Research League, 1970). Norwood's monograph is the most extensive work available on the subject. A second edition, coauthored with Sabrina Strawn, was published in 1984.

of the state (see Chapter Nine), and they remain integral to the state judicial system. Many state records, such as titles, deeds, and court records, are kept by the county; many state taxes are collected by the county; and counties handle state elections. Counties also distribute many of the federal funds that pass through the state government en route to individuals, such as welfare recipients. Thus, most dealings that citizens have with the state are handled through the county. Yet, strangely, state government exercises virtually no supervisory authority over county governments. They are left to enforce the state's laws and administer the state's programs pretty much as they choose.

County officials are elected by the people of the county and have substantial discretion in a number of areas. For example, they can appoint some other county officials and set the tax rate. The result is a peculiar situation in which the county is a creation of state government, administering state laws and programs—with some discretion on the part of its officers—while county officials are elected by the people of the county and are in no real way accountable to the state government for the performance of their duties. Not surprisingly, county officials view themselves not as agents of the state but rather as local officials. One result is that enforcement of state law varies considerably from county to county.

Organization and Operation of County Government

The Constitution of 1876, which established the state government, also set out the organization and operation of county government. The same concerns apply to both governments, and there are close parallels in their organization and operation. For example, the decentralized executive found at the state level is reproduced at the county level in the county commissioners[3] court and semi-independent county agencies.

Structure.   Since the county is the creation of the state and has no home-rule authority, the organization and structure of county government are uniform throughout Texas. Tiny Loving County, with a population of 114, and enormous Harris County, with a population of 3.2 million, have substantially the same governmental structure—a structure that, unfortunately, is a burden to both.

---

3. Although one often sees commissioners court written as "commissioners' " (with an apostrophe), Chapter 81 of the *Texas Local Government Code* is explicit about the lack of an apostrophe.

Counties have often found themselves saddled with unnecessary offices, such as treasurer, school superintendent, or surveyor. In November 1993, Texas voters were asked not only to eliminate the county surveyor office in McLennan and Jackson Counties but also to eliminate the need for a statewide vote in all counties wishing to abolish this office. The vote was more than six to one in favor of eliminating the office.

FIGURE 9.1

Organization of County Government in Texas   SOURCE: George D. Braden, *Citizens' Guide to the Texas Constitution,* prepared for the Texas Advisory Commission on Intergovernmental Relations by the Institute of Urban Studies. The University of Houston (Austin, 1972), 51. Used by permission.

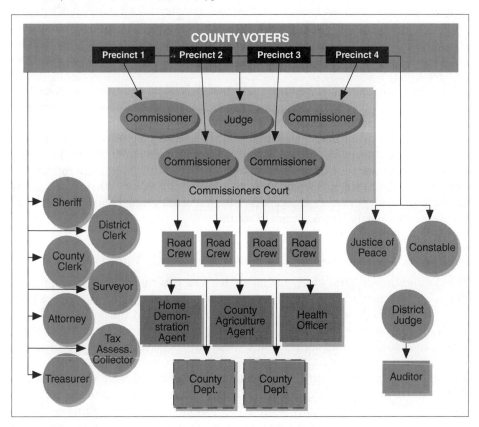

Figure 9.1 illustrates the organization of Texas county government. A county is divided into four precincts, each of which elects a commissioner to the commissioners court. A county judge, who presides over the commissioners court, is elected on a countywide basis. The county commissioners and the administrative agencies constitute the executive branch of county government, but, as we shall see, the commissioners court performs as a legislature as well.

Apportionment.   When county commissioners drew precinct lines, they used to draw them on some basis other than population. Unlike gerrymandering, where the object is to perpetuate the position of the dominant party or faction, county precinct apportionment was for the purpose of reelecting incumbent commissioners and dividing the county road mileage on an equal basis. Roads, a major county function, were often more important than people. Not only were roads the lifeline for the state's rural population, which was once in the majority, but also contracts for road work represented the best opportunity for individual commissioners to wheel and deal. As a result, county commissioners often created precincts with great disparities in population.

In 1968, one precinct in Midland County, composed of the city of Midland, contained 97 percent of the people in the county; the remaining 3 percent were distributed among the other three precincts. The U.S. Supreme Court, in a case against Midland County, ruled that all counties had to abide by the one-person, one-vote rule that had been applied earlier to the U.S. House of Representatives and to state legislatures (*Avery v. Midland County,* 88 S.Ct. 1114, 1968). The ruling resulted in some commissioners courts voluntarily redistricting on the basis of population; in other counties, judges ordered population-based redistricting. County apportionment has resurfaced as an issue in recent years in disputes over adequate opportunities for ethnic minorities to contend for county offices, in counties with substantial political party competition, and in urban counties with fast-growing suburbs.

Commissioners Court.   *Commissioners court* is a misnomer. This "court" is not a judicial body but an executive (policy-administering) and legislative (policy-making) body for the county. Each of the four commissioners is elected from a district called a *precinct.* All county elections are partisan; that is, candidates run as Democrats, Republicans, or minor-party candidates.

Although technically the county is nothing more than an administrative arm of the state, the commissioners court does have functional latitude in several areas. In addition to setting the tax rate for the county (a legislative function), it exercises discretion in the administration of state programs (an executive function). Some of these state programs are mandatory, but the county may choose among others and may determine the amount of money to be allocated to each. For example, the state and counties are responsible for health care for indigents, including care for individuals not qualified for the federally funded Medicaid program, and counties must ensure that hospital service is provided. An individual county, however, may choose among operating a public hospital, paying a public hospital in an adjacent county for services, or paying a private hospital for care of the indigent. Counties also are responsible for building and maintaining county jails and generally for providing health and safety services in rural areas. Perhaps the most important power of the commissioners court is that of controlling the county budget in most areas of county government. If it so chooses, a variety of different programs may be instituted, including major undertakings such as county hospitals, libraries, and various welfare programs. Counties also are active in economic development activity.

Chapter Five described how the county commissioners court has the responsibility for conducting general and special elections. The court also has the power to determine the precinct lines for the justice of the peace precincts, as well as the precincts of the four commissioners themselves. As indicated by the malapportionment in the Midland case noted earlier, these are powerful political weapons that can be used to advance the cause of some individuals and groups and to discriminate against others.

County Officials.   The *county commissioners* also perform important functions as individuals. Each is responsible for his or her own precinct, including the establishment of road- and bridge-building programs, which represent a major expenditure of county funds. Since 1947, counties have had the authority to consolidate the functions of building and maintaining roads and bridges. In twenty-four counties, a countywide unit system has been established, enabling commissioners in those counties to take advantage of volume purchasing, share heavy road equipment, and so on. But in more than 90 percent of Texas's counties, individual commissioners tend to the roads and bridges in their individual precincts. One reason is the importance of these transportation facilities to residents in outlying areas, and thus the potential effect on the commissioner's reelection. Another reason is that individual commissioners simply like the power implicit in hiring personnel and letting contracts for road and bridge work. They also like the political advantage to be gained from determining just where new roads will go and which existing roads and bridges will be improved.

The *county judge* is selected in an **at-large election;** *at large* means jurisdiction-wide. The position does not require legal credentials other than "being well-informed in the law." The county judge performs many functions. As a member of the commissioners court, the judge presides over and participates fully in that body's decision making. As a member of the county election board, the county judge receives the election returns from the election judges throughout the county, presents the returns to the commissioners court for canvassing, and then forwards the final results to the secretary of state. In any county with a population of less than 225,000, the county judge also serves in the administrative capacity as county budget officer. County judges also have the authority to fill vacancies that occur on commissioners courts. They are notaries public, can perform marriages, and issue beer, wine, and liquor licenses in "wet" counties. Many citizens see the county judge as a representative of the people and ask him or her to intervene with other elected officials and county bureaucrats. Many county judges have strong countywide power bases and are influential politicians.

The county judge also presides over the county court, although the position does not require legal credentials other than "being well-informed in the law." County judges devote time to such matters as probate of wills, settlement of estates, appointment of guardians, and, in many counties, hearing lawsuits and minor criminal cases. However, in larger counties the county commission usually relieves the judge of courtroom responsibilities by creating one or more county courts-at-law (see Chapter Eight for a discussion of the Texas judiciary).

The two major nonjudicial legal officers of the county are the *county sheriff* and the *county attorney;* both are elected at large. The sheriff has jurisdiction throughout the county but often makes informal agreements involving a division of labor with the police of the municipalities in the county. Particularly where large cities are involved, the sheriff's office usually confines itself to the area of the county outside the city limits. The county sheriff has comprehensive control of departmental operations and appoints all deputies, jailers, and administrative personnel. Depending on the size of the county, the sheriff's department may have a substantial annual budget. As the head of the county's legal department, the county attorney provides legal counsel to the county and represents it in legal proceedings. The attorney also prosecutes misdemeanors in the justice of the peace and county courts.

Another important elective office in the county is that of *county clerk,* who is elected at large. The county clerk is recorder of all legal documents, such as deeds, contracts, and mortgages; issues all marriage licenses; and is the clerk of both the county court and the commissioners court. Many of the responsibilities for the conduct of elections, which formally rest with the commissioners court, actually are performed by the county clerk. For example, absentee voting is handled by the county clerk (see Chapter Five).

The *assessor-collector of taxes* collects the ad valorem (general property) tax for the county, collects fees for license plates and certificates of title for motor vehicles, and serves as the registrar of voters. This last duty is a holdover from the days of the poll tax, which was a fee paid to register to vote. The assessor-collector's job has been changed in recent years by the creation of the uniform appraisal system, to be discussed later in this chapter. In counties of 10,000 or more population, a separate assessor-collector is elected at-large; in smaller counties, the sheriff serves as assessor-collector.

Other legal officers of the county are the *justices of the peace* (JPs) and the *constables*. Most but not all counties have at least one justice of the peace and one constable for each of the four precincts. Larger counties may have as many as eight JP districts. In the largest counties, numerous deputy constables assist the elected constables. The justice of the peace is at the bottom of the judicial ladder, having jurisdiction over only minor criminal and civil suits. The constable has the duty of executing judgments, serving subpoenas, and performing other duties for the justice of the peace court. Like the commissioners, the constables and JPs are elected for four years on a partisan basis by district.

The county has a number of other officers, some of whom perform important functions. In counties with a population of more than 35,000, state law requires that an *auditor* be appointed by the district judge having jurisdiction in the county for the purpose of overseeing the financial activities of the county and assuring that they are performed in accordance with the law. A *county health officer* to direct the public health program is also required by state law, and in most counties, a *county agricultural agent* and a *home demonstration agent* are appointed by the commissioners court for the purpose of assisting (primarily) rural people with agriculture and homemaking. Both of the latter officers are appointed in conjunction with Texas A&M University, which administers the agriculture and home demonstration extension programs.

An Evaluation of County Government

When industrial firms experience problems, they call in teams of management consultants who make a searching examination and a critical evaluation of the firm's operation. If a management consulting firm could be engaged to make a thorough examination of county government in Texas, its report would very likely include the following topics.

Structure and Partisanship. The county in Texas is a nineteenth-century political organization struggling to cope with twenty-first-century society—hence the title of this section, "Counties: Horse-Drawn Buggies?" In many states, counties have the same flexibility as cities to choose a form of government that is appropriate for the size and complexity of that particular jurisdiction. In Texas, all county governments are structured the same way, and the emphasis is on *party politics* because all officials are elected on a partisan basis. The positive aspect of partisanship is that the average voter can understand more clearly what a candidate's approximate political position is when the candidate bears the label "Republican" or "Democrat" than when the voter has no identifying tag. One negative aspect is a heavy reliance on a spoils system—that is, on the appointment of deputy sheriffs, assistant clerks, and road workers on a political basis.

Nationally, although most counties operate with a commission, urban counties serving the majority of the nation's citizens operate with a county manager or appointed administrator. Texas, of course, offers no such flexibility for the larger counties. Although the current structure is uniform and simple, it also makes it difficult to produce decisions for the benefit of all or most county residents because of the emphasis on precincts. In turn, the precinct focus makes it difficult to enjoy economies of scale such as purchasing all road paving materials for the county at one time.

The partisanship and restrictive structure can lead to governance problems. Commissioners often squabble over petty matters. Citizens have difficulty deciding whom to blame if they are dissatisfied with county government, since the commissioners serve as a collective board of directors for the county. For example, a troublesome sheriff—a not uncommon phenomenon—may be reelected by the voters, who blame the county commissioners for the sheriff's performance. Similarly, the voters may focus on the county judge, who has one vote on the commissioners court just like the other members, when other members of the court should be the object of attention. Such confusion can happen in any government, but the large number of elected officials—mirroring the state pattern—compounds the problem.

A plus for counties is that they are less bureaucratic than other governments, so the average citizen can deal more easily with a county office. One reason for this ease of use may be that, unlike the state government, county government does not have a clear-cut separation into legislative and executive branches and functions. The merger of executive and legislative functions, which is called a unitary system, also is found in some city and special district governments. It can sometimes produce a rapid response to a citizen problem or request.

One county judge assessed county government by noting that many county officials are highly responsive to public demands when they must face competitive elections. In fact, he argued, counties are the last true bastions of "grassroots politics," whereby government is close to all the people in the county. Although the court sets much of the policy and the tone for the conduct of county operations, it lacks the authority to give explicit orders to subordinate officials. Nevertheless, this county judge pointed out that by controlling the budget, the commissioners court can often dictate the behavior of other elected officials. Additionally, counties have the lowest tax rates of all the governments in Texas.[4] Another county judge put it this way: "We do meat-and-potatoes government . . . not flashy, press-release government, but good government."[5]

Thus, the evaluation of county organization and politics is mixed. The public often shows little interest in county government. Voter turnout is low, and even the media tend to ignore county government and focus instead on big city, state, and na-

4. Bell County Judge John Garth, in a conversation with one of the authors on February 21, 1991.

5. Travis County Judge Bill Aleshire in "Elected County Officials—Unlike City—Actually Run Government," *Austin American-Statesman*, September 26, 1996, p. A15.

tional political events. The county is a horse-drawn buggy in structure. It is often highly democratic, especially when it advocates the interests of groups ignored by other governments, since the commissioners must secure support for reelection. However, the willingness of commissioners and other elected officials to attend to the needs of individuals and to deal with details can easily lead to corruption.

Management Practices.   With the exception of a few of the larger counties, county government in Texas is one of the last bastions of the *spoils system,* under which persons are appointed to government jobs on the basis of whom they supported in the last election and how much money they contributed. While a spoils system helps to ensure the involvement of ordinary citizens in government, it also leads to the appointment of unqualified people, especially in jobs requiring specialized training. A spoils system can also lead to a high turnover rate if the county tends to usher new elected officials into office on a regular basis.

From a management standpoint, a merit system—a *civil service* or *merit system* of recruitment, evaluation, promotion, and termination is one based on qualifications—and a pay scale that can attract and hold competent personnel would help to improve governmental performance. This also would be fair, both to employees, as they would be properly paid for their labors and to taxpayers, as they would get a return on their dollars. Only a handful of Texas counties have made significant strides toward developing professional personnel practices such as competitive hiring, merit raises, and grievance processes.

Two other features of county government illustrate its tendency toward inefficient management: decentralized purchasing and the road and bridge system. *Decentralized purchasing* means that each commissioner and each department makes its own purchases. Quantity discounts, which might be obtained if there were a centralized purchasing agent, are unavailable on small-lot purchases. Also, the possibility for graft and corruption is great. To be sure they will get county business, sellers may find themselves obliged—or at least feel that they are—to do a variety of favors for individual officials in county government. This situation is not unknown in the other governmental units but becomes more widespread in highly decentralized organizations.

Unless a Texas county belongs to the elite 10 percent that have a unit system for county-wide administration of the *roads and bridges,* individual commissioners may

In rural areas, the lack of county ordinance power has created a new kind of "range war." The 800 indoor and outdoor gun ranges in the state are primarily in rural areas, and counties lack the authority to control the noise or even the straying bullets.

SOURCE: Tara Trower, "Range War," *Austin American-Statesman,* March 4, 1967, B1, B6.

Texas counties have no authority to pass ordinances that, for example, could regulate land use in rural areas.

SOURCE: Courtesy of Ben Sargent.

plan and execute their own programs of highway and bridge construction and maintenance at the precinct level. The obvious result is poor planning and coordination, as well as duplication of expensive heavy equipment. These inefficiencies are important because counties, like other local governments, must cope with taxpayer resistance to providing more funding for government. Thus, efficient performance is a "must."

Lack of Ordinance Power.   Texas counties have no general power to pass ordinances—that is, laws pertaining to the county. They do have the authority to protect the health and welfare of citizens, and through that power they can regulate the operation of a sanitary landfill and mandate inoculations in the midst of an epidemic. They can regulate subdivision development in unincorporated areas, sometimes sharing power with municipalities and, for flood control, with the federal government. However, the lack of general ordinance power means that, for example, they cannot zone land to ensure appropriate and similar usage in a given area.

Recommendations.   Having reviewed Texas county government, the mythical management consultants probably would recommend greater flexibility in this form of government, particularly in heavily populated areas, to encourage more professional management of personnel, services, purchasing, and all other aspects of county government. They would urge counties to take advantage of economies of scale by centralizing purchasing and adopting a unit system of road and bridge construction and maintenance. They probably would not yet explore any of the forms of city-county cooperation that exist in such areas as San Francisco, Honolulu, or Nashville, since counties in Texas are not yet ready to function as cities. The exceptions are El Paso County, where the county and city have explored consolidation, and Bexar County (San Antonio), where the county judge has advocated merger. The largest Austin newspaper has also urged some consideration of "government modernization" on the Travis County commissioners.[6] Such changes would require a constitutional amendment.

Prospects for Reform.   Given these obvious disadvantages, what are the prospects for changing county government in Texas? County commissioners, judges, sheriffs, and other county officers, acting individually and through such interest groups as TACO (Texas Association of County Officials), are potent political figures who can and do exercise substantial influence over their state legislators. Unfortunately for the taxpayers, most county officials have shown little willingness to accept changes in the structure and function of county government. The exceptions are usually county commissioners in more heavily populated counties, who have taken a number of steps to professionalize government, including the appointment of personnel and budget experts. They are outnumbered ten to one by commissioners in less populous areas. Thus, substantially more citizen participation will be necessary if change is to occur. If city residents, who tend to ignore county politics, were to play a much more active role, reform might be possible because of the sheer numbers they represent when approaching legislators.

CITIES: MANAGED ENVIRONMENTS

State legislatures traditionally have been less than sympathetic to the problems of the cities, partly because of rural bias and partly because they wished to avoid being caught in the quagmires of city politics. Therefore, the states (including Texas) established *general laws* for the organization of city governments, to which municipalities were required to conform. But these general laws were too inflexible to meet

6. Richard Oppel (editor of the paper), "Time to Ask Right Questions about County Government," *Austin American-Statesman,* September 22, 1996, E3.

the growing problems of the cities, and around the turn of the century there was a movement toward municipal **home rule.** The home rule laws permitted the cities, within limits, to organize as they saw fit.[7]

The home rule amendment to the Texas Constitution was adopted in 1912. It provides that a city whose population is more than 5,000 be allowed—within certain procedural and financial limitations—to write its own constitution in the form of a city charter, which would be effective when approved by a majority vote of the citizens. Home rule cities may choose any organizational form or policies as long as they do not conflict with the state constitution or the state laws.

Two legal aspects of city government in Texas that are growing in importance are extraterritorial jurisdiction (ETJ) and annexation. ETJ gives cities limited control over unincorporated territory contiguous to their boundaries; that is, cities get some control over what kind of development occurs just outside the city limits. The zone ranges from a half-mile in distance for cities under 1,500 in population to 5 miles for those over 25,000. Within these zones, municipalities can require developers and others to conform to city regulations regarding construction, sanitation, utilities, and similar matters.

Annexation power allows cities to bring adjacent unincorporated areas in the ETJ into the municipal boundaries. Doing so helps prevent suburban developments from incorporating and blocking a larger city's otherwise natural development. It also allows a city to expand its tax base. In the 1950s and 1960s, municipalities could make great land grabs without any commitment to providing services, but over the years annexation powers have been curbed. The legislature in 1999 tightened requirements considerably with the passage of SB89. Effective September 1, 1999, cities have more restrictions about notifying individuals in the area to be annexed. Beginning in 2002, they must immediately provide fire, police, and emergency services to the annexed area and must improve such infrastructure as roads, water supply, and sewer systems within two and a half years. The old annexation law required notification by public announcement, not by apprising individual residents, and it required provision of services but over a four-and-a-half-year period. The new law set

---

7. Provisions covering how both home rule and general law municipalities can organize are found in Chapters 9 and 21–26 of the *Texas Local Government Code.*

Houston has long been known as the only major American city without zoning ordinances that dictate what can be built where—homes, offices, factories. In the past, city leaders have used such terms as "Communist plot" and "socialized real estate" to describe zoning. Voters have explicitly and repeatedly rejected it, most recently in 1993. As a result, a church, office tower, and home can be found adjacent to one another. The city has begun to rely instead on carefully crafted deed restrictions.*

*SOURCES: See, for example, "'Anything Goes' Houstonians May Go the Limit: To Zoning," *New York Times,* October 27, 1993, 1, and Patrick Barta, "To Limit Growth, Houston Turns to Deed Restrictions," *Wall Street Journal,* May 12, 1999, T1, T3.

FIGURE 9.2

Council-Manager Form SOURCE: Adapted from *Forms of City Government* (Austin: Institute of Public Affairs, University of Texas, 1959), 23. Used by permission.

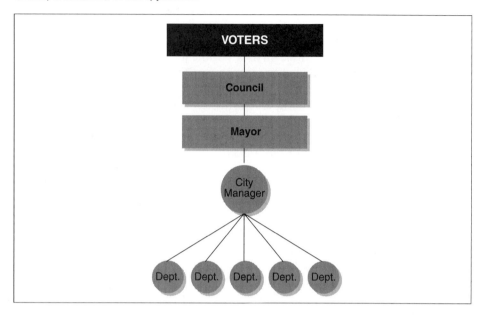

off an explosion of annexations, particularly in the Dallas–Fort Worth area, prior to the notification provision going into effect in 1999.

Much of the economic and residential growth around the larger cities in the state has been in "edge" cities—those on the edge of the metropolitan center. Thus, municipalities are likely to rely on ETJ and annexation even more in the future in an effort to control growth and development.[8]

Organization of City Government

As of 1999, Texas had 304 home rule municipalities. These municipalities overwhelmingly describe their form of government by standard terms such as *mayor-council, commission,* and *council-manager.* Occasionally, one finds a city council that calls itself a commission or a board of aldermen. In a few cases, two of the standard forms of local government have been combined. However, one of the standard forms of municipal government is most prevalent: 271 of the 304 home rule municipalities prefer council-manager government. Only nineteen operate with the mayor-council form, and fourteen use the mayor-manager form. None uses a straight commission form.

The Council-Manager Form. Dallas and San Antonio are two of the largest cities in the country—along with San Diego, California—using this organizational model (Figure 9.2) but smaller cities such as Bay City, Gainesville, and Yoakum also operate with this

8. See Robert H. Wilson, "Understanding Urban Texas," *Discovery: Research and Scholarship at the University of Texas at Austin* 15, no. 2 (March 1999), 34–37.

form of government. Under the **council-manager form,** a city council of five to fifteen members, elected at large or by districts, appoints a city manager who is responsible for the hiring and firing of department heads and for the preparation of the budget. A mayor is elected at large or by the council; the mayor is a member of the council and presides over it but otherwise has only the same powers as any other council member.

Proponents of council-manager government, including many political scientists, traditionally have argued that this form of government allows at least some separation of politics and administration. They believe the council makes public policy and, once a policy is set, the manager is charged with administering it. In reality, however, politics and administration cannot be separated; the city manager must make recommendations to the council on such highly political matters as tax and utility rates and zoning,[9] as the brokering role cited by Alan Ehrenhalt in the opening quotation indicates. Nevertheless, some citizens claim to perceive a distinction between politics and policymaking on one hand and administration on the other in this type of government, and many are convinced that it is the most efficient form of city government.

For all its efficiency and professionalism, council-manager government does have some problems. First, council members are part time and their tenure is often short; thus, they may rely heavily on the manager for policy guidance. Because the manager is not directly responsible to the voters, this practice makes it more difficult for the average citizen to influence city hall, and many citizens react negatively to reading in the local newspaper about the city manager's policy recommendations, even though the council must approve them. Second, the comparison is frequently drawn between council-manager government and the business corporation because both involve policy-making "boards" and professional managers. When coupled with the emphasis on efficiency, this image of a professionally trained "business manager" also tends to promote the values of the business community. The result is that festering political problems, especially those involving ethnic minorities and the poor, may not be addressed in a timely manner. However, the increasing number of council-manager cities with district elections and mayors directly elected by the people has tended to mute this problem somewhat, as representation on city councils has become more diversified. Also, city managers are now trained to be sensitive to all citizens.

9. A thorough look at modern council-manager government can be found in George Frederickson, ed., *Ideal and Practice in Council-Manager Government,* 2d ed. (Washington, DC: International City/County Management Association, 1995).

On Becoming a City Manager

How does one become a city manager? A city manager usually has a master's degree in public administration, public policy, or public affairs. The most common route is an internship in a city while still in school, followed by a series of increasingly responsible general management positions: administrative assistant, assistant to the city manager, assistant city manager, then city manager. Alternatively, an individual may begin in a key staff area—for example, a budget analyst, then budget director, then director of finance—or in a major operating department—for example, as an administrative assistant in the public works department, then as an assistant director, then director. Usually the individual holds these positions in more than one city.

FIGURE 9.3

Strong Mayor-Council Form

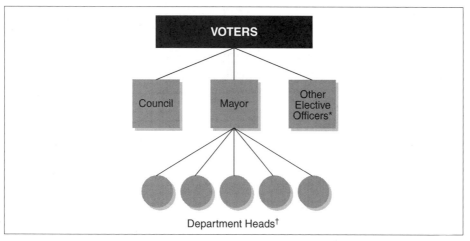

SOURCE: *Forms of City Government* (Austin: Institute of Public Affairs, University of Texas, 1959), 10. Used by permission.

*In a number of strong mayor-council cities, the chief of police and some other department heads are elected, although that is not the case in Texas.

†Common departments are fire, police, streets and sanitation, utilities, parks and recreation.

The Mayor-Council Form.   In the mayor-council form of municipal government, council members are elected at-large or by geographic districts, and the mayor is elected at-large. The mayor-council form has two variants: the weak mayor-council form and the strong mayor-council form. In the *weak mayor-council form,* other executives such as the city attorney and treasurer are elected also, while in the *strong mayor-council form,* the mayor has the power to appoint and remove other city executives. In the strong mayor-council form, the mayor also prepares the budget, subject to council approval. In both mayor-council forms, the mayor can veto acts of the city council, but typically fewer council votes are needed to override the mayor's veto in a weak mayor-council city than in a strong mayor-council city. An individual city charter may combine elements of both strong and weak mayor-council government—for example, giving the mayor budget control while also allowing for some other elected positions. Figure 9.3 illustrates the strong mayor-council form.

The words *strong* and *weak* are used in reference to a mayor's powers in the same way that the word *weak* is applied to the Texas governorship. The terms have to do with the amount of formal power given the chief executive by the city charter. An individual mayor, by dint of personality, political savvy, and leadership skills, can heavily influence local politics regardless of restrictions in the city charter.

The strong mayor form is most common among the nation's largest cities, while the weak mayor form prevails in smaller communities. In Texas, among the state's largest cities, only El Paso and Houston operate with mayor-council government. The other large cities have council-manager government. Small city examples include Hitchcock and Olney.

Many political scientists favor the strong mayor-council form of government because it seems most likely to provide the kind of leadership needed to cope with the growing problems of major urban areas and because it focuses on an elected, not an appointed, official. One reason for this belief is that the mayor and council members, especially in larger cities, are full-time paid officials who can devote their time to the development of public policy and oversight of governmental services. Thus, policy proposals come directly from elected officials. If these officials represent a broad public interest, as opposed to narrow interest groups, democracy is well served.

The Mayor-Manager Form.   The *mayor-manager form* of municipal government, also called the *chief administrative officer (CAO) form,* is growing in popularity nationwide. This plan has generated interest because it combines the overt political leadership of a mayor-council plan with the professional management skills identified with council-manager government. Typically, it arises when the mayor realizes a need for managerial assistance. In this form, the city manager reports only to the mayor, not to the council as a whole, and focuses on fiscal/administrative policy implementation. The mayor provides broad policy leadership in addressing major problems such as crime and economic development. In Texas, some smaller cities use a *city administrator plan,* but often only until a charter election can be held to adopt council-manager government. Houston comes closest to a CAO plan in that the mayor and budget director have something of a mayor–city manager relationship. Elsewhere, mayor-manager government is practiced in major cities such as San Francisco and New Orleans.

A variant of mayor-manager government is arising in larger municipalities. In Texas and across the country, large cities using the council-manager plan have seen disputes develop among the mayor, council members, and managers as assertive mayors work to carve out a larger role for themselves. The growing interest of big-city mayors in controlling both the political and the administrative aspects of city government is illustrated by events in Dallas. First, in 1992–1993, Mayor Steve Bartlett—a former U.S. congressman—and City Manager Jan Hart struggled for control, with Hart ultimately leaving in 1993 to enter the private sector. In 1997, Mayor Ron Kirk struggled more with the Dallas city council, which resisted his bid for greater power, than he did with City Manager John Ware, but his intent was the same as Bartlett's: to gain control of the city's executive establishment. A more cooperative mayor-manager relationship existed in San Antonio during the mayoralty of Henry Cisneros, who enjoyed widespread popularity as an elected official but who also worked well with City Manager Lou Fox.[10]

The Commission Form.   Under the *commission form* of organization, elected commissioners collectively compose the policy-making board and function, as individuals, as administrators of various departments such as public safety, streets and transportation, finance, and so on. They are usually elected at large. Although initially

10. See Melvin G. Holli, "America's Mayors: The Best and the Worst since 1960," *Social Science Quarterly,* 78, no. 1 (March 1997): 149–157. Holli's survey ranks Cisneros as the second best mayor of the modern era and the best minority mayor in the United States since 1960. Richard J. Daley of Chicago was ranked number one.

widely copied, the commission system has more recently lost favor because many think that individual commissioners tend to become advocates for their own departments rather than public interest advocates who act on behalf of the entire city. Also, the city commission form is subject to many of the same problems as the county commission, including corruption and unclear lines of responsibility. Although some cities still call their city councils "commissions," Texas home rule cities have abandoned this form of government, which was invented in Galveston to cope with the cleanup and rebuilding made necessary by the great hurricane of 1900. Some general-law cities still have a commission government.

Forms Used in General-Law Cities.   There are 873 *general-law* cities in Texas: cities whose population is less than 5,000 and somewhat larger cities that for one reason or another have not opted for home rule. These cities can organize under any of three basic forms of government: aldermanic (a variant of the mayor-council type), council-manager, or commission. However, state law limits the size of the council, specifies other municipal officials, spells out the power of the mayor, and places other restrictions on matters that home-rule cities can decide for themselves. Because of their small size, most of the general-law cities have chosen the aldermanic model, although the municipal clerk often acts as chief administrative officer for the city.

What Form Is Preferable?   The only clear answer is that council-manager government seems to work best in middle-sized cities (from 25,000 to 250,000 or so in population). These cities are largely suburban and prefer this form's emphasis on businesslike efficiency and the distance it maintains from party politics and from state and national political issues. Smaller cities that can afford a city manager also often do well with that form, but most use a mayor-council form. The really large cities often fare best with either a mayor-council form or a mayor-manager form, since they need the political focus provided by the elected mayor.[11]

City Politics

The discussion of forms of city government and their characteristics provided a substantial amount of factual information about the operation of the city, but it said little about how city government really works. Who gets the rewards, and who is deprived? Which individuals and groups benefit most from city government, and which groups bear the burdens?

The electoral system used by Texas cities is an indication of how the rewards and deprivations are distributed. Although the party identification of candidates is well known in cities like Beaumont and El Paso, all Texas cities hold **nonpartisan elections.** In most Texas cities, municipal elections are held during the spring in a further attempt to separate city government from party politics. In this electoral setting,

11. See, for example, Robert B. Boynton, "City Councils: Their Role in the Legislative System," *The Municipal Year Book,* 1976 (Washington, DC: International City Management Association, 1976), 67–77; Tari Renner and Victor S. DeSantis, "Contemporary Patterns in Municipal Government Structures," *The Municipal Year Book, 1993* (Washington, DC: International City/County Management Association, 1993), 57–68; and Daniel R. Morgan and Robert E. England, *Managing Urban America,* 4th ed. (Chatham, NJ: Chatham House, 1996), 58–80.

private interest groups such as local Realtors' associations or homeowners may sponsor a slate of candidates for municipal office, just as a political party would, under the guise of a civic organization that purportedly has no goals except efficient and responsive government. Such a claim is misleading, however. These groups do have goals and are highly effective in achieving them. In some cities, a charter association or good government league exists; these organizations inevitably reflect the interests of conservative business elements in the community. In other cities, environmentalists or neighborhood advocates or antitax groups may launch well-organized single-issue campaigns. In addition, a number of more or less ad hoc groups usually appear at election time to sponsor one or more candidates; and in all Texas cities, independent candidates also come forth with their own campaigns to seek public office.

Closely associated with nonpartisan elections is the system of electing candidates for the city council at large. All voters select all the members of the council and vote for as many candidates as there are positions on the council. In another practice widely followed in Texas cities, the **place system,** the seats on the council are designated as Place One, Place Two, and so on. In this type of election, candidates who file for a particular place run against only other candidates who also file for that place. Voting is still citywide. The at-large, by-place system predominates in smaller cities.

Increasingly, however, Texas cities whose population is 50,000 or more are amending their charters to provide for a district system, wherein candidates are required to live in a particular geographic area within the city and run against only those candidates who also live in the district. Voters choose only among candidates within their district, although the mayor is usually elected at large. In some cities, the council is composed of some members elected by district and some elected at large. Often the change to **district elections** occurs as the result of a successful court suit based on discrimination against minorities, who find it difficult to win election in a citywide race (see Chapter Eight). Running in districts costs less money and has the advantage of al-

Changes in Texas politics are most evident in the major cities, where leaders and interest groups reflect newer interests and where the sacrosanct principle of nonpartisanship is sometimes violated. Austin, San Antonio, Houston, Dallas, El Paso, Fort Worth, and Galveston have had women mayors, as have more than 200 smaller communities. El Paso and San Antonio have elected Mexican-American men as mayors, and Houston and Dallas have elected African-American males.

Austin, Houston, and Dallas have become the homes of large groups of politically active homosexuals. In all three cities, politicians of many ideological persuasions seek the support of the Gay and Lesbian Political Caucus.

In the big cities, the importance of neighborhood representation and ethnic representation has intensified to such an extent that it is difficult to gain a workable consensus for establishing public policy. Instead, individual council members sometimes advocate the needs of their districts to the exclusion of concerns about the city as a whole.

lowing minority candidates to concentrate their campaigning in neighborhoods with large numbers of individuals who share the candidate's ethnic background. Often, additional council seats are created when a city switches to district elections.

Advocates of at-large and by-place elections argue that the council focuses on citywide concerns and that having district elections results in a fragmented council whose members concentrate on only the problems of their electoral district. They also think that district elections are incompatible with council-manager government, which predominates in the state's home rule cities, because they make local elections "too political." Advocates of district elections think that the council is more representative when members are elected by wards or districts because minorities, spokespersons for citizens groups, and individuals without personal wealth have a better opportunity to be elected and will be more inclined to address "local district" problems. They believe that government by its very nature is political, and so all political viewpoints should be represented.

Questions about the organization of elections and the nature of representation are at the heart of the democratic process. One measure of a city's democratic morality is the extent to which the council is diversified ethnically, economically, and geographically. Thus, democratic theorists sometimes recommend district over at-large elections except in small municipalities, where candidates are likely to be known by most voters.[12]

Controversy also exists over whether elections should be nonpartisan. As discussed in Chapter Five, nonpartisan elections rob the voters of the most important symbol that they have for making electoral choices: the party label. Without knowing whether a candidate is a Democrat, a Republican, or a member of some other party, how does the voter decide how to vote?

In answering this question, critics of nonpartisan elections say that voters depend on personalities and extraneous matters. For example, television personalities and athletes frequently win elections simply because they are better known than their opponents are. These critics also think that nonpartisan elections rob the community of organized and effective criticism of the government in power. Since most candidates win as individuals rather than as members of an organized political party with common goals and policies, their criticism is sporadic and ineffectual, and meaningful policy alternatives seldom are stated. Chapter Four pointed out that Texas political parties are not well organized. The blame for weak party organizations is often placed on nonpartisan local elections because the parties have no strong grassroots input. A fourth criticism is that nonpartisan elections encourage the development of civic organizations that are, in essence, local political parties whose purposes and policy goals are not always clear to the voters.

Advocates of nonpartisan elections obviously disagree. They think that the absence of a party label allows local elections to focus on local issues, not on national issues about which the municipal government can do little or nothing. They note that their television personalities, athletes, and actors are also elected under party banners. Moreover, they point to the fact that local civic groups clarify, not confuse, local issues. Homeowners, taxpayers, and consumers have become political forces that

---

12. John Nalbandian discusses local representation in "Tenets of Contemporary Professionalism in Local Government," in Frederickson, *Ideal and Practice*, 157–71.

TABLE 9.1

Number of Units of Local Government in Texas, 1967–1997

Type of Government	1967	1977	1987	1997	% change
Counties	254	254	254	254	0
Municipalities	884	1,066	1,156	1,177	+33.1
School Districts	1,308	1,138	1,111	1,087	−16.9
Other Special Districts	1,001	1,425	1,891	2,182	+118
Total	3,447	3,883	4,412	4,700	+36.3

SOURCES: U.S. Department of Commerce, Bureau of the Census, *Statistical Abstracts of the United States*, 88th, 98th, and 108th eds. (Washington, DC: 1968, 1978, 1988) and *1997 Census of Governments*, vol. 1, *Government Organization*, issued August 1999.

stand in contrast to the traditional business-oriented civic associations. As a result, participation is enhanced, although resolving political disagreements has become more difficult.

At-large elections, nonpartisan voting, and holding elections in the spring apparently do contribute to low voter turnout. A municipal election with as many as 25 percent of the eligible voters participating is unusual. Many local elections are decided on the basis of the preference of only 5 or 10 percent of the eligible voters. Moreover, in all elections, the older, affluent whites vote more frequently than do the young, the poor, and ethnic minorities. The structure of municipal elections in Texas, particularly when those elections are at large, tends to perpetuate the dominant position of the white middle-class business community. Thus, when we measure municipal government against the criteria for a democratic government, we find some problems of participation, especially among the less affluent and among ethnic minorities.

SPECIAL DISTRICTS: OUR HIDDEN GOVERNMENTS

Perhaps the best way to introduce the topic of special districts is to look at the changes in Texas local government shown in Table 9.1. The number of counties has been stable for most of the twentieth century; the number of school districts has steadily declined as districts consolidate to gain greater economy and efficiency. The number of municipalities has increased largely because of the incorporation of suburban areas on the edge of central cities as the population has shifted out of the metropolitan core. The big increase is nonschool special districts, which have more than doubled in number in a thirty-year period.

What Is a Special District?

A *special district* is a unit of local government created by an act of the legislature to perform limited functions. Its authority is narrow rather than broad, as in the case of the city or the county. Any further definition is almost impossible; special districts vary enormously in size, organization, function, and importance.

Texas has about two dozen different types of special districts. About one-fourth of these are housing and community-development districts, while another fourth are concerned with problems of water—control and improvement, drainage, navigation, supply, and sanitation. Other types of frequently encountered special districts are airport, soil conservation, municipal utilities, hospital, fire prevention, weed control, and community college.

No single state or county agency is responsible for supervising the activities or auditing the financial records of all these special districts. Such supervision depends on the type of district involved. For example, community college districts are supervised by the Texas Higher Education Coordinating Board and the Texas Education Agency. Average citizens, however, have a hard time keeping track of the many special districts surrounding them. This lack of uniformity and resulting confusion are caused in part by the various ways in which special districts can be created: through special acts of the legislature or under general laws; by general purpose governments (cities and counties) in some instances; and even by state agencies.

Why Special Districts?

Why do we have so many special districts? And why is this form of government growing so rapidly?

First, *our established governments—the cities and counties—are inadequate to solve many of the increasingly diverse problems of government.* The problem of flood control can seldom be solved within a single city or county, for example, and it frequently transcends state boundaries. Too, special districts are part of the price we pay for governmental institutions such as counties that were fashioned a century ago and are not always capable of addressing complex modern problems such as water supply.

Second, part of the attraction of special districts is that *they are easy to organize and operate.* Political leaders of cities and counties frequently promote a special district as a solution to what might otherwise become "their problem," and the legislature is willing to go along. Creating a hospital district, for example, means that the city and the county don't have to raise their taxes.

Third, in a few instances, *special districts have been created primarily for private gain.* Land speculators and real estate developers create special districts called municipal utility districts (MUDs) on the outskirts of urban areas to increase the value of their holdings. Once enabling legislation has been obtained from the state, it requires

Every county has a tax appraisal district that is responsible for assessing property and providing up-to-date tax rolls to each taxing jurisdiction—county, municipalities, school districts, and other special districts. This system began in 1982 to eliminate the confusion caused by different taxing jurisdictions setting different values on property. In addition to assessment, the uniform appraisal district may have a formal agreement with one or more of the taxing jurisdictions to collect taxes. In many counties, the appraisal district makes all of the tax collections.

only a handful of votes in the sparsely settled, newly created district to authorize a bond issue for the development of water, sewer, and other utilities. MUDs are a good example of the consequences of a lack of effective state regulation of special districts.

Fourth, *special districts offer great flexibility to government organizations* and have the added attraction of rarely conflicting with existing units. A two-city airport such as Dallas–Fort Worth International is the result of a flexible airport authority.

Fifth, with highly technical problems such as flood control, *the special district offers the opportunity to "get it out of politics."* In other words, it is possible to take a businesslike approach and bring in technical specialists to attack the problem.

Assessment of Special Districts

Special districts other than school and appraisal districts are *profoundly undemocratic.* They are indeed "hidden governments," with far less visibility than city or county governments. It is not an exaggeration to say that every reader of this book is under the jurisdiction of at least one special district. Yet it will be a very rare reader who knows the districts that affect her or him, how much they cost in taxes, who the commissioners or other officials of the districts are, whether these officials are elected or—as is more frequently the case—appointed, and what policies they follow. Special district government is hidden government, unseen and frequently unresponsive to the people. Thus, when we apply the test of democratic morality, we find that special districts fail to meet the standards of participation and public input.

Most special districts are small in size and scope. Because of this, they are *uneconomical.* Their financial status is often shaky, so that the interest rates taxpayers must pay on bond issues used to finance many types of special district projects are exceptionally high. Economies such as large-scale purchasing are impossible.

Finally, one of the most serious consequences of the proliferation of special districts is that *they greatly complicate the problems of government, particularly in urban areas.* With many separate governments, the likelihood is greater that haphazard development, confusion, and inefficiency will occur. No single government has comprehensive authority, and coordination among so many smaller governments becomes extremely difficult. Texans have been reluctant to experiment with a comprehensive urban government. Their individualism demands retention of the many local units, although metropolitan areas such as Miami and Nashville have succeeded with comprehensive government.

Instead Texans rely on one of the twenty-four *regional planning councils,* also known as *councils of governments* (COGs), to provide coordination in metropolitan areas. These voluntary organizations of local government provide such functions as regional land use and economic planning, police training, and fact-finding studies on problems such as transportation.

Given the inadequacies of comprehensive planning and periodic revenue shortfalls at the local level, special districts will surely continue to proliferate. Under current conditions, they are too easy to create and operate as short-range solutions to governmental problems. Such continued proliferation without adequate planning and supervision will result not in a solution but rather in a worsening of the problems of local and particularly urban government.

School Districts

School districts are an exception to much of the foregoing discussion of special districts for several reasons. First, school board members are publicly elected, most commonly in an at-large, by-place system. Second, their decisions are usually well publicized, with the local newspapers and broadcast media paying careful attention to education decisions. Third, considerable public interest in and knowledge about school district politics exist. Indeed, although county or city public hearings sometimes fail to attract a crowd, as soon as a school board agenda includes a topic such as determining attendance districts—basically, who gets bused and who doesn't—or sex education, the public turns out for the debate. Fourth, the number of school districts has been steadily declining for fifty years. Finally, although the local boards have a substantial amount of control over such matters as individual school management, location of schools, and personnel, the state is the ultimate authority for basic school policies and shares in the funding of public schools.

LOCAL GOVERNMENT FINANCE

County Finance

The financing of local government varies a great deal depending on the type of government. Counties depend heavily on local property taxes and on intergovernmental transfers, chiefly welfare money that is passed down from the national government to the Texas Department of Human Services to the counties. The intergovernmental money is beyond the control of the local government. The commissioners court is required to meet annually to set the property tax rate, which may not exceed the prescribed 80 cents per $100 valuation. Rates in excess of that evaluation, if authorized by the legislature and approved by the voters of the county, can be imposed for special projects such as farm-to-market roads. Counties receive funding from federal grants other than welfare and from various state programs. State maintenance of rural farm-to market roads and state highways is an important financial aid to Texas counties. Counties get miscellaneous income from local charges collected from hospitals, toll roads, and recreation facilities and from fines, special assessments, and

Large urban school districts have had the same struggles over district versus at-large elections that cities have had. At-large proponents argue that "children," not "politics," should prevail. District proponents argue for "representation." In Dallas, the board is elected by district and has been sharply divided. Bill Rojas, a new superintendent hired in the fall of 1999, had already grown crosswise with several board members before Thanksgiving and was dismissed in July 2000. Amarillo has used an experimental voting procedure to try to find a compromise between district and at-large elections.

FIGURE 9.4

Typical Texas County and City Revenues and Expenditures

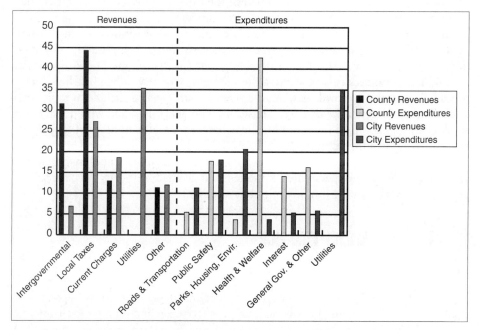

interest earned. Selected counties also have been authorized to collect a sales tax. Figure 9.4 illustrates revenues and expenditures for units of general purpose local government—counties and cities—in Texas.

As Figure 9.4 illustrates, a typical Texas county spends the largest share of its budget on health and welfare programs. Not only are counties the "pass-through" agencies for implementing welfare programs, but they also are responsible for indigent health care. Another cost that has risen over the past decade is that of jails, as counties struggle to meet court-imposed minimum jail standards. County law enforcement costs depend on how much unincorporated land there is in the county. For example, in Dallas County, little unincorporated land exists, thereby minimizing the sheriff's enforcement range. In Harris County, much of the county is unincorporated and dependent on the sheriff's office.

Of course, individual Texas counties vary greatly in both revenue and expenditures, depending on whether they are rural or urban, rich or poor, large or small. They also vary according to the services demanded by the residents.

City Finance

The most important sources of municipal funding are the property tax, sales tax, borrowing through bonds, and user fees, especially for utilities such as water, solid waste pickup, wastewater, and electricity. Other sources include intergovernmental transfers, miscellaneous fees and fines such as liquor licenses and traffic fines collected by the municipal court.

Figure 9.4 shows that cities spend their money on diverse services. The largest areas of expenditure are utilities (laying all those water lines cost a lot of money!); police and fire protection; parks, recreation, and environmental compliance; and streets. Interest on debt is significant in many municipal budgets.

School and Other Special District Finance

School districts depend on two revenue sources—property taxes and state assistance. In Texas, however, state aid pays for only about half the cost of public education, thereby putting considerable pressure on property tax. Chapter Eight discusses the legal issues surrounding public school finance in Texas, including efforts to distribute some dollars from rich to poor districts. The two largest differences in spending in richer versus poorer districts is in facilities (posh buildings, full computerization versus bare bones) and enrichment activities (choir trips to Europe versus a poor-quality field for athletics and band).

Other special districts have a variety of funding sources depending on their purpose, and their expenditures vary just as widely. One really cannot generalize about them. For example, a transit authority will depend on fees and grants and will spend its money on equipment and people to operate it. A junior college district will depend on property taxes, state aid, and student funds and will spend its money on programs and to some extent buildings. A water district will depend on fees and will spend its money on infrastructure to a large extent.

Both cities and counties face resistance from taxpayers over increased property taxes, a vexing issue because general-purpose governments have been able to maintain or even lower the property tax, but special districts, especially school districts, have continued to increase the rate. All local governments face federal and state policy changes that result in shifting local priorities. The quotation at the beginning of the chapter that "somebody forgot to tell Amarillo to duck" refers to all Texas municipalities—indeed, to local government in general.

As a result of political-fiscal pressures, local governments have become creative in identifying new revenue sources, such as impact fees charged to developers for putting in infrastructure (streets, utilities) in new subdivisions or athletic fees charged to students who want to participate in sports. Public-private cooperation has stretched local dollars for everything from park construction to Fourth of July celebrations. Sometimes, however, local governments, have had to curtail services such as allowing lawn clippings to be hauled to the landfill or providing fine arts programs in the high school.

LOCAL GOVERNMENT: PROSPECTS FOR THE FUTURE

There is little doubt that the trends toward urbanization and suburbanization will continue, with the result that metropolitan problems will become more acute than they are today. Nowhere is the problem of rapid growth and dealing with a sprawl that even cuts across county lines more obvious than in the Austin Metropolitan Area, which topped 1 million in population in 1996. What are the prospects for local governments in Texas under these circumstances?

There are several developments worth noting. As urban problems and local finance problems become more acute, national and state governments are being forced to pay more attention to them. One major consideration in the 1999 legislative struggle over utility deregulation was the recognition that the legislature would have to find a way for both cities and private companies to retire their debt on power plants. This recognition came about in part because *the legislature is becoming more "citified."*

Another significant development occurred in August 1978, when the voters of Houston and six of its suburbs approved the creation of a Metropolitan Transit Authority with taxing power and authority to establish transit systems as alternatives to Houston's increasingly congested freeways. Other Texas metropolitan areas such as Dallas are following suit. It has long been obvious that the practice of virtually every person's using his or her own motor vehicle for personal and business travel is incompatible with increasing urbanization. Smog, congestion, even rush-hour gridlock do not make for a high quality of life. *Mass transit systems* must be established if the trend toward further urbanization is to continue, especially given the inability of the state to build roadways fast enough to move traffic at peak times.

Another development is that of *strategic planning,* a type of planning that focuses on identifying a mission and pursuing it in an opportunistic manner, i.e., taking advantage of any favorable situation that comes along. A community that strives to attract high-technology companies might aggressively recruit electronics plants, perhaps even ignoring some of their environmental problems.

A fourth area of concern for the future is *interlocal cooperation.* COGs are one example of how local governments—counties, cities, special districts—are working together to solve their common problems. Cooperative ventures such as city-county ambulance service, city-school playgrounds and libraries, and multiple-city purchasing are other examples. Indeed, interlocal agreements are the most dynamic element of modern intergovernmental relations and can help to overcome some of the negative effects of the growing number of governments.

A fifth area of concern is *ordinance-making power for counties.* The lack of ordinance-making power is becoming a serious problem in various areas, including safety, environmental, and aesthetic standards, as well as other matters. For example, an issue of growing concern is the lack of control over adult bookstores and massage parlors that set up shop just outside a municipality, where control of them becomes a problem for the county. Indeed, counties asked for legislative relief in 1989 on this specific issue. Counties want and need ordinance-making power but have thus far

The air quality problem in the state's major metropolitan areas is acute. The Environmental Protection Agency put Houston in the same category as Los Angeles in 1999, and the Dallas–Forth Worth area was scheduled for a downgrade to "severe" without major remedial steps by 2002. Much of the problem is the result of automobile emissions.

been denied it, primarily because of the opposition of the real estate developers who can, for example, create developments in unincorporated areas that do not have to meet rigorous city building codes.

A sixth major problem that will continue to plague local governments is *funding*. With an improved economy, some of the financial strains have been alleviated, but, unlike costs in many enterprises, local government costs are not subject to economies of scale. In manufacturing, for example, producing more cars or soap bars results in lowered unit costs—the cost of one car or soap bar. This principle doesn't hold true for picking up more bags of garbage or cleaning more streets or teaching more children. Burgeoning populations that move farther and farther away from the central city make delivery of services more costly.

SUMMARY

Local governments are the governments that are most likely to have a daily impact on the citizen, and much of this effect is critical to the quality of life. Will our children get a good public education, or should we save to send them to private school? Is our neighborhood safe, or will we have to live behind triple-locked doors with a guard dog for a companion? Will we enjoy a reasonably efficient and economical transportation system, or will we have to fight dangerous and congested freeway traffic two or three hours a day to get to and from our jobs?

The answers to these and a hundred other critical questions are given by the units of local government. And Texas counties, cities, special districts, and COGs seem ill prepared to provide optimum solutions. County governments are anachronisms—holdovers from an earlier, nonindustrial, nonurban period of American political history. City governments are better organized and have more comprehensive powers, yet they too are handicapped by a variety of factors, including the rapid increase in

How to Get Involved in Local Government

Local government is the logical starting point for exercising your democratic rights and getting involved as a participant in government. Here are a few suggestions for how to go about getting involved:

- Go to the party precinct conventions held immediately after the primary elections (see Chapter Six).
- Attend a public hearing and speak out.
- Organize a petition drive on a matter of importance to you—saving the trees along a planned freeway route, for example.
- Attend a neighborhood meeting.
- Attend a meeting of the city council, county commission, or school board.
- Talk to the city clerk or the county clerk to find out how to volunteer for an advisory committee or citizen task force.
- Volunteer to work for a local candidate during an election.

urban population, the proliferation of independent special districts, and the limited and frequently reluctant cooperation of state and national government. COGs, as voluntary organizations, provide only very limited solutions to problems arising from the need for organized, coordinated planning. All local governments will face serious revenue problems for the foreseeable future.

Texas, like most states, will undoubtedly continue to become more and more urbanized. Consequently, problems such as congestion, poor housing, inadequate schools, and crime will grow. It is imperative that local governments both represent the diversity of the state and govern effectively. Democracy is about both participating and getting things done.

STUDY QUESTIONS

1. What is a home rule city? What are the forms of government used in home rule cities? Why do you think most home rule cities have council-manager government?
2. Pretend you are consultant to a city of 250,000 people. Your advice is sought on how to structure municipal elections. How would you advise this city about the time when city elections should be held and whether to have nonpartisan candidates and at-large elections? Why?
3. Why does Texas have so many special districts, and what are some of the problems associated with them?
4. Which type of local government do you think is truly at the "grassroots"; that is, which type most nearly represents all the citizens and works hardest to solve human problems?
5. Attend a meeting of your local city council, school board, or county commission. Then describe for your fellow students what you learned by attending the meeting.

SURFING THE WEB

Instead of "name," type in the name of a Texas city of your choice.
   www.ci.name.tx.us

Instead of "name," type in the name of Texas county of your choice.
   www.co.name.tx.us

Visit the home page of the Texas Department of Housing and Community Affairs (roughly the equivalent of the U.S. Department of Housing and Urban Development).
   www.tdhca.state.tx.us

Check out the Texas Municipal League site for legislation affecting local governments.
   www.tml.org

10

eople want JUST taxes more than they want LOWER taxes. They want to know that every man is paying his proportionate share according to his wealth.

Will Rogers,
legendary American humorist

Texans are like the tea bags of life. They perform when the water's hot.

Carolyn Pesce, reporter,
USA Today

Texas will . . . outpace U.S. economic growth by an average of 1.4% a year.

Carol Keeton Rylander,
Texas Comptroller of Public
Accounts, 1999

THE STATE ECONOMY AND THE FINANCING OF STATE GOVERNMENT

INTRODUCTION

The ability of any government to generate the revenues needed to provide the programs and services that citizens want is directly tied to the economy. Are most people working? Are wages good? Are profits high? Is money available for loans to finance business expansion and home ownership? This chapter begins by sketching the robust economy at the beginning of 2000. It has emerged from the economic troubles that began in 1983 when oil prices plummeted, wreaking havoc on the Texas economy and on state finance. In 1997 and 1999 Texas had a sizable surplus at the beginning of the legislative session, causing long-time observers of the Texas political scene to recall fondly the 1970s, when every year brought with it a surplus.

A major issue for the revenue system is its fairness. As Will Rogers noted in the opening quotation, citizens always seek fairness. Yet as we shall see, the poor in Texas pay a higher proportion of their incomes in taxes than do the wealthy. The fairness of the Texas revenue system raises questions about how democratic the state system is and constitutes a major theme of this chapter.

The chapter also looks at how the state spends its money, including how elected officials struggle to agree on what the budget will be. Because the budget is the best guide to policy priorities, it is a practical test of how well citizens' interests are accommodated in state spending.

Texas has grown from 14.2 million people in 1980 to slightly over 20 million people at the beginning of 2000—an increase of more than 40 percent in just twenty years. During that same period, the state budget has increased from $22.5 billion for fiscal years (FY) 1980–81 to $98.1 billion for FY 2000–2001[1]—an increase of 336 percent. However, when adjusted for population growth—more people require more services—and **inflation**—that is, increases in what things cost—the Texas budget was relatively flat across this period. Budget growth has been only about 2.4 percent a year, less than the inflation rate for the period as a whole.[2]

THE TEXAS ECONOMY

The Past

Historically, the Texas economy was based on natural resources, chiefly oil, land, and water. Indeed, Texas has been characterized as the state where "money gushes from the ground in the oil fields and grows on the citrus trees in the irrigated orchards."[3] Texas is still an important producer of oil and gas, and listings of its principal products continue to include petroleum, natural gas, and natural gas liquids.[4] Chemicals, cotton, and cattle also contribute their share of wealth. In fact, the economy is robust

---

1. *Fiscal Size Up: Texas State Services, 1982–83 Biennium* (Austin: Legislative Budget Board, 1982), 5, and *Text of House Bill No. 1 (General Appropriations Act)*, with gubernatorial vetoes (1999).

2. *Fiscal Size Up: Texas State Services, 1998–99 Biennium* (Austin: Legislative Budget Board, 1998), 1–9.

3. Wayne King, "Despite Success, Sun Belt Oil Patch Is Finding It's Not Immune to Recession," *New York Times,* June 9, 1981, 11.

4. See, for example, "Texas, The Lone Star State: Business," *Texas Almanac and State Industrial Guide, Millennium Edition* (Dallas: *Dallas Morning News* 1999), 5.

and complex enough that the *Wall Street Journal* noted in 1998 that the state could not identify its largest industry.

The state's natural resources are finite—that is, once used, they cannot be replaced. Furthermore, the global economy is shifting from one based on natural resources to one based on information and technology. In 1997, the overall Texas economy was $776 billion a year. Of that, $8.8 billion—slightly over 1 percent—came from agriculture, forestry, and fisheries. Although the percentage of the state economy from agriculture has declined, only California has a larger agribusiness economy. By 1997, oil and gas production—once 27 percent of the state's economy—had shrunk to less than 6 percent. Both of these figures are somewhat misleading because the manufacturing (25% of the economy) and construction (another 3%) segments of the economy included projects such as petrochemical plants, drill sites, and agricultural processing factories.[5]

Nevertheless, the erosion of the natural resource–based economy meant that hundreds of thousands of Texans found themselves out of work. In June 1986, the state unemployment rate reached 9.6 percent, compared with a national rate of 7.3 percent. The collapse of financial institutions made the problem worse. In 1988–1990, Texas led the nation in the number of banks and savings and loans that failed. At that time the defense industry was depressed by the end of the Cold War in the early 1990s.

State government worked to shore up the shaky economy by consolidating economic development programs, developing aggressive marketing campaigns for farm and ranch products, and selling the high-technology capability of the state through industry-university partnerships. Nevertheless, in 1991 Texas was given a grade of "D" by the nonprofit Corporation for Enterprise Development, with the educational system, economic performance, international marketing, and state policies cited as particular weaknesses.[6] In 1996, the same rating source graded the state "A" for business vitality, but "C" for development capacity and "D" for economic performance.[7] That same year, however, the Development Counsellors International, based on a poll of 173 executives in top firms on sites they would consider for relocation, called Texas one of the top places for business locations, running second only to North Carolina in the "business beauty pageant."[8]

The state comptroller frequently noted that the state should outperform the nation economically during much of the 1990s.[9] State leaders talked about the history of the state and the ability of Texans to overcome adversity—"perform when the water's hot," as one of the chapter opening quotations says.[10] In 1993, state leaders

5. Anne Reifenberg, "Biggest Industry in Texas? You'll Be Sorry You Asked," *Wall Street Journal,* January 28, 1998, T1.

6. Mark Tatge, "Texas Fails to Make the Grade," *Dallas Morning News,* April 24, 1991, 1D, 4D. This rating measures public policies promoting economic development.

7. Michael Totty, "It May Be Time for Texas to Rethink Business Plan," *Wall Street Journal,* September 24, 1997, T1.

8. Steve Brown, "Texas No. 2 on List of Best Business Sites," *Dallas Morning News,* October 2, 1996, 1D, 10D.

9. See, for example, "The Texas Economic Outlook," *Texas Economic Quarterly,*" a publication of the Comptroller of Public Accounts, March 1994, 1–4; and John Sharp, *The Changing Face of Texas: Texas through the Year 2026: Economic Growth, Cultural Diversity* (Austin: Comptroller of Public Accounts, August 1992).

10. See Diane Jennings, "Extracting a Lesson: Texas Emerges from Economic Bust Wary, Wiser," *Dallas Morning News,* August 8, 1993, 1A, 34A, 35A, and the four-part series, "Texas in the Last Decade: From Boom to Bust—and Back Again," *Dallas Morning News,* March 17–20, 1996, for in-depth looks at economic recovery in the state.

strongly supported passage of the North American Free Trade Agreement (NAFTA), which economically links all of North America, because Texas is a major gateway to trade with Mexico.

The Present

The optimism proved to be well founded. The state's economy continued to improve. During the entire decade of the 1990s, Texas outpaced the rest of the country in economic growth. As the comptroller's comment at the beginning of the chapter attests, the boom was expected to continue into the new century.[11]

By the fall of 1999 Texas was creating 26,000 new jobs a month, although some concern was expressed about the number of those jobs that were in low-paying service industries. College-educated workers who found jobs in the growing technology industry were doing well. Restaurant workers and less-skilled employees in the health care industry often earned below-average wages.[12] The distance between highly skilled and unskilled workers seemed to be growing.

In November 1999, unemployment statewide was 4.2 percent—a figure last seen in 1979. High-technology centers such as Austin, Dallas, and Bryan–College Station had virtually full employment, with only 1.5–2.9 percent of workers unable to find work. Petrochemical centers and border cities were less fortunate; unemployment in McAllen-Edinburg-Mission stood at 13 percent.[13] New and expanded corporate facilities in 1994–1996 numbered 1,968, second only to Ohio.[14] High technology, financial services, manufacturing, and communications were the economic engines for the job growth. As we shall see, one reflection of the newly booming economy was the $98.1 billion budget approved by the legislature in 1999.

Analysis

At least six reasons help explain the ups and downs of the Texas economy and the growth in the state budget over the past quarter century. First, overproduction of oil worldwide in the early 1980s, and again in the 1990s, led to price slides that placed a strain on the Texas economy, especially in the earlier period. However, oil prices experienced a resurgence in 1999. Second, federal assistance to the states has waxed and waned over the past twenty years and is likely to decline again as a result of changes in federal social programs that first took effect in the fall of 1997. Third, Texans responded to the challenges posed by the economic doldrums of the 1980s and diversified the economy. Fourth, at times during the 1970s, double-digit inflation prevailed; both public and private spending increased in proportion to the inflation rate. During the 1980s and 1990s, the nation continued to experience some inflation, but at a much lower rate. Fifth, the Texas revenue system, particularly its tax structure, lacks **elasticity,**

---

11. "Rainy Day Fundamentals: Economic Good Times Offer Texas Chance to Build Reserves," *Fiscal Notes*, January 1999, 6–9.

12. See, for example, "Texas Tomorrow," the special section of the *Dallas Morning News* published on December 19, 1999.

13. Larry Bollinger, "County Jobless Rate Low," *Denton Record-Chronicle*, December 17, 1999, 16A.

14. "Expanding in Texas," *Fiscal Notes*, May 1997, 16.

that is, it is not easily adjusted to ups and downs in the economy. In the mid-to-late 1990s, the most important factor was the booming economy, but only cautious optimism should prevail since the inelastic revenue structure coupled with spending demands and federal cutbacks could be a problem in the new century if the economy should sag. Sixth, when state government did enjoy a surplus in 1997, it chose to rebate the money to taxpayers in the form of reduced local school taxes; the 1999 surplus partly went for improved services but also included tax cuts. This action was in line with strong conservative trends to reduce taxes rather than increase spending.

WHERE DOES THE MONEY COME FROM?

State finance consists of raising and spending money. For most of those who are involved in government, the budget is the bottom line, as it is for the rest of us. Policy decisions regarding state financing are made in the glaring light of political reality—what political scientist Harold Laswell called "Politics: Who Gets What, When, and How." Whenever money is raised, it comes from someone; whenever it is spent, someone gets it. Struggles over who will pay for the government and who will receive dollars from it are at the heart of politics in Texas, as elsewhere.

Figure 10.1 gives us an approximate idea of the sources of state revenue for FY 2000–2001. It shows that 56.2 percent of all revenues comes from sources deposited as general revenue. These include the sales tax, the severance tax, vehicle sales and rental taxes, motor fuel taxes, and miscellaneous other taxes such as those on alcohol and tobacco, as well as fines, fees, interests, and dividends. In addition, portions of some revenues are dedicated to particular purposes, most notably the portion of the motor fuel taxes that goes to public schools and the oil and gas lease royalties that go to the Permanent University Fund; there are about 200 funds with such particular purposes, and the revenues that feed these funds account for 6.4 percent of the total revenue of the state. Another 28.2 percent comes from federal revenue, especially for highways, health, and welfare. Also, 9.2 percent of revenues comes from other sources such as the lottery, bond funds, the state highway trust, interagency contracts, and "local" income (such as tuition and fees) collected by colleges and universities.

The revenue picture of the state shows many fluctuations. In 1979, the severance tax—the oil and gas tax—produced 22 percent of state revenues. By 1999, that tax produced only 1.6 percent, testimony to the glut of oil on the international market that caused falling prices as well as the state's own decline in production. In FY 1984–85, federal funds contributed only 19.4 percent of state revenues. In FY 1996–97, federal sources peaked at 30.3 percent and began to decline in keeping with national balanced budget initiatives. The state lottery, which began in FY 1992–93, quickly reached 5.1 percent of the state budget at the beginning of FY 1998–99 and was called the most successful lottery in the country. Since then, it has been declining as a source of revenue, in part because of public disenchantment with the payoffs. Lost revenues from these sources have been made up by economic growth that generated added tax revenues, by higher and more expensive fees, and sometimes by requiring local governments to fund some activities previously paid for by the state.

FIGURE 10.1

Recommended Funding for the 2000–2001 Biennium by Fund Source (in Millions)*   SOURCE: Legislative
Budget Board, *HB 1 Conference Summary,* May 24, 1999, 4.

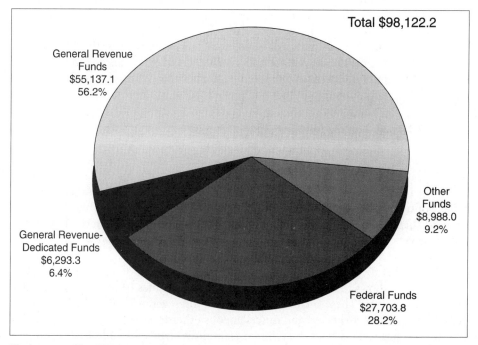

*Totals may not add to 100% due to rounding.

Nontax Sources of Revenues

Federal Grants.   The state has sources of revenue other than the checks oil producers write to the state comptroller and the pennies, nickels, and dimes that citizens
dig out of their pockets to satisfy the sales tax. Monies also come to the state treasury
from federal grants. In fact, beginning in the 1960s, state and local governments became heavily dependent on national budgetary policies that distributed monies to the
treasuries of states, cities, and other local governments. Originally these dollars came
to states in the form of **categorical grants-in-aid,** which could be used only for specific programs such as community-health centers. Under President Richard Nixon,
revenue sharing was enacted. Distributed by formula, general revenue-sharing funds
could be used by state and local governments for whatever projects these governments wanted—police salaries, playground equipment, home care for the elderly. In
addition, the federal government began to fund **block grants,** which provide money
for general use in broad programs such as community development. However, federal funding of state and local programs reached a peak in 1978; after that, President
Jimmy Carter's administration began to phase the national government out of some
programs. General revenue sharing for states ended in 1979 and for cities, in 1986.

When President Ronald Reagan was elected, he emphasized the concept of block grants even more. State and local governments gained considerable flexibility under Reagan's version of "New Federalism" because more and more categorical grants were consolidated into block grants. The state gained more control because many funds were no longer channeled directly to local governments but first "passed through" a state agency. This flexibility came at a price, however, as the amount of funding for many programs, especially those affecting the poor and urban development, was reduced. For the first time in a third of a century, states had a dollar drop in federal aid in 1982 as a result of Carter-Reagan fiscal federalism.

Recent increases in federal funding have been attributable to interstate highway construction and maintenance spending following the increase in the national motor fuels tax in 1983. In the early 1990s, additional federal funds were forthcoming as a result of the state's aggressive pursuit of Medicaid funds to assist with hospital care for the needy and the school lunch program. However, critics of state policy processes have continued to criticize Texas officials for not taking full advantage of national programs. Although expressing sympathy for the nation's cities and their problems, President Bill Clinton had to contend with the need for budget balancing. The "implication of this budget-balance strategy is that by 2002 grants to state and local governments will need to be about 25 percent less."[15] National welfare reform legislation signed shortly before the 1996 presidential election has resulted in the states being asked to take on new responsibilities for health benefits for the poor and to emphasize job placements instead of cash assistance as the focus of welfare programs (see Chapter Eleven).[16] Figure 10.2 illustrates the fluctuations in federal funding over six biennia. While a drop from 30.3 percent (FY 1996–97) to 28.2 percent (FY2000–2002) may not seem significant, in dollar amounts a 4 percent difference is about $4 *billion.*

Borrowing.   Governments, like private citizens, borrow money. The reasons are varied. Political expediency is one. Borrowing allows governments to implement new programs and extend existing ones without increasing taxes. A second reason is that borrowing allows beneficiaries of a state service to pay for that service. Students who live in residence halls, for example, help pay off the bonds used to finance those halls through their room fees.

State government indebtedness is highly restricted in Texas, however. The framers of the state constitution strongly believed in "pay-as-you-go" government. A four-fifths vote of the legislature is needed to approve emergency borrowing, and the state's debt ceiling originally was limited to $200,000. A series of amendments has altered the constitution to allow the issuance of state bonds for specific programs, particularly land for veterans, university buildings, student loans, parks, prisons, and water development. At the end of fiscal year 1996, total state indebtedness was almost

15. Andrew Reschovsky, "A Balanced Federal Budget: The Effect on States," *The LaFollette Policy Report,* 8, no. 1 (Winter 1997), 8.

16. See, for example, Carl Tubbesing and Sheri Steisel, "Answers to Your Welfare Worries," *State Legislatures,* January 1997, 12–19; Rob Gurwitt, "Cracking the Casework Culture," *Governing,* March 1997, 27–30; and William McKenzie, "Texas Tries to Pick Up the Federal Burden," *Dallas Morning News,* May 20, 1997, 13A.

FIGURE 10.2

Federal Funds as Percentage of State Revenues, 1990–91 to 2000–2001   SOURCE: *Fiscal Size Up,*
1990–91 through *1998–99 Bienniums* (Austin: Legislative Budget Board, 1990, 1992, 1994, 1996, 1998), fig. 1 in chapter 2; and
Summary, Conference Committee Report on House Bill 1, Appropriations for the 2000–01 Biennium, May 24, 1999.

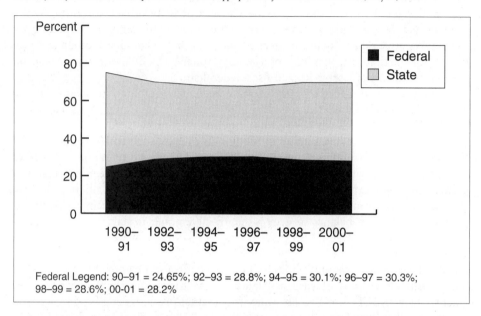

Federal Legend: 90–91 = 24.65%; 92–93 = 28.8%; 94–95 = 30.1%; 96–97 = 30.3%;
98–99 = 28.6%; 00-01 = 28.2%

$14.6 billion. Although this figure may seem high, on a per-person basis, only five
states had a lower level of indebtedness than Texas.[17]

Other Nontax Sources.   Because taxes are unpopular in Texas (and elsewhere),
government inevitably looks to nontax revenue sources whenever possible. The
prospective budget deficits that began in 1985 have led the state to raise money by increasing fees for almost everything, looking to gambling as a source of public revenue, and even manipulating state pension funds. An excellent example is college
tuition, a type of *user fee*—that is, a sum paid in direct exchange for a service. Senior
college tuition has risen from $4 a credit hour in 1985 to a base of $120 plus $40 per
semester hour in 2000–2001. Institutions can and do charge considerably more for
graduate and professional education. Each community college district sets its own
rate since community colleges are financially supported not only by state revenues
but also by local taxes. Originally, the community/junior colleges kept tuition on the
low end, but by 2000 most community colleges were charging $17 to $35 per credit
hour. What college students have really noticed is the great increase in fees, with universities in particular charging a separate fee for almost everything—for each course,
for publications, for building use, for computer use, and so on. These fees speak to
institutional desperation to overcome inadequate state funding and to deal with the
"privatization" of higher education—that is, a steady erosion of public support in

17. *The Book of the States, 1998–99,* vol. 32 (Lexington, KY: Council of State Governments, 1998), 262.

One of the arguments against establishing a state lottery was that the people who could least afford to wager in a lottery would be most enticed to do so. Nevertheless, a lottery was approved by the voters and began in 1992. It has proved to be the most successful state lottery in the country, but revenues had begun to decline by 1999.

SOURCE: Courtesy of Ben Sargent.

favor of students, grant givers, and donors covering more of the cost of education. The legislature finally called for many of these fees to be rolled into tuition to cause less confusion for those paying the bills.

Another revenue measure that you as a college student will notice is that a driver's license costs $24 but is valid for six years. Other fees for everything from car inspections to water permits, from personal automobile tags to day-care center operator licenses continue to increase. Fines for various legal infractions have risen. Even the cost of fishing licenses has gone up.

Other nontax sources of state revenue include the interest on bank deposits, proceeds from investments, and sales and leases of public lands. Having a surplus increases investment income. A lack of robustness in the oil industry decreases income from land leases.

The 1987 legislature proposed a constitutional amendment, approved by the voters in November of that year, that permitted pari-mutuel betting on horse races and, in three counties, on dog races on a local-option basis. By 1991, however, track betting had contributed virtually nothing to state coffers because the state's share of the proceeds—5 percent—was so high that track developers declined the opportunity to invest. Even though the 1991 legislature lowered the state's share to a graduated rate beginning at 1 percent, first-class tracks have been slow in coming.

A state lottery also was debated but was not approved by the legislature in 1987, 1989, and 1991. Ann Richards and her Democratic primary opponent Jim Mattox had both campaigned on a pro-lottery platform in 1990. Governor Richards apparently was able to work out a deal with enough legislators—allegedly supporting their redistricting concerns—to get a lottery on the November 1991 ballot. Voters approved the lottery, which began in summer 1992. Since then, whether the revenues were to be dedicated to education has been an issue. The 1997 legislature did dedicate the revenues, but moved other funds previously earmarked for education back to the general fund. Administrative scandals and some falloff in betting have caused the lottery not to live up to expectations.[18]

Taxation

Taxes are the most familiar sources of governmental revenue and the most controversial. Since colonial days and James Otis's stirring phrase, "No taxation without representation," citizens have sought justice in the tax system. Texas's conservative heritage has not always made justice easy to find.

Taxes are collected for two principal reasons. *Revenue taxes*—for example, the general sales tax—are the major source of governmental income. They make it possible for government to carry out its programs. *Regulatory taxes*—for example, the taxes on tobacco and alcohol—are designed primarily to control those individuals and/or organizations who are subject to them and either punish undesired behavior or reward desired behavior.

Who Pays?   The question of who pays which taxes raises two issues. The first is ability to pay, and the second is whether individuals and businesses both really pay.

Ability to Pay.   A matter of some importance to taxpayers is whether their taxes are progressive or regressive. **Progressive taxation** is characterized by a rate that increases as the object taxed—property, income, or goods purchased—grows larger or gains in value. Progressive taxation is based on ability to pay. The best-known example is the federal income tax, which progresses from relatively low rates for those with the least income to increasingly higher rates for those with larger incomes. Note, however, that loopholes in the federal tax laws and ceilings on special taxes such as Social Security still result in a proportionately heavier tax burden for the middle class than for the wealthy.

Regressive Taxation.   Although technically a tax system that involves a higher rate with a declining base, **regressive taxation** has come to refer to a system in which lower-income earners spend larger percentages of their incomes on commodities subject to flat tax rates. The best example of Texas's reliance on regressive taxes is the general retail sales tax. Almost one-third of Texas revenues from all sources come from this sales tax, which is assessed at 6.25 percent on a wide variety of goods and

---

18. See George Kuempel, "Reversal of Fortunes," *Dallas Morning News,* February 19, 1999, 29A.

FIGURE 10.3

Percent of Income Paid in Sales Taxes, Selected Income Levels SOURCE: Constructed from information in Robert Elder, "Study Shows Who Really Bears the Sales-Tax Burden," *Wall Street Journal,* February 3, 1999, T1; the article in turn was based on official estimates of the comptroller in the "Tax Exemptions and Tax Incidence Report" published prior to the 1999 legislative session.

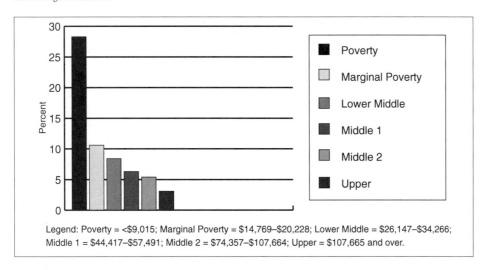

Legend: Poverty = <$9,015; Marginal Poverty = $14,769–$20,228; Lower Middle = $26,147–$34,266; Middle 1 = $44,417–$57,491; Middle 2 = $74,357–$107,664; Upper = $107,665 and over.

services at the time of sale, regardless of the income or wealth of the purchaser (see Figure 10.1). Municipalities can levy a 1 percent additional tax, as can mass transit districts and county economic development districts. Municipalities can also add additional sales tax percentages of a half percent each for economic development and in lieu of reduced property taxes. The additional selective sales (excise) taxes—those levied on tobacco products, alcoholic beverages, and motor fuels, for example—also are regressive. The $18,000-a-year secretary and the $150,000-a-year executive who drive the same distance to work pay the same 20-cent-a-gallon tax on gasoline, but who is better able to bear the tax burden?

Citizens for Tax Justice, a Washington, D.C.–based research and lobbying group, examined tax structures in all fifty states in 1996. The group dubbed ten states, including Texas, "the terrible 10" for the regressivity of their tax structures. Only Washington and Florida have higher tax rates for their poorest citizens than does Texas, and only Washington, Florida, South Dakota, and Tennessee tax their richest citizens as lightly as does Texas.[19] Figure 10.3 shows the sharp drop in percentage of income paid in sales taxes in Texas as income itself increases. This figure factors in the effects of exemptions as well as taxes paid. The poorest Texans pay 28.3 percent of their income in sales taxes, while the richest pay only 3.1 percent.[20] The gap, while large, has grown somewhat narrower during the 1990s. Also, Texas, unlike some states, does not tax "lifeline items"—food purchased at a grocery store, prescription medicines, or work clothes.

19. Michael P. Ettlinger, *Who Pays? A Distributional Analysis of the Tax Systems in All 50 States* (Washington, DC: Citizens for Tax Justice, 1996), 2–3. All these states rely on sales taxes rather than a personal income tax.

20. Robert Elder, "Study Shows Who Really Bears the Sales-Tax Burden," *Wall Street Journal,* February 3, 1999, T1.

Texas is one of only seven states with no personal income tax and one of five with no corporate income tax, although many people consider that the corporation franchise tax (to be discussed) serves as a corporate income tax.[21]

At this stage, Texas cannot claim to have a progressive tax system. Yet a fair tax system is a value associated with democratic government. Many observers believe that a progressive income tax would be fairer than the general sales tax and could replace all or part of it. But the state's conservatism and the dominance of business lobbies in the state government have thus far precluded the adoption of a progressive tax policy, either based on ability to pay or a flat percentage of total income. However, some business leaders have begun to advocate a state income tax, and changes in the corporation franchise tax in 1991 were a first step toward a corporate income tax.

One may also note that, while the terms *progressive* and *regressive* are most commonly applied to taxes, they can apply to other forms of revenue as well. No good example exists for a progressive revenue source that is not a tax, but a set fine for a traffic violation is regressive in that it is not based on ability to pay.

Taxes Paid by Individuals.   A number of taxes are levied directly against individuals—for example, the inheritance tax collected at the time beneficiaries inherit estates, the motor fuels tax paid each time a motorist buys gasoline, and the ad valorem property tax collected on real property, buildings, and land by local governments.[22] Businesses also pay the motor fuels tax and local property taxes, of course, but by increasing prices, they let their customers pick up the tab.

Most authorities also would include all sales taxes in the category of taxes paid by individuals on the assumption that businesses pass them on to the consumer just as they do local ad valorem and state vehicle registration taxes—whether that is the intention of the law or not. There are three types of sales taxes:

1. The *general sales tax* is a broadly based tax that is collected on most goods and services and must be paid by the consumer.
2. *Selective sales taxes (excise taxes)* are levied on only a few items, comparatively speaking, and consumers are often unaware that they are paying them. These taxes are included in the price of the item, not computed separately. Tobacco products, alcoholic beverages—tobacco and alcohol taxes are sometimes called "sin taxes"—automobiles, gasoline, and admission to amusements—movies, plays, nightclubs, sporting events—are among the items taxed in this category.
3. *Gross receipts taxes* are levied on the total gross revenues (sales) of certain businesses: cement producers, telegraph and telephone companies, and private clubs' and bars' sales of liquor by the drink, for example. Technically, they are business taxes that are paid directly by the business. Nonetheless, in most cases, these taxes are actually passed on to the consumer, either directly or indirectly.

Taxes Levied on Businesses.   Taxes levied on businesses in Texas produce considerable revenue for the state but are often regulatory in nature. One example is the *sev-*

21. "State Individual Income Tax Rates" and "State Corporate Income Tax Rates" (Washington, DC: Federation of Tax Administrations, 1999), available at www.taxadmin.org under "Tax Rates."

22. The state ad valorem (property) tax was abolished by a 1982 constitutional amendment.

erance taxes levied on natural resources, such as crude oil, natural gas, and sulfur, that are severed (removed) from the earth. This removal, of course, depletes irreplaceable resources, and part of the tax revenue is dedicated to conservation programs and to the regulation of production; thirty other states have similar taxes. Severance taxes once were the backbone of the state's revenue system, but the steady decline in the oil business for more than a decade has resulted in these taxes contributing less than 2 percent of current revenues.

The major Texas business tax today is the *corporation franchise tax,* which is assessed against corporations as the price of doing business in the state. Some people regard it as a type of corporate income tax because the business pays tax on invested assets (capital) or income, whichever amount is greater. This tax was overhauled substantially in 1991 to make it fairer, since it originally emphasized taxes on capital-intensive businesses such as manufacturing and collected little from labor-intensive businesses such as computer software firms, financial institutions, and even the big downtown law firms. The tax is expected to provide about 7 percent of state revenue for FY 2000–2001.

Another tax levied directly on businesses in Texas is the *insurance premium tax,* levied on gross premiums collected by insurance companies. Businesses also pay *special taxes and fees* for such varied activities as chartering a corporation, brewing alcoholic beverages, and selling real estate. These taxes are largely paid by consumers in the form of higher prices. Indeed, other than a corporation net profits tax, it is almost impossible to construct a tax that cannot and will not be passed on to the consumer, at least so long as consumers are willing to pay higher prices.

Who Benefits?   To address the question of who benefits from tax policies, we must consider the kinds of services the government provides. Nothing would seem to be more equitable than a tax structure resulting in an exact ratio between taxes paid and benefits received, and in Texas some taxes are levied with exactly that idea in mind. The motor fuels tax, 20 cents per gallon on gasoline and diesel fuel, is paid by those who use motor vehicles, and three-fourths of the revenues from this tax are spent on maintaining and building highways and roads. The remainder goes to public schools. However, this same motor fuels tax also points up a paradox in the "benefit theory" of taxation: People who do not own automobiles and do not buy gasoline also benefit from those big trucks hauling goods to market over state highways.

The Tax Burden in Texas

Texas has prided itself on being a low tax state, and the George W. Bush legislative agenda for 1997 and 1999 pushed tax relief—a popular short-term approach during a boom economy. When the *state only* tax burden is considered, Texas ranks 44th in the country, indicating that it is, indeed, a low-tax state.[23] A further indication of the Texas tax effort is the ranking of the Tax Foundation, a Washington think tank. The Foundation listed Texas as 41st in combined state and local taxes for 1999.[24] The 41st

23. Mary J. Sprouse and Teresa Tritch, "Stop Paying 50% in Taxes," *Money,* January 1995, 92–93, and "1998 Texas Fact Book" available at www.lbb.state.tx.us by clicking on "Fact Book."

24. Curt Anderson, "Few Changes Seen in Tax Code," an Associated Press report, *Dallas Morning News,* January 9, 2000, 6A.

place ranking indicates that the state may not be so supportive of its local governments as some other states, causing local taxes to be proportionally higher. However, the school property tax relief measures begun in 1999 had a dramatic effect. In 1996, the combined state and local tax burden placed the state 30th.

One irony of the Texas tax situation is that the state does not fare well under many federal grant formulas, which include tax effort—the tax effort already borne by citizens—as a criterion. The state does least well on matching grants for social services and welfare. Although the state is third in total federal receipts, mainly from defense spending at military bases and with military contractors, only nine states have lower *per capita* federal expenditures than Texas.[25] Typically, Texans contribute more in federal taxes to get back a dollar in federal grants than other states. Moreover, because of the way that deductions work in the federal income tax system, the Texas tax system, as of 1997, costs Texans an estimated $331 million a year in extra federal taxes that would not have to be paid if the state relied on an income tax rather than

25. "Texas Is 3rd in Receipt of Federal Money," *Austin American-Statesman*, April 3, 1997, A10.

From Bust to Boom: A Summary of Revenue and Spending Measures in the FY 1984–85 to FY 2000–2001 Period

FY 84–85: Broad-based $4.8-billion revenue package to provide additional funding for highways and public schools; major increases in user fees

FY 86–87: $512 million in budget cuts, $872 million in new taxes

FY 88–89: $5.7 billion in new taxes; intensive study by a Select Committee on Tax Equity, whose recommendations were subsequently ignored

FY 90–91: Legislative authorization of a 12 percent *spending* increase by fiscal sleight-of-hand tricks such as using the money reserved to settle lawsuits against the state; another tax study that was ignored

FY 92–93: Initiation of the governor's Texas Performance Review (TPR) spearheaded by Comptroller John Sharp leading to $382 million in budget cuts—not all of which materialized, leading to other cuts in agency budgets for FY 93; thirty new revenue measures, including a major restructuring of the corporation franchise tax, totaling $2.6 billion; voter approval of a state lottery

FY 94–95: $2 billion in increased revenues without any tax increase due to measures such as TPR savings on Medicaid and changes in tax collection schedules; voter approval of a constitutional amendment limiting the possibility of an income tax to simultaneous local property tax relief

FY 96–97: $9.8 billion in increased revenues without any tax increase due to an improved economy, more federal contributions, more lottery revenues

FY 98–99: Constitutional amendment to triple the homestead tax allowance for school districts, with the revenue loss to be made up with surplus state funds; more than a $7 billion *spending* increase due to a strong economy, federal funds; failure to produce a bill incorporating recommendations from the governor's tax study

FY 00–01: $506 million in tax breaks, including some for business (research and development tax credits, no severance tax for small producers when prices are low) and some for consumers (the end of the sales tax on over-the-counter medicines and some Internet services plus a back-to-school tax holiday on some items of clothing); continuing pressures on local governments to raise the property tax to make up for a lack of state revenues allocated to them; also, an $11 billion spending increase due to the continuing strong economy

sales taxes.[26] New Mexico is at the top of the list in terms of getting more money back than it paid; New Jersey is at the bottom.[27]

The Dawn of the Twenty-first Century

Perspectives from the Past.   For a half century, Texas relied on oil and gas production taxes as the major source of state revenue, with most of these being paid by out-of-state purchasers. How good were the good old days? "Texas went from 1971 to 1984 . . . without an increase in state tax rates, or new taxes" while the population was growing 42 percent.[28] After the world oil market crashed, Texans were ill prepared to develop a responsible and responsive revenue policy to provide dollars for state services. As the previous box shows, the state got better at revenue measures, then benefited subsequently from a booming economy and some added federal funds.

What's Next?   Texas will be no different from other states in its need to find adequate *and* equitable revenue sources to support the services needed by a rapidly growing citizenry and to make up for federal funding cuts that will have a major effect on the states. One strategy that the state will pursue is *performance evaluation and management,* including funding cutbacks that are recommended in the biennial Texas Performance Review. The importance of the Texas Performance Review can only grow. For FY 2000–2001, Comptroller Carol Keeton Rylander published *Challenging the Status Quo: Toward Smaller, Smarter Government,* which called for a variety of cutback measures including a 1.25 percent general revenue decrease for each state agency with 100 or more employees, selling or leasing surplus land, and eliminating overlapping programs and agencies. Her proposals totaled $207.4 million. Rylander said, "I am committed to lean, efficient government and to the recognition that government cannot and should not be all things to all people."[29] The performance evaluation/cutback approach is grounded in a national movement to "reinvent government."[30] This demand emerged from strategic planning and quality management movements in the private sector as sluggish industries had to downsize—or, in the new terminology, "rightsize."

Performance reviews speak not only to "smaller" but also to "smarter." In 1999, *Governing* magazine gave Texas good marks for its management practices. Texas got a "B" for financial management, human resources, and information technology; a "B+" for managing for results; but a "C" on capital management because of the lack

---

26. Dave McNeely, "No Texas Income Tax Means More for Feds," *Austin American-Statesman,* April 15, 1997, A11.

27. "Do You Subsidize New Mexico?" *Money,* January 1998, 23.

28. "Bullock's Tax Speech Serves as a Warning for State," *Austin American-Statesman,* January 27, 1991, A8.

29. Carol Keeton Rylander, *Challenging the Status Quo: Toward Smaller, Smarter Government,* vol. 1, available at www.window.state.tx.us/tpr/tpr5/vol1/vol1.html, 1.

30. See, for example, David Osborne and Ted Gaebler, *Reinventing Government* (Reading, MA: Addison-Wesley, 1992), especially chapter 5 on "Results-Oriented Government"; Jonathan Walters, "The Cult of Total Quality," *Governing,* May 1992, 38–41; and the many reports stemming from the Texas Performance Review and the National Performance Review.

of a coherent capital plan or identifiable capital budget. The state's overall grade was "B," placing it in the top third of all states.[31]

Another strategy is *privatization.* Two examples are the private prisons that now serve the state and the increasing rate of tuition and fees paid by college students. The first is direct private provision of service; the second is passing along the cost to private citizens rather than burdening the revenue system.

A third strategy is to *change the revenue structure* in order to avert the **revenue shortfalls** that plagued the state in the 1980s, especially by making the system more elastic, and adequately to fund state services. The major change to date is the restructuring of the corporate franchise tax discussed earlier in this chapter. The dominant issue of the 1997 legislative session was revenue restructuring to lower school property taxes, but the lower property taxes did not stem from a new revenue system. Instead, the difference between the revenues formerly raised by the school districts and what they raise now is made up by state surpluses, with uncertainties about what happens when there is not a surplus.

Democratic theory recognizes the equality of the citizenry, and many people think that a tax system that extracts more from people the poorer they are seriously compromises equality. Since 1991 business is paying a greater share of taxes, but, as previously noted, the tax system in Texas still is regressive, placing a proportionately heavier burden on those with the lowest incomes. The reality is that without an income tax, the state will always have difficulty meeting its revenue needs in anything other than a booming economy. Historically, Texas attracted businesses because they found the state's tax structure favorable. However, the experience of other states with economic development indicates that many modern industries are also concerned about stability in providing for state services. Such stability is difficult in the absence of a flexible tax structure.

Another aspect of revenue structure is the competition among governments for tax sources. National and state governments both tax motor fuels, tobacco, and alcohol, for example, and both levels of government keep increasing tax rates. Both the state and local governments have general sales taxes. The upshot is that the combined

---

31. "Texas," *Governing,* February 1999, 80; see also "Report Card of the States," *Fiscal Notes,* published by the Comptroller of Public Accounts, April 1999, 3–4.

Round Two

Texas experimented with private prisons from 1871 to 1882. The state leased to private companies all of the land, prison buildings, and prisoners for an annual payment. The system was short lived because of rampant abuse of prisoners.

SOURCE: David M. Horton and Ryan Kellus Turner, *Lone Star Justice* (Austin: Eakin Press, 1999), 217–18.

tax rates begin to vex citizens after a while. Ironically, federal income tax rates were cut in the 1980s, enhancing the income tax as a logical new source of state revenue.

For tax restructuring to occur, state politics would have to change. Businesses, including partnerships, would have to accept some sort of business activity tax that functions as an income tax, whatever it is called. Ultimately, private citizens would have to be willing to accept a personal income tax. Businesses accepted major changes in the corporation franchise tax in 1991, but the 1997 tax reform efforts ran into buzz saws wielded by groups such as law partnerships that escape the present system and demands by large corporations that dividends and interest they received from out of state be exempted from the franchise tax. Only about one-third of private citizens now file an itemized federal tax return, so that one argument that in the past has favored an income tax—the ability to deduct state income taxes but not sales taxes from one's federal income tax return—may be dead, too. Changes in public attitude are critical to legislative action, since in the past mere advocacy of an income tax was a sure ticket out of office. However, as Jared Hazleton, former director of the Texas Research League, stated: "The more the sales tax is broadened, the more it looks like an income tax in drag."[32] Thus, in theory the state might just as well consider a real income tax on personal income, corporate net profits, or both.

32. Robert Reinhold, "For Texans, the Unthinkable: State Income Tax on the Horizon," *New York Times*, April 6, 1987, 1.

The work of the 75th Legislature in 1997 illustrates the difficulty of tax restructuring. The governor made reduction of the local school property tax and elimination of the Robin Hood system of rich school districts making financial contributions to poor ones his number one concern. He proposed that the state pick up the slack for the schools by imposing a business property tax for school maintenance and operations, expanding the franchise tax to include all partnerships, eliminating exemptions from the sales tax, and increasing the motor fuels tax.

Although political observers claimed that the governor's plan was dead on arrival, both the House and the Senate produced tax bills. The bills varied significantly in the amount of local property tax reductions, the amount of the increase in sin taxes, whether to include new motor fuels taxes, and special business fees. The business lobbies went to work and effectively prevented the emergence of a compromise bill.

In the end, all that happened in the 1997 session was a proposed constitutional amendment that would increase from $5,000 to $15,000 the amount of valuation of a homestead that could be protected from taxation. The resulting revenue deficit for school districts was covered by a budget surplus (and perhaps by future taxes when no surplus exists). Legislators themselves were frustrated by the huge amount of work they had done with such a small result.

SOURCES: See, for example, Wayne Slater and Richard A. Oppel Jr., "Legislature Abandons Tax Efforts: Bush Turns Focus toward Raising Homestead Break," *Dallas Morning News*, May 25, 1997, 1A, 32A; Shannon Noble, "Countdown to June 2," *Legislative Newsletter of the League of Women Voters of Texas*, May 29, 1997, 1–2; and Michele Kay, "Tax Overhaul Is Dead, Bush Declares," *Austin American-Statesman*, May 25, 1997, A1, A14–15.

Former Lieutenant Governor Bill Hobby was fond of saying that "the [legislative] session is all about the budget; the rest is poetry." The budget is not just spending, but also revenues. In 1988, 1991, and 1996, high-level special committees studied the state's revenue system. Although Governor George W. Bush made tax reform his number one legislative issue in 1997, only minor tinkering resulted.

SOURCE: Courtesy of Ben Sargent.

WHERE DOES THE MONEY GO?

Occasionally an argument is heard in the state's legislative chambers that reflects serious concern about budgeting a particular program—who will benefit from it, whether it is needed by society, and how it will be financed. More generally, however, whether funds are allocated for a proposed program depends on which interests favor it and how powerful they are, who and how powerful the opposition is, and what are the results of compromises and coalitions between these and "swing vote" groups. The political viewpoints of the legislators, the governor, and the state bureaucracy also have an impact on budgetary decisions. In short, decisions about spending public money, like decisions about whom and what to tax, are not made objectively. Rather, they are the result of the complex relationships among the hundreds of political actors who participate in the state's governmental system. The biases of the political system are thus reflected in the biases of state spending.

This section outlines the stages in the budgetary process, then describes the major expenditures of the state.

Budgetary Process

The budgetary process consists of three stages: planning and preparation, authorization and appropriation, and execution (spending). Budget planning and the preparation of the proposed budget is a function of the chief executive in the national government and in forty-four states, but Texas has a **dual-budgeting system.** The constitution makes the legislature responsible for the state budget. The legislature is aided in this task by the Legislative Budget Board (LBB) and its staff, who prepare a draft budget. The LBB is made up of four senators and four representatives; it is chaired by the lieutenant governor, and the speaker of the House serves as the vice chairman. However, modern governors have understood the importance of the budget as a political tool, and with the aid of the Office of Budget and Planning, the governor also prepares a budget. This duplicate effort is wasteful, but it does allow for different political perspectives on state spending to be heard. The LBB and governor's staffs hold joint budget hearings at which agency representatives justify their requests.

The authorization and appropriation stage consists of the authorization of programs to be provided by the state and the passage of a bill appropriating money—the state budget. The House Ways and Means (revenues), House Appropriations (spending), and Senate Finance (both revenues and spending) committees are the key legislative players. Agency representatives, the governor's staff, interest group representatives, and private citizens testify on behalf of the particular agency or program of concern to them. There is considerable forming and re-forming of coalitions as legislators, lobbyists, and committee members bargain, compromise, trade votes, and generally endeavor to obtain as much for "their side" as possible. Past campaign contributions begin to pay off at this stage, and the relative power of different interest groups is reflected in the state budget. For example, political campaigns frequently include a call to "get tough on crime" and to build more prisons; in turn, prisons are typically well funded. The four main teachers' groups in the state expend considerable effort in trying to influence legislators, and schoolteachers usually get raises, albeit often small ones. The success of the business lobby is the most problematic. In 1995, business got virtually everything it wanted. In 1997, business buried the tax bill it did not want but also found itself on the receiving end of a lot of negative legislation. In 1999, business got some tax breaks and the ability to shop for competitive electric rates.

The authorization and appropriation stage is a lengthy one, and the Appropriations and Finance committees submit their reports—the two versions of the appropriations bill—near the end of the session. The two versions are never identical, so a ten-member conference committee made up of an equal number of senators and representatives carefully selected by the presiding officers must develop a single conference report on the budget. The two houses must accept or reject the report as it stands, including adequate revenue measures to fund the proposed spending, since Texas has a balanced-budget requirement.

The approved appropriations bill then goes to the governor for signature. The governor has a very powerful weapon: the line-item veto, which allows him to strike individual spending provisions from the appropriations bill if he disagrees with them. However, the governor cannot add to the budget or restore funding for a pet project that the legislature rejected.

The final budget stage, execution, is a rather technical one. It includes shifting money into various state funds, issuing state warrants (which are like checks), and auditing expenditures.

Major Expenditures

To the average citizen, which programs and services are funded by the budget are of far greater interest than the details of the budget process. Figure 10.4 shows that health and human services plus education account for almost three-fourths of the FY 2000–2001 Texas budget of $98.1 billion.

Education.   For FY 2000–2001, 45.3 percent of the state budget was slated for public schools and higher education. More than three-fifths of the education budget— $28.6 billion—was for elementary and secondary schools in the state's 1,087 independent school districts[33] and for state schools for the deaf and visually impaired. The state provides textbooks as well as special services such as programs for disabled children and vocational courses, the Texas Assessment of Basic Skills (TABS) achievement tests, school buses, operating costs, and teacher salaries. The state does not pay the total costs of public education, however. Local school districts share the cost and also are responsible for buildings and other school facilities. Those that can afford it provide supplements to attract the best teachers, buy additional library books, develop athletic programs, and offer students enrichment opportunities. As was summarized in Chapter Eight, financial equality is the dominant issue affecting public schools. As of 1998–99, Texas ranked 8th among the states in per capita spending for public education.[34]

The other large slice of the education dollar pie—$12 billion—supports higher education: the operations of thirty-six general academic institutions, including five upper-level institutions and a marine science institute, three lower-division centers, fifty-six community/junior college districts, a technical institute with three campuses and four extension centers, ten medical and dental schools plus related programs, and such services as agricultural and engineering extension programs. Higher education did not fare well in the state funding game for more than a decade, but, with a rebounding state treasury in 1997, the legislature paid some attention to higher education. For both junior and senior colleges, a formula based on such factors as semester credit hours determines the basic level of state support, with the formula funding supplemented by special program funding and affected by performance norms originally adopted in 1992. One positive piece of legislation in 1997 was creation of a greatly simplified funding formula. The community/junior colleges also are supported by local districts.

---

33. School districts continue to consolidate over time, but population growth and new communities have led to the creation of a few new districts.

34. *Fiscal Size Up: 1998–99*, 3–1. All the comparative data in this section are drawn from table 16.

FIGURE 10.4

Biennial Recommendations for 2000–2001, All Funds (in Millions)* SOURCE: *Summary, Conference Committee Report on House Bill 1, Appropriations for the 2000–01 Biennium,* May 24, 1999. *Note:* Although the full text of the appropriations bill was available (www.1bbb.state.tx.us, click on CSHB 1) when this figure was prepared, it was less clear on the distribution of funds because of the many special provisions, the governor's vetoes, and numerous contingency statements.

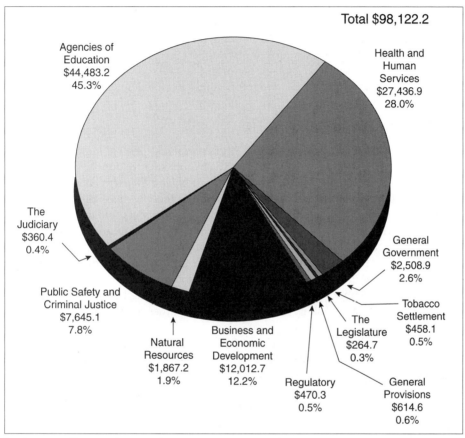

Total $98,122.2

Agencies of Education $44,483.2 45.3%

Health and Human Services $27,436.9 28.0%

The Judiciary $360.4 0.4%

General Government $2,508.9 2.6%

Public Safety and Criminal Justice $7,645.1 7.8%

Tobacco Settlement $458.1 0.5%

Natural Resources $1,867.2 1.9%

Business and Economic Development $12,012.7 12.2%

The Legislature $264.7 0.3%

Regulatory $470.3 0.5%

General Provisions $614.6 0.6%

*Totals may not add to 100% due to rounding.

As Chapter Eleven will show, higher education funding is a continuing issue in Texas. Texas ranked 38th among the states in higher education funding although it may have improved its ranking somewhat with the attention paid to higher education in 1997. New initiatives funded by the 75th Texas Legislature included a "Back to Basics" program to assist the institutions in recruiting and retaining students, especially ethnic minorities.

These figures do not include the cost of teacher certification or the Telecommunications Infrastructure Fund. Neither do they include payments for retirement and insurance contributions.

Health and Human Services.   Over $27 billion—28 percent of the budget—is allocated for human services programs, including welfare, unemployment compensation, employment services, workers' compensation, services for special groups such as the blind and the elderly, and health programs such as mental health and retardation programs, treatment of substance abuse, contagious-disease control, and treatment for catastrophic illnesses such as AIDS, cancer, and kidney failure. Of the $27 billion total, about 60 percent of the funding comes from the national government. Chapter Eleven, will discuss the health and welfare systems.

Although expenditures for health and human services are the second largest segment of the state budget, Texas ranked 38th among the fifty states in welfare services and 24th in hospital services. A major factor in the state's low ranking is the fact that the majority of funding for these programs comes from federal grants, not from the state's general revenues. However, the state has moved up in these two service areas since FY 1990–91, when it was 47th and 36th, respectively.

Business and Economic Development.   Texas's expenditures for business and economic development for FY 2000–2001 are $12 billion, slightly over 12 percent of the total budget. This category includes transportation; the Department of Economic Development, which promotes the state's economy; the efforts of the Housing and Community Affairs Department on behalf of local governments, and employment and training services. Slightly more than one-quarter of the expenditures in this category come from federal highway matching funds to maintain and upgrade the 3,233 miles of federal interstate highways in Texas. In 1977 the legislature capped highway expenditures, with the result that the transportation portion of the state budget has declined from 21 percent to about 9 percent. Texas ranks 39th among the states in per capita spending on highways. Rankings are not available for other services in this category.

Other Major Expenditures.   The next largest category of expenditures is public safety, at $7.6 billion, or 7.8 percent of the total budget. This category includes law enforcement, prisons, and related programs. Texas ranks fifth in the country in prison spending.

The remainder of the budget, $6 billion, accounts for 6.1 percent of state expenditures. Services, programs, and agencies in this category include general government—the legislature, the judiciary, the governor, and various management offices—as well as parks, natural resources, and regulatory agencies.

SUMMARY

E conomic conditions, the political climate, and power plays are all part of the game of generating revenues for state government and determining how that income will be spent. Both taxing and spending are usually incremental, with major changes rarely occurring. However, the state's poor economic health through much of the 1980s and early 1990s meant more tax and fee increases than usual and less budget growth. That "downer" scenario clearly reversed itself by the late 1990s, when both revenue and spending decisions were driven by a robust economy.

In comparing Texas with other states, we find that the combined state and local tax burden is relatively low, with Texas ranked in the bottom fifth of all states. We also note the significant absence of any personal or corporate income tax, although business has been asked to pay a larger share of the tax burden through the corporation franchise tax. The fundamental difference in the Texas revenue system from that of many other states is the disproportionate burden borne by the poorest citizens. This regressive system raises serious questions about how democratic the tax system is in the state.

Democracies are also responsive to the citizenry. The state's spending may not meet the needs of all its citizens, particularly when one considers that Texas ranks in the bottom quarter of all states in its per capita spending for higher education, welfare services, and highways. It ranks in the top 10 percent only in prison spending.

The Texas budget process differs procedurally from the ones used by most other states. These differences include the dual-budgeting system, the extraordinary dominance of the presiding officers in the appropriations process, and the virtually absolute veto power of the governor because of the short legislative session.

Important aspects of state finance in Texas are:

1. The reliance on taxes paid directly or indirectly by the individual
2. The reliance on regressive taxes such as the sales tax as a major revenue source for the state
3. The restrictions on borrowing
4. The importance of federal funds to the state budget
5. The extent to which the budgetary process is dominated by the legislature, and the legislature, in turn, is dominated by the presiding officers
6. The obvious need for diversified revenue sources

The largest category of expenditure is for education, followed by health and human services, business and economic development, public safety and criminal justice, and "other," which includes everything else. Critical issues affecting some of these state service areas are discussed in the next chapter.

STUDY QUESTIONS

1. What are the different sources of nontax revenue in Texas? How have these changed in recent years?
2. Give two reasons why you think Texas should adopt an income tax. Then, give two reasons against the state's adopting an income tax. With which side do you agree? Why?
3. This chapter has criticized both the regressiveness and the lack of elasticity in the Texas tax system. What does each of those terms mean? Give and discuss an example of each, then indicate what some of the revenue considerations are as we prepare to enter the twenty-first century.
4. What pitfalls do you think exist because of the dual-budgeting system? Do you think there are any advantages to such a system?
5. If you could increase spending in any one of the categories shown in Figure 10.4, which would it be? What if the total amount available had to remain the same? Would you still increase spending in that category? If so, in what

category would you decrease expenditures to offset this increase? Discuss the likely effects on services in both the increased and the decreased categories of expenditure.

SURFING THE WEB

The site with official budget data.
www.lbb.state.tx.us

The comptroller's site, which includes both revenue estimates and performance data.
www.window.state.tx.us

Under "Tax Rates," good comparative date for all fifty states.
www.taxadmin.org

Sites for looking at illustrations of progressive and regressive taxes.
http://cc.kzoo.edu/~k98ww01/progressive.html and
http://cc.kzoo.edu/~k98ww01/regressive

11

*T*he new federal welfare
law gives states wide
flexibility to create
solutions for getting
people into jobs. It also
sets parameters,
prescribes standards and
penalizes states if they
don't comply.

Carl Tubbesing and Sheri Steisel,
State Legislatures, 1997

*Water is like sex.
Everybody thinks that
there's more of it around
than there really is and
that everybody else
is getting more than his
fair share.*

Old Wyoming Saying

ISSUES IN PUBLIC POLICY

INTRODUCTION

POVERTY AND WELFARE

HIGHER EDUCATION

THE ENVIRONMENT

SUMMARY

STUDY QUESTIONS

SURFING THE WEB

INTRODUCTION

Texas, like all other states, has an array of programs and services that it needs to address. These constitute the policy agenda for the state. When elected officials develop **public policy,** they are establishing priorities for programs that provide services and benefits to the public. However, agreement on what those priorities should be rarely exists. People even argue, sometimes intensely, about whether government should address some problems at all. Consequently, many controversial issues confront state policymakers. This climate of disagreement and debate is part of a democratic society. Also, even when there is agreement on a particular issue, the fiscal health of the state (see the previous chapter) can complicate the policy agenda considerably. Rarely does a state have enough money to fund all the desired programs, and state finance itself becomes a major policy issue.

The development of public policy begins with the emergence of a problem that needs to be addressed. When someone in government recognizes the need to deal with a problem, it is placed on the policy agenda. One way in which a prospective program or service makes its way onto the policy agenda is through the efforts of the governor and key legislators (see Chapters Six and Seven). Often gubernatorial and legislative viewpoints conflict. In 1999, legislators of both parties were reluctant to slow down the governor's push for a presidential nomination—having a president from one's state yields all sorts of benefits. Thus, Governor Bush was successful in his social and business initiatives but still failed to get through a school voucher program. That program would have allowed students greater choice of elementary and secondary schools. However, voucher programs are complicated because they can also have a detrimental effect on low-performing schools that most need state help, and the governor's plan died in the state senate. A similar disagreement occurred in 1997, when the governor was successful on most counts but could not get everything he wanted for tax cuts. Tax cuts, too, are controversial because reducing state revenue may not please individuals and groups who want an expansion of or improvement in state services such as highways or parks.

A second way in which a prospective program or service gets onto the political agenda is through the political processes described in Chapter Three. Interest groups and lobbyists make known the priorities they think the state should set. These individuals and groups work through both elected officials and the bureaucracy, but they are especially vigorous in pursuing legislative support for their demands. The water policy discussed in this chapter is an example of the coming together of legislative, bureaucratic, and interest group concerns.

Another avenue for setting the policy agenda is through the *intergovernmental* system (the complex relationships among federal, state, and local governments) and the *intragovernmental* system (the relationships that cut across the different branches of government). Often these relationships result in a **mandate,** a term that refers to an action of one government or branch of government that requires another government to act in a certain way. National clean air standards that must be implemented by state and local governments are an example. Intergovernmental and intragovernmental mandates help policymakers to identify and define issues even when they would prefer to ignore them. Mandates are often burdensome to the lower level of government, which is required to act but receives no funding to help implement the new programs.

Mandates have several possible sources. These include the courts, administrative regulations, legislative actions, and/or highly publicized shifts in national priorities. For example, changes in Texas public school finance began in 1973 with a federal court order and continued with a 1987 state court order to provide a more equitable and "efficient" system of funding public schools[1] (see Chapter Eight). Similarly, the state prison system was tied up in a long-running court suit from 1971 until 1993, when the suit was dismissed because the state seemed headed in the right direction to correct historic problems such as overcrowding, abuse of prisoners, and poor health facilities.[2]

The welfare system in Texas is a product of the state's emphasis on efficiency, national budget cutting and changing national priorities, and state efforts to gain administrative approval from the federal bureaucracy. All states are struggling to provide adequate welfare services in the midst of federal changes. The transition from welfare to workfare is discussed in this chapter.

An example of intergovernmental influence through administrative regulations is environmental standards. Across the country, states are trying to deal with provisions of the Clean Water Act, the Safe Drinking Water Act, and the Clean Air Act. As this chapter explains, Texas is one of the states furthest from meeting the national standards.

Another example of how public policy gets set is the intragovernmental example of state-assisted higher education in Texas. A public university is a state agency, just as is the Department of Human Services or the Department of Parks and Wildlife. As we will see later in this chapter, the 1997 legislature, after years of ignoring higher education, mandated a number of procedures previously regarded as local business for the institutions. In doing so, the legislature was giving explicit instructions to executive branch agencies.

Although mandates may be difficult to implement, they are not the causes of society's problems. Urbanization, industrialization, inflation, depletion of natural resources, the world oil market, citizen demand, and the curtailment of federal funds to state and local governments are among the causes of the policy problems that confront Texas. Because new and different problems constantly emerge, no one can conceive of all the challenges that may be on the future Texas policy agenda.

Neither is it possible to explore all the major items on the present agenda. Some issues—the fiscal crisis, campaign finance, redistricting, school finance, the crisis in the courts, and civil liberties, for example—have already been discussed elsewhere in this book. Other issues that are not discussed here include the need for economic diversification, juvenile crime, placement of the mentally retarded in group homes, child care and child abuse, care of the elderly, the fact that many persons cannot afford health insurance, illegal aliens, substance abuse, and acquired immune deficiency syndrome (AIDS). Simply put, this chapter samples the diverse issues on the

---

1. See *San Antonio Independent School District et al. v. Rodriguez,* 411 U.S. 1 (1973) for the appeal. The case was originally styled *Rodriguez v. San Antonio ISD,* since Rodriguez instituted the suit. Then see *William Kirby et al. v. Edgewood Independent School District et al.,* 777 S.W. 2d 391 (1989) for the state case on appeal. Originally, the Edgewood ISD sued Kirby, who was commissioner of education.

2. *Ruiz v. Estelle* (666 Fed. 2d 854, 1982, and 650 Fed. 2d 555, 5th Cir., 1981). Ruiz was a prisoner and Estelle was the head of the prison system.

agenda, selecting *poverty and welfare, higher education,* and *the environment* to illustrate policy-making in the nation's second-largest state.

The issues the state chooses to address and how state policymakers attempt to solve public problems once again allow an examination of how democratic the Texas political system is. Do policymakers try to deal with a wide variety of issues affecting all citizens, or do they mainly look at issues placed on the agenda by political elites? Can they solve contemporary problems in the context of a conservative political culture when many of the issues stem from the needs of the "have-nots" of society, who traditionally have been supported by liberals? Do they consider alternative viewpoints? Can their policies be implemented effectively, or are they merely "smoke and mirrors" that only seem to address the problem?

Overall, state policymakers have coped reasonably well. It is true that Texas, when compared with other states, tends to rank toward the bottom in many service areas. It is equally true that the state is sometimes slow to respond to emerging issues. However, state officials can proceed at no faster pace than the public is willing to move and to fund. One of the awkward aspects of democracy is that following majority opinion does not always lead to wise or swift policy decisions.

POVERTY AND WELFARE

Conservative agendas dominated national and state politics in the 1990s, and they have long shaped Texas politics. In short, for reasons discussed throughout this book, the viewpoints of individuals in upper-income brackets often dominate public policy. This political fact of life is particularly important when we examine the issues of poverty and welfare. Whenever the government attempts to improve the quality of life for the poor, it is producing *redistributive public policy*[3]—that is, policy that redistributes wealth from those who have the most to those who have the least. Inevitably, then, poverty and welfare politics produces strong emotions and sharp political divisions.

In Texas, as elsewhere, some policymakers and ordinary citizens think that poor people could be more effective at helping themselves through job training, education, and looking for work. Even when compassion exists for those too ill or infirm to work, it does not spill over into sympathy for individuals seen to be shirkers. Other people think that, in addition to well-documented reasons such as debilitating physical or mental illness, people are poor because they have never been given an opportunity to have a good education or relevant job training. In truth, all of these opinions are correct. The reasons for poverty are many. The task at hand is to determine how the state of Texas addresses poverty issues.

Any state's role in combating poverty and seeing to the welfare of its citizens is a mix of both state policy and federal programs. Because of changes in national policy, Texas, which has traditionally relied on federal funds for its welfare programs, has had to make changes in its own welfare system.

---

3. See, for example, the policy discussion Randall B. Ripley and Grace A. Franklin, *Congress, the Bureaucracy, and Public Policy,* 5th ed. (Monterey, CA: Brooks/Cole, 1991), chapters 1 and 6.

The two fastest-growing homeless groups are families with children and the deinstitutionalized mentally ill. The "hidden homeless" are so difficult to count that the national estimate of homeless people ranges from 470,000 to 2,000,000.

SOURCE: Courtesy of Ben Sargent.

Poverty in Texas

The poverty threshold for a family of three was $13,880 in 1999,[4] and 18.5 percent of all Texans fell below this line compared to 13.8 percent nationally. Texas was fifth in the percentage of the state population living in poverty, with only Mississippi, Louisiana, New Mexico, and West Virginia ranking higher.[5] Ironically, even though Texas led the country in the number of new jobs created, many of those jobs were low paying. As a result, the average income per person in Texas was $1,454 less than the national average; the median household income was more than $2,500 below the national average.[6] Ten of the forty-nine poorest counties in the country are in Texas; six counties—Starr, Zavala, Maverick, Willacy, Cameron, and Dimmitt—had poverty

4. U.S. Department of Health and Human Services, "The 1999 HHS Poverty Guidelines," January 30, 2000, available at http://aspe.hhs.gov/poverty/99/poverty.htm. For an additional family member, add $2,820. These numbers are revised in March each year.

5. Diane Jennings, "Prosperity Fails to Reach Many," *Dallas Morning News,* February 12, 1999, 1A, and Richard Wolf and Beth Belton, "Household Income at New High, *USA Today,* October 1–2. 1999, 1A, 3A.

6. *Fiscal Size Up: Texas State Services, 2000–01 Biennium* (Austin: Texas Legislative Budget Board, 2000), 34.

rates above 40 percent.[7] One-fourth of Texas children live in poverty, and almost half are eligible for the free/reduced-rate school lunch program. Half these poor children live in families that have at least one working parent. The reality is that the very young and the very old are the most likely to be poor. One measure of that phenomenon is the 1.34 million children and over 300,000 aged persons who received Medicaid assistance in 1998.[8] Rural south and southwest Texas and the ghettos and *barrios* of the largest cities have the highest number of poor people.

One question that arises when the stark numbers of Texas poverty are stated is, "What about the homeless?" Neither the state nor the national government has a very accurate measure of the number of homeless people because the homeless are a mix of people who sometimes have work, sometimes do not, and include a substantial number of mentally ill people. When adequate help is provided, the majority of homeless move into housing and find a job, according to the U.S. Bureau of the Census.[9] The Bureau conducted a large-scale study of homeless persons and providers of services to the homeless in 1995 and 1996 that estimated almost 2 million homeless persons nationwide. It determined that "overall the homeless were deeply impoverished and most were ill." Two-thirds had some type of chronic illness, with more than half of these beset with mental illness. More than a quarter had a childhood history of living in an institution or being in foster care. Given the population size of Texas and the entrenched poverty in some parts of the state, one can safely assume a sizable homeless population.[10]

The Players and the Major Programs

The key players in delivering services to the needy in Texas are ten administrative agencies that provide health, welfare, and social services. These agencies are: Department of Human Services, Department of Health, Department of Mental Health and Mental Retardation, Department on Aging, Commission on Alcohol and Drug Abuse, Commission for the Blind, Commission for the Deaf and Hard of Hearing, Interagency Council on Early Childhood Intervention Services, Texas Rehabilitation Commission, and Department of Protective and Regulatory Services. Overall policy setting is done by the Health and Human Services Commission, which acts through a commissioner appointed by the governor. Employment services and benefits are handled through the Texas Workforce Commission.

In Texas, programs to help needy citizens long have been funded primarily with federal dollars supplemented by whatever additional funds the state was obligated to provide to be eligible for the federal dollars. The Texas Constitution places a ceiling on welfare expenditures. Since a 1982 amendment, that ceiling has been 1 percent of the state budget for general public assistance, so long as the state ceiling did not con-

---

7. The poorest of the poor are 400,000 residents of the *colonias* along the Mexican border. See Ralph K. M. Haurwitz, "Scant Relief from Filth, Disease for the Poorest of Texans," *Austin American-Statesman,* July 12, 1998, A1, A8.

8. *Fiscal Size Up: 2000–01,* 102.

9. "Study Provides Look at Homeless," *Dallas Morning News,* December 8, 1999, 3A.

10. An in-depth look at homelessness in the Dallas–Fort Worth area can be found in "Left Out of the Good Times," *Dallas Morning News,* November 24, 1999, all of Section P.

FIGURE 11.1

Cash Value of Typical TANF Family's Monthly Benefits and Services, Fiscal Year 2000 SOURCE: Texas Department of Human Services, in *Fiscal Size Up: 2000–01*, 109.

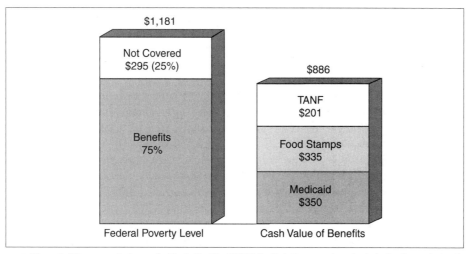

NOTE: The typical Temporary Assistance for Needy Families (TANF) family in Texas consists of a single female caregiver and two children who receive no child support. The federal poverty level for a family of three is estimated at $1,181 per month for fiscal year 2000.

flict with federal welfare program requirements. However, this provision is more flexible than the previous one, which was expressed in dollar amounts.

The national Social Security Administration provides direct case assistance for aged, disabled, and blind Texans through the Supplemental Security Income (SSI) program and channels funds to the state Department of Human Services (DHS) for the Temporary Assistance to Needy Families (TANF) program, which replaced the old Aid to Families with Dependent Children (AFDC) program. TANF is a program for families with needy children under age 18 who have been deprived of financial support because of the absence, disability, unemployment, or underemployment of both parents. The U.S. Department of Agriculture administers the food stamp program, passing dollars through the DHS. Medicaid, a program of medical assistance for the needy, is a joint federal-state program administered through the DHS. Medicaid's principal programs are for children, the aged, the blind and disabled, and maternity care. TANF, food stamps, and Medicaid are the largest welfare programs. These programs all work in conjunction with one another so that a person eligible to receive help from one program is sometimes eligible to receive help from one or more of the others. Although most states supplement these programs, Texas historically has chosen to provide "bare bones" programs. Figure 11.1 illustrates for FY 2000 the assistance that a typical welfare family received—$350 for Medicaid, $335 for food stamps, and $201 for TANF. This typical family consisted of a mother and two children who receive no child support. Thus, the typical Texas payment of $886 to a qualifying family left the family short of moving beyond the poverty level.

TABLE 11.1

Texas TANF and Food Stamp Households, 1996–2001

Program	1996	1997	1998	1999	2000*	2001*
TANF households	256,956	219,475	173,426	137,390	126,614	113,603
Food-stamp households	913,438	784,408	627,858	536,291	500,134	499,871

*Figures are estimated.

SOURCE: *Fiscal Size Up: Texas State Services, 2000–01 Biennium,* 109.

Table 11.1 shows the decreasing dependence of many Texans on food stamps and TANF at the turn of the twenty-first century. The requirements for food stamps are different than they are for the TANF program, and the recipients include many working poor. A recipient who qualifies for both TANF and food stamps receives somewhat more food stamp assistance. As Figure 11.1 indicated, the average was $335 for TANF families; for all families, food stamp assistance in 2000 averaged $237 a month for a household of three. Discussion of state welfare policy later in this chapter addresses reasons for the declining number of recipients of TANF and food stamp help.

In addition to the three largest welfare programs—TANF, food stamps, and Medicaid—other social services include day care, foster homes, energy assistance for low-income persons (to help with heating bills), and job training. Health care is, of course, a problem affecting everyone, and problems shared by persons from all social classes tend to have a higher degree of political support.[11] The Texas Department of Health and the Texas Department of Mental Health and Mental Retardation are the two largest agencies providing for the health needs of Texas citizens. State services range from programs for crippled children and for individuals with devastating diseases, such as cancer and tuberculosis, to rehabilitation of trainable mental retardates and the control of rabies in skunks. Although such programs are not restricted to the poor, there existence eases the burden of medical costs for less well-off Texans. Additionally, a joint state-county system of indigent health care has existed since 1985.

Another related service is unemployment compensation—that is, payments to unemployed workers administered by the Texas Workforce Commission, which also assists individuals in finding jobs and keeps records of employment in the state. Unemployment compensation is a joint federal-state effort. The basic funding method is a tax on wages paid by employers, plus any surcharge needed to make the system fiscally sound, and reimbursements from governmental units for any unemployment benefits drawn by their former employees. If a state has its own unemployment compensation program and an agency to administer it, the employers can charge off most of the tax on their federal tax returns. If the federal government administers the program directly, employers cannot take advantage of the tax writeoff. In Texas, unemployment benefits vary according to previous wage and disability status. In 1998, the average weekly unemployment benefit paid in Texas was $186.81

11. For an excellent discussion of the importance of middle-class attitudes in the development of social programs, see Robert Morris, *Social Policy of the American Welfare State* (New York: Harper & Row, 1979), chapters 1 and 2. Morris, along with C. John E. Hansan, also offers useful commentary on welfare philosophy in the United States in *Welfare Reform, 1996–2000: Is There a Safety Net?* (Westport, CT: Auburn House, 1999).

(the disabled received about twice that amount), which was 25th in the nation. However, Texas was 43rd in the United States in the percentage of the unemployed who actually received benefits. Benefits are payable for a period up to twenty-six weeks except when the federal government extends the period. The average benefit period in Texas was fifteen weeks, which was 13th in the country.[12]

Recent Policy Developments

Early in the 1990s, many states including Texas had addressed the issue of welfare reform, all of them with emphases converting welfare to work fare, forcing "deadbeat dads" and "misanthrope moms" to provide child support, and employing modern electronics to aid in tracking those in the welfare system. In 1996, Congress passed and the president signed the Personal Responsibility and Work Opportunity Reconciliation Act, otherwise known as welfare reform. Fundamentally, this legislature followed the lead of the states in getting people off welfare and onto payrolls. The *work fare* approach carried with it not only such positive values as helping welfare recipients regain their self-esteem by becoming better trained and gainfully employed and freeing up money for other programs but also such negatives as more rules and regulations. Coupled with a devolution of responsibility to the states, these features explain the opening chapter quotation about the new federal welfare law.[13] The federal reform allowed five years of welfare support, but the time clock begins to tick from the first date a recipient receives a check even though the person might have extensive training to undergo. Texas provides for only three years of assistance although the average time on welfare is less than two years. The federal requirement is that the individual be working within two years, without the flexibility of the earlier Texas plan that includes job training, parenting or life skills training, and education or literacy training within the definition of work.[14]

In their concern for reducing welfare fraud, putting people to work, and generally moving one step away from Big Government, the politicians failed to address the fundamental reality of welfare reform—namely, that the legislation forces single mothers of dependent children to go to work and may cost their children health care through Medicaid. Since work fare means that their children will either be left alone all day or placed in day care, this consequence would seem to contradict the much-touted "family values" espoused by many politicians. Less parental care is also likely to have the further consequences of more juvenile crime, poorer school performance, and thus, paradoxically, even more welfare dependency. Welfare reform illustrates how complex social issues are. In trying to fix one set of problems, it is all too easy to create another set.

The federal bill created a "cafeteria-style" welfare system for the states, with each state receiving a block grant for welfare support that a state could apportion among

12. Michael Totty, "Unemployment Benefits Benefit Few, Critics Say," *Wall Street Journal,* October 21, 1998, T1, and table 35, "Average Duration of Unemployment Benefits (Weeks), 1997–98," *Just the Facts 1999–2000,* February 5, 2000, available at www.ppinys.org/jtf99/table35.htm.

13. For an excellent explanation of the federal legislation and its consequences, see Carl Tubbesing and Sheri Steisel, "Answers to Your Welfare Worries," *State Legislatures,* January 1997, 12–19.

14. "Welfare Reform, Part Two: A Kinder, Gentler Plan for Texas," *Texas Government News,* September 23, 1996, 2.

programs that the state judged as having the highest priority. AFDC was transformed into Temporary Assistance to Needy Families (TANF), with the stipulation that individuals have no automatic entitlement to welfare support.[15] States had until July 1, 1997, to file a plan for TANF, with block grant funding to begin on that date or six months after submission of the plan, whichever was later. Proportionately less money now flows from Washington, and the states are allowed under the national legislation to slash their own welfare payments by 20 percent with no loss of federal funds.

Implementation of the federal legislation in Texas was delayed for several months because the state and the federal government tangled over the state's plans to privatize parts of the welfare system. The state budget passed in 1997 included state funds to support the Medicaid and food stamp needs of legal immigrants, who had been omitted from the national program.

Analysis

Signals sent during the 1995–97 period were not entirely clear. One reading is that despite a set of elected officials even more conservative than those of the past, the state had developed a social conscience with regard to the needy. An alternate interpretation is that the state was mainly interested in money—finding ways not to spend state dollars on the poor and finding ways to get a bigger piece of the federal welfare pie. Beyond dispute is the fact that Texas has a welfare problem that is tied to social divisions that rest on ethnic conflicts and struggles between the haves and the have nots.

A combination of stringent qualifications for recipients and a booming economy has resulted in one effect desired by state and federal welfare reformers—namely, a sharp drop in the number of aid recipients. Table 11.1 shows that the number of TANF families fell by more than 50 percent and the number of food stamp recipients declined by 45 percent between 1996 and 2000. Between 1994 and 1998, Medicaid recipients declined by 7.5 percent.[16]

The second effect was that Texas, like other states, is not spending all the money to which it is entitled by federal programs. According to *State Legislatures* magazine, of the five states mentioned earlier in this chapter as having the highest poverty rates,

15. Mary Jo Bane, "Stand By for Casualties," *New York Times*, November 10, 1996, 13.

16. *Fiscal Size Up: 2000–01*, 102, and *Fiscal Size Up: Texas State Services, 1996–97 Biennium* (Austin: Texas Legislative Budget Board, 1996), 5–19.

Many Texans asked, "Why should the welfare system exclude support for legal aliens who are poor? They have all the necessary and proper approvals for permanent residence in the United States and were at one point encouraged to emigrate here. They pay taxes. They contribute in many other ways to society. They deserve humane consideration."

Texas and the others—Mississippi, Louisiana, New Mexico, and West Virginia—were spending less than 69 percent of their allotted funds. The states as a whole were spending only 76 percent of their block grant funds.[17] This publication, which is published by the National Conference of State Legislatures, points out two important facts about the underspending. First, those individuals who remain on welfare will be very difficult to place in jobs for reasons such as domestic violence, little training, lack of transportation, and lack of child care. Second, innovative states—Arizona, Colorado, Florida, Maine, Michigan, New York, Washington—have used the funds not spent on TANF recipients to provide a variety of solutions to hard-core unemployment and chronic welfare-ism.

Several factors make it likely that welfare is an issue that will be heard again in 2001 and beyond. First, the economic boom can slow down at any time; even at its peak, it resulted in many "working poor" jobs. Second, the state's immigration rate is among the highest in the country, and many of the immigrants lack essential job skills. Third, early studies of the impact of the 1996 federal legislation show that the poorest 20 percent of welfare families have lost income and become even poorer and that Texas, while moving hundreds of thousands of people off the welfare rolls, has had some trouble placing them in jobs.[18]

HIGHER EDUCATION

Higher education, more than any other policy area, seems to ride a roller coaster in Texas. In the 1970s and early 1980s, when the state was flush with funds from oil and

17. Jack Tweedie et al., "Window of Opportunity for Welfare Reform," *State Legislatures*, April 1999, 22.

18. Laura Meckler, "Study: Under Welfare Reform, Some of the Poor Get Poorer," *Austin American-Statesman*, August 22, 1999, A11, and Christopher Lee, "Study Faults Texas' Job Help for Welfare Recipients," *Dallas Morning News*, June 28, 1998, 39A, 42A.

A Kinder, Gentler Legislature

Governor George Bush sought harsh penalties from the 1999 legislature for those mired in the welfare system and seemingly unwilling to find work. The 76th Legislature seemed to be in a gentler mood. Legislation included:
- Retention of some benefits during the transition from welfare to work
- More child care for welfare mothers
- More outreach for Medicare
- Pilot program of group homes for unmarried teen mothers
- Intensive caseworker services to welfare mothers with special problems such as learning disabilities
- Training for jobs that pay better than minimum wage
- One-time payments plus social services for grandparents providing care to welfare grandchildren

The legislature also reduced the work exemption for parents with young children from four children in 1999 to one in 2002.

SOURCE: Christopher Lee, "Texas Continues Welfare System Reform," *Dallas Morning News*, May 31, 1999, 19A.

gas taxes, Texas hired so many scholars away from out of state colleges that the practice inspired a rueful national joke about "locking up the faculty so a Texas school won't get them" was told. When the state's budgetary surpluses turned to revenue shortfalls in the mid-1980s, higher education was the first program area to suffer, and it continued to suffer for a decade. Simply put, higher education represented the largest budgeted amount available for reallocation. Public education, prisons, and mental health and retardation were all under court mandates to improve services. Welfare and highway programs were dominated by federal funding, not state dollars. Essentially, except as a source of funds for other programs, higher education was ignored until 1997.[19]

The Dark Decade

Some pluses did exist during the "dark decade" of the 1980s. A 1984 constitutional amendment provided a wider distribution of Permanent University Funds (PUF) to satellite campuses of the University of Texas System and the Texas A&M System and established a Higher Education Assistance Fund (HEAF) for non-UT and non-A&M institutions for capital expenditures. These expenditures include equipment, library materials, land, rehabilitation of older buildings, and new construction. In 1985, legislators created a science and high-technology research fund linked to the state's interest in attracting high-technology industries as a means of moving away from the oil-dominated economy.

The legislature also created a Select Committee on Higher Education to review higher education with a wide-sweeping agenda. The select committee report took the form of a Texas Charter for Public Higher Education, which was adopted by the 70th Legislature in 1987. Although the study and the recommendations were broad, the major outcomes were increased research funding and modest increases in operating funds following the 1987 legislative session. Two-year colleges received little benefit from the charter.

From 1989 through the 1995 legislative session, higher education got modest increases that allowed it to stay more or less even with 1985 operations—but 1985 and 1986 were the primary budget-slashing years. The legislature seemed particularly willing to give small increases if the colleges and universities supported tuition increases.

To keep pace with enrollment growth, inflation, and other factors resulting in cost increases, the institutions began to raise dollars wherever possible. Particularly at the universities, students found themselves paying fees for almost everything as the institutions sought adequate dollars to provide operating funds, and graduate students on most campuses were asked to pay tuition rates above the state minimum.[20] Some two-year colleges strove to keep tuition and fees low, but in others tuition neared the rate assessed by universities. In short, the state was moving to *privatize* "public" higher education by investing proportionally fewer tax dollars in its support. The universities were forced to increase student tuition and fees as well as to search for private donations. In other states, the same development was occurring. The fact

19. Higher education, K–12 education, Medicaid, and corrections are the "big four" of spending for state governments in the United States. See Ronald K. Snell, "The Budget Wonderland," *State Legislatures*, February 1998, 14.

20. Finance 101: Who's Footing the Bill for College Education," *Fiscal Notes*, May 1992, 1, 8–13.

that higher education funding was troubled in a majority of the states by the early 1990s, however, prevented another faculty drain such as Texas experienced in the mid-1980s.

In 1992, higher education had its own constitutional dilemma paralleling the *Edgewood* decision on public school finance described in Chapter Eight. The League of United Latin American Citizens (LULAC) filed suit against state officials, the Coordinating Board, and the officials of predominately Anglo universities claiming that South Texas institutions were discriminated against in the allocation of graduate and professional programs in the state. Ten days before the Texas Supreme Court's final ruling in the *Edgewood* case, District Judge Benjamin Euresti Jr., of Brownsville ruled that the Texas system of higher education discriminated against the predominantly Mexican-American border area of Texas and gave the state until May 1, 1993, to solve the problem or risk an order barring all higher education funding.[21] Judge Euresti's ruling followed the logic of the *Edgewood* case—namely, using the language of the Texas Constitution to determine that the educational system was unconstitutional because it was not efficient. After the *LULAC* case, the state directed higher education dollars to remedy the problems. However, efforts to fix a problem once again caused other problems in that the attempt to upgrade historically Hispanic institutions merely made worse an already precarious funding situation. In 1992, the state ranked 44th among all states in its funding per full-time student—$3,210 a year— about $1,100 below the national average. It ranked ninth among the ten most populous states in faculty salaries.[22]

As the state economy improved, higher education did receive increased funding for FY 1994–95 and FY 1996–97, although much of the money went to continue the South Texas initiatives mandated by the court. However, the HEAF program was reauthorized, and increasing enrollments were covered by the funding.

The Setting for the 1997 Legislative Session

At the end of the 1995 legislative session, four situations in higher education were obvious. First, higher education had an *image problem* that plagued it during legislative sessions. Elected officials often saw higher education as composed of a group of affluent institutions that salted away their private contributions and revenues from auxiliary enterprises such as student unions, bookstores, and athletics while constantly seeking more state dollars. Governor Ann Richards was widely quoted as saying, "The average Texan is far more concerned about taking care of the kids and their elderly parents and the bills than they are about research on cold fusion."[23] By

21. See *LULAC et al v. Clements et al.*, Cause No. 12-87-5242-A, in the District Court of Cameron County, 107th Judicial District; *Clements et al. v. LULAC et al.* (Appellees), Cause No. 13-90-146-CV, in the Court of Appeals, 13th Supreme Judicial District, Corpus Christi, Texas; and Final Judgment, *LULAC v. Richards*, January 20, 1992. (The style of the case changed when Ann Richards succeeded Bill Clements as governor.)

22. "Notes from the Joint Select Committee," January 28, 1992, prepared by Wanda Mills for the Council of Public University Presidents and Chancellors.

23. See, for example, Katherine S. Managan, "College Officials Are on the Defensive in Texas as They Lobby against a Budget They Say Will Devastate Higher Education," *Chronicle of Higher Education*, July 31, 1991, A15.

implication, she was saying that universities are best known for esoteric, impractical research and not much that is useful.

A second characteristic was *continued marginal funding*. Enrollments grew by 35 percent in the fourteen-year period from 1977 through 1991[24] before finally slowing down. Faculty and staff did not grow as rapidly. Thus, many institutions have experienced an increased reliance on part-time faculty and graduate assistants, a development that made the image problem worse. Other problems also resulted from inadequate funding such as larger classes, fewer book and journal purchases by the libraries, and some buildings still in poor repair in spite of PUF and HEAF expenditures. Community colleges had an additional problem in that their districts often coincided with those of public schools; given the massive reorganization of public school finance, the college boards were likely to be reluctant to seek a tax increase to generate more funding of the local two-year colleges. In short, while public and higher education were both vital to the state's economic recovery, higher education's consistent underfunding meant that the needed quality is almost impossible to achieve.[25]

Former Lieutenant Governor Bill Hobby, when he was interim president of the University of Houston System, noted at the beginning of the 1995 legislative session that Texas ranks 49th in appropriations plus tuition, almost $1,000 per student below the national average ($5,084 versus $6,019). He also remarked that higher education's share of the state budget had shrunk from 18 percent in 1985 to 12 percent in 1995. He applauded the legislative leadership for preventing out-and-out cuts but pointed out that higher education funding had "remained flat compared to criminal justice, health and human services, and public schools."[26]

Third, *higher education was being privatized* steadily. This phenomenon occurred in several ways. Institutions were encouraged to sell long-standing university operations such as bookstores and residence halls to private companies. They developed partnerships with private corporations to build parking garages, hotels, and residence halls. Depending on the spending patterns of the institution, the state has paid less than a third of the actual costs for some institutions, but more than half for most. Finally, students were now constantly being asked for more dollars—that is, to support their state institutions with private dollars.

The fourth situation was that *higher education was rarely high on the policy agenda*. Although it is clearly linked to economic development since it provides valuable human resources trained to conduct the business of business, the legislature did not pay much attention to higher education since the *Edgewood* ruling invalidated public school funding. At the end of the 1995 legislative session, some key senators indicated that higher education might begin to receive attention in 1997. They proved to be prophetic.

24. "Finance 101," 8.

25. Harry Reasoner, "Texas Is Underfunding Higher Education," *Dallas Morning News,* May 12, 1991, 8J. Reasoner was chair of the Texas Higher Education Coordinating Board at the time, but was removed by Gov. Ann Richards because he was so ardent in support of the institutions.

26. Bill Hobby, "Stealth Budget Cuts Hurt Higher Education," *Austin American-Statesman,* February 9, 1995, A15.

The 75th Legislature

When the 75th Legislature convened in January 1997, higher education clearly had a place on the policy agenda. The political fact of life that placed it there was the difficulty of coping with an increasingly diverse state.

Hopwood.   Two related racial and ethnic diversity issues confronted higher education: (1) a court case that struck down an *affirmative action* admissions program—that is, a program that gives advantages to certain classes of people, including ethnic minorities, because of historic discrimination against them, and (2) a concern by the universities that enrollments would plummet unless ways to attract more students, including ethnic minorities, to higher education were identified. In turn, Texas would lag even farther behind in creating a well-educated populace. The *Hopwood v. State* case involved a suit by four white students who sued the University of Texas law school for reverse discrimination after they were denied admission in 1992. At the time the suit was filed, the UT law school was reserving some admissions slot for minorities, and, like virtually all law schools, had a maximum enrollment. That procedure had been abandoned when the case was heard. The decision of the Fifth Circuit Court of Appeals that the race-based admission policy was unconstitutional was allowed to stand by the U.S. Supreme Court in July 1996.[27]

Attorney General Dan Morales issued guidelines in August 1996 advising all Texas educational institutions to use "race-neutral" criteria. In February 1997, in response to a University of Houston query about the legality of race-based financial assistance, Morales issued a twenty-four-page Attorney General's Opinion[28] on *Hopwood,* the essence of which was that the only situation in which an educational institution could take race into consideration was to demonstrate past discrimination with ongoing effects and specific remedies to address that particular discrimination (see Chapter Eight on the role of this statement in Texas government). Morales specifically ordered the universities to stop making financial aid decisions based on ethnicity and race and cited the possible loss of $1.8 billion in federal funding if state institutions violated the federal court decision. The potential funding loss had been suggested by a former federal deputy solicitor general who was an attorney for the *Hopwood* plaintiffs.

The universities were unhappy: None wished to admit to past discrimination, and all—especially the urban ones—saw a future of sliding enrollments and an inability to serve their clientele. The ethnic minority communities were also unhappy—they saw fewer opportunities for admission and fewer opportunities for scholarship assistance. And the U.S. Department of Education was unhappy: Norma Cantú, assistant secretary for civil rights in DOE, notified the state in March 1997 that she thought other federal court rulings upholding affirmative action allowed race still to be considered as a factor. Thus began a series of angry exchanges between Morales and Cantú.[29]

---

27. *Hopwood v. State,* 78 F.3d 932 (5th Cir. 1996), rehearing en banc denied, 84 F.3d 720 (5th Cir. 1996), certiorari denied, 116 S.Ct. 2581 (1996).

28. *Attorney General's Letter Opinion No. 97-001.* February 6, 1997.

29. Letter from Texas Attorney General Dan Morales to U.S. Secretary of Education Richard W. Riley, April 2, 1997, 2.

In the wake of a federal court decision declaring a University of Texas law school admissions plan unconstitutional because it was race based, the Texas attorney general interpreted that decision broadly and prohibited scholarships and financial assistance awarded on the basis of race. Concern was expressed about a return to whites-only universities.

SOURCE: Courtesy of Ben Sargent.

Whatever the reasons for the controversy, the short-term results were plain to see. Black and Hispanic enrollment in professional schools dropped sharply.[30] In some cases, the students simply sought an environment in which they felt more comfortable, often out of state. In others, the students sought admission to schools where scholarship opportunities were greater. In still other cases, their place was taken by students with stronger admission credentials.

The majority of Texans approved the *Hopwood* decision and its implication that race was no longer a valid criterion for university admission or financial assistance although the decision was less-well supported by ethnic minorities than by Anglos.[31] The case is merely symbolic of American struggles with the concept of affirmative action (AA). At its simplest, AA merely calls for ensuring that all individuals have an opportunity to be part of the "pool"—whether the pool of talent is for work or admission. At its most complex, AA results in quotas for hiring or admission based on one of the protected categories—race, ethnicity, gender, disability, age, or veteran's status. Thus, a concern for equal opportunity can be interpreted as favoritism or reverse discrimination. Issues such as affirmative action illustrate why democracy, however desirable, can be such a difficult form of government.

30. A. Phillips Brooks, "Law, Medical Schools Hurting for Minorities," *Austin American-Statesman,* October 17, 1997, B1, B7.

31. Jayne Noble Suhler, "58% Back Ruling on Race, College Entrance," *Dallas Morning News,* November 16, 1997, 45A, 50A.

Back to Basics.   The other major issue confronting the 1997 legislature was the need to address pent-up funding needs in higher education. Begun as an initiative of the chancellors of the six public university systems (University of Houston, University of Texas, Texas A&M, Texas Tech, University of North Texas, Texas State University), who called themselves The Coalition, the "Back to Basics" movement became the theme of a united higher education.[32] The Back to Basics proposals laid out a strategy to achieve a competitive edge for the state by:

- Increasing partnerships between higher education and public schools
- Increasing efforts to help at-risk students who are most likely to drop out or "stop out" (interrupt their education)
- Reversing the trend of less experienced faculty members teaching lower-division courses
- Providing more state financial assistance

The information provided to legislators called attention to the need for a better-educated workforce if Texas was to continue to prosper economically. It pointed out that the state's college graduation rate was 16 percent below the national average and that this problem would get worse if corrective measures were not taken because the fastest-growing populations are those with low educational attainment historically. The report pointed out the below-average income of the state, the growing number of unskilled workers, and the importance of a highly productive workforce to provide the state with adequate public revenues.

What did The Coalition ask for? The answer is $1 billion to fund full professors teaching lower-division courses, to provide student financial aid, to boost health-related institutions, to improve reading in primary grades and develop preparatory programs for secondary students, and to develop workforce skills programs and fund research. Texas A&M Chancellor Barry Thompson summed up the request by saying, "If we do not do something, the problems will become irreversible."[33]

What the Legislature Did.   Legislators were spurred by thoughts of economic decline, the consequences of not accommodating a growing segment of the population, and having more money to spend than usual. As a consequence, over 1,000 bills dealing with higher education were introduced during the 1997 session. Some addressed *Hopwood.* Some addressed Back to Basics. Some addressed pent-up needs of institutions. Overshadowing all of the measures was a legislative desire to gain more control over the institutions, to treat them more like other state agencies. The result was typical politics—give a little, get a little.

The following list includes most of the better-known measures passed in 1997. The 75th Legislature voted to:

- Mandate a performance review system for tenured faculty members in each institution.
- Place a cap of 100 hours on the number of credit hours that would be funded by the state for a doctoral student.

32. This section relies heavily on *Back to Basics: The Role of Higher Education in the Economic Future of Texas,* a set of proposals for the 75th Texas Legislature prepared by The Coalition (of public university chancellors), January 1997.

33. Todd Ackerman, "Back to Basics," *Houston Chronicle,* January 10, 1997, 1A.

- Place a cap of 170 hours on the number of credit hours that would be funded for an undergraduate degree student.
- Revise the formula by which universities are funded, both simplifying it and providing greater rewards for institutions already achieving efficiencies.
- Combine certain fees with tuition.
- Mandate a new core curriculum, more or less common to all institutions, to make transfers easier.
- Simplify admissions applications for individuals wishing to apply to multiple institutions.
- Create a new admission system that requires an institution to accept any student in the top 10 percent of his or her graduating class and encourages accepting the top 25 percent and that mandates that eighteen race-neutral criteria be considered for other admissions, including, for example, academic record, whether the applicant was in the first generation of a family to attend college, the applicant's extracurricular activities, whether the applicant is bilingual.
- Force universities to eliminate the double standard of admitting athletes on one standard and denying other students with the same credentials.
- Give staff raises for the first time in five years and tell universities to find the money to give faculty raises.
- Fund more than half of the Back to Basics program—$593 million dollars.

The 76th Legislature

The issues in 1999 were little changed from those of 1997. Higher education sought more resources and got them—$940 million more. In exchange, both four-year and two-year institutions were expected to yield more control to Austin and to be especially attentive to issues of how accessible college is to anyone who wants to attend. Legislators wanted almost universal access and wanted four-year graduations. The nagging problem of the percentage of the state's population with college degrees worsened. The national average in 1998 was 24.4 percent; in Texas, 20 percent.[34] Texas had slipped another couple of percentage points in the race for an educated workforce. Texas faculty pay had dropped to 10th among the ten largest states.[35] The legislature wanted a progress report on their 1997 mandates to diversify the factors considered in admissions, to get rid of some of the bureaucracy that plagues almost all students, and to discourage "professional students." An issue from the 1980s resurfaced—namely, whether institutions should be put into tiers in the state, with more flagships such as the University of Texas at Austin and Texas A&M, a middle range, and a basically undergraduate tier.

However, not much happened during the 1999 legislative session. The 76th Legislature focused on public education, electric deregulation, tax breaks, and other

34. U.S. Bureau of the Census, "Current Population Report," March 1998, available at www.census.gov/population/ www.socdemo/edu-attn.htm and Lieutenant Governor Rick Perry, "Remarks at the First Meeting of the Special Commission on 21st Century Colleges and Universities," October 27, 1999, available at www.senate.state.tx.us/75r/LtGov/pr/p102799a.htm.

35. Thomas Hoffman (president of the Texas Association of College Teachers, a lobby group), "A Message to Gov. Bush: Higher Education Needs Your Attention, Too," *Austin American-Statesman*, August 31, 1998, A7.

issues, not higher education. Thus, following the session, Lieutenant Governor Rick Perry formed a Special Commission on 21st Century Colleges and Universities. The commission was charged with looking at workforce development (graduates), the role of technology, accessibility and affordability, the long-term role and mission of higher education in Texas, and improved accountability measures.[36]

Analysis

State policymakers finally began to pay attention to higher education in 1997 and gave it considerable prominence in late 1999 with the formation of the 21st Century Commission. Whether the institutions will get what they want in 2001 is another question. The fourteen-member commission membership is a mix of long-time, knowledgeable lawmakers, the secretary of state, six businesspeople, two persons from education, and one religious leader. University leaders were quick to try to make points with the commission, the most pointed being former University of Texas Chancellor Bill Cunningham, whose views were published throughout the state's newspapers in January 2000. Some of his points were generic—Texas is now $2,000 below average in per-student spending in higher education—but others were very specific in laying out a four-institution flagship proposal.[37] Other chancellors and presidents would follow in making their own points.

THE ENVIRONMENT

The 1990s dawned with the return of Earth Day, initially celebrated in 1970. The return of Earth Day symbolized for many people that the 1990s would be a decade of environmental consciousness and renewed activism. For Texans, environmental issues are particularly important. The state lived off the environment—land, water, air, and minerals—for much of its history but increasingly finds that environment to be deteriorating (land, water, air) or being used up (minerals). The situation is made worse by the booming population of the state. Too, Texas is a place where nature is often hostile—tornadoes, flash floods, hurricanes, even occasional earthquakes confront its citizens, not to mention rattlesnakes, killer bees, and fire ants. Moreover, Texans, as the proud inheritors of a frontier past, remain unclear on whether to nurture the environment or conquer it.

Furthermore, the national government has required a cleanup of the environment. Texas, like other states, is finding environmental cleanliness to be another one of those well-intentioned but costly federal programs. Three key pieces of national legislation are the Safe Drinking Water Act of 1996, the Clean Water Act of 1972, and the Clean Air Act of 1996. These laws include standards that are expensive to implement. Federal funding adequate to assist state and local governments in meeting the new criteria was not forthcoming, although these laws are examples of the mandates discussed earlier in the chapter.

36. "Perry Forms Special Commission on 21st Century Colleges and Universities," press release, Office of the Lieutenant Governor, September 27, 1999, available at www.senate.state.tx.us/75r/ltgov/pr/p092799a.htm.

37. Christy Hoppe, "Proposal Would Elevate Colleges," *Dallas Morning News*, January 12, 2000, 31A–32A.

Is There Any Water? Is It Safe to Drink?

Texas has three basic kinds of water problems: water quality, water supply, and water damage. All remain perennial contenders for the policy agenda.

Under average rain conditions, the rule of thumb is that for every 20 miles one moves westward in the state, annual average rainfall diminishes by an inch. Since Texas is a very wide state indeed, by the time one reaches El Paso, the average rainfall is only 8 inches a year, compared with 55 inches in the southeastern part of the state. Consequently, West Texas politicians have kept the issue of *water supply* in the forefront for thirty years. They made water a critical issue in the 1969, 1981, 1983, 1985, and 1993 legislative sessions, and the state produced various schemes and plans for providing water and engaged in extensive water planning.[38] Texans are very conscious of that old Wyoming saying that opens this chapter.

Drought plagued the state in 1996, 1998, and 1999, and 2000 began as a warm, dry year. Only two weeks into 2000, seventy-five of Texas's 254 counties had been declared drought disaster areas.[39] Agriculture was imperiled; small towns without good water resources found themselves without water; images of a repeat of the seven-year drought of the 1950s began to loom.[40]

The drought of 1996 made water supply a focal point of the 1997 legislative session, even though 1997 proved to be an extraordinarily wet year, with severe spring floods.

In 1997, lawmakers came prepared to deal with water, and they produced a comprehensive, 220-page bill covering most aspects of water in the state. The exception

---

38. See *Water for Texas Today and Tomorrow—1990* and *Water for Texas Today and Tomorrow—1992* (Austin: Texas Water Development Board, 1990 and 1992, respectively). The 1990 volume focuses on a detailed analysis of each water basin and aquifer, with emphasis on specific plans to meet water resource needs in the state. The 1992 volume focuses on legislative issues, progress toward meeting the state water plan, and recommended amendments to that plan.

39. George Kuempel, "Drought's Impact Could Be Extensive," *Dallas Morning News,* January 15, 2000, 1A, 24A.

40. Ralph K. M. Huarwitz, "In Drought, Towns Left Out to Dry," *Austin American-Statesman,* February 16, 1997, A1, A10, dramatically points out how drought can affect an area that is usually considered to be water rich.

The old adage "When it rains, it pours" certainly holds true in Texas. In one week in June 1997, the area south of Austin saw more than 21 inches of rain. Texas's infamous thunderstorms and the deluges that come from them are the reason that Texas ranked far higher than any other state in the number of deaths from flash floods in the 1960–1995 period: Texas had 610 deaths. California followed with 255, then came South Dakota with 248.

SOURCE: "Texas Leads in Flash-Flood Deaths," *USA Today,* June 23, 1997, 14A.

was a failure to address the 400 or so inadequate dams in the state—dams that could give way during any heavy rain.[41] Lawmakers agreed to the following measures:[42]

- Requiring local, regional, and statewide planning for water supply, conservation, and drought management
- Requiring economic and environmental studies before water can be transferred out of a river basin and discouraging such transfers
- Streamlining procedures for creating groundwater districts, *but*
- Leaving intact traditional Texas law that allows unlimited pumping of groundwater that is not part of a water district
- Exempting water conservation equipment from the sales tax
- Creating an electronic mapping system for natural resources
- Consolidating water management dollars, subject to voter approval since previously approved bonds are involved, in order to maximize their effect and garner federal funds
- Increasing fines for illegal water usage

Implementing the plan was somewhat rocky, particularly because of the creation of a host of new water districts. Rural areas were especially prone to try to safeguard water supplies through the creation of more governmental units.[43] With reservoirs at a twenty-two year low as 2000 dawned, the plan was more critical than ever.

Another 1990s issue was *water quality.* The oft-cited bottom line for water and for air quality in Texas is that, since 1988, Texas has ranked either first or second in the country in the millions of tons of toxic pollutants it spewed into the air (let seep into the ground) and dumped into the water.[44] Everything from runoff of fertilizer used in agriculture to inadequate storm water control can cause water quality problems. The Texas Natural Resource Conservation Commission (TNRCC)—created in 1993 as the result of a merger between the Texas Water Commission (TWC) and the Texas Air Control Board[45]—oversees quality concerns. TNRCC (called "Ten-Rack" or sometimes "Train-Wreck") adopts regulations to ensure that Texas communities comply with the standards of the Environmental Protection Agency, which administers the national policy. Taking the necessary steps to avoid toxic pollutants such as pesticides,

41. Ralph K. M. Huarwitz, "Hazards of Dams Continue to Loom," *Austin American-Statesman,* June 3, 1997, B1, B5.

42. The summary of legislation relies heavily on Ralph K. M. Huarwitz, "Legislature Takes Stand for Water Planning," *Austin American-Statesman,* A1, A4.

43. Analyses of the 1997 plan can be found in Patrick Barta, "Texas Is Better Prepared for the Next Big Drought," and "Rural Counties Try to Guard Water by Creating More Special Districts," *Wall Street Journal,* December 1, 1999, T1, T3 and March 3, 1999, T1, T3, respectively. See also "Improving Drought Preparedness," *Texas Water Resources* [published by the Texas Water Resources Institute at Texas A&M University] 24 (August 1999): 1–6.

44. See, for example, Bruce Nichols, "Houston, We Have a Problem," *Dallas Morning News,* November 7, 1999, 45A, 57A; H. Josef Hebert, "Texas Air Quality One of the Worst," *Denton Record-Chronicle,* January 13, 2000, 7A; Jennifer Files, "Texas Tops List on Toxic Emissions," *Dallas Morning News,* June 27, 1997, 1D, 10D; and Michelle Mittelstadt, "Toxic Chemicals: Texas Near Top of List," an Associated Press story appearing in the *Denton Record-Chronicle,* May 27, 1993, 9A.

45. The creation of the Texas Natural Resource Conservation Commission was the final step in a series of steps to consolidate the variety of agencies dealing with water, wastewater, and air quality beginning in 1991.

heavy metals, and raw sewage is up to communities. TNRCC itself has had very mixed reviews—plaudits from industry and pans from environmentalists.[46]

Is the Air Safe to Breathe?

The Texas Natural Resource Conservation Commission also sets standards and emission limits for the abatement and control of air pollution. This agency is responsible for state compliance with the national Clean Air Act. The national legislation, originally passed in December 1990 and modified in 1996, regulates emissions that cause acid rain and affect the quality of air in metropolitan areas, and it also controls the release of toxic pollutants into the air.

Much work must be done to clean up the state's air, particularly in major metropolitan areas, where motor vehicles emit a large volume of toxic gases, and in areas where the petrochemical industry operates. Sixteen counties failed to achieve the national clean air requirements through most of the 1990s: Denton, Collin, Tarrant, and Dallas in north Texas; El Paso in far west Texas; and Montgomery, Waller, Harris, Fort Bend, Brazoria, Liberty, Hardin, Orange, Jefferson, Chambers, and Galveston in southeast Texas. The metropolitan areas of Austin, San Antonio, Longview-Marshall, and Tyler joined the list of problem areas in 1998. In 1999, Houston joined Los Angeles as the two U.S. cities with the poorest air quality. In addition, Texas, like everywhere else in the world, faces the various effects of global climate change, holes in the ozone layer, and the "greenhouse" effect in general. (The *greenhouse effect* is the buildup of gases that retain heat reflected from the earth's surface; this heat retention then causes climatic changes.)

The 1995 legislature, one of the least environmentally sensitive on record, did its part for clean air by revoking the state's auto emissions testing program. This failure to comply with federal environmental standards not only may be costly in the allocation of future federal dollars, but also immediately caused a $160 million law suit

46. Steve Scheibal, "Agency Gets Mixed Review for Efforts to End Pollution," *Austin American-Statesman,* September 3, 1996, B1, B7.

When it comes to the environment, sometimes the state is its own worst enemy. In 1991, the legislature was set on encouraging an insurance company to develop a large resort on environmentally sensitive Padre Island despite a fourteen and a half-hour filibuster from Senator Carlos Truan, who represented that area. The bill finally died at the last minute, but, had it been needed, Governor Ann Richards had promised a veto. In 1995, a similar situation occurred when the legislature overrode Austin's strict environmental regulations to allow the Freeport McMorRan corporation to develop the Circle C area in spite of potential degradation of the Barton Creek watershed. Austin Senator Gonzalo Barrientos's twenty-one-hour filibuster went for nought, and Governor George Bush did not veto the law.

by the firm that held the contract for emissions testing.[47] Texas political leaders, however, were perceptive in reading a lack of national impetus to enforce some of the aspects of the Clean Air Act, including emissions testing, and decided to spend the state's money elsewhere regardless of any long-term consequences. In 1996 Texas was one of only five states listed as "no progress" with regard to clean-air compliance.[48] In December 1999, TNRCC published prospective air quality regulations in the *Texas Register*. These regulations stressed industrial clean ups, a move toward California standards of motor vehicles anti-pollution devices, and even restrictions on the times of day when heavy construction equipment could be operated.[49]

The Land: Is It Safe to Walk Here? Is There Room?

Where does one put solid waste, whether that waste is toxic chemicals, radioactive by-products, or just simply the paper, plastic, bottles, and cans that are the residue of everyday living? Four possible solutions are recycling, composting, incineration, and landfill disposal.[50] In Texas, landfills are by far the most common solution. Consequently, the municipalities of the state are facing major problems with their landfills, both because of the amount of land needed to dispose of wastes—and the resistance of citizens to having a landfill in their part of town—and the need to meet stringent new federal regulations as of 1991. The federal regulations evolved from the Resource Conservation and Recovery Act. The TNRCC has jurisdiction over solid waste disposal in the state.

One of the reasons the state has such a problem with wastes is that Texas has so many "dirty" industries. For example, Texas is a major producer of petrochemical products such as fertilizers, paints, and motor fuels, all of which have hazardous by-products. It is a big mining state, with the slag from mineral production a danger in itself. These same industries intensify the water pollution problem because of the runoff of toxic materials into the storm water drains and waterways of the state.

With two nuclear power plants on line—Commanche Peak south of Dallas and South Texas near Houston—and other radioactive materials such as those from medical facilities and defense plants, the state must also be concerned about the disposal of radioactive materials. Furthermore, the national government periodically has looked to the state as a potential national storage site for radioactive wastes. Texas for years tried to deal with this problem in isolation, ignoring other states, but burying one's head in the sand doesn't work when an 18-wheeler carrying nuclear waste is speeding along a Texas highway. The legislature entertained a bill in 1999 that would have opened the state to private companies in the nuclear waste disposal business, but the bill ultimately failed.

47. Steve Scheibal, "Emissions Case Costs Texas $160 Million," *Austin American-Statesman,* April 5, 1997, A1, A10.

48. Gary Lee, "The Clean Air Act Evaporates, One Program at a Time," *Washington Post Weekly Edition,* March 11–17, 1996, 11.

49. Texas Natural Resource Conservation Commission, "December 16, 1999 Air Quality Proposals," available at www.tnrcc.state.tx.us/oprd/991216.html. See also Patrick Barta, "EPA Rules Could Delay New Roads," *Wall Street Journal,* September 8, 1999, T1, T4.

50. John McNurney, "Solid Waste Disposal Options: The Pros and Cons," *Texas Town & City* (February 1990), 6, 23.

Analysis

Operating dirty industries and dirty municipal waste facilities is cheaper than operating clean ones, but the real problem is not a venal unwillingness to protect the environment but, rather, the very high costs of doing so. Anyone who has watched the haze settle in over Houston or Dallas or Austin in the afternoon rush hour knows that there is a problem, as does anyone who has seen dead fish floating belly up in the state's rivers. However, environmental policymaking often tends to produce diametrically opposed views and make compromise difficult. Interests from ranches to factories that lower their costs of production by polluting air and water resist government attempts to order them to clean up their operations. And, as explained in Chapter Three, because these polluting interests tend to be organized and well represented among Austin lobbyists, they can often put up a serious resistance to pro-environmental forces. Environmental policymaking is thus an issue well suited to illustrate the difficulties encountered by democracies in achieving the public interest. In Texas, the politics of special interests often dominate land, water, and air policy to the detriment of society as a whole. Thus, Texas state environmental policy does not meet the test of democratic theory.

Nevertheless, Texas is still spending considerable money on environmental matters—an apparent reflection of its size and the magnitude of its problems. In 1993, the state ranked in the top ten for expenditures for air pollution controls (4th), wetlands protection (9th), and support for solid-waste programs (6th). It was not a top-ten state in helping local governments with recycling.[51] More recently, the TNRCC budget for 2000–2001 was just under four-fifths of a billion dollars.

SUMMARY

This chapter has not attempted to deal with all the issues facing the state. Rather, three policy issues—poverty and welfare, higher education, and environmental quality—illustrate the continuing and often interrelated problems of Texas and the complexity of public policymaking. These issues also point out the intergovernmental and intragovernmental aspects of modern public policy.

The resolution of each issue is important to the future of Texas, and each is linked to other significant issues not outlined in this chapter. Without addressing the considerable poverty of the state, Texas may find it difficult to resolve other policy issues such as economic diversification and sound public education. Moreover, abject poverty tends to foster crime. Education has long been seen as the key to the proverbial better future. However, Texas has allowed its higher education system to lag behind that of the nation as a whole, and its economic future depends on catching up. Everyone needs clean water, air, and land, and environmental quality also is tied to the need for economic diversity to avoid further expansion of high pollution industries. None of the issues is new. All are costly to deal with, so much so that solving one problem may worsen another.

51. Todd Sloane, "Environmental Survey of the States: Survey Finds States Still Going Green," *City and State*, July 5, 1993, 9.

Texas policymakers have dealt with all these issues to some extent, but problems remain on the public policy agenda:

1. The transformation of the welfare system to work fare is a national priority with which Texans can agree. However, the change in philosophy and the reduction in federal social spending has been both boon and bane to Texas. Texas enjoys greater flexibility to make decisions on what program to offer its neediest citizens. It will not enjoy having to spend more state money to pay for those programs. Additionally, the state continues to have one of the highest proportions of poor people in the country.

2. Higher education in Texas continues to be plagued by a bad image, underfunding, privatization, and, in most years, an inability to rank high on the policy agenda. The 1997 legislature did pay attention to higher education, providing it with not only improved funding but also a bundle of new regulations; the 1999 legislature followed suit. However, improving the state's degree production is heavily tied to the ability to recruit, admit, and provide financial assistance for ethnic minority students.

3. Texas has always been proud of its resources, but it has materially damaged those resources. Now the state must find an integrated, comprehensive approach to environmental quality. It keeps trying to find a workable solution and has emphasized clean industry in its economic development efforts. In 1997, the state once again legislated a comprehensive water act (the *sixth* such effort in slightly less than thirty years).

The three issues discussed in this chapter—poverty, higher education, and pollution—affect all citizens, albeit in different ways. They bring to mind the "haves" and "have-nots" of our society, disparities among ethnic groups, and even problems of mortgaging our children's future by failing to address current problems.

Combined, these issues have major tax and quality-of-life implications for citizens. They also will help shape the future economy of Texas. They all reflect problems that will cause the governor and the legislators, as the principal policymakers of the state, many anxious moments. They are all grounded in the conservative political culture of the state and, like other issues, reflect the influence of special interests in the policy process. More participation, more concern for society as a whole, and more concern for future generations might have helped to prevent some of the problems in the first place.

The state has shown stinginess in trying to mitigate poverty, inconsistency in its approach to higher education, and, until forced into federal compliance, a cavalier attitude toward the environment. In each approach, powerful interests tended to dominate the policy arena, and the average citizen's perspective was not always considered. As we have argued elsewhere in this book, Texas, when judged by standards of democratic theory, seriously falters.

STUDY QUESTIONS

1. As we argued throughout this book, Texas public policy has long been dominated by special interests. Do you agree or disagree with this notion? Why? What

effect would domination by upper-income groups have on state policy toward the poor? What effects do you think the conservative political culture has?

2. How do you think that the Texas political culture has affected Texans' attitudes toward the environment? What evidence have you personally seen that reflects an attitude that the environment is something to conquer or subdue? What evidence have you seen that reflects an attitude that the environment is something to be treasured and preserved?

3. Think back to what you have learned about the revenue system and revenue shortfalls in Texas. Given the revenue problems of the state, which of the issues discussed in this chapter—poverty and welfare, higher education, and the environment—would you address first? Should the state find new revenue sources to solve all the problems?

4. Consider any one of the three major issues discussed in this chapter. How well do you think democratic ideals such as participation, equality, and concern for the general welfare are reflected in state policy?

5. What do you think about the legislation to end some people's practice of being "professional students"? Can you think of circumstances in which an undergraduate student might be justified in taking more than 170 hours to get a bachelor's degree?

SURFING THE WEB

All about the Department of Human Services.
   www.dhs.state.tx.us/about

Poverty guidelines.
   http://aspe.hhs.gov/poverty/poverty.htm

Information on higher education in Texas.
   www.thecb.state.tx

Air quality regulations.
   www.tnrcc.state.tx.us/oprd/991216.html

APPENDIX

A Research Guide to Texas Politics

The original research guide was written in 1983 by Arnold Fleischmann, then of the University of Texas at Austin. It was updated and rewritten in 1992 by Geneva Johnson of the University of Texas at Austin and by the text authors. Additional material was added by the authors in 1995, 1997, and 2000.[1]

TEXAS POLITICS: A GREAT PLACE TO DO RESEARCH

People frequently study Texas politics as part of a course, to further their interest in the subject, or because of personal involvement in an issue or campaign. No matter which reason applies to you, this essay can serve as a road map so that you can do your research thoroughly and efficiently. The first section of the essay includes some common-sense reminders about doing research papers. The second section helps you develop a bibliography that includes not only books but periodicals, newspaper articles, government documents, and other publications that can help you narrow your research topic and develop some background in it. The third section includes reference books and periodicals that can provide you with up-to-date statistics and other information about Texas politics. The fourth section will help you do original research by directing you to the great wealth of information that is generally not available in books. Finally, following this essay is a list of locations where you are most likely to obtain important references and competent assistance for your project.

GETTING STARTED

You have an almost unlimited range of topics from which to choose. The most important thing to do at the outset of your project is to narrow the topic or question you want to investigate. You need not worry in the beginning about what information is available—you can do good research without burying yourself in the state archives. An important first step is to consult with your instructor and a reference librarian. They can provide you with suggestions or manuals on how to write a good research paper. They can also discuss the limitations of your library and other problems you might encounter. Once you have defined your topic somewhat, you can begin to develop your bibliography, read to broaden your knowledge of the subject, and then narrow the questions to be examined in your paper. To some extent, the

---

1. Copyright 1983, Arnold Fleischmann. My special thanks to Malinda Allison and Bonnie Grober for their encouragement, careful review, and suggestions. The authors of the textbook have updated the basic 1983 guide—A.F.

headings and citations in this book can serve as a starting point for developing a topic and a bibliography.

DEVELOPING A BIBLIOGRAPHY

Where to Start

To cover a wide range of references and to avoid wasting time, you need a good library. A general source of information about the libraries in your area is the *American Library Directory,* which is arranged alphabetically by state and city. It includes the addresses of public, university, and some private libraries, along with information about their holdings and rules. If you will be looking for historical information, you can consult the *Directory of Historical Societies and Agencies in the United States and Canada.*

Much of the information you will need will be located in a library's reference area, periodicals section, or documents department, or in a special collection labeled "local history," "Texana," or some similar title. Your reference or research librarian can give you valuable advice about your library's card catalog or on-line catalog, reference works, special collections, documents, and the like. Getting professional advice early can save you time and improve the quality of your project, especially since your library may not have all the references that pertain to your research.

The best general guide to research about Texas is *Texas Reference Sources: A Selective Guide* (1978), which surveys general reference works, the humanities, the social sciences, history, and the physical sciences. Ask your librarian to order this volume if it is not available. It can be purchased for $8.50 from the Texas Library Association, 8989 Westheimer #108, Houston 77063. The 1984 Supplement can be purchased for $6 from the same source. The 1986 Supplement is available for $3.00 from the Texas Library Association, 3355 Bee Caves Road #603, Austin 78746. Suggestions and/or questions can be sent to the general editor, Lois Bebout, 3304 Bridle Path, Austin 78703. You can also locate valuable books and articles by using a variety of published bibliographies, indexes, and special library services, in addition to the card or on-line catalog in the library.

Bibliographies

There is only one recent bibliography:

- Arnold Fleischmann, Manley Elliot Banks, Richard H. Kraemer, and Allen Kupetz, *A Bibliography of Texas Government and Politics* (Policy Research Institute, The University of Texas at Austin, March 1985).

Other sources that can help you identify useful books and articles include the following:

- Institute of Public Affairs, University of Texas, *Bibliography on Texas Government,* rev. ed. (1964). This book emphasizes history, government structure and organization, and the concerns of public officials. It represents the last effort at a comprehensive bibliography on the subject, but it was published prior to the social changes, population and economic shifts, and behavioral research of the past generation.

- Robert B. Harmon, *Government and Politics in Texas: An Information Source Survey* (1980). This book provides a good overview of reference works and general books on Texas politics, but omits many articles. It is available for $8.75 (plus $2.00 for book-rate postage) from Vance Bibliographies, P.O. Box 299, Monticello, IL 61856 [phone (217) 762-3831]. A photocopy of the 1980 edition can be made; write a letter requesting P401 and enclose a check or money order for $7.60 plus $2 postage (no credit cards).
- *Texas: A Dissertation Bibliography* (1978). This work covers Texas-related doctoral dissertations and master's theses completed since the 1920s. The bibliography is divided into 142 categories, with authors listed alphabetically with their dissertation title, degree date, and institution. It frequently omits dissertations and theses if the title does not indicate a Texas focus, however. The bibliography is available free from University Microfilms International, 300 North Zeeb Road, Ann Arbor, MI 48106, which also sells copies of the dissertations. The dissertation hot line, (800) 521-3042, operates 8:30 A.M. to 5:00 P.M., eastern standard time; the fax number is (313) 973-1540. Datrix search by subject is available at $20.00 for 500 titles; call extension 3732 to order by credit card. There is no update to the 1978 edition.
- *Texas State Documents.* This valuable resource is published monthly and lists the publications of Texas state agencies, including annual reports, technical reports, and special studies. Documents are listed both by agency and in a subject/title index. The catalog also gives you information on how to borrow copies of the reports listed. Some of these reports have been photographically reduced and copied on microfiche cards, and these can be purchased at a nominal charge (an order form is included). The monthly catalog also lists the forty-eight depository libraries around the state to which documents are shipped. (They are also listed at the end of this essay). If your library does not receive *Texas State Documents,* inform your librarian that it is sent free to libraries on request. You can also consult *Texas State Documents Periodicals Supplement,* which is published yearly and lists all periodicals received by the State Library's Publications Clearinghouse.
- *Catalogue of the Texas Collection in the Barker Texas History Center, the University of Texas at Austin* (1979). This fourteen-volume set is a reproduction of the Barker Center's subject and author/title card catalogs. Call ahead to make sure a library has this source, since many will not have spent the $1,375 to buy it. You may call the Barker Center directly at (512) 459-4515 to see if the material you want is available, whether it can be made available to your library on interlibrary loan, and if not, whether it can be duplicated. The sales agent for the catalogue, the G. K. Hall Publishing Company in Boston, Massachusetts, can be reached at (800) 343-2806.

Indexes

You are bound to do poor research if you limit your use of indexes to the *Reader's Guide to Periodical Literature.* While the *Reader's Guide* includes numerous references to popular magazines, it does not provide coverage of newspapers, documents, or the more detailed studies usually published in journals. You can locate such articles in the following sources:

- *Social Sciences Index.* As the title suggests, this index covers books, articles, and reviews in history, political science, sociology, and related fields.
- *P.A.I.S. Bulletin.* This index specializes in political science, public policy, selected law reviews, and some documents.
- *Index to Legal Periodicals.* The index surveys law reviews and can be a great asset if you are interested in a legal issue or controversy.
- *Current Law Index.* This index was begun in 1980 and provides good information on legislation and legal articles.
- *Business Periodicals Index.* This index focuses on business and industry, but also includes topics related to government management and bureaucracy.
- *Newspapers. The Houston Post,* which ceased publication in 1995, was the only Texas newspaper with a widely available index, published by Bell & Howell from 1976 to the year of the paper's demise. The *Post* gave extensive coverage to matters of statewide interest, but did not provide in-depth reporting of local politics outside the Houston area. Do not despair if you are interested in some other city or region. Many newspapers are indexed, usually in a special card catalog at the main public library in the city where they are published. For a list of newspaper indexes, their locations, and years covered, see Anita Cheek Milner, *Newspaper Indexes: A Location and Subject Guide for Researchers* (1977), vol. 2 (1979), vol. 3 (1982), with subsequent volumes. Submit questions/suggestions to Anita Cheek Milner, 1511 Rivcon Villa Drive, Escondido, CA 92027. Also, almost all daily newspapers maintain libraries, which include files of articles according to subject matter. The larger dailies have librarians who maintain these files and who can answer questions. If you want to use newspapers that are not well indexed, you can often use the *Post* index to locate the date of an event and then scan other newspapers for the same period. You may also find it helpful to consult *Newspapers in Microfilm,* which the Library of Congress published for 1948–1972 and 1973–1977. The 1948–1983 volume combines the 1948–1972 publication, the 1973–1977 publication, the quinquennial issue for 1978–1982, and the report of 1983. There are annual issues for 1978 to 1982.
- *Texas Observer Index.* Indexes have been published for 1954–1970 and 1971–1981. The *Observer* is a biweekly political magazine with a liberal perspective. Its stories cover national, state, and local political issues. It does a good job of covering the legislature and some of the larger state agencies.
- *Access.* This index has been published since 1975 and concentrates on periodicals not covered by the *Reader's Guide,* including *The Texas Observer, Texas Monthly,* and local magazines.
- *Texas Index* (vol. 3, no. 3, Spring 1990), Sharon Giles, ed. The index was first published in 1987. There are four issues per year—fall, winter, spring, and summer. It is a periodical index or reader's guide to more than 120 magazines and newsletters about Texas, Texans, Texana, and topics specifically of interest to Texans. Topics are separated into fifty-six broad categories with subheadings and extensive cross-referencing.

- *Index to Texas Magazines and Documents* (1986, 1987, 1988, 1989, 1990, and current). This index, a noncommercial venture on the part of librarians on the Victoria College/University of Houston–Victoria library staff, was developed as a way to answer questions from students, the business community, and the general public about topics specific to Texas, with emphasis on business, education, and government. Magazines of general interest are included.

Special Library Services

There are a number of ways in which your library can help you identify and obtain references. One is the bibliographic search. Usually for a fee, libraries will have a computer scan a national "card catalog" for books or articles that meet criteria you specify. A second important service is the interlibrary loan, mentioned above. Under such an arrangement, your library borrows or gets a photocopy of an item you want from another library. If your library does not have a reference you want, you can ask the librarian to borrow it for you through interlibrary loan. (Be sure to find out beforehand if there is a charge for this service.) In addition, many libraries are becoming more and more electronic. Not only does that allow you to access the library catalog from a terminal, but it also allows you access to many materials located at other sites.

RESEARCH USING COMPUTERS

Computer Databases

- *Texas Innovation Network System (TINS).* This commercial service provides a number of services through Internet linkages. They include Texas Research Centers, a search through research installations across the state, and Texas Guide to Business Resources, a service for small businesses. In addition, if your university/college library is not equipped with a readily available computer search system, you might be interested in the Online Library Card Catalogue, which provides direct access to many university library catalogues. Other such services will continue to develop.

Information on the World Wide Web

Extensive information is available to those with computer access to the World Wide Web. Since this area of cutting-edge technology changes rapidly, we can supply only the most basic web addresses.

Texas Government Websites.   Any state government agency can be accessed at this address: http://www.texas.gov/agency/agencies.html.

Once you get to this site, you will see a menu that will enable you to move anywhere in the cyberstate. Here are the web addresses of a few of the most important governmental institutions:

House   http://www.house.state.tx.us/
Senate   http://www.senate.state.tx.us/

Office of the Governor	http://www.state.tx.us/agency/301.html
Attorney General	http://www.state.tx.us/agency/302.html
Supreme Court	http://www.state.tx.us/agency/201.html
Court of Criminal Appeals	http://www.state.tx.us/agency/211.html
Ethics Commission	http://www.state.tx.us/agency/356.html

Universities.   By logging on to university websites, you will be able to access library files, plus much more. Here are addresses for some of the state's major universities:

Southwest Texas State	http://www.state.tx.us/agency/754.html
Texas Tech	http://www.state.tx.us/agency/733.html
Texas A&M	http://www.state.tx.us/agency/711.html
University of Houston	http://www.state.tx.us/agency/730.html
University of North Texas	http://www.state.tx.us/agency/752.html
University of Texas at Austin	http://www.state.tx.us/agency/721.html

KEEPING UP WITH TEXAS POLITICS

Statistics and Background Information

- Robert I. Vexler and William F. Swindler, eds., *Chronology and Documentary Handbook of the State of Texas* (1979). This is part of a series by Oceana Publications. This volume lists significant events from 1519 to 1977. It also gives the names, birth and death dates, and years of service of Texans elected to the governorship and Congress.
- U.S. Department of Commerce, Bureau of the Census. The *Statistical Abstract of the United States* is published annually and includes brief information about population, government, and the economy. It also lists its sources so that you can consult them for more detailed information. Information on Texas is available in the *1990 Census of Population,* vol. 1, *Characteristics of the Population,* Chapter A, "Number of Inhabitants," and Chapter B, "General Population Characteristics" (Texas is part 45). These two chapters provide data about education, race, poverty, income, and similar economic or social characteristics for the state, counties, metropolitan areas, and municipalities. The bureau also publishes agricultural and economic (manufacturing, retail trade, etc.) censuses for years ending in "2" and "7." *The Census of Governments, County and City Data Book,* and *State and Metropolitan Area Data Book* provide detailed information on cities and counties, including population, economic activity, government finances and employment, and elections. Normally, you also can get such data by contacting the local chamber of commerce, city planning department, or regional council of government. The Census Bureau also publishes the *Congressional District Data Book,* which includes district maps, population and housing characteristics, and vote totals for recent elections. Your library may have much of this census information available on CD-ROM.

- A. H. Belo Corporation, *The Texas Almanac and State Industrial Guide.* This "everything you ever wanted to know about Texas" book is published biannually and gives records and other statistical information about a wide range of subjects, including Texas elections.
- Mike Kingston, Sam Attlesley, and Mary Crawford, eds., *The Texas Almanac's Political History of Texas* (1992). This book has election results since 1845, as well as sections on African-American politics, women's political issues, and scandals. Veteran journalists have compiled noteworthy factual material.
- Texas State Directory, Inc., *Texas State Directory.* This volume is published annually and is a great resource when you need to know something about a public official or agency. It has sections on each branch of state government; county, city, and federal officeholders; political party officials; and the state capital press corps. Useful information includes maps; officials' names, titles, addresses, telephone numbers, and brief biographies; and Texas House and Senate membership, seniority, committee membership, and county delegations. It features a compendium of state agencies, boards, and commissions, including administrative heads, board members, addresses, and phone numbers. Capitol employees consider it their "bible." At the beginning of each regular session, the company also publishes a pocket-sized guide to the Texas legislature. In addition, it publishes *Capitol Update,* a political newspaper published twenty-five times a year, and the *Texas Legislative Manual,* a guide to the functions and inner workings of the legislative process.
- Texas Advisory Commission on Intergovernmental Relations, *Handbook of Governments in Texas.* This was published until 1987, when the agency was dissolved. It contains information about the state, county, municipal, special, regional, and federal governments. The information includes agency descriptions, general responsibilities, membership qualifications, top officials, spending and employment levels, and laws governing operations. The Lyndon B. Johnson School of Public Affairs *Guide to Texas State Agencies, 1990,* serves the same purpose.
- Legislative Reference Library (LRL), *Chief Elected and Administrative Officials.* This list is updated regularly and includes the names of state and federal officeholders, the office locations and telephone numbers of Texas senators and representatives, and the membership of each House and Senate committee.

Important Periodicals

There are several periodicals that you should review on a regular basis. Some publish cumulative or annual indexes that will make your task easier.

- *Texas Business Review* (six issues per year). Published by the Bureau of Business Research at the University of Texas at Austin, this journal contains short, crisp articles on economic conditions, population changes, and public policy. Articles have examined the 1981 Houston mayoral election, the effects of federal cutbacks on Texas cities, and changes in the state's African-American population. It includes an annual index.

- *Southwestern Historical Quarterly.* This journal is published by the Texas State Historical Association and covers a wide range of subjects and historical periods. Its best feature is "Southwest Collection," a list of articles on Texas that have appeared in other recent publications. The *Quarterly* has a four-volume cumulative index covering its first eighty volumes. Students can join the association and receive the *Quarterly* for $10, half the regular rate. The association also sponsors the Walter Prescott Webb Society on college campuses to encourage the study of state and local history.
- *Social Science Quarterly.* This journal covers all the social sciences, but concentrates on sociology and political science. Although it does not specialize in Texas-related research, it is the most likely of the regional political science journals to include topics on the state and the Southwest.
- *Texas Journal of Political Studies.* This journal is published semiannually by Sam Houston State University, and focuses on Texas state and local politics.
- Law reviews. Each of the state's eight law schools publishes one or more journals with annual and occasional cumulative indexes. Law reviews specialize to some extent. If you want to focus on some key issues in Texas politics, it might be helpful to skim the "Annual Review of Texas Law" in the *Southwestern Law Journal,* published by the SMU Law School [phone (214) 692-2594].
- Specialized periodicals. Periodicals that regularly include information about Texas government as well as the governments of other states include *Governing,* published monthly by Congressional Quarterly, Inc.; *State Legislatures,* published monthly by the National Conference on State Legislatures; *City & State,* published every two weeks by Crain Communications; *The Book of the States,* published in even-numbered years by the Council of State Governments; and *Significant Features of Fiscal Federalism,* published yearly by the U.S. Advisory Commission on Intergovernmental Relations.
- *The Texas Poll Report.* This is the most important source of information about public opinion in Texas. The polls are conducted by the Public Policy Resources Laboratory of Texas A&M University, and the report is available in most libraries. It is published quarterly by The Texas Poll, Harte-Hanks Communications, Inc., 815 Brazos #800, Austin 78701, phone (512) 428-9646. Subscriptions are $40 for one year, $75 for two years. Reports of Texas public opinion in the 1960s and 1970s can be found in some libraries in *The Belden Poll.*

Professional Meetings

Another way to keep abreast of Texas politics is to attend conventions that discuss the subject. The Texas State Historical Association meets each spring. To find out the location and dates of its annual convention, ask a member of your history faculty, check the *Southwestern Historical Quarterly,* or contact the association. Another interesting conference is the annual convention of the Southwestern Social Science Association. This group meets each March, usually in Dallas, Fort Worth, Houston, or San Antonio, and includes political scientists, economists, sociologists, and other social scientists as well as historians. To find out about this meeting, ask a member of your government department, check *Social Science Quarterly,* or contact the Southwestern Social Science Association.

The above suggestions should help you to develop and get copies of a good set of secondary sources—other people's research. If, however, you would like to contribute something new to our knowledge of Texas politics, the following section should be useful.

DOING ORIGINAL RESEARCH ON TEXAS POLITICS

Doing original research is often more interesting than summarizing existing studies, as well as possibly giving you a chance to present your findings to a meeting or publish them in a newsletter, newspaper, or journal. This section contains suggestions for studying the electoral and policy processes at the state and local levels, the judicial and legal systems, or some aspect of a political figure's career.

State Politics: The Electoral Process

There are a number of sources to help you do original research on state campaigns and elections.

- *Election data.* The *Texas Almanac* includes state, district, and county vote totals for state and federal offices. Data for individual precincts are more difficult to obtain, however. Registration figures, precinct maps, and vote totals for primary and general elections for president, U.S. senator, governor, and lieutenant governor from 1966 to 1976 were published in two series of volumes, *Texas Precinct Votes* (1966, 1968, and 1970) and *TexaStats* (1972, combined volume for 1974 and 1976). These studies were discontinued, so you will have to get other election totals from the state archives, the secretary of state, or county clerks. In addition, you usually can obtain unofficial returns from your local newspaper the day following an election. The state archives has election tally sheets dating back to the days of the Texas Republic, and the elections division of the secretary of state's office maintains more recent returns, some of which are computerized and are for sale. The elections division operates a nationwide toll-free number (1-800-252-8683) from 8:00 A.M. to 5:00 P.M., Monday through Friday. You may leave a message for a callback. During primary, general, and constitutional amendment election times, Election Central [(512) 463-5701] is in operation, and callers can get raw data or percentages, plus polling-place activity. The best source for precinct maps is your county tax assessor-collector, city clerk, or elections administrator (Texas has nineteen combined city clerk and tax assessor-collector offices), planning department, or public works department. The Texas Legislative Council, located in the John H. Reagan building of the capitol complex, also has maps. Call (512) 463-1151 for information.
- *Campaign finances.* Candidates and contributors are generally required by law to report their financial transactions. Newspapers are your best source of current information on who contributes large amounts to candidates and how

candidates spend their money. News accounts are seldom very detailed, however. The elections division of the secretary of state's office maintains the official, complete reports of candidates, lobbyists, and political action committees (PACs).

- *Candidates.* You usually can get extensive information about candidates from newspapers. The Texas State Library also has two services that can help you if you want a reasonable amount of information. The state archives maintains an index to biography and can refer you to works about particular individuals. The Public Services Division maintains clipping files and can copy limited amounts of material at 15 cents per page. This division can also send some materials through interlibrary loan.

- *Issues.* Newspapers are undoubtedly the best source of information on the issues in a campaign. You should use them cautiously, however, since most newspapers are not completely unbiased in their reporting and normally endorse candidates. In addition, candidates and local political party officials may have copies of campaign literature that can help you identify election issues.

State Politics: The Policy Process

There is a wealth of sources on the policy process in Texas. Where you turn for information, though, depends in part on whether you are interested in the development of alternative policies, the legislative or bureaucratic process of choosing a policy from a number of options, or the problems of implementing or enforcing a policy once it is enacted.

- *Newspapers and periodicals.* Newspapers, of course, can help you understand the background of an issue. In addition to news stories, you should pay attention to editorials and columns by a newspaper's regular political writers, who often discuss the inner workings of the policy process. You can also obtain important information about policy alternatives and the legislative process from the publications of interest groups. Dozens of organizations, such as the Texas Medical Association, the Texas State Teachers Association, and the Sierra Club, publish magazines or newsletters for their members. Most of these are listed in *Legislative Library Resources,* published by the Legislative Reference Library, or *Texas Publishers and Publications Directory,* published by the S&S Press of Austin. Also try Georgia Kemp Caraway, ed., *Writers and Publishers Guide to Texas Markets, 1991,* for city and category indexes of book and magazine publishers; daily, weekly, and minority newspapers; publisher organizations; writers' groups; and radio and TV programs (some with public affairs content).

- *Legislative Clipping Service.* This service of the Legislative Reference Library (LRL) includes copies of articles on government and politics clipped from newspapers throughout Texas. Each Friday the service also includes a section titled "Recent Articles of Interest," which lists articles in any newspaper or periodical that pertain to public policy in Texas. This service is an excellent source of information, but few libraries subscribe to it. If it is not available at your library, ask your librarian to inquire about obtaining it. The clipping service is distributed on a daily basis to each legislator's capitol office, one copy to each House member and three to each senator. Library copies cannot be checked out but can be read there. The LRL loans out items to state officials, members of the legislature, and their staffs. From time to time the LRL puts out a compilation of recent articles, sorted by issue and subject category. This is also distributed to House and Senate capitol offices.

- *Texas Legislative History: A Manual of Sources* (1980). This manual, produced by the LRL, provides excellent tips for doing research on the legislative process and is a good place to turn before examining the history of specific legislation.
- *Texas House and Senate journals.* These journals trace the history of all bills and resolutions considered by the legislature. They are limited, however, to actions that occur on the floor of each house or are reported there. Contact your state representative or senator if you want to get on his or her limited journal mailing list. The floor debate in both houses is recorded, and these tapes may be listened to in the LRL.
- *Legislative Information System of Texas (LIST).* LIST is a database with basic information about bills and resolutions introduced in the legislature since 1973, including author, sponsor, short description, and the like. It also has a subject index, author and sponsor index, and committee index. Texts of proposed legislation can be printed out on a member's printer, or on the printer in the LRL, during the sessions. Material from the 71st and 72nd legislatures, regular and special sessions, is in the LRL. Material prior to the 71st legislature is in hard copy in the LRL. During a legislative session, you can find out about the status of current legislation by calling a toll-free number, (800) 252-9693 (475-3026 in Austin), between 8:00 A.M. and 5:00 P.M. weekdays or whenever either house is in session.
- *Original bill files.* The state archives and the LRL also maintain complete files on all bills and resolutions introduced in the legislature. Each file contains not only the original bill, but often other documents such as notes on its fiscal effects, detailed explanations, and committee reports. Files on bills prior to 1973 are kept at the state archives; those since 1973 are at the LRL.
- *House Research Organization reports.* The House Research Organization (HRO), formerly known as the House Study Group, issues general reports on issues, as well as detailed analyses of individual bills that summarize the legislation, describe the arguments for and against it, and list its major supporters and opponents. Many reports are provided only to House members who belong to the study group. Its special legislative reports on general issues are distributed to depository libraries, and analyses of bills are usually included in the original bill files mentioned above.
- *Legislative hearings.* The proceedings of committees in the legislature are tape-recorded, not written. The dates of hearings can be obtained from LIST. Hearings can be very instructive in understanding policy alternatives and decisions because of the testimony and debate that occur there. They can also provide information about the implementation of policies when legislators question officials of state agencies. Minutes of committee meetings are kept, however. Senate minutes are maintained by the LRL and House minutes by

the House committee coordinator. Because of the general inaccessibility of committee proceedings, you may be forced to rely on secondhand accounts of committee actions by the press, the House Research Organization, or other sources. If you live in Austin, however, you can listen to tapes of the committee hearings, either at the LRL or in the House committee coordinator's office, once requests have been made and if the minutes and tapes are available. There is sometimes a rule-allotted time lag for the committee clerks to prepare documents for processing. While the minutes reflect only the action or nonaction taken, the tapes reveal interesting dialogue.

- *Interest groups.* Lobbyists and political action committees are required to register and file reports with the elections division of the secretary of state's office. Their activities are often discussed in newspapers and periodicals such as *The Texas Observer* or *Texas Monthly.* The positions of groups are usually discussed in bill analyses, and House study-group reports are included in original bill files. In addition, interest groups often publish their positions on issues in magazines or newsletters distributed to their members.
- *Legislative votes.* Votes on the floor of the House and Senate are included in the journal of each house. In addition, the *Texas Government Newsletter* has published a *Voter's Guide* to recent legislative sessions. This volume does not cover all floor votes, but provides background on major votes along with the actual head count.
- *The Texas Legislative Council.* This is a vital component of the legislative process. Drafts of legislation emanate from its staff of attorneys who put the members' concepts into proper form for introduction. The council publishes a cumulative number, subject, and author index throughout the session, with a final one at the end of the session (or special session); after the session is over, it distributes a "Summary of the Legislative Session." It also publishes a *Legislative Manual,* showing how to draft legislation correctly. In 1988, it published the two-volume *District Profiles: Congressional, State Senate, and State Board of Education Districts* and the companion *District Profiles: State House of Representatives.* These show configurations and compositions of four types of districts drawn by the Texas Legislature following each federal decennial census. For each type of district, there is a short history of the evolution of the statewide plan and a population/size analysis of the plan. For each individual district, there is a locator, and detailed boundary maps and tables of selected 1980 census data. This first edition is a prototype for a district publication that the council plans to update for the 1990 census. The publication has not yet been printed because redistricting plans are in litigation.
- *Agency reports and hearings.* The annual and periodic reports of state agencies are indexed in *Texas State Documents.* Hearings are listed by agency name in the *Texas Register,* which reports the activities and publishes the rules of bureaucratic agencies. These reports and hearings are a good way to gather information about the enforcement of policies.
- *Texas State Comptroller.* The comptroller's office issues both regular and special reports. Among these is *Fiscal Notes,* which is a bimonthly publication on the economy and fiscal picture of the state.

- *Institute of Public Affairs, University of Texas.* The institute published more than eighty-five books and monographs between 1950 and 1971, when it was disbanded. These included summaries of several legislative sessions and an overview of the lieutenant governorship. Its activities have been continued by the Lyndon B. Johnson School of Public Affairs, which issues a variety of reports on issues facing the state. The school's publication office issues free cumulative and yearly catalogs of its publications.
- *Other bureaus, centers, and institutions.* Many college and university campuses have research and public service bureaus, centers, and institutes that can provide you with valuable information. These are too numerous to list, but you should check your campus telephone directory to see what appropriate offices exist on your campus or a nearby campus. Look for organizations with the word *Texas* in the title, as well as for such designations as "public management," "Texas culture," "economic development," and "urban affairs."
- *Your legislators.* The Legislative Reference Library and legislative committees exist to serve the legislature and do not have time to do your research. If you need limited advice or information in Austin, however, you often can get some help by calling or writing your senator or representative, who has staff members who can assist you. Use *Chief Elected and Administrative Officials* to find the correct spelling of your legislators' names if you do not find them on the editorial/opinion page of your local newspaper.
- *State agencies.* State agencies frequently issue reports and conduct special studies that may be of interest to you. The Office of the Comptroller of Public Accounts is perhaps the most prolific. These offices are not equipped to do your research for you, but if you hear or read about a report issued by one of them, you may be able to obtain a copy. The comptroller's office can be reached at (800) 531-5441, extension 3-4900, or 463-4900 in Austin.

Local Politics: The Electoral Process

- *Election data.* Voting returns are available from the city secretary (called city clerk in some municipalities). Precinct maps and voter registration totals can be obtained from the city secretary or the county tax assessor-collector. This overlap occurs because counties draw precinct boundaries and oversee voter registration. The city secretary or planning department may have detailed census data about precincts, although this information has become generally available only recently as many cities began electing their council members from districts.
- *Candidates.* One of the best ways to find out about candidates and issues is from the local League of Women Voters (LWV), which usually prints a "Voter's Guide" before each election. Although the league does not endorse candidates, it promotes voter education and occasionally takes positions on issues. Since the league is a volunteer organization, it does not always maintain a permanent office or old records. If you cannot reach the local chapter by phone or mail, ask if the city clerk knows the names, addresses, and phone

numbers of its officers. Contacting the LWV is well worth the effort, since the "Voter's Guide" includes detailed biographical information about candidates and analyzes both sides of referendum, charter, and bond elections. You can also get information about the occupations and addresses of candidates from the alphabetical listing in the city directory.

- *Issues.* Many libraries, newspapers, and interest groups maintain files of articles, press releases, letters, and similar material. These clipping files can hold a wealth of knowledge and save you a lot of time, especially if the local papers are not well indexed. The first place to look for these clipping files is the main branch of the local public library. As with state and federal elections, candidates often keep material that can prove helpful to you.

Local Politics: The Policy Process

Local politics is often the easiest realm in which to do research, since you hear about it daily and the resources for a good project are readily available.

- *Newspapers.* As mentioned earlier, indexes and clipping files are extremely important sources for understanding policy making. They can help you identify the nature of a controversy or issue, the people or groups involved in it, and their goals and political maneuvers.
- *Official records.* City council minutes are valuable, since they indicate who made and seconded motions and how council members voted on specific questions. If verbatim minutes are kept, you can also analyze council debates to expand your understanding of an issue. Most city secretaries also maintain files on each ordinance and council meeting, and these usually include substantial background information on issues. Most city secretaries also have a subject index of council meetings and ordinances, copies of agendas, lists of citizens who sign up to address the council, and copies of petitions. All these records can help you identify the significant participants in a policy decision and their positions and strategies. In larger cities, tapes or radio broadcasts may be available. Check with the city clerk's office.
- *Organizations.* There are several things, in addition to lists of speakers at council meetings, that can help you analyze the role of organizations in the policy process. Neighborhood groups and other organizations often register with the city secretary, planning commission, or city manager. You can also find the names, addresses, and phone numbers of political and social organizations in a very handy source, the yellow pages of the telephone directory.
- *Reports and studies.* Budgets, department reports, and board or commission studies often provide insights into the formulation and implementation of policies. Contacting the relevant department is usually the best way to gather such information about an individual city. Comparing cities is a somewhat more difficult task. *Texas Town and City,* the official publication of the Texas Municipal League, often reports data for the state's cities. In addition, the *Index to Current Urban Documents* covers reports and studies done by the nation's largest cities, many of which are available in the *Urban Documents Microfiche Collection.* A regional council of government (COG)

may also have some of the information you need and be willing to assist you in your research.

- *Local magazines.* Most large Texas cities have at least one local magazine. These are typically published by the chamber of commerce and promote economic activity in the area. They sometimes carry interesting accounts of local politics, however. Several of these magazines, including *D* and *Houston City,* are indexed in *Access.*
- *Interviews.* Do not hesitate to ask questions of people who participate in local politics. You should do so, however, only after doing careful background research on an issue and consulting with one of your instructors who is experienced in interviewing.

Law and the Judicial System

If your college library does not include a law collection, the county law library will include the basic volumes for doing research on the Texas legal system.

- Marian Boner, *A Reference Guide to Texas Law and Legal History: Sources and Documentation* (1976). This is a good starting point if you intend to do research on some aspect of the law. It includes a detailed bibliography and helpful tips.
- *Vernon's Texas Constitution.* These three volumes include the text of the Texas Constitution, commentary, citations of important court cases and articles, and a thorough subject index.
- *Vernon's Texas Codes Annotated, Vernon's Annotated Revised Civil Statutes, Vernon's Annotated Code of Criminal Procedure.* These volumes include the text of laws plus commentary, citations, and an index. Be sure to check the pamphlet supplement at the back for important developments since the volume was published.
- *Southwestern Reporter.* Federal and state cases involving Texas are reported in this series. Citations are in the form *City of San Antonio v. State ex rel. Criner,* 270 S.W.2d 460. To find the decision in the case involving these two parties, you would go to volume 270 of the *Southwestern Reporter* second series, and locate the beginning of the court's opinion on page 460. This is not a book for browsing—you need a case citation before you can refer to it.
- *Shepard's Citations.* These citations to cases give the complete judicial history of every reported case and how it has been affected by decisions of both state and federal courts. If you are wondering if the decision in a particular case is still valid or has been superseded, *Shepard's Citations* will answer your question. Check with your reference librarian about how to use *Shepard's.*
- Texas Department of Criminal Justice, *Annual Report.*
- The Office of Court Administration of the Texas Judicial Council, *The Texas Judicial System: Annual Report.*

Biographies

You may also want to study an individual political career. To a large extent, you can start by reviewing existing accounts of the individual and then supplementing them.

A quick way to begin is to look up the individual in such biographical references as the following:

- *The Handbook of Texas Online.* This joint project of the General Libraries at the University of Texas at Austin and the Texas State Historical Association contains important biographical information on deceased Texans in an alphabetical format. http://www.tsha.utexas.edu/handbook/online/
- *Who's Who in the South and Southwest.* This volume includes short biographical information about prominent persons.
- *Dictionary of American Biography.* This series is published under the auspices of the American Council of Learned Societies, and has been updated frequently. Each entry includes a short life history and brief list of references. To locate someone, go to the most recent volume, which will refer you to the proper volume.
- R. R. Bowker Company, *Biographical Books, 1950–1980* (1980). This collection includes subject/name, author, and title indexes.

You can supplement these sources with the materials mentioned above for studying local politics, particularly newspapers and clipping files. Another invaluable tool is personal papers, which many individuals donate to libraries. In addition to the *American Library Directory,* there are several other ways to locate biographical information.

- Texas State Archives, Biographical Index. You can contact the archives to find out what materials have been published on an individual, as well as what sources the archives have available.
- Chester V. Kielman, ed., *The University of Texas Archives.* This includes an alphabetical list and index of the many manuscript collections at the University of Texas at Austin.
- Library of Congress, *The National Union Catalogue of Manuscript Collections.* This annual series is organized by state and city, and will help you locate both personal papers and oral histories. Among the latter is the Oral History Collection at the University of North Texas, which includes interviews with Texas governors and legislators.
- Philip M. Hamer, ed., *A Guide to Archives and Manuscripts in the United States* (1961). Although somewhat dated, this volume covers some major collections. It is organized by state and city, and includes a description of each institution's holdings.

CONCLUSION

Although none of the preceeding suggestions guarantees a good research project—which depends on some work on your part—this research guide should make your work easier. It should also allow you to analyze carefully some important political questions facing Texas citizens and their elected representatives.

HELPFUL LOCATIONS FOR GETTING INFORMATION

Texas Depository Libraries

Abilene:
Public Library, Documents Department
202 Cedar Street
Abilene 79601
(915) 677-2474

Alpine:
Sul Ross State University
Bryan Wildenthal Memorial Library, Documents Department
Alpine 79832
(915) 837-8125

Amarillo:
Public Library, Documents Department
P.O. Box 2171
Amarillo 79189-2171
(806) 378-3050

Arlington:
University of Texas at Arlington Library,
Government Publications/Maps Department
P.O. Box 19497
Arlington 76019
(817) 463-1252

Austin:
Legislative Reference Library
1110 San Jacinto, Room 260
Box 12488
Austin 78711
(512) 463-1252

Texas State Library and Archives, Reference/Documents
Box 12927
Austin 78711
(512) 463-5455

University of Texas at Austin, Center for American History
2.109 Sid Richardson Hall
Austin 78713-7330
(512) 471-5961

Beaumont:
Public Library, Reference Department
P.O. Box 3827

Beaumont 77704
(409) 838-6606

Lamar University
Gray Library, Documents Department
Box 10021, Lamar University Station
Beaumont 77710
(409) 880-8261

Brownsville:
University of Texas at Brownsville
Documents Department/LRC
1614 Ridgley Road
Brownsville 78520-4991
(956) 983-0295

Canyon:
West Texas State University
Library, Documents Department
P.O. Box 748, WT Station
Canyon 79016
(806) 656-2204

College Station:
Texas A&M University
Sterling C. Evans Library
Reference Division (Texas State)
College Station 77843-5000
(409) 845-5310

Commerce:
East Texas State University
Library, Serials Department
Commerce 75249
(903) 886-5734

Corpus Christi:
Public Library, Documents Department
805 Comanche Street
Corpus Christi 78401
(512) 880-7005

Texas A & M Corpus Christi
Library, Documents Department
6300 Ocean Drive
Corpus Christi 78412
(512) 994-2341

Dallas:
Public Library, Government Publications Division
1515 Young Street
Dallas 75201

(214) 670-1460
Southern Methodist University
Fondren Library, Documents Department
Dallas 75275
(214) 692-2331

Denison:
Public Library
300 West Gandy Street
Denison 75020
(903) 465-1797

Denton:
University of North Texas
Library, Documents Department
P.O. Box 5188, NT Station
Denton 76203-5188
(940) 565-3869

Texas Woman's University
Library, Documents Department
P.O. Box 23715, TWU Station
Denton 76204
(940) 898-3708

Edinburg:
University of Texas
Pan American Library, Documents Department
1201 W. University Drive
Edinburg 78539-2999
(512) 381-3304

El Paso:
Public Library, Documents Department
501 North Oregon Street
El Paso 79901
(915) 543-5475

University of Texas at El Paso
Library, Documents and Maps Section
El Paso 79968-0582
(915) 747-5685

Fort Worth:
Public Library, Government Publications
300 Taylor Street
Fort Worth 76102
(817) 871-7724

Texas Christian University
Burnett Library, Documents Department
P.O. Box 32904

Forth Worth 76129
(817) 921-7669

Houston:
Public Library, Texas Room
500 McKinney Avenue
Houston 77002
(713) 247-1664

Rice University
Fondren Library, Documents Department
P.O. Box 1892
Houston 77251
(713) 523-2417

Texas Southern University
Library, Documents Department
3100 Cleburne Street
Houston 77004
(713) 527-7147

University of Houston
Library, Documents Department
4800 Calhoun Street
Houston 77204-2091
(713) 749-1163

University of Houston—Clear Lake
Neumann Library, Documents Library
2700 Bay Area Boulevard
Houston 77058-1083
(713) 283-3910

Huntsville:
Sam Houston State University
N. Gresham Library, Department of Government Documents
Huntsville 77341
(409) 294-1629

Kingsville:
Texas A&M Kingsville
Library, Documents Department
Kingsville 78363
(512) 595-2918

Laredo:
Laredo State University
Library, Documents Section
1 West End Washington Street
Laredo 78040-9960
(956) 722-8001, ext. 402

Lubbock:
Texas Tech University
Library, Documents Department
M.S. 2041
Lubbock 79409-0002
(806) 742-2268

Nacogdoches:
Stephen F. Austin State University
Library, Documents Department
P.O. Box 13055, SFA Station
Nacogdoches 75962-3055
(409) 568-1574

Odessa:
Ector County Library, Documents Department
321 West 5th Street
Odessa 79761
(915) 332-0634
University of Texas of the Permian Basin Library
4901 E. University Boulevard
Odessa 79762
(915) 357-2313

Prairie View:
Prairie View A&M University
John B. Coleman Library, Documents Department
Prairie View 77446
(409) 857-2612

Richardson:
University of Texas at Dallas
Library Documents Department
P.O. Box 830643
Richardson 75083-0643
(214) 690-2627

San Angelo:
Angelo State University
Porter Henderson Library
2601 W. Avenue N.
San Angelo 76909
(915) 942-2222

San Antonio:
St. Mary's University
Academic Library, Documents Department
One Camino Santa Maria
San Antonio 78228-8608
(512) 436-3441

Public Library (Main Branch)
Business and Science Department
203 S. St. Mary's Street
San Antonio 78205
(512) 299-7802

Trinity University
Library, Documents Unit
715 Stadium Drive
San Antonio 78212
(512) 736-7430

University of Texas at San Antonio
Library/Documents
San Antonio 78249
(512) 691-4583

San Marcos:
Southwest Texas State University
Library, Documents Department
San Marcos 78666-4604
(512) 245-3686

Stephenville:
Tarleton State University
Dick Smith Library/Education Library
Stephenville 76402
(254) 968-9869

Tyler:
University of Texas at Tyler
Muntz Library, Documents Department
3900 University Boulevard
Tyler 75701
(903) 566-7344

Victoria:
Victoria College/University of Houston at Victoria
Library, Documents Department
2602 N. Ben Jordan
Victoria 77901
(512) 576-3151, ext. 283

Waco:
Baylor University (Texas Collection)
B.U. Box 97142
Waco 76798-7142
(817) 755-1268

Wichita Falls:
Midwestern State University
Moffett Library, Documents Department

3400 Taft Street
Wichita Falls 76308-2099
(940) 692-6611, ext. 4165

Other Depository Libraries:
Library of Congress, State Documents Section
Exchange and Gift Division
Washington, DC 20540
(202) 707-9470

Texas State Library

P.O. Box 12927, Austin 78711
Reference: (512) 463-5455
Archives: (512) 463-5480
Public Services: (512) 463-5455

The Legislature and Legislative Agencies

Legislative Reference Library
P.O. Box 12488 Capitol Station
Austin 78711-2488
(512) 463-1252
Bill Status: (800) 253-9693
(463-1251 in Austin)

The Honorable _____
Texas Senate
P.O. Box 12068 Capitol Station
Austin 78711

House Research Organization
Texas House of Representatives
P.O. Box 2910
Austin 78769-2910

The Honorable _____
Texas House of Representatives
P.O. Box 2910
Austin 78769-2910

Secretary of State

Elections Division
P.O. Box 12060
Austin 78711-2060
(512) 463-5650

Texas Ethics Commission
P.O. Box 12070
Austin 78711-2070
(512) 463-5800

Support Services Division,
Texas Register Section
P.O. Box 13824
Austin 78711-3824
(512) 463-5561

Professional and Educational Organizations

Texas State Historical Association
2.306 Sid Richardson Hall
University of Texas
Austin 78712-1104
(512) 471-1525

Southwestern Social Science Association
University of Texas
P.O. Box 7998
Austin 78713-7998
(512) 471-4384

Office of Publications
Lyndon B. Johnson School of Public Affairs
Drawer Y, University Station
Austin 78713-7450
(512) 471-4962

Texas University Presses

Seven universities in the state maintain presses that publish books on virtually all aspects of Texas: The University of Texas, Texas A&M University, The University of North Texas, Texas Christian University, Southern Methodist University, Rice University, and Texas Western. Each university press provides catalogs of its publications, and each can provide information on the publications of the other presses. Addresses and telephone numbers are available at your local library.

INDEX

1